SOLDIERS AND CIVILIZATION

SOLDIERS AND CIVILIZATION

How the Profession of Arms Thought and
Fought the Modern World into Existence

REED ROBERT BONADONNA

NAVAL INSTITUTE PRESS
ANNAPOLIS, MARYLAND

Naval Institute Press
291 Wood Road
Annapolis, MD 21402

Library of Congress Cataloging-in-Publication Data is available.
ISBN 978-1-68247-067-1 (hardcover)
ISBN 978-1-68247-068-8 (eBook)

♾ Print editions meet the requirements of ANSI/NISO z39.48-1992 (Permanence
of Paper).
Printed in the United States of America.

25 24 23 22 21 20 19 18 17   9 8 7 6 5 4 3 2 1
First printing

For Sue, Luke, Devon, and Erik,
who mean more and more to me every day

These, in the day when heaven was falling,
The hour when earth's foundation fled,
Followed their mercenary calling,
And took their wages, and are dead.

Their shoulders held the sky suspended;
They stood, and earth's foundations stay;
What God abandoned, these defended,
And saved the sum of things for pay.

"Epitaph on an Army of Mercenaries"
—A. E. Housman

Contents

Illustrations

Acknowledgments

This work evolved over a period of years from a draft for a single article spreading over the centuries of military history and gathering to itself the results of years of reading, experience, teaching, and conversation. I decided to write this book when, designing and teaching a course on military professionalism, I realized that no such work existed and that my own understanding of the evolution and impact of military professionalism was incomplete. The research, teaching, and writing all fed one another. I want to thank a number of people who have been very helpful. Dr. Jeffrey Forgeng, formerly curator of the Higgins Armory Museum, Worcester, Massachusetts, read the chapter on medieval military professionalism, making valuable comments on writing and sources. Dr. Elizabeth K. Holmes, Captain, USN (Ret.) encouraged me to submit a draft manuscript to a publisher. Dr. Clifford J. Rogers, History Department, U.S. Military Academy, read the draft on early modern military professionalism and made valuable suggestions. The staff of the Bland Memorial Library at the U.S. Merchant Marine Academy library were unfailingly friendly and helpful, especially head librarian Dr. George Billy and Mr. Donald Gill. My students among the midshipmen at the U.S. Merchant Marine Academy cheered me up and prevented me from getting too sure of myself.

My students of the Marine Corps Command and Staff College Distance Education Program were my comrades in arms and among the most admirable group of individuals I've ever met. Most of them were majors in the Marine Corps Reserve, although the active component, other branches, and greater and lesser grades were also represented. Many had considerable deployed and "gun time" in addition to impressive educational and civilian credentials. Often our discussions turned to a consideration of the nature and essentials of military professionalism, and more of their observations have made it into this work than I can ever enumerate. In particular, an understanding of the relationship between the profession of arms and the humanities grew out of conversations I had with my Command and Staff students. The rest of my brothers and sisters in arms in the U.S. Marine Corps bequeathed to me an understanding of the profession of arms that words alone cannot convey. *Semper Fidelis*.

HISTORY AND MILITARY PROFESSIONALISM

The life of man is a soldier's service, and that long and various.
—Epictetus

The soldier is both the least civilized and the most civilized of persons. Soldiers walk the weird wall at the edge of civilization, but they are prepared to serve their civilization and society without stint or limit.[1] As the French theorists Gilles Deleuze and Felix Guattari remark, soldiers are constantly in danger of forsaking that which they serve and of forgetting the nature of what they do. That paradox of the soldier's profession is the central concern of this book. The soldier has played a vital, inescapable, and neglected role in the formation of human civilization, and must have a part in its future survival. One of the constitutive aspects of Western civilization has been its distinctive tradition of military professionalism. Western civilization has been significant both for its own diverse member nations, cultures, and peoples and for the rest of humankind. Not all of this influence has been for the good, but much of it has been and is. I side with Niall Ferguson in his conclusion that the West has tended to more of the positive attributes of civilization than have those cultures outside the Western tradition. This may be attributable to a variety of reasons, and it is likely not the product of innate capacities or necessarily superior wisdom. Civilization may be largely a matter of luck, climate, natural resources, and the catastrophes of plague and extreme weather.[2] As Victor Davis Hanson frequently and persuasively argues, however, the civilization of the West could not have flourished had it not created a uniquely effective style of war fighting. This Western way of war has been primarily the creation of professional militaries in a tradition beginning with the Greeks and Romans. In this book, I want to argue that, while the creation of war-fighting principles and practices contributing to the defense of Western civilization has been an important and traceable achievement of Western military professionals, the contribution of these professionals has gone beyond war fighting. It has also been cognitive, cultural, ethical, and even ontological.[3] The Western

1

military profession has not only allowed the West to flourish, it has also contributed to the goods for which Western civilization is responsible and of which it remains an important repository. In some significant ways, however, the modern military profession is only partially equipped to fulfill its civilizing role in an unstable and uncertain present and future. In order to meet its challenges, the military profession must engage in a thoughtful and focused reconsideration of its own past. This history, properly considered, contains important knowledge on the role of the military profession in the times ahead.

A Soldier's Story

For me, soldiering has always meant reading. I was a late but avid reader, and for as long as I can remember I have read books about soldiers. I remember one book in particular, a series of historical fiction vignettes by Ernest Tucker called *The Story of Knights and Armor*. For years, until I finally reacquired a copy, I could summon up much of the book from memory. As a boy I had tried to copy the illustrations of knights and legionaries with pencil. In a sense, those childish artistic efforts were among my first attempts to fashion myself as a soldier, to put myself in the place of a Roman legionary or medieval knight. I felt a kinship with these men. I wanted to be someone like them. Unlike some other youthful enthusiasms, this one never left me, but it was words rather than pictures that proved the deeper and more durable form of connection to the soldiers of the past. As a teen I graduated to more grown-up books. *Stilwell and the American Experience in China* by Barbara Tuchman, *The Swordbearers* by Corelli Barnett, Robert Leckie's *The Wars of America* series, and Winston Churchill's biography of his ancestor John Churchill, the 1st Duke of Marlborough, were favorites. When the time came for me to choose a college and branch of the service, I attended Virginia Military Institute (VMI) and then joined the U.S. Marine Corps, choices I made largely because I had been inspired by biographies of George S. Patton and Marine general Lewis "Chesty" Puller. I also read Patton's poem "Through a Glass Darkly," a haunting if fanciful account of his military reincarnation throughout the ages, and an extended metaphor for the soldier's sense of military history. Both VMI and the Marine Corps were and are institutions in love with their own past. Attending the institute and serving in the Corps was like living with history every day. I chose to serve in the infantry, the military branch least affected by technological change and therefore the most continuous with the past. Not only do VMI and the Marine Corps recall and respect their own histories, they also see themselves as preserving a venerable narrative of military excellence. In terms coined by literary critic Harold Bloom, these institutions may be said to create a strong poetics of leadership, discipline, esprit de corps, and physical vigor, each generation adding new verses in varying cadences but returning to common themes as old as the fifes of the Spartans.

As a cadet and Marine I kept on reading: books in my rooms in barracks, in my pack in the field, maybe especially in my bunkroom on the amphibious ships where Marines spend much unoccupied time. Army combat historian S. L. A. Marshall's writings on small-unit combat were great favorites in my days as a junior infantry officer. I was honored to meet Eugene Sledge after reading his memoir, *With the Old Breed*, while I was stationed on Parris Island. While still on active duty, I wrote my master's thesis on the World War I poets Robert Graves and Siegfried Sassoon.

Young adult restlessness and a desire for a doctorate led me to leave the active-duty ranks of the Marine Corps as a captain, but (in a sense that will resonate within this work) I never left the military profession. I stayed in the Marine Corps Reserve for another twenty years. I had participated in one small war on active duty (the 1982 U.S. intervention in Lebanon), and as an activated reservist I was in one big one (the 2003 invasion of Iraq). By the time of the Iraq campaign, I had come full circle, serving as a field historian with an infantry brigade—a chronicler of and participant in war at once. Even apart from my duties as a reserve officer, my interests continued along military lines. I wrote my doctoral dissertation on war literature, taught for the Marine Corps Command and Staff College as a civilian adjunct, and eventually became the director of ethics and character development at the U.S. Merchant Marine Academy, a federal service academy that educates both maritime and military officers. I taught an elective course at the academy called "Leadership in Action: War and the Military Profession" and another (in collaboration with colleague Dr. Melanie Ross) called "Pen, Cutlass, and Sword: Humanities and Officership," both of which provided me with the opportunity to develop ideas that have found their way into this book.

My job at the academy has thrown me into close contact with representatives from the other four federal service academies, and from some of them I learned about the scholarly work being done on the nature of military professionalism. This was of considerable interest to me as a presumptive professional who teaches professional leaders in embryo, but the contemporary writings on military professionalism seemed to me to lack the depth, historical rootedness, narrative, and poetic quality of my early reading experience. This book is an attempt to fuse modern ideas on professionalism and culture with an earlier, humanist tradition on the subject. It is even perhaps a rewriting of the book by Ernest Tucker that I first read long ago in that it is a work of military history told as collective biography. One thing that this biography reveals is that to be a soldier is both more and less than to be a member of a profession. Ernest Hemingway once said of bullfighting that it is not a sport but a tragedy. It might be said that war is too much a tragedy, and one of historic, even metaphysical dimensions, to be confined within the definition of a profession. At a minimum, a consideration of the military profession needs a broad canvas and wide context in the history of events, arts, and ideas. The need for a thorough appreciation of the military profession, its place in history, and its relationship to society strikes me as especially relevant in our time, for reasons that may be obvious but that I will discuss in greater details in the pages that follow.

The Military Profession Today

The U.S. armed forces are the most formidable and versatile on the face of the earth and in the history of humankind. In the past decade they have acquired valuable experience and expertise across a wide spectrum of military operations. Standards once expected only of special forces have become the norm, and special forces units regularly achieve wonders only dreamed of by the special operators of the twentieth century. The American armed forces also set the standard of professional education and training, schooling thousands of foreign soldiers on their own ground and in American military bases. However, a number of discouraging details dim this bright picture. Since 9/11, the American military has expended resources, effort, and lives in pursuit of uncertain objectives and still-unconfirmed outcomes. The utility of military force as an answer to problems of strategy and policy has sometimes seemed dubious. The American military finds itself up against unfamiliar, asymmetric adversaries and allied with strange partners. "The American Way of War" is not what it once was.[4] At home, as noted by former chairman of the Joint Chiefs Admiral Mike Mullen, the military is respected but little known or understood; and it is increasingly isolated geographically, demographically, and perhaps culturally.[5] This state of affairs offers particular challenges to the American military profession, which is both triumphant and uncertain, confident but uncomfortably self-conscious. The twenty-first-century military professional may feel at times like a champion boxer who steps into the ring expecting to see a similar opponent but instead finds the ring empty, with ominous noises in the remote corners of a large arena hidden behind bright lights. For soldiers—not only American soldiers but those all over the developed and developing world too—the present situation is disorienting, and the future is more than usually obscure.

Some writers have seen the challenges to the armed forces of today as characteristic of postmodernity. Jeff Geraghty, writing on the work of military sociologist Charles Moskos, identifies five aspects of the postmodern military. First, the postmodern military increasingly blends civilian and military spheres. Second, it diminishes differences that are based on branch of service, rank, and combat versus support roles. Third, it changes its primary use from fighting wars to performing missions other than major combat operations. Fourth, it is used more often than before in internationally authorized or legitimized missions. The fifth and final change is the multinationalization of armed forces, such as the Eurocorps and the multinational divisions within some North Atlantic Treaty Organization (NATO) countries.[6]

In this work I will argue that the current situation of the military profession is far from unprecedented, that the past contains clues and guidelines to its current state of affairs, and that an enlightened reconsideration of the nature of historical military professionalism is required in order to understand the challenges of the twenty-first-century military profession. I am not the first to suggest that postmodernity recapitulates the premodern and early modern. The wider one's historical perspective, the more the current situation can be seen as representing, in varying degrees, a return or revival of some past trend, of facts and challenges soldiers have faced many times in the past. In this work I will argue for a broadly historical and humanist approach to the military profession. Before I do so I will briefly discuss sociological and previous historical works on this subject, in order both to acknowledge my debt to them and to show where my ideas build on and synthesize with those of previous writers on the subject.

The Sociologists

Scholarly consideration of the military profession began in the 1950s with the appearance of seminal works by Morris Janowitz and Samuel Huntington.[7] These social scientists initiated a consideration of the status of soldiers, of officers in particular, as members of a profession. Since then, the U.S. Army and other military branches have adopted the study of military professionalism as a tool to define and refine the education, self-perception, careers, and societal expectations of military leaders. Janowitz and Huntington established the discussion of military professionalism in the terms of sociological studies of other professions that began with the work of Max Weber in the early twentieth century. In purely pragmatic terms, the sociological discourse of military professionalism has not been without its uses. It has enhanced the quality and value of military service for many— for example, helping the armed forces to reclaim some of the idealism and high-mindedness of military service in the wake of the Vietnam War.

Sociologists define professions as groupings of persons who earn their professional status through lengthy advanced (undergraduate) and professional (graduate) education. This extensive education arguably grants members of a profession the ability both to reason abstractly and to exercise focused expertise. Professionals are supposed to be motivated by a sense of public duty, to be regarded by society with a considerable degree of trust and respect, and to retain control over the standards for entry and advancement within their own ranks. Medical doctors probably constitute the best fit for the sociologists' definition of a professional, with lawyers and clergy second and third. Engineers and architects qualify, as do most teachers. The idea of "a profession" is sometimes distinguished from that of "professionalism." While some workers who are lower on the ladder of occupational qualifications may not qualify as "members of a profession" according to the sociologists' definition, they are still capable of acting with "professionalism"—that is, in a manner that would do credit to a member of a profession. It may even be that some workers outside the strict professional ranks have a better claim to be called professionals than some of those who are nominally members but lacking in experience, expertise, commitment, understanding, or public spirit. The idea of professionalism has broad significance in that it seems to denote an attitude about work—perhaps any worthwhile work—that is pursued with a sense of responsibility and accountability.

Despite the efforts of the military sociologists, the status of the military as a profession is more often acknowledged within the armed forces than without. Some have argued that since military professionals are employed to "kill people and blow things up," the social benefit of their activities is much less clear than that of people who heal the sick or build useful structures. Military professionals cannot claim to control or predict outcomes to the degree expected of a civilian professional. Operations in war regularly go awry; one side of a war (not always the side with the less able or professional military) typically loses, and even victory often has unintended, unforeseen consequences and broad effects. As I have suggested, the military vocation may stretch past, as well as fall short of, the outlines of professionalism. It arguably possesses elements of the historical, tragic, and sublime that transcend the sociologists' professional model.

One difficulty with the social science model is that it stresses the nominal aspects of a profession, inclining the definition more in the direction of careerism and neglecting the inner and essential aspects of professionalism. Most sociologists would deny professional status to enlisted members because of their lack of advanced education. In the armed forces themselves the debate goes on as to whether at least some enlisted members qualify as professionals or the title is limited to officers, and perhaps only to career officers of the active components, omitting both reserve officers and short-service junior officers. This study generally will reflect a broad and flexible definition of military professionalism, one that might admit some enlisted members and reservists and omit some career officers. It will treat as the sine qua non of military professionalism a deep understanding of armed conflict. The military professional knows war.

By defining military professionalism in terms created with civilian professionalism in mind, the social science model of professionalism may also omit distinctive or special aspects of the profession of arms. The *professional* status of the military professional is not the esoteric specialist knowledge of a surgeon or physicist, but rather a combination of knowledge, experience, ethos, outlook, personal example, and character.

Another limitation of the social science perspective is that it seems not merely to omit but to block off the historical past. The soldiers of history did not meet all of the social science criteria for professionalism. Before the nineteenth century few of them had higher education. The standards for professional membership and advancement were not always written down. Although military orders and communities existed, they did not function in the same way as do modern professional associations. By other measurements, however, such as degree and duration of commitment, the soldiers of history sometimes rate very high.

Historian David J. Ulbrich defines the debate between the main camps of American military sociologists in terms of the contrasting views expressed by Huntington and Janowitz.[8] Huntington sees the military profession (at least in America) as developing in isolation from the rest of society. Janowitz (and also historian Walter Mills) thinks that civil and military societies are interdependent. The complete answer may lie in between, or in both. The lethal skills practiced in an atmosphere of maximum stress and friction— the "how" of the military profession—make the military a thing apart. No one else does this, or should. On the other hand, in order that it not forsake the thing it serves, the "why" of the military profession must remain strongly connected to the rest of society and to the idea of civilization itself.

The Historians

Several historians have written on military professionalism, among them Russell Weigley, coauthors Williamson Murray and Richard Hart Sinnreich, William B. Skelton, and (for early American naval officers) Christopher McKee.[9] If a social science approach to professionalism has the virtues of clarity and categorization, a historical approach may be said to add depth and inclusiveness. History provides examples and exceptions, richness and complexity. A historical consideration of the military profession can provide scope for scholars and professionals to study an ancient calling. It permits both a focus on essentials and the rediscovery of neglected but still useful ideas and imagery, perhaps especially in an era of change and uncertainty. A historical consideration of military professionalism also allows us to trace the genealogy of these ideas and to critique the modern conception of professionalism itself. The work of the historians has largely focused on specific historical periods. This book will take a broader view in an effort to paint the trends and tendencies that have defined the nature of the military profession in its long history. Military history has demonstrated the role of soldiers and armies in state formation, especially in the years leading up to and following the Treaty of Westphalia in 1648, which marks the emergence of the modern nation-state and state system. By taking a broader perspective I will be able to indicate the role of armies, not just in the formation of particular nation-states, or even of nation-states in aggregate, but in the idea of civilization as it has developed. The military profession may fall under the consideration of social scientists, but in essence it is a branch of the humanities. It is the least specialized of all professions. Risqué examples aside, it is also perhaps the oldest. Since the military profession is connected to an extent that is unique among professions to the narrative of history, to the rise and fall of states and their causes, and to the idea of civilization, only a comprehensive view of human experience and knowledge will suffice for complete military professionalism. At the core of military professionalism is the humanist's comprehension of human nature, relationships, culture, values, and language. Only words, narrative, even a poetics can take in the totality of what the soldier does. When Kipling wrote in "The Young British Soldier," "Now all you recruities what's drafted to-day, / You shut up your rag-box an' 'ark to my lay. / An' I'll sing you a soldier as fair as I may," he understood that it takes words to make a soldier—in fact, that a soldier is made of the words of history, poetry, and the laws and language of the calling.[10] The challenges facing the military profession require professional soldiers to be artists and narrators as well as warriors, and, by instinct, more creative than destructive. This may be true now more than ever, although, as I hope this book will illustrate, it was ever so.

"Paid Professionals"

All professions are vexed by the paradox that to be a professional is to be paid, while to be a professional is also to be someone who is not motivated primarily by pay. The question of remuneration—"the money motive"—and its relative importance is a problem for military professionals on a number of levels. Soldiers who desire monetary gain may be unlikely to restrain themselves given the opportunity for plunder in wartime. Soldiers are expected to risk life and limb, and a soldier who is motivated mostly by a desire for money probably wants to live to enjoy that wealth (as noted, although perhaps with questionable examples, by Machiavelli). Also, soldiering is usually associated with some form of political, or at least cultural, membership, values, and loyalty, and in the money-motivated soldier remuneration seems to take the place of these less buyable inducements. Perhaps most important, material greed by its nature seems incompatible with the character expected of soldiers: their willingness to endure danger and discomfort and their separate economy of soldierly virtue, which should place prowess over money as a sign of personal worth and self-denial and endurance over self-indulgence as defining a desirable way of life.

The ambiguity of the money motive is only one reason, I will argue, why the everyday definition of the professional as someone who acts for pay is particularly inapt in the case of professional soldiers. In fact it will be part of my redefinition of military professionalism to argue that, paradoxically, societies often have been best served by part-time or temporary military "professionals" or by full-time, long-service professionals who have equipped themselves to play their role broadly, avoiding the trap of narrow concerns that has been the nemesis of many professions but is especially insidious for professional soldiers. In this sense those who are less professional in the objective terms of remuneration, specialization, and duration of involvement often are more professional in the more subjective (and important) areas of knowledge, ethos, and connection with the larger society. The reasons for this are complex and often historically rooted and contingent. One enduring reason is that military professionals require much more than purely military knowledge. They are best served and serving under an ethos that strongly adapts the values of the larger, civil society and those of civilization in general. Professional soldiers require both the deep, personal, and abstract understanding of war that is their special province and an appreciation for the culture, institutions, and aspirations of their own society, and even of those of an adversary. History provides examples of the dangerous tendency of some military professionals toward isolation, specialization, and a narrow technical or technological focus. The most successful military professions and professionals have contextualized their calling in historical, political, and cultural terms. The military profession has always been highly interdisciplinary, with different forms or tropes of knowledge dominating at different times. It has been seen as art, science, and business; as a subset of engineering; and as an expression of faith. In fact, it encompasses all of these areas of human endeavor and understanding, and much more besides. There is a separate place for what might be called "soldiers' wisdom," a distinct form of understanding that is perhaps rare even among military professionals but is unique to soldiers. These are soldiers who have caught a glimpse of eternity behind the smoke and fire, the sublime landscape of war. The Western military profession will need wisdom allied with professional competence to be equal to the enormous demands likely to be placed on it, responsibilities that may amount to nothing less than the survival of the concept of civilization that it has helped to create and fought to protect.

Soldiers in History

Soldiers of every age have studied those who came before them. Like philosophy, the military profession can be seen as being involved in a long conversation with its own past. In part this conversation is an effort to adapt the techniques, tactics, and strategies of the past to modern conditions. Soldiers have gone to history and to biography for instruction, for a renewal of the idealism of their occupation, and for inspiration from the leadership and character of their forebears in arms. For the soldier, the study of military history involves the acquisition of a certain outlook and mindset.[11]

Military history has also fascinated the layman. For the soldier and the civilian alike a great appeal of military history has been the desire to identify with soldiers of the past. The study of military history may be seen as a kind of inoculation against the rude shocks of military life or as vicarious military experience for its own sake. In their collective history, soldiers have known more than the clash of arms. They have been leaders, teachers, writers, and judges; they have practiced statecraft, psychology, art, and science. Every age has produced exemplary soldiers who by a combination of commitment, knowledge, and ability might be called professionals. These men and women present a rich source for study, and not by soldiers alone. History tells us that the military profession has played a unique and varied role in Western civilization. Soldiers certainly helped to develop the "Western way of war" argued by writers such as Hanson, and to adapt to and sometimes to adopt the military practices of non-Western societies. Soldiers have done terrible things, preying on the helpless, inciting conflict, and turning their weapons on those they were pledged to protect. Sometimes they have seemed Samson-like in pulling the temple down on themselves and everyone else in reach. They also have been responsible for much of the restraint shown in war, for advances in useful knowledge, and for a collective and instructive memory of the realities of warfare. The challenge facing any society that arms itself is to create capable military organizations that will remain loyal and connected to civil authority and that adopt a soldier's ethos while upholding civil and civilized values.

What has been the role of military professionals in history? As figures of the imagination and as living actors on the historical stage, they have meant different things at different times, although some continuities emerge. In delineating their contributions I will sometimes make a distinction between the military profession and the profession of arms. "Military profession" is the more inclusive term, and it includes professionals who are auxiliary to the military undertaking: medics, administrators, scientists, manufacturers, and policy makers as well as soldiers. By "profession of arms" I mean those professionals who bear arms and who exercise leadership over military organizations in war. I thus focus on the officer ranks and their historical equivalents, although I do not necessarily exclude those who are not distinguished by formal command authority, by knighthood or commissioning. Soldiers and those who have supported them with supplies and services have all contributed to the sum of human achievement and knowledge. Necessity was often the mother of invention, but invention was often fathered by the uniquely focused and adaptive capacity developed by members of the military profession. Soldiers have not only played an important role in state formation; they have also contributed to state maintenance. Soldiers hold states together, not just by protecting them from external and internal threats to security, but also by helping to create national identity and self-image. An educated, enlightened officer corps is one of the requirements of a healthy society, while an excessively politicized, praetorian, narrowly professional, or militaristic officer body can be a civilization's nemesis. The armies they lead can be schools for citizenship or nurseries of nihilism.

Elements of Military Professionalism

I will define a profession as an occupational institution that makes a broad contribution to a society by means of a transmittable body of knowledge, some of it abstract, and an ethic that is both specific to the profession and relatable to the larger society. The elements of military professionalism are knowledge, cognition, beliefs, compensations, communication, leadership, trust, and character. Military professionalism is the combination of these elements, considered qualitatively and quantitatively, and both in the context of their times and as part of a narrative of gains and losses, development and decay. In the following paragraphs I briefly discuss each of these elements in turn.

Knowledge

The military professional's most essential knowledge is an understanding of armed conflict—its feel, function, and impact. Military professionals have always cultivated a body of specialist knowledge, from the simple and mechanical to the abstract and theoretical. The branches of military knowledge might be divided into techniques and tactics, operations, strategy (respectively the art of winning battles, campaigns, and wars), leadership, and logistics (a broad category encompassing housekeeping, subsistence, transport, and medical care). For the soldier, knowledge involves the humble professional prerequisites of acquired manual and physical skills: weapons and equipment handling, riding and driving, strength and endurance. Military professionals often possess knowledge that goes beyond the purely military. They gain knowledge in governance, organization, and technology that can be translated to civil uses. Soldiers also experience revelations and self-insights as well as glimpses of the sublime and the eternal in the course of their occupation. Like the returning crusading knight in the 1957 Ingmar Bergman film *The Seventh Seal*, a soldier can be both a representative of order and civilization and a charismatic reminder of change and mortality. The knowledge possessed by soldiers of the past was limited by the tools of inquiry and dissemination of their times, but it may also be said that what these soldiers knew they knew intensely in a personal, corporeal, even spiritual way. Military knowledge is tasted in the soldier's issued or improvised field rations, felt in burning thigh and back muscles, remembered through scars and in dreams.

Cognition

The military profession presents a unique variety of cognitive challenges. Soldiers must continually process and adapt to new conditions and information by considering previous experience and recalling whatever they have had in the way of training and education. They make decisions on the strategic, operational, and tactical levels, and they impart and receive advice and commands. Military thought rarely takes place in professional isolation from the larger culture. In its more sophisticated forms it may be considered in the context of the intellectual activity of its time.[12] In a way that moderns, the products of a more future-oriented society, might find difficult to understand, a more remote past weighed heavily on many soldiers of the past. The gaps in their knowledge were often filled in by superstition, their limited capabilities by fatalism. Still, just as the knowledge of soldiers of the past could be impressive, we know too that they were also capable of astonishing ingenuity and invention. They built things, solved problems, organized, and planned. Who among us will claim to be smarter than Caesar? The great soldiers of the past expanded the cognitive reach of the profession, extending the literal reach of operations and sometimes seeing war and its impact in new ways. Alexander the Great executed a far-ranging strategy that went far beyond that of any previous Greek soldier. He also saw the relationship between military force and culture as it had not been perceived before. Although we will never know what Alexander would have accomplished if he had been spared (or if his demons had not gotten the better of him), even his short career resulted in the spread and hybridization of Hellenic culture in an unprecedented manner. Some soldiers' thought processes can perhaps be intuited from their actions; some expressed their reasoning in words that have been preserved. The planning of military operations has been described as the most distinctively professional form of military thought because it is reserved to soldiers whose experience and expertise qualify them as professionals. Military planning and execution are unique among forms of professional thought in that they take place in a complex and changing four-dimensional space. In this, soldiers are perhaps more akin to physicists and astronomers than to lawyers, whose professional world is largely verbal; or to engineers, whose spatial realm is less prone to rapid change; or to doctors, who think mostly (although not solely) of what is happening inside the human body. Another special feature of military thought is the presence of an adversary intelligence. Carl von Clausewitz famously saw the competitive nature of war as constituting a similarity with business, which also involves competition; but even the most intense business competition lacks the direct win/lose or winner-take-all aspect of most military operations.

Beliefs

Like those of other people, soldiers' beliefs are likely to be complex, even inconsistent, and sometimes incoherent. They have personal values and aspirations, passing allegiances and commitments. In this work I am most concerned with those beliefs that define military professionals and influence them in the performance of their role. For the most part these may be described as their professional ethos. The soldier's professional ethos has been defined by codes of honor and of conduct; by personal, tribal, or family loyalties; by obligations of service to city or state; and by international conventions, unwritten or written, such as chivalry and the law of war. These beliefs may be contradictory or conflicting. It is clear that the soldier holds certain important beliefs that are almost uniquely military and others that are shared with civilians, although a soldier may sometimes experience, hold, or express these beliefs in peculiarly military ways. Soldiers often adapt or express the civic or religious beliefs of their times to their own needs and outlook.

Compensations

Why be a soldier? What are the motives and compensations that lead men and women to seek out, take on, and retain the status of soldier? The social science model for professionalism usually does not include a discussion of its inducements and rewards, but it may be an especially interesting and important consideration for the military occupation because the drawbacks are so obvious and unpleasant. Some of the inducements may be timeless. Others are more particular to time and place. The military professional's motive for service has sometimes been compared to a "calling" like a priestly vocation. Of course, many soldiers and some professional soldiers have served out of compulsion or dire necessity. Soldiering has been viewed as a passage to manhood; a path to adventure, social promotion, or wealth; or simply a way to bring meaning and identification to one's existence. Some have seen it as an escape from unwanted ties or responsibility or as an excuse for license and even criminality. Other soldiers have been moved by their better angels; by more idealistic and even altruistic motives; by a desire to serve; or by a wish to test and develop their courage, judgment, and moral strength. Some soldiers have continued to "trail the pike" despite other opportunities and sufficient acquaintance with war's reality. Others have been like the British subaltern after Waterloo who is said to have announced, "I have often expressed my desire to witness a general engagement. I have, and I am perfectly satisfied."

Communication

By "communication" I mean the process of articulating, passing on, and reinforcing knowledge, belief, and habits of thought. Communication in this sense comprehends training and education, both formal and informal. The soldiers of the past were less likely to receive formal education and training than to learn by emulation and through experience. The literate might read books on military history, tactics, organization, and technology. A rich tradition and treasury of works exist on these subjects, beginning with the Greeks, a body of knowledge that has been attenuated at times of upheaval but never lost.[13] Command may also be seen as relying on communication or even as a form of communication. In some ways methods of command in the past were less autocratic than are those of modern armies, in which the principle of unified command has become an article of faith. Ancient commanders held councils of war where all those present might feel free to air their views. The lack of official written doctrine potentially created an atmosphere that was less doctrinaire. The lack of formal schooling was a weakness, but it could also be a strength by creating more openness to the original ideas of subordinates or those outside the profession. Verbal communication, including the arts of discourse and rhetoric, could be very important to commanders of previous centuries. The means of control were generally more fluid than in the highly organized societies of modern times. Officers and commanders often had to make personal spoken appeals to their men before and during battle, and the terrifying, intensely physical nature of close-in combat meant that these appeals bore repeating and reinforcement by way of personal intervention and example, which might be considered forms of military "speech-act." Standardized commands and terminology may have simplified the modern leader's task, and remote communications by signal, wire, and radio have expanded its reach, but the need for a leader's command of hortatory, expressive, and even poetic language is a lesson of the past because it is an enduring, if sometimes neglected, component of leadership.

Leadership

If planning is the most distinctive activity of the military professional, leadership is perhaps the most comprehensive. Leadership may be defined as the exercise of personal control under conditions of change.[14] If we distinguish leadership from management—which is a more impersonal form of control under more static, and in that sense less challenging, conditions—it will be clear that warfare and other kinds of armed conflict make particular demands on leadership. The military profession has cultivated the art of leadership to a greater extent than has any other professional group. In a sense, leadership is a form of professional knowledge, but to varying degrees it intersects with all of the elements of professionalism listed above. The exercise of leadership will be influenced by belief, or ethos. Leadership is closely tied to cognition, and to problem solving in particular. Leadership involves communication and is an important topic of professional instruction. It is both form and content, medium and message. Discipline and morale may be said to be the necessary complements to leadership—making soldiers receptive to leadership and allowing those in the ranks to perform their functions just as leadership allows officers to perform theirs—but more than discipline is required for leadership to be effective. The leader has to understand and help to define what motivates both himself or herself and other soldiers to serve, fight, and strive for victory.

Trust and Character

A distinguishing feature of any profession is that its members are conscious of themselves as a distinct group. However, a group of individuals cannot simply lay claim to professional status.[15] No matter how extensive their knowledge and wide-ranging their minds; no matter how secure and admirable their ethos; and no matter what mechanisms they have in place to instruct, reward, or sanction, no profession can properly be so called unless the larger society approves this designation. Professional practice, requiring as it does a high degree of individual and corporate autonomy, must be based on the trust and confidence of those outside the profession. The trust placed in military professionals is to a degree dependent on the presumption that they possess specialist knowledge. The military profession may be unique in the degree to which both the public trust and the self-image of military professionals are based on character, on the possession of certain beliefs and the will to act on them even under conditions of stress and sometimes of considerable license, since, as Tolstoy observes in *War and Peace*, "nowhere is a man freer than during a life and death struggle."[16] Character is central to military professionalism, but military professionals are not alone in possessing it. The soldier is not the sole repository of virtue in a society. More than other professions, the military profession requires inclusiveness as well as distinctness. If soldiers are to thoroughly fulfill their role, the line between citizen and soldier must remain permeable from both sides. Soldiers' specialized knowledge and insight should be made available to the society at large. The professional soldier must also be open to ideas, control, and critique from the larger society and to the contributions of citizen-soldiers whose character and abilities may be greater than those of the lifetime or career professional.

The Soldier as Historian

The military professional, in the role of educator, leader, and war fighter, is like the historian in navigating a labyrinth of knowledge that is endless and uncertain. In this realm of doubt he or she must decide and act. The soldier's calling is an ancient one with a long memory. Military institutions are in a sense made up of history and literature and of traditions and symbols (as Marine colonel John W. Thomason notes) "such as regiments hand down forever."[17] But individual and institutional memories are selective and imperfect. The military professionals of the past knew things that were not passed on to those of the present or have been neglected. They held beliefs that are often not to be despised in themselves, and they held them in a way and to a depth that the soldiers of a more skeptical and distracted age can profitably ponder and admire. More important, perhaps, history offers examples of the complex ways knowledge is gained, adapted, and discarded or forgotten and the ways beliefs are held, strengthened, and modified. How is a "profession," a public utterance of competency and commitment, internalized, enacted, perceived, and developed? In the case of military history these questions relate to the mysterious nature of war as both an extension of humankind's evolutionary origins and a component of nearly all civilizations, no matter how advanced or expressly peaceable they have been. Members of the military profession, the very existence of a military profession, have undoubtedly contributed to the fact that certain wars have been fought or prolonged; indeed, the existence of the profession of arms is tied up with the persistence of warfare as a constant theme in human history. But the military profession, with its collective knowledge of war's reality, of its tendency to escalate beyond any stated goals, intentions, or control, has also been responsible for keeping the lid of the Pandora's box of armed destruction from flying open. Professional soldiers have been responsible for practicing much of whatever humanity and restraint have existed in war. They have instructed nonprofessional or unprofessional warriors in the various codes of conduct that professionals have developed and often followed.[18] Professional soldiers have carried with them some of the highest aspirations of the societies they served and of the times in which they lived. Although war is destructive of both civilized structures and civilized attitudes, every advanced society, and perhaps especially those of the West, has valued and even revered the profession of arms in a special way, acknowledging its particular challenges, significance, and importance to a society and to civilization itself.

Armies build as well as destroy. Soldiers are often involved in the restoration of peace after victory. At the times when members of the profession of arms have made their greatest contributions, they have viewed themselves and been viewed as serving a larger societal, cultural, and ethical function. It would not be too much to say that at such times the soldier has been in the vanguard of civilization. At other moments soldiers have become what they beheld and given way to callousness, ambition, and love of slaughter. The dangers of narrow professionalism have also been, in their way, as dangerous as those of lack of professionalism. This legacy challenges modern military professionals to view their inheritance with a mixture of respect and skepticism and to be instructed by the positive examples of soldiers of the past as well as by their errors and omissions.

A great benefit of the study of history lies in the efforts to understand and to empathize based on incomplete knowledge. Any form of mastery involves this extension and involvement of the imagination. Any leader or follower must have the ability to understand others across distances of time, culture, and experience. The effort to understand the past gives us tools, cognitive and affective, for grasping the present and ourselves. To study history is to enter a labyrinth, a place of endless uncertainty and discovery where every corner presents an opportunity for the unexpected. The more we see of this place, the more we realize what we do not know and how much remains to be known. Perhaps through further reading, through some uncovering of lost texts or artifacts, or through a deeper understanding of existing knowledge and material we may gain in the ability to see the world of the past in all its difference, strangeness, and complexity and, without simplifying this distinctiveness, to relate the past to the history of human-kind being lived today.

Soldiers and Civilization

I have claimed that the soldier is at once both the most and the least civilized of persons, one who serves society in a condition of "unlimited liability" while often being a marginal figure on the fringes of civilization. The war zone can be a lawless and licentious place. What has often distinguished militaries with a claim to professionalism from mere groups of marauders or bands of warriors has been the former's emphasis on the need for both self-control and external controls, for character, discipline, and organiza-tion. Military professions of this kind have arisen mostly in the West—in Europe and in the Americas—in North America especially. The West has been an important repository of the idea of civilization, of settled and stable societies that provide individuals with a reasonable chance at a high quality of life, including self-expression and the enjoyment of leisure.

Soldiers have contributed to civilization in three functional areas: defense, state formation and support, and leadership and innovation. Sol-diers, perhaps military professionals in particular, have served the cause of civilization by defending the civilizations of their time. Soldiers also have helped to bring down civilizations. Sometimes the barbarians won. More commonly, however, it was the more advanced civilizations of their times that possessed the most professional militaries, both because the develop-ment of a professional military was conducive to the stability and prosperity that are necessary to civilized works and attitudes, and because professional militaries could and often did contribute directly to the development of the civilizations of their time and place. The more professional militaries have tended to prevail in war. Armies have served as nascent state institu-tions providing organizational impetus and expertise. They have also been engines of social change, expanding the ties of citizenship and serving as a means of upward mobility.

This work will proceed in a chronological order. Internally, the organi-zation of the chapters will vary depending on where the main subdivisions of the military profession seem to fall along thematic, regional, and temporal lines. Generally I will examine the military professions of each successive historical period by assessing the cultural and historical context of the military profession under discussion and then the specifically military culture of the time—how it was developed, organized, and perpetuated, and how it in turn influenced the larger society. Next, I will examine how the profession functioned as a war-fighting entity, addressing the challenges of strategy and the battlefield. Last, I will address the legacy of the military profession of the time for soldiers, for civilians, and for the ideal of civilization itself.

Throughout this work I hope to address a number of questions, specifically:

- Were there soldiers of this time who qualified as members of the profession of arms and military profession? If so, who were they?

- Does the example of this period illuminate any essential, enduring, or neglected aspects of military professionalism?

- How did soldiers contribute to the growth of human knowledge, of their societies and civilization?

- Can a consideration of the past or this particular past indicate a path of future progress or regress for the military profession?

1

GREEKS AND MACEDONIANS
Poetry, Philosophy, and the Phalanx

We begin with the ancient Greeks and *The Iliad*. Homer's war poem forms the ethical and theoretical underpinnings of Greek warfare and of the embryonic but prodigious military professionalism of the ancient Greeks. In the seventh century BCE, with *The Iliad* well established as a touchstone of Greek civilization, a number of factors combined to evolve a distinctive form of warfare: a heavily armed infantry of men called hoplites who fought in tight formations, or phalanxes, battling on an open field. In its ideal form, classic Greek warfare was a highly cultural, almost ritualistic practice. This ideal filled the needs in Greek society for constant competition and for the persistence of mythic and dramatic elements in everyday life. The reality of Greek warfare was more complicated than the idealized version of hoplite battle writers such as Demosthenes and Polybius refer to nostalgically, but the ideal exerted an undeniable influence on the reality.[1] My position on the significance of Greek warfare may be said to lie between that of Victor Davis Hanson and others, such as Hans van Wees, who paint a more complex picture.[2] Following Hanson, I argue that the Greeks are responsible for the origins of Western military practice and professional theory. Drawing on work by van Wees, I see these origins as mixed and complex. From the Greeks we get not only the legacy of decisive battle but also that of asymmetric warfare, and not only a rational approach to warfare but also an acknowledgment of its irrational factors that Carl von Clausewitz would call "friction" two thousand years later. The Greek military legacy is many faceted, and it is inseparable from the broader Greek cultural and cognitive achievements. In the period of Greek intellectual flowering, interest in warfare and the nature of military professionalism attracted the attention of the best minds of the time. Given the nature of Greek society, the philosophers, dramatists, and historians were often also soldiers of considerable experience and repute. The list of classic Greek thinkers and writers who also served notably as soldiers includes Socrates, Aeschylus, and Herodotus. All of these men wrote about their military experiences in the context of the history and issues of the time. Plato's *Republic* requires that all members of the governing class of Guardians perform military service as a prerequisite to assuming their roles as philosopher-rulers. One of the senses in which the Greek military profession is seminal is that Greek society and philosophy conceived the Western idea that military service is not just necessary but also uniquely edifying for the individual and conducive to the moral well-being of the state. Most of the Greek soldiers I have mentioned and will discuss were not professionals in the sense that they worked at soldiering full time (the Spartans and Macedonians were exceptions in this sense), but in times of frequent, sometimes annual warfare many part-time soldiers gained considerable military experience at the "sharp end of the spear." In addition, many Greeks specialized in military matters as teachers and practitioners, including the Athenian *strategos* Laches, who gave his name to an early Socratic dialogue that moves through the subjects of courage, education, and military training. The Greeks possessed an extensive military literature as well as a class of educators who claimed to possess communicable expertise in military matters. Members of the larger Greek military profession included these military teachers and also scientists and engineers such as Hero and Archimedes, who lent their skills and intellect to the practice of warfare. Greek civilization suffused the practice of warfare with an ethical code, a literary and cultural narrative, a scientific discourse, and an evolving war-fighting tradition.

Eventually the competitive and innovative spirit of the Greeks won out over the conventions established for hoplite battle in phalanx formation. Ironically, the greatest challenge to these conventions came not from the Greeks' mortal enemies the Persians, but from their poor relations the Macedonians. Philip II and his famous son, Alexander III, created and fielded a more lethal and offensive version of the phalanx. This organization was capable of more sophisticated tactics than its predecessor was, creating a need for greater theoretical and practical knowledge among the military professionals of the day. The ethos of Greek soldiers underwent changes along with those in organization and tactics, but there were also strong continuities. Greek soldiers saw themselves as fighting for unique values that were inherent in individual city-states and also across Greek society, with its rich mix of drama and myth, tradition and innovation, discipline and debate.

Ancient Greek military knowledge may be said to have expanded in volume and in scope from the early heroic and Homeric periods of Greek history through the classical and Hellenic periods. The expansion of knowledge coincided with cognitive growth, a more expansive sense of the uses of warfare, and a movement from individual combat, to the simple tactics of the classic phalanx, to the complex combined-arms operations and ambitious, far-ranging strategies of Alexander. Those with the greatest claim to be called military professionals in the time Homer depicts were aristocrats who were filling a role that was expected of all members of their class (an idea that I will explore more fully in the following section on *The Iliad*). Great stress was placed on the need to demonstrate individual prowess, but in the course of *The Iliad* it also becomes clear that military professionals must be able to lead competently and to have some understanding of tactics and strategy (words that are Greek in origin). The proto-military professional par excellence of *The Iliad* is Ulysses. Ulysses not only shows courage on the battlefield in leading his own contingent of Ithacans, he also functions as a staff officer in guiding the actions and correcting the mistakes of Agamemnon. As a man who is capable with words and ideas as well as action, he sets the pattern for military professionalism in the West for nearly three millennia.

The Iliad as Military Doctrine

In the following pages I will discuss *The Iliad* as a work of military doctrine that informed Greek soldiers' understanding of warfare as well as that of their conquerors and successors, the Romans, and that still suffuses thought on the subject of warfare today.[3] *The Iliad* began the West's long inquiry into the nature of armed conflict and retained a strong hold on the attention of Greek soldiers throughout antiquity.[4] It was ancient Greek military doctrine in that the Greeks understood it as an instructive work on the nature of warfare and on why and how to fight. Considered as doctrine, it may be seen to have advantages over more recent and modern, less poetic and more prosaic works. *The Iliad* presents a complex, even problematized, picture of warfare in all of its tragedy, error, and mischance.

Implicit in Homer's work is a definition of war that could serve to supplement Clausewitz's famous belief that war is politics pursued by other means, and to Sherman's simple assertion that it is hell unrefined. In Homer there is an understanding that war is a self-reflexive cultural activity, one defined by evolving cultural beliefs that also itself constitutes a critique of those beliefs. A reading of Homer contributes to the sense that war is about the status and value of certain kinds of meaning: that each war is an inquiry into the efficacy and even the possibility of such ideas as courage, prowess, leadership, and victory. Since to address issues of meaning is also to raise questions of value, Homer's work focuses attention on the moral aspect of warfare. This is something the later Greeks profoundly understood, as evidenced by the fact that they went to Homer as to no other source for moral paradigms as well as for military instruction. He was their scripture and interpreter in one. The Greeks were also famously enamored of the contest and the debate. War is the ultimate contest, and it may be understood in terms of an argument, both between the two opposing sides and among competing views of war's significance, views that may appear in either opposing camp. It should be understood that like any form of doctrine or discourse, *The Iliad* cannot be perfect.[5] Its teachings can be both valuable and misleading, as we shall see. The argument of *The Iliad* (and, to a lesser degree, of *The Odyssey*) can be broken down into four parts: causes and victory; courage, prowess, and heroism; friction and the battlefield; and leadership and language.

Causes and Victory

The Trojan War is fought for a complex array of varied and even contradictory causes. Some goals it sets out to achieve are eventually realized (for the victors), but others, unstated but perhaps even more important, are not. In this sense, as in many others, the Trojan War resembles most of those fought in human history. The Trojan War may be viewed as an illustration of Clausewitz's "paradoxical trinity." It is fought for reasons combining the rational and irrational. Chance—fortune and misfortune—plays a sizable role in the conduct and ultimate outcome of the war. The Trojan War is fought, first, to restore Queen Helen to her rightful husband, Menelaus. On the Trojan side, the decision to back Paris in his abduction of Helen is the subject of considerable debate and continuing dissension. What begins as a matter of pride becomes a question of necessity as the Trojans come to believe that they are unable to meet the Greeks' demands for compensation if they surrender. The ostensible causes for the war may seem quixotic by modern standards, but queens are politically important. Also, Helen is likely not the only reason for war. As *The Iliad* often illustrates, the aristocrats who run Mycenaean society are heavy consumers and generous gift givers. In this culture, material goods are neither merely symbols nor items of luxury; they are the stuff of honor. Such a culture would require frequent sustenance. The raid for booty was the most common form of warfare in this time.[6] In fact, the historical basis for Homer's fictionalized Trojan War may have been a large-scale raid, which then became with the telling the epic ten-year conflict that we know.[7]

For Menelaus and Agamemnon, the chief belligerents, the conflict is an opportunity to assert both their temporal authority and their reproductive rights. For them the great matter to be settled in this war is who is the *man*? Like the epic combat fought over the corpse of Patroclus, the ostensible cause of the Trojan War is possession of a person, the living person of Helen; but in both cases the greater matter is honor. For Agamemnon in particular the war offers an occasion to enforce a discipline that is both necessary to the conduct of the war and desirable in itself. The war gives him the opportunity to assert his authority over the sometimes turbulent Greek lordlings, to remind wives of their duty, and to crush a rival state whose prince is guilty of conduct unbecoming a gentleman. Although he may not see it this way, it is also an occasion for Agamemnon to learn the arts of leadership. War is the sport of kings; it is their playing field and training ground. As Nietzsche and others have reminded us, the idea of nobility is inseparable from demonstrated success on the battlefield. Kings have gained their positions by war and must continue to justify themselves through war.

Going beyond the text of *The Iliad* to the subsidiary legends it has gathered to itself, we may learn something of the divided nature of victory. The Greeks gain much by this war: Agamemnon learns some important lessons as a leader at Troy; Menelaus recovers his wife; and the Greeks' cause and manhood are validated by their willingness to fight, by their successes in battle, and by the favor of the gods. But the justifications and rationale for victory begin to unravel even before the war is won. Arguably, the Greek victory is won not by superior prowess but by a clever stratagem. Agamemnon establishes himself as fit to be king, only to be killed by his wife, Clytemnestra, and her lover, Aegisthus, upon his return home. These events repudiate the larger principles behind the need to retrieve Helen—

those of wifely loyalty and proper conduct as a guest. On the other hand, Homer is clearly holding up the world of Mycenaean culture as superior in many ways to that of his own time. Later Greeks would come to view the Trojan War as the historical, and literary, event that would unite the Hellenic world, a preamble to their victory over the Persians and to the age of accomplishments as the cradle of Western thought. Victory, it seems, may come in many forms. Both defeat and victory are temporary, temporal, and therefore rooted in time, which is the stuff of narrative. They are therefore phenomena that the narrative form of *The Iliad* was perhaps uniquely suited to enable the Greeks to understand, because *The Iliad* is storytelling as doctrine.

Courage, Prowess, and Heroism

Twentieth-century commentaries on the age Homer describes routinely stress that it was a heroic age, one marked by an unapologetic regard for the heroic virtues of physical strength, courage, spirit, and military skill.[8] The men of Homer's time are said to have valued these qualities beyond the estimation placed on them perhaps at any other time. This way of interpreting Homer's work seems to have a firm basis in the text. Many scenes in *The Iliad* appear to glorify war and conquest; Sarpedon's speech on noblesse to his friend Glaucus is often cited as an example. But as writers from Simone Weil to Sheila Murnaghan note, there are also many incidents in *The Iliad* that wear away at the dominant ethos of the warrior-aristocrat.[9]

The glorification and the interrogation of the warrior ethos are both centered in the person, actions, character, and fate of Achilles. Because of his status as their most puissant warrior, Achilles often bears the identifying tag "best of the Achaeans," but the text also sometimes assigns this title to others, casting reasonable doubt on the preeminence of Achilles.[10] Although he is the strongest, fastest, most dangerous man on the field, on either side, he is hors de combat for most of *The Iliad*. When he finally does enter battle, it is not to retrieve the Achaean cause but to exact personal revenge for the death of his only friend, Patroclus. Achilles is the complete warrior, and in a heroic society this would seem to make him the complete man. By denominating him the "best of the Achaeans" there is a sense that the poet desires to accept this simple, heroic view of virtue. Like Menenius declaring the fractious Roman Coriolanus in Shakespeare's play to be "right noble," of Achilles some seem to think that (surely) so great a warrior must be a great man. Such demonstrations of nobility as Achilles could perform in battle could not come from a nature that had anything of the petty, petulant, or immature.

Surprisingly, Achilles sometimes appears to be all of these things, and worse. He violates even the rough-and-tumble standards of his day for conduct toward the enemy by sacrificing large numbers of prisoners and refusing (for a time) to allow Hector's father to have his son's corpse for burial. The best of the Achaeans is also the beast of the Achaeans: an outcast and outlaw.

Would these doubts cast on Achilles' preeminence have dethroned, for Greek soldiers, the heroic values? The nearest competitor to Achilles for the title of the best of the Achaeans in *The Iliad* is Ulysses, who as protagonist of *The Odyssey* is in effect promoted to the top position. In the long run it is the clever Ulysses, not swift Achilles, who is the Homeric ideal. In elevating him, Homer infuses the Ulysses of *The Odyssey* with martial abilities that in *The Iliad* take a backseat to his cleverness and skill with words. As Telemachus searches for his father in *The Odyssey*, the tales of Ulysses at Troy that he hears from the veterans of Troy mostly concern his father's prowess rather than his intelligence. Ulysses regains his household by cunning but also by sheer physical strength. Only he can bend the bow that he uses to kill the importunate suitors. This is itself reminiscent of Achilles, who carries a spear that no one else can wield. Ulysses cannot be quite the best man of his world unless he is also one of its most formidable warriors. The humbling, death, and antiheroic speech from Hades of Achilles (when Ulysses visits the underworld) have not changed this. The warrior's preeminence is cast into doubt, but it is not discarded.

Another comment on the value of purely martial qualities is implied in *The Iliad*. If the Trojan War is later (after the conclusion of Homer's poem) decided by an amphibious feint and a covert operation, in *The Iliad* the death of Hector at the hands of Achilles has made the defeat of the Trojans a foregone conclusion. Simply put, the Greeks have several heroes of the first rank but the Trojans have only one, and when Hector is killed it is taken for granted that the Trojans are lost.

Friction and the Battlefield

The term "friction" has its origins in Clausewitz, who uses it to describe the tendency of things on the battlefield to go wrong under the pressure of confusion, violence, fatigue, and fear. "In war all things are simple," he says, "but even the simplest thing is difficult."[11] Clausewitz likens the effect of the combat environment on the soldier to that of water on a swimmer. The actions of the limbs, respiration, even the workings of the mind are slowed and disordered. Panic can set in more easily in water than on land. The battlefield, even more than the storm-tossed, wine-dark sea, is an essentially alien, hostile, even ineffable place.

In *The Iliad* friction can be said to visit the battlefield in the form of the gods. Whenever a spear unaccountably misses its mark or an apparently cornered enemy suddenly makes his escape, both sides seem to attribute this remarkable happening to divine intervention. Those who go about unscathed are thought to be in a god's favor; but the immortals are fickle, and such good fortune may be suddenly withdrawn. The gods are divided as to which side they support, and they even fight among themselves. The goddess Panic, sister of Fear, may grip the soldiers' hearts at any time. The Greeks call upon Zeus to disperse a fog that is helping the Trojans, and he grants their request, surprisingly, because he has usually favored the Trojans.[12] The intervention of the gods in combat in *The Iliad* may seem to be an anachronism, but it is really a profound comment on the nature of war. War is both human relations gone sour and the place where everything goes wrong. The only perfect war is the one that is not fought. War is a testament and a demonstration of human error. It is hubris to think that we can completely control what happens in war, or that it will not in some way rebound on us if we choose to wage it, even if it is forced upon us. The most successful warriors are not only those the gods most favor; they have an appreciation of the battlefield as a place where they are in the hands of gods. In book eight of *The Iliad*, when Hector seems unstoppable, the veteran Nestor and heroic Diomedes agree that "Zeus has given this man the glory today. Another day he may give it to us, but no one can change the purpose of Zeus." In *The Iliad*, to yield to the inevitable, to recognize the tide of battle when it is for or against one's own side, combines common sense, wisdom, and piety.

Leadership and Language

The Iliad addresses the paradoxical, sometimes inverse relationship of war and language. War both depends on and is hostile to language. War calls for the arts of exhortation and narration and the voice of command. The commander who issues a plan of battle or who exhorts his men may be said to be engaging in a tale of victory, one that will be effective only if it demonstrates the same traits of coherence and verisimilitude that make for good narrative. Speech in war must be active and convincing. Agamemnon learns this early on in the poem when his attempt to manipulate his men backfires. "The usual drill—order them to beat a retreat in their ships."[13] Instead of inspiring his men, Agamemnon is surprised when they turn the retreat into a rout that almost clears the beaches of Achaean ships. Insincere, unmotivated, perfunctory speech is not an effective tool of command. Later, Agamemnon's speech seems to improve. In book seven he is reputed to have "said all the right things" to dissuade Menelaus from an ill-considered combat with Hector. Both he and Achilles learn to moderate their speech, with each in the latter books of the poem discussing rather than merely exchanging insults. Excellence in council is second only to battlefield prowess as the trait most valued in *The Iliad*. Even Achilles concedes that although he is the best at fighting, "some do speak better," so that for all of his commitment to action he possesses a perhaps increasing recognition of the value of speech.[14] The paean and the exchanges of taunts, threats, and lineages that precede most of the important individual combats in the story are important forms of war-speak in Homer.

In *The Iliad* there is also a tendency for men in war to eschew speech entirely, as illustrated by the poem's foremost warrior's temporary abandonment of speech and social contacts. Some significant utterances in the poem are not speech at all. A frequent tag for warriors is "good at the war cry." And there is the magical, inspiriting or demoralizing speech of the gods, which mortals experience as a kind of internal rhetoric.

Homeric themes and images continued to appear in Greek art and drama for centuries. The golden age fourth-century Greek culture writers and artists depict war and the soldier almost obsessively, underlining the nature and importance of armed conflict for generations of Greek soldiers and citizens. Historians and dramatists show how wars are fought, won, and lost, and also depict the feelings and motives of soldiers in war. The warriors whose images are preserved on vases are lithe and deadly, both lethal and vulnerable. The compendium of Greek art and writing on warfare is too rich to summarize here, but it can at least be said that the Greeks saw war as a tragic and inevitable ritual of human and social existence that could be faced only head-on.

After *The Iliad*: Hoplite and Phalanx

The warfare Homer describes is difficult to fix in time. It mixes features of different periods, from the Mycenaean age, in which the Trojan War putatively took place, to Homer's own time, roughly the seventh century BCE, when hoplite warfare began to emerge. There are intimations in Homer of the phalanxed, close-in, heavy infantry combat of hoplite warfare as opposed to the missile and chariot combat that more likely characterized fighting in the Mycenaean age. Homer's work both presages and underlies the work of later military writers while offering a unique and still unmatched assessment of the nature of warfare. *The Iliad* continued to be treated as doctrine for centuries. Although the conduct of war changed, Greek soldiers tried to order their conflicts to give scope for the demonstrations of prowess described in *The Iliad*.[15] The classic combat of the hoplite (named for the *hoplon*, his equipment of helmet, breastplate, greaves, spear, and shield) and the deep, dense formation of the phalanx laid emphasis on individual and collective will, allowing little scope for maneuver and less for stratagems or trickery. In the time of kings, a few aristocrat-champions determined the fitness of a society. In a still class-bound but somewhat more egalitarian society, fitness and victory would be upheld by the aggregate moral and physical strength of its citizen population. The combat of the phalanx was in effect a democratized, collectivized form of Mycenaean warfare. Still a test of strength and fitness, it now put to the test not only warrior-aristocrats but also the free and property-owning adult manhood of the city-state and of Greece.

We cannot be certain exactly how the phalanx developed. It may be that Greek soldiers developed an early version of the phalanx formation that the evolution of the *hoplon* refined. A lightly armored soldier in close-range combat in a dense formation would have been very vulnerable. A heavily armored infantryman in the phalanx, whether fighting others like himself or different (and likely less protected) fighters, was able to fight to a decision without the need to incur heavy casualties. A battle could be fought in less than an hour. The losing side almost always lost more men, but the winners were prevented from pursuit and annihilation of the losers—possibly by convention, and certainly by fatigue and the weight of the *hoplon*. This method of fighting suited Greek strategic needs in a number of ways. When Greeks fought Greeks it could be for modest objectives, even merely for kudos. The low casualty rate was sustainable even in a time of frequent warfare. Hoplite battle spared enough economically useful citizen-soldiers and their crops to sustain the local Greek economies.[16] It also helped to usher in Greek democracy and egalitarianism by empowering a large middle class who provided the hoplites and their equipment. These social changes took time and had to overcome the resistance of conservatives (e.g., Aristotle), but they represented an important departure from the past. Once the rich and middle class fought side by side, it became more difficult for the wealthy to insist on a monopoly of political power.

Recent historical and archaeological work, along with experiments using reconstructed *hoplon*, has created a more complex picture of classical Greek phalanx warfare.[17] First, the idea of Greek battles as agreed-upon matches in which both sides disdained to capitalize on any advantages other than strength or *arête* (excellence in character) is at least oversimple. The Greeks may have wanted warfare to be conducted this way, and they may even have chosen to depict it as such, but the ideal of Greek warfare often gave way to necessity. For the weaker side, a test of strength could be a disaster, even given faith in the superiority of one's own cause or character. The Greeks were not above ambushing a superior force or refusing battle in favor of more indirect or asymmetrical approaches. The depiction of phalanx combat as essentially a shoving match of two opposing scrums is also likely an oversimplification. Although difficult to control—in fact, not subject to command and control in the modern sense (with the exception of the Spartans)—the Greek phalanx was capable of a high degree of cohesiveness as well as small-group and individual action. The spacing between men was great enough to permit visibility and the use of weapons. Hoplites would have had to depend on one another, but they also would have had to look out for themselves, pick their opponents, and push forward or hold back. If not really a scrum, neither was the phalanx a wide-open rugby backfield. A better analogy may be to a football line, with its protected players acting both in cooperation and as individuals. Phalanx battle was likely an interconnected series of individual and group combats, with small groups sometimes acting in unison and then breaking up, each man trying to hold his own, performing at a level dictated by an interplay of pride and shame, skill level and confidence, and whatever reserves of courage, strength, and aggressiveness he could summon on that day, at that hour and moment. If the men in front got the idea to backpedal, they had the ranks behind them barring the way, as

The Push of the Spear. Two hoplites square off in close combat with the near support of spearmen in the second rank. *"Closeup of Vase" by Grant Mitchell/CC BY 2.0*

long as the latter held. The rear-rankers might use their shields to push into line anyone in front who fell back. Victory rested on the cumulative effects of small combats. Defeat was likely to be the result of a loss of confidence rippling through the formation until enough men, having had enough for one day and afraid of being left behind to face an advancing enemy without adequate support from comrades, gave ground, turned, and fled, leaving shields and other encumbrances on the field.

The classical Greeks' attachment to the ideal of the citizen-soldier helped to define their version of culturally inclusive military professionalism. The Greeks wanted victory based on their cultural DNA, as an extension of civic virtue, and at the height of Greek civilization this was not an entirely deluded hope. Greek society proved able to pass on sufficient knowledge and ethos to enable the Greeks to field armies ready and able to fight one another regularly and to repeatedly defeat the numerically superior Persians. Although regular training occurred only in Sparta until the fourth century BCE, social and familial relationships among male citizens provided a means to transfer knowledge, instill beliefs, and reinforce cohesion on the battlefield. This knowledge included a glossary of military terms that the Greeks used to describe and discuss warfare.[18] There is considerable evidence that a segment of Greek society took a focused interest in military matters and regularly sought positions of military leadership. The Athenians elected ten *strategos* annually to lead the contingents of the Athenian army. Socrates recommended taking advantage of the teaching offered by professional military instructors, although he also warned his pupils not to take their advice uncritically. According to the officer and military writer Xenophon, one of Socrates' students, Dionysodorus, opened a military academy. Thanks to the nature of Greek civil society, that of Athens in particular, the professionalism some of the ancient Greeks cultivated could not be narrow or insular. The professionals benefited from contact and conversation with the amateurs: the majority of Greek citizens who served in the army but did not specialize in military matters. Perhaps the most famous example of this is in the early Socratic dialogue *Laches*. This work is named for an Athenian general with whom Socrates discusses the purpose of education and of military training and the nature of courage. Socrates is remarkably and unironically respectful of the *strategos*, of Laches especially, as they are of him, based partly on his reputation for excellence and courage as a hoplite. The dialogue is a seminal example of military professionalism in the wider context of culture and ideas.

A form of professionalism existed even in the city-states, such as Athens, where amateurs were exalted and outnumbered the professionals. Two Greek states developed superior levels of military professionalism that were both exemplary and cautionary for their contemporaries, as they are for moderns: Sparta and Macedonia. Both were outsider communities in the larger Greek civilization that came to be imitated by and to dominate their neighbors. They may be said to express a militarism latent in all of Greek civilization, an addiction and commitment to arms that proved to be fatal. The Spartan state rested on a narrow base of highly professionalized citizen-soldiers who were granted the leisure and impetus to engage in intensive, lifelong military training by the existence of a slave, or helot, class that outnumbered the citizens by as much as ten or twenty to one. The highly militarized culture of Sparta, with its communal messes and autocratic style of government, produced an uncompromising military ethos and a system of sanctions to ensure compliance. A Spartan male who failed in combat was guaranteed a life on the margins without wife, comrades, or the right to public utterance. Their militaristic culture gave the Spartans major advantages in the areas of training, discipline, and command and control. The full-time preoccupation with soldiering made certain that Spartans were physically fit and adept at weapons handling, two areas left to chance and the individual in other Greek city-states. An even greater advantage may have derived from the organization of the Spartan phalanx. A Spartan army was divided into large and smaller units, all with leaders and commanders, so that Spartan officers were said to be "commanders of commanders." The Spartans organized their phalanx into *mora* of five hundred men. Each *mora* contained four *lochoi*, each containing two *pentecostys* that were in turn divided into two *enom-oties*.[19] The file of about eight men was the smallest unit. Each man in the file had his assigned place, with the most experienced and reliable positioned front and rear. Training and organization gave Spartan formations a great degree of flexibility. They could execute complex maneuvers on the move, reacting to threats of ambush from sides and rear.[20] Military organization in the other cities appears to have been similar but much looser. Men fell in where they chose and were not subject to a chain of command. Military orders in the field carried much less weight and authority in a typical Greek army than among the Spartans.

The Spartans fought the same battle as the rest of the Greeks; they just fought it better. Eventually the advantages of the Spartan military system became so manifest that the other Greeks widely imitated it. Regular train-ing was instituted among the citizen-soldiers, and mercenaries were some-times preferred for their superior training. Innovation among the Spartans was limited by their deep religious conservatism and perhaps by their ten-dency toward minimalist speech. (We now call those of few words "laconic," after the Laconians, or Spartans.) Both of these tendencies may have con-tributed to the Spartans' excellence as warriors and soldiers, but they reflect a narrow form of military professionalism. Sparta's strategic ambitions were limited by the need to control the helot population, upon which the Spartan economy and militarized way of life depended. Their dependency on the helots would prove to be the Spartans' strategic vulnerability. The need to guard the restive slaves forced them to outsource military operations that might take them away from home, turning the Spartans from soldiers into overseers and ending both their days of military dominance and their claims to moral superiority. Eventually the Spartans would be beaten at their own tactical game by the innovating commander of a more egalitarian society, Epaminondas of Thebes.

In contrast to the Spartans, the Macedonians created not just a temporarily perfected form of traditional Greek war fighting but a new system of tactics, and eventually a new approach to strategy. The Macedonians under King Philip II and his son Alexander the Great developed a combined-arms army with a different, more lethal, and less-protected hoplite; a decisive cavalry arm; and effective torsion artillery. This army was far more adept at engineering and siege craft. Under Alexander it became capable of long-range power projection, driven by the young king's ambitions and conceptual reach and fueled by an impressive system of logistics.[21]

The change from Greek to Macedonian hoplite was signaled by an increase in the length of the spear. The old *dory* was seven to eight feet long. The *sarissa* Philip introduced could be up to twenty-one feet in length. The new spear took both hands to manage, so the large shield, the *aspis*, of the classical hoplite was abandoned. Helmet and breastplate became smaller, sacrificing protection for greater ease of movement and field of vision. In the old phalanx only the front rank had been able to directly engage the enemy. The new formation probably permitted three or four spear points to extend past the front rank at normal intervals, more if the intervals between ranks were closed. The files on the flanks could be faced outward or pulled back ("refused") to meet the threat of an envelopment, but the main, formidable combat power of the Macedonian phalanx was to the front, and it was meant to keep moving. In the hands of the Macedonians the phalanx became an offensive weapon.

As lethal and mobile as it was, however, the phalanx was only the anvil to the Macedonian hammer, the cavalry.[22] Alexander would normally place himself at the head of his Companion cavalry, a band of armored and well-mounted aristocrats. Typically, Alexander led the charge that won the day. Combining with the mobile, lethal infantry and cavalry was a new generation of torsion artillery.

The greatest military leader of the age, Alexander the Great is also an equivocal, confusing, and even murky figure. Opinion of him on the part of soldiers and historians is notably divided. His campaign of conquest in the name of glory resulted in tens of thousands of deaths, but by the standards of the time he could be merciful.[23] His empire was short-lived in political terms, but it helped to spread Hellenic civilization. A Macedonian educated in the Greek manner (by his fellow Macedonian Aristotle, among others) and a devotee of Homer, Alexander ended up an Eastern-style despot, debasing and killing his former friends and purging the ranks of his most experienced commanders, the unlucky along with the disloyal or disillusioned. Historian Peter Tsouras credits Alexander with an excellence across all matters of command that is exceptional even among the great captains.[24] He was a strategist, logistician, tactician, combat leader, negotiator, and ruler. At his best he was nearly impossible to beat as a war fighter. Some of his acts of leadership still have the ability to inspire, even when we know how the story ends. Alexander at the head of his cavalry may be the prime example of an ancient Greek military commander's ability to set an example of skill and aggressiveness. Alexander leaping first into the fortress of Gaza, or publicly pouring out a helmet full of water that had been offered to him during the scorching passage of the Balochistan desert, show leadership at its most elemental and its most theatrical.

Greek Military Discourse

In a way both reflecting and expressive of their attachment to *The Iliad* as a form of military doctrine, the military thinking of the Greeks often represents a conflict between continuity and innovation. Classical Greek warfare was generally conservative in that its purpose was to preserve the traditional values of Greek society as reflected in *The Iliad*, in Greek myths, and in the worship of the gods. Sometimes the desire to preserve the values represented by religious observances could delay a campaign, as in the preliminaries to the Battle of Thermopylae when the Spartans, Thespians, and a few other contingents were forced to defend Greece against the Persian Empire unaided because of a festival taking precedence over military victory. The aristocratic, heroic, and pious values of *The Iliad* (institutionalized by Sparta and reconceived by Plato and Alexander) came into conflict with emerging democratic and scientific ideas. This was a debate that concerned all of Greek society, and the soldier was at the center. There was a conflict between the desire to wage war according to Iliadic doctrine and a growing perception that its emphasis on the battlefield as a place where warriors squared off in combat against one another under the close refereeing of the gods was being eroded by the social diversity of Greek and Macedonian armies, developments in weaponry, and an increasing variety in military operations. Added to this were changes in Greek and Hellenic civilization that made it harder to see warfare as a preservative. Thucydides records the changes in Greek warfare and civilization in his history of the Peloponnesian War between Athens and Sparta. That account may be seen as a pragmatic, historical caveat to the mythological idealism of Homer, reflecting the two sides of the divided Greek mind.

The Greek Military Legacy

Collectively, Greek civilization may be given credit for establishing the terms and outline of military professionalism. If one follows the argument of Victor Davis Hanson in his various works (perhaps most especially *Carnage and Culture*), the ancient Greeks established a way of warfare that came to dominate in the West and eventually throughout the world. They bequeathed this approach to warfare partly by contextualizing it in ways that would be accessible to the soldiers and military professionals of the future. Warfare was both the impetus and the arena for much of the vitality of classical Greece, but the Greeks' approach to warfare eventually failed them. Greek civilization was spread by victories in warfare, most notably those of Alexander, and eventually by defeat. Rome conquered Greece in 146 BCE, the Greeks losing to a civilization that was in many ways a descendant of their own and that they went on to Hellenize. The cognitive Achilles' heel of the Greek military profession was perhaps its attachment to the past, but its cultural embeddedness was also a source of strength.

The example of the Greeks sheds light on the idea of military professionalism in a number of ways. One of the most important is the relation of the military profession to defeat. A modern, instrumentalist view of the military profession is that its first responsibility is to deliver victory. This is surely an important function, but the Greeks, in their understanding of hubris and tragedy, knew that no matter how clever, virtuous, or god-favored the protagonist, city, or civilization, all success is temporary. Thucydides notes that the Greeks could be flexible in their approach to war and victory, often preferring truce over the pursuit of victory at high cost. It is a lesson from the ancient Greek military profession that the profession of arms has an obligation not only to deliver victory, but also to warn, anticipate, accept, and accommodate the sometimes unavoidable conditions of defeat. A military profession that holds victory as its ideal may instead serve up disaster. Some victories may simply not be worth the cost in human, political, or historical terms. The honorable defeat may sometimes be preferable to the battering, self-wounding, or corrupting victory. Like the retreat, the honorable defeat is a hard thing to do well. The Greek *polis* could be tough on military commanders who failed to deliver victory, but it could be equally censorious of victorious commanders who failed in their responsibility in some other way. Athens executed eight generals for failing to rescue survivors after the naval victory at Arginusae.[25] An advantage of the Greek system was that those who had spoken in favor of the military campaign also often led it and thus bore the sufferings and uncertain outcome of warfare up close. In addition, just as victory is never final, so is defeat at least rarely final. Even lost civilizations leave their trace, like the memorials of the fallen soldiers of past armies, whether victorious or defeated. The memorials of Greek civilization are many, and some of the most significant have to do with the military profession.

For much of their military history, most Greeks were determinedly amateur in their approach to soldiering. As I have tried to demonstrate and will again, amateurs may be professionals in the sense of possessing many of the traits that are at the heart of professionalism; in possessing knowledge and belief of considerable quality and quantity; and in being able to transmit, instill, and put into operation what they know and believe about waging war. Like soldiers of other times, Greek soldiers, sometimes aided by their amateur status, were able to make contributions that often drew on their military experience but went far beyond purely military tasks. They spoke and wrote, led, and envisioned, displaying wisdom as well as skill and courage, sometimes making their societies and noncombatant brethren better informed and even wiser. But the Greeks also provide a cautionary tale of extreme professionalism in the Spartans and Macedonians. Finally, for all of the claims made by contemporary and recent writers about the innate superiority of the citizen-soldier, the benefits of training became undeniable.

The Greeks wanted warfare to be a test of character, but it became increasingly a matter of skill and money. Just as the Greeks sought moral justifications for victory, they attributed special ethical qualities to the warrior. This was reflected in their veneration of the citizen-soldier and in their desire to wage war in such a way as to foreground moral virtues, courage foremost among them. On the other hand, the Greeks recognized that this approach to warfare was not inevitable. Indeed, it represented an idealization of warfare at least as much as a perception of its reality. The gap or overlap between the real and the ideal drove much of Greek thought in art, poetry, drama, and philosophy. The soldier was the imperfect embodiment of the Greek ethical and aesthetic ideal. The Greek theory of war was powerful but incomplete, although in a sense it still represents the most perfect fusion of soldier and citizen; of body, mind, and spirit; of an ideal impelling and imposing itself on a stubborn reality of deadly, crafted weapons borne by mortal men. In Greek mythology even the eternal gods are feckless and undependable when they wage war. Perhaps it is the Greek conception of war that approaches perfection and war's reality that falls short, like death itself, which Ralph Waldo Emerson predicted would be the ultimate anticlimax. For a time war was as fine a thing for the Greeks as it ever could be. Starting with a poetics of military doctrine, and building on a tragic tradition of drama and a historic philosophical turn, the Greeks developed a seminal theory and practice of warfare in the West. The theory of Greek citizen-soldiers fighting other hoplites on equal terms was instigated by Homer, imperfectly perpetuated for a time in practice, and given philosophical basis by Socrates and Plato (in *The Republic* especially). Alexander's Macedonian professionals are a dead end of the ideal, mercenaries clothed as citizens.[26]

If the main cognitive problem of the ancients was an excessive concern for the past, coupled with practical impediments to innovation, for moderns the fault may lie on the other end, with an exaggerated perception of change, an excessive respect for newness, and a lack of regard for the past. The means of war change, but the causes for which soldiers fight have changed less, and the mortal, fearful, fighting heart of the soldier is much the same.

ROMANS

Legis et Legio

The Roman army of the late republic and empire represents what is in some ways a still-unmatched achievement. In many respects it was a modern army, even an anachronistic precursor of modernity in the ancient world. It had standardized units, ranks, and specializations; voluminous records and awards; and a systematic, pragmatic approach to warfare. The Romans developed a large body of instructive military literature and a poetics and culture of military virtue. They expanded the ties of military service and citizenship developed by the Greeks, and for a time they were able to cure themselves of the habit of fratricidal warfare that had so bedeviled the Hellenes. Under the republic, the Roman army was composed of militant citizens who were able and willing to achieve a level of discipline, training, and tactical proficiency worthy of any professionals.[1] During most of the empire the army consisted of long-service professionals who considered themselves citizens or on the path to citizenship. The achievements of the Roman army in creating, maintaining, and policing an empire are all the more remarkable when one considers the limitations of the period. This was an army that largely moved and fought on human muscle power. All of their discipline and organization would have availed them nothing if the Romans had not arrived on the field mentally and physically ready to engage in lethal combat and to efficiently kill sizable numbers of the enemy with the sharp-edged projectile and handheld weapons of the time. This called for a kind of tightly controlled savagery that is characteristic of combat forces in general, but that perhaps reaches the height of tension in a highly disciplined, hand-to-hand combat force like the Roman legion. Even so, the Roman soldier was more than a war fighter. Many upper-class Romans were the ancient equivalent of reserve officers, serving in alternating civil and military posts. Soldiers doubled as magistrates, police, and engineers. In the years of empire, the army's civic role eventually overlapped onto a political one, and it went from serving the civic authority to bestowing and wielding political power. In the end the army became an abettor of

41

disorder; perhaps it might be said that its commitment to violence and to its commanders won out over a more abstract dedication to Roman order and to civilization. Eventually the army seemed to pull the edifice of Roman civilization down on itself.

At its best, the Roman way of war was a unique fusion of the paradoxical elements of war that the Romans well understood long before Clausewitz enumerated the trinity of reason, passions, and chance. Through a combination of hard experience, ideology, and organization the Romans constructed a military machine that harnessed and directed the capacity for violence of a wild beast and subordinated it to reasons of state. Roman culture, a kind of urbane paganism, could hold the primal and civilized elements of organized combat together in one thought in a way that is perhaps inaccessible to moderns, just as the union of cruelty and splendor of the gladiatorial arena is incomprehensible to us. As in all times, the paradox of military force for the Romans always threatened to become a contradiction, its parts finally irreconcilable and incapable of coexistence. Even at its height, the emperor Tiberias compared control of the Roman army to holding a wolf by its ears. Like the Greeks, the Romans eventually paid a heavy price for the professionalism that necessity appeared to force on them. The professionalization of the Roman army secured the expansion and survival of the empire but also ensured its violent, unsettled, strife-ridden history and its eventual demise.

Roman military professionalism was distinguished by a number of key factors: cultural, tactical, organizational, strategic, and ethical. In this chapter I consider the trajectory of each of these factors from its development through its fulfillment, and on to its decline and fall.

Roman Military Culture

Roman culture contributed to Roman military professionalism in a number of important ways. The republican Romans virtually equated citizenship with eligibility for military service, and virtue with military prowess. The Romans' language was shaped by the country's history and came to determine their character. In a language in which the nearest match and cognate for our word "virtue" was *virtus*, which denoted manly strength and courage (and whose root is *vir* = man), it was difficult for Romans to conceive of personal excellence without the military virtues. Latin with its inflections can also achieve an admirable and soldierly compression, expressing what in English might take twice as many words. Latin lent itself to imperatives and exhortations such as the famous *Carthago delenda est*, and it is still the language of epitaphs and school and services mottos such as *Semper Fidelis*.

Early Roman legends and narratives reinforced the inescapability of war and combat in service to the state. The proto-Romans Romulus and Remus are suckled by a she-wolf, the beast to which Tiberius later compared the Roman army. When Romulus kills his brother for overstepping the city walls, at this point marked only by plow lines, the message is clear: the sanctity of the city is to kill for; it comes before kinship or any other consideration. Horatius not only readily volunteers to defend the Tiber bridgehead in the face of fearful odds, but he also kills his sister when she mourns the death of one of Rome's enemies.

Cultural factors gave the Romans some of the ingredients for military excellence, but it took some time to complete the formula. The very early Romans showed few signs of their later military greatness. They learned from their Etruscan adversaries and eventually adopted a form of Greek hoplite and phalanx warfare in the sixth century BCE.[2] A distinctly Roman form of warfare may have begun its development following the disastrous encounter with the Gauls at Allia in 390 BCE. The Romans endured the disgrace of a foreign invader in their capital for the last time until 410 CE, when the Goth Alaric sacked the city. After Allia they would relentlessly pursue the defeat of any enemy they saw as a danger or serious obstacle to their plans. The Roman way of war was spurred to development through the First Punic War with the powerful Carthaginian Empire. Hemmed in and beset by strong enemies, the Romans learned the hard way how to muster, organize, and employ the literal manpower on which the military operations of the time directly depended. It is interesting to speculate why the Romans were able to do these things better than their neighbors and competitors, states that were subject to similar pressures. We will examine some of their wars, campaigns, strategy, and tactics for signs of an answer. Contributing to the development of Roman military excellence was the banishment of kings and the development of the Roman republic in the fifth century. The republic provided a new, inclusive form of statehood and citizenship. Much of early Roman expansion was in the form of treaties, and even the residents of conquered territories were offered degrees of Roman citizenship, an arrangement that was unusual at the time and is still advanced compared with the practice of many modern countries where citizenship is dependent on ancestry, birth, and ethnicity. Roman diplomacy and inclusiveness exemplified the Romans' realistic understanding of human nature and motivations. The Roman system extended the ideal of civic militarism to new members and allies.[3] Throughout the republican period Roman civic and military authorities were closely connected, and citizenship was tied to military service. The alliance practices of the early republic were in effect extended to conquered peoples, who were allowed within limits to keep their own culture and social organization. Military service was the sine qua non and bottom line of extended Roman citizenship. This ensured a supply of recruits to replace casualties or expand the army as needed.

In a sense the Romans followed a pattern of cultural and professional development similar to that of the Greeks. Spurred by the need to develop and sustain a high level of military proficiency, the Romans institutionalized military excellence, creating specialized structures and a community that was in effect a military subculture of the larger society. The story of the development of the Roman army throughout the republic and the empire is one of expanding and then narrowing and diminishing professionalism. In his *Decline and Fall of the Roman Empire* historian Edward Gibbon remarks that the Romans elevated war to an art but then debased it to a trade.[4] The Romans' fusion of the needs and strengths of the larger society with those of the army had strong and weak points. The key to this fusion often seems to have been strong leadership at the national level. Soldier-politicians such as Scipio Africanus and Julius Caesar and emperors such as Augustus, Hadrian, Diocletian, and Constantine were able to forge armies that were effective in combat and biddable to command, and to organize social institutions so as to support the army in a rational and efficient way. What we would call today civilian control of the military was ever a challenge for the Romans. It was both a strength and a vulnerability of the Roman system that civil authority and military authority were often mixed in the same man. This system could place inexperienced and incompetent men in command, as happened at Cannae in 216 BCE. Hanson believes this was the inevitable and acceptable price the Romans paid for their unique form of civic militarism. It is also the case that efforts to make the army more professional tended to estrange the army from society.

Livy's (also Shakespeare's) Coriolanus is an example of the sometimes uncertain terms on which military and civic virtues coexisted. A soldier who was contemptuous of the civil population for what he viewed as their lack of martial qualities, Coriolanus was eventually forced into exile and sought refuge in the enemy city of Corioles, whose name he had borne as an honorific. He was killed there, unable to control himself in the face of any insult or challenge. The military career of another republican general, Caius Marius, may illustrate the double effect of professionalization. Marius introduced a number of useful measures that made the legion both more efficient as a fighting instrument and more socially equitable. He standardized equipment and introduced the eagle standard that became the rallying point and emotional heart of the legion. He eliminated property qualifications for military service, expanding the recruiting base and making military rank less dependent on wealth. Marius was perhaps the archetypal hard-knocks plebian Roman commander: tough and experienced but also (especially in his later career) brutal and contemptuous of civil authority.[5] It was a weakness of the Roman system that since the days of the republic, soldiers would enlist in order to serve a certain general, not the state. Although the legion standard bore the initials *SPQR*, for *Senatum Publicamque Romanum* (the Senate and the people of Rome), the *sacramentum* sworn by soldiers even in imperial times was to their general. Unlike the constitutional oath sworn by members of the American armed forces, the oath of Roman soldiers stressed military obedience but not social responsibility. This contributed to the endemic civil wars of the later republic and to the rise of the soldier-emperors of the later empire. Not only would the soldiers follow the man to whom they had sworn their oath, even to the detriment of the interests of the state, but the men they followed were unlettered, often foreign-born soldiers themselves. Rome eventually outsourced its army, turning the defense of the empire over to barbarians and recent adversaries.[6]

Roman literature tended to reinforce the martial aspects of Roman society. Historians such as Livy extolled military virtues. The poet Virgil also dwelled on patriotic and military themes, most famously in his *Aeneid*, which arguably filled a place in Roman imperial society similar to that of *The Iliad* for the Greeks. Virgil wrote his masterpiece just as Augustus was bringing the empire into existence. The voyages and successive allegiances of Aeneas as he flees from Troy to found the city destined to be the Roman state in embryo illustrate the complex problems of empire. Aeneas is more a pragmatic Roman commander than a romantic young warrior or hero. His desertion of the Carthaginian princess Dido is perhaps a prediction of Rome's difficulties with the African state and a rejection of the Greeks' and Trojans' obsession with Helen (a part rewritten for Cleopatra). Other writers comment unfavorably on soldiers and on the militarism of Roman society. Plautus lampoons the swaggering but cowardly soldier in *Miles Gloriosus*, although it may be significant that his characters are Greek, not Roman, and at a time when the Greeks might be seen as enemies and rivals.[7] The satirist Juvenal, writing in the late first or early second century, actually complains of the privileged legal status afforded to soldiers, the chances for advancement and enrichment from an army career, while he also acknowledges the risks:

> *Find me a lucky star to watch over my enlistment*
> *And I'd join up myself, walk in through those barrack-gates as*
> *A trembling recruit. One moment of fortune's favor does us*
> *More good with the God of Battle than a letter on our behalf*
> *From Venus, or Juno her mother.*[8]

The Romans also understood the power of spectacle and of impressive structures to instill martial pride in the citizen and soldier and to overawe the subject or potential adversary.[9] Although their gladiatorial contests appear to us as forms of decadent, idle cruelty, for the Romans they were meant to be reminders of a glorious past and of the continuing need for Rome to produce fighting men. Roman military commanders attended the gladiatorial schools to learn the latest killing techniques.[10] In addition, Rome produced a library of specialist books on military subjects. Marius was characteristically dismissive of book-taught generals, but in the absence of formal military schools, books provided a valuable means of preserving and communicating professional military knowledge and ethics. Marius' comment also suggests a large number and considerable currency of Roman military writings, most of them now lost, long before the birth of the empire.

The Army of Polybius

The surviving work of Polybius (a Greek by birth, like many writers on Roman military affairs) presents a picture of the Roman army of the Second Punic War (218–201 BCE). Although the armies of this time were not

THE VERSATILE LEGION. In a detail from Emperor Trajan's triumphal column, some Roman soldiers build a fortress and others depart city gates on a pontoon bridge, watched over by Danuvius. On the left, Emperor Trajan addresses a group of legionaries and standard-bearers. *"Trajan's Column: detail of frieze reliefs" by Minneapolis College of Art and Design Library/CC BY 2.0*

the permanent standing forces that would serve the empire, Roman military culture was already characterized by an extraordinary degree of standardization, set procedure, and discipline. When they were on campaign, Roman legions fortified their camps and held to a fixed routine of security and maintenance. Romans' commitment to these practices was literally religious. Discipline and order were almost as respected as courage. When introducing the section of his work on the construction and layout of army camps, Polybius has this to say: "I cannot imagine anyone so indifferent to things noble and great as to refuse to take some little time to understand things like these; for if he once heard them, he will be acquainted with one of those things genuinely worth observation and knowledge."[11]

The Romans' attachment to order was reinforced by the fact that in the ancient world, any order was tenuous and exceptional. The Romans represented an advanced state of civilization in their time, but they enjoyed little if any technological superiority over their often larger and more numerous enemies, and the civilized advantages they enjoyed were hard-won and easily forfeited. The army was like an aqueduct, controlling strong forces rather than allowing them to run on wastefully or self-destructively. Everything literally depended on the efficiency of the army's organization and on the strength and skill of its human components. Interestingly, the legions of this period did not have a single commander, but were led by a commission of six tribunes "working by a system of rosters and committees."[12] To modern soldiers imbued with the idea of necessity of unified command this might seem a glaring deficiency. On the other hand, there may have been wisdom in distributing authority among citizen-officers, none of whom necessarily had a clear advantage in terms of experience or ability. The system may also suggest a common outlook or unwritten doctrine that was so pervasive as to make unified command less effective than willing cooperation among peers, as well as a desire to avoid concentrating too much power in one person. Caesar began the practice of assigning the senatorial officers called *legati* to command of legions. Under Augustus this practice would become official and the legion commanders referred to as *legati legionis*.[13] The system of cooperative command perhaps survived in the centuriate, among whom the senior centurion in a legion, the *primus pilus*, was referred to as the *primus inter pares* (first among equals).[14] The similarity of the words *legatus* and *legio* suggests a common root in the Latin words for "law" and for the principal unit of the army. The root of this word also refers to reading, and can be seen in the English word "legible," suggesting a fusion of law, military organization, and reading or literacy.

More Roman Writing

After Polybius, and with the exception of Caesar's writings (about which more later), there was a long period from which little military writing survives. The production and dissemination of military writing appears to have seen a rebirth with the empire. Augustus took an interest in military writing, helping to draft the now-lost army regulations called *The Constitutions*. Toward the end of the first century, Frontinus and Onasander wrote works on military leadership that have survived. Frontinus, a military commander and colonial governor, wrote the *Strategemata*, a collection of instructive anecdotes that has been compared to Napoleon's *Maxims*, in addition to works on civic administration and engineering.[15] In keeping with its title (usually translated as "The stratagems"), most of Frontinus' military writing is concerned with tricks and ruses of one kind or another. Even the sections on leadership and discipline treat these subjects as matters of "spin," or the manipulation of perceptions.[16] His contemporary Onasander takes a more theoretical approach in the *Strategicus*, discussing the traits of the ideal commander and then describing how this paragon would act in different tactical situations, some of them perhaps drawn from historical examples.[17] Military writers of the second century included Aelian and Arrian, respectively authors of *Tactical Studies* and the *Anabasis of Alexander*.

The work of the most significant writer on Roman military affairs did not appear until the fourth century. *De Re Militari* by Vegetius seems to be motivated by a sense that the military excellence of the republic and early empire was being neglected and forgotten. It appears to have been written to extol the past and to revive the ancient, proven practices. Vegetius describes in practical detail the hows and whys of the old Roman military system. The neglect he notes in such areas as selection, discipline, training, and security may have stemmed from the fact that the empire was no longer expanding. The empire enjoyed periods of peace of which the late republic had known little. Soldiers in this period became absorbed with civic duties: construction, cultivation, tax collecting, and policing. Also, by the fourth century the legion and legionary were themselves declining in importance within the Roman military establishment, with nonlegion units of cavalry and auxiliaries now playing a larger role. A long period of peace can erode any army's fighting spirit and realism in training. Beyond the specific tactical or administrative details, what Vegetius perhaps most identifies is a moral malaise, a decay in the seriousness of purpose that had characterized the earlier army.

Roman philosophical writings both reflected and influenced the culture that for centuries produced the best armies in the world. Most important among the schools of philosophy in the eclectic world of Roman thought was Stoicism. Stoicism was Greek in origin, but as an idea and in practice it attained fulfillment in Roman civilization. Stoicism taught an alignment with the natural world, especially with the inevitability of suffering and death, and stressed practice over theory. Writers such as Cicero, Seneca, and Marcus Aurelius deemed it essential to live the values the Stoics espoused. Seneca chides himself for his failures to do so, eventually redeeming some of his past self-indulgence by the courage of his suicide. The Stoic philosophy is also expressed in the works of Epictetus, whose words on the similarity of life to a soldier's service precede the introduction to this book. Like a soldier, the Stoic was expected to bear wounds, the death of comrades and loved ones, sudden departures, and the approach of the unknowable shores of death with composure. The Stoic philosophy evolved from an articulation and elaboration of the Roman citizen-soldier's code of strength and honor into a proto-Christian expression of the universality of virtue and of humankind.[18]

Roman Training, Tactics, and Organization

Like the Spartans and their Greek imitators, the Romans understood the importance of regular training. Even the part-time soldiers of the republican period willingly submitted to tough training because they knew that training meant success and survival. As Gibbon points out, the word for army in Latin, *exercitus*, was borrowed from the word for "exercise." Roman soldiers ran and swam. They threw projectiles and jabbed their handheld weapons against targets, fenced with one another, and fought mock battles.[19] They were expected to meet certain standards when, for example, conducting timed marches under heavy loads. The Romans emphasized physical fitness for practical reasons. Modern armies conduct physical training partly as a metaphor. The soldier operating a self-propelled rocket launcher or working in the personnel office doesn't need to be able to run three miles or do push-ups to function, but his or her willingness to maintain and demonstrate a standard of fitness is considered a sign of commitment, self-discipline, and general good health and habits. For the Romans, victory depended directly on physical strength and skill, and few soldiers would have been excused or exempt from combat. Modern soldiers train with close-combat weapons and techniques that they will probably never use, but for centuries the Roman recruit faced a strong possibility of seeing combat face-to-face with a large, hairy, enraged barbarian. While it waged war, the Roman *exercitus* was an army of the strong and brave.

Roman tactics evolved from an undistinguished imitation of the Greek phalanx to the combination of discipline and flexibility of the legion, to the use of combined arms that united the strengths of the legion with the complementary capabilities of mounted and missile auxiliaries and torsion artillery. In addition, each legion could serve as a brigade both of infantry and of engineers. The Roman legion was initially a tribal organization like that seen among the Athenians. It began to assume a more permanent form in the second half of the fourth century BCE, with a strength of about five thousand. The legion developed into a more flexible formation than the phalanx, but the early Romans fought in straight-ahead style, scorning trickery or stratagems. Their devotion to mass and aggressiveness came to a *reductio* during the Second Punic War against the Carthaginians at Cannae, where Hannibal's army lured a large Roman army attacking in a dense formation into an encirclement and destroyed it. After this, the Romans were more open to clever tactics and adopted a more intellectual approach to generalship. The Roman general Fabius Maximus, who had been derisively labeled "Cunctator" (Delayer) for his unpopular defensive tactics, was recalled to command after Cannae.

This period also saw the adoption of the manipular legion, a more articulated and flexible formation than the phalanx. Historian J. E. Lendon wonders at the excessive complexity of the manipular legion, with its divisions into front-to-rear formations of *velites*, *hastati*, *principes*, and *triarii*. It may be, as he speculates, that the Romans created a formation that would give the maximum opportunity for heroic, Homeric-style individual combat. But the manipular legion also may have been designed to prevent the kind of impotent herdlike panic of Cannae by keeping forces distributed and in a position to provide for effective mutual support.

In a sense the Romans approached war literally and figuratively as an engineering problem. To gain an advantage they would move mountains of earth and stone and build siege engines, torsion field artillery, and fortifications. They engineered their formations and tactics to minimize exposure and maximize flexibility, lethality, mutual support, and a combination of arms. Romans' realism and ingenuity when it came to preserving the physical and moral powers of soldiers fighting in hand-to-hand battle continued to define their approach to warfare. It has been said of the Greeks that they were goaded into military excellence partly by poverty, as indicated by the number of Greek men who hired themselves out as mercenaries (and echoed by the impoverished Irishmen and Germans who later did likewise). The Romans grew from adversity, even from defeat, and perhaps also from lack of physical stature. Often outsized by some of their formidable North African and northern European enemies, and confronted by elephants or heavy cavalry, the smaller, infantry-centric Romans had to develop organizations and tactics that negated or reversed their enemies' size advantage in hand-to-hand fighting. The legion and army continued to evolve. The manipular legion was gradually replaced in the second century BCE by the legion of ten cohorts, each of about six hundred men. This arrangement preserved the flexibility of the manipular legion while simplifying command and control.

Manipular and cohortal legions are sometimes depicted as laid out in checkerboard formation with large gaps between units. Most historians agree that the Romans would not have fought this way because the gaps would have been fatal against an aggressive enemy, creating multiple interior "flanks" for exploitation.[20] It is possible that the gaps were left open to provide room for turning movements and could be closed for combat by units in the rear echelons moving forward. Anyone who has ever seen or participated in a parade involving a mass formation will have some idea of the difficulty in turning such a dense collection of soldiers in a way that preserves the ranks and the positioning of guides and unit leaders.

In addition to their standard legion order of battle, the Romans had specialized formations to deal with threats and to exploit opportunities. The best known of these was the "tortoise" formation, which provided a shield wall at the front, sides, and top of a unit. The interior of the tortoise would have been dark and confused, more like the rugby scrum that some have imagined the phalanx to resemble. The formation also would have limited the use of weapons. The tortoise was used primarily to approach a defended wall or fortified position, affording maximum protection while the unit moved across the "danger area" of increased exposure to missile attack, and then deploying into a more open offensive formation at the point of direct contact with the enemy. Other specialized formations included the "wedge" for attack and the "saw" for defense. The saw was a kind of reserve or reaction force that shuttled behind the front lines to restore gaps or penetrations.

The Romans' tactical problem was to create a formation that was cohesive enough for mutual support and unity of action but also gave impetus and advantage to individual soldiers taking on opponents and using their weapons to cut and kill. Soldiers standing in formation and brandishing their weapons could not win battles. Unlike the phalanx, the legion could engage at varying ranges. The *pilum* carried by legionaries was a highly lethal spear that was about half wooden handle and half iron shaft and point, and could be thrown up to one hundred feet. The shaft directly behind the spear point was designed to bend after impact, rendering it useless to the enemy and catching fast if it struck a shield. The iron shaft made the *pilum* difficult to cut away from a shield, so an enemy fighter with a Roman *pilum* in his shield would have the choice of holding on to a heavy and unbalanced shield or throwing the shield away and doing without its protection. The *pilum* could also be used in close combat, although for close-in fighting the Romans generally preferred the short sword called the *gladius*, a weapon Scipio Africanus had adopted in Spain. Given the short length of his *gladius*, which he was trained to use to jab rather than to slash, a Roman soldier was encouraged to be aggressive, to move forward and throw the enemy off balance. On the other hand, the Romans understood that this style of fighting would take its toll on any man, no matter how fit or disciplined. The Romans fought in relays to preserve the physical powers of the legionaries, to maintain forward momentum, and perhaps to afford as many of them as possible the opportunity to go "toe to toe" with the enemy to win glory and awards.

The technique of the relay handover has been lost to time. Factors to consider would have included maintaining protection for the soldier in contact and keeping pressure on any enemy fighters opposite. It was probably considered at least desirable that the movement be conducted by the reliever surging forward rather than by the relieved man falling back. Did the reliever come up on the right or left, or was this dependent on the situation? Was there a signal to commence the movement and perhaps another to say, "I/you got it"? The change of relays was supposed to be conducted on command, but the conduct of the handover in contact with an adversary must have been dicey, and we should not imagine it being conducted with the precision of a drill movement. The shields probably came into use to push or hold the enemy and create a protected space. We may imagine that for a moment the two soldiers involved stood side by side, maybe with the right-hand sword of one and the left-arm shield of the other actually in play, before the fresh legionary took over. In the Greek system the rear ranks may also have provided replacements for worn-out first-rank fighters, but the emphasis in the phalanx appears to have been more on the rear ranks providing impetus and momentum. The Roman system produced fresh combat power, preventing physical exhaustion of the individual from bringing on a "culminating point" until victory was achieved.

The Roman shield evolved from a round or oval shape into a rectangle with notched corners to permit its use with weapons. The curved shield shown in some illustrations would have enabled a Roman soldier to forge ahead of the men on his left and right to engage an enemy and use his weapons with greater freedom without completely losing cover on his flanks. The shield could also be used as an offensive weapon. It appears to have been a common technique for a legionary to rush at an enemy, using the shield, which also sometimes had a center boss that would have been useful to provide greater punch, to push an enemy off balance. In addition, the metal edges of the shield could be used for cutting.[21] Roman fighting techniques also seem to have exploited both the instinct to protect the face and the vulnerability of the unprotected face and neck. A feint to the face could be combined with a strike to the throat, cutting the trachea or jugular.

Each imperial legion had ten large catapults and forty-five smaller *carroballista*, crew-served crossbows. Gibbon says that the use of artillery weapons designed for use as siege weapons increased on the battlefield in the later empire as Romans' valor declined.[22] The Romans also used flame weapons, again mostly in sieges. The use of artillery and flame weapons recalls the statement by Adrian Goldsworthy that the Romans were masters of practicality and spectacle.[23] They gave themselves every advantage in battle, and they knew how to overawe their opponents, staging demonstrations of seemingly divine power: buildings, parades, festivals, the lightning bolts of Zeus or Odin shooting through the sky over the battlefield.

The Romans had no standing military organization above the legion, but they did group legions together along with their auxiliaries. An army commanded by a Roman consul under the republic normally consisted of two legions. Under the empire, legions were assigned according to province, so the governor of the province would have operational control over perhaps two or three legions.[24] With auxiliaries and perhaps reinforced by allies, a reinforced Roman legion approximated the strength of a modern division of ten thousand to twelve thousand soldiers. The force assigned to a governor could be the equivalent of a modern corps or even an army. The military organization of the empire in a sense resembled the regional combat command structure of the modern U.S. military.

Roman Military Administration

In perhaps no other sense is the similarity of the Roman army to a modern military organization so striking as in the area of administration. This becomes most apparent when examining the empire, when standing units both allowed and impelled the development of written regulations, record-keeping, regular pay, permanent ranks and qualifications, awards, and transfers. The long-lost Imperial Roman Army regulations, *The Constitutions*, were written under Augustus and revised by Hadrian.[25] Enough army records survive to form an important historical source and to give an idea of their voluminous original extent. Reports were written and retained on even small-unit actions. One surviving document, apparently an annual strength report by a cohort stationed on the Danube, lists the reasons for various soldiers' absences from the fort. In so doing it gives a glimpse of some of the diverse duties to which Roman legionaries might be assigned. Quite a few of the absent soldiers were off seeking and guarding food supplies in the form of crops, grain, and animals.[26] Under the empire a copy of the personnel file of every serving centurion was kept in Rome. Some records were reproduced in triplicate. The army may have been almost over-bureaucratized, but without extensive recordkeeping it would have been impossible to exercise any degree of control over an organization approaching half a million men spread out over an empire of 2.2 million square miles. Caesar Augustus is sometimes credited with creating the first true mail system, the *cursus publicus*, and a separate system for government correspondence.

The Roman army gave both individual and unit awards for outstanding conduct, in a system of *dona* (awards) that reached its height in the first two centuries of empire.[27] The nature and evolution of the awards system reflected the ethos of the Roman army and state. Significantly, the top two awards were for saving lives rather than taking them. The highest award was the *corona obsidionalis*, awarded for raising a siege. Second to this was the *corona civica*, for saving the life of a Roman citizen. Other *coronae*, or crowns, included the *muralis*, for being the first over the wall of a city or town under attack, and the *aurea*, given for more general acts of courage. Other forms of decoration included the *hastae*, a spear, and the *vexillum*, a flag. *Torques* were rings attached to the armor of the decorated soldier, apparently a borrowing from the barbarian tribes who wore them around the neck. The Romans also attached disks called *phalerae* to the armor as a form of award. Although the Romans generally considered the wearing of bracelets by civilians a sign of effeminacy, *armillae* were used as military decorations. Eligibility for awards sometimes varied by rank, but the Roman system did allow for some forms of decoration at nearly every level of the hierarchy. Perhaps the highest award that could be bestowed on an ally or auxiliary was Roman citizenship. After the second century the imperial system of *dona* declined in status and then disappeared. Afterward, soldiers were more likely to receive tangible awards of money, land, promotion, or, for non-Romans, citizenship. It is tempting and perhaps plausible to view this as a decline in the ethos of the army from one based on honor to one of remuneration, from an army still retaining its civic character to one more mercenary. It may also reflect demographic changes in an army that consisted more of the disadvantaged and noncitizens.

Regular payment does not suffice to make for a profession; in fact, as I have argued, a professional is a person whose motives are ethical or broadly social rather than monetary. Still, the ability of an army to provide regular pay to its members is itself a professional accomplishment, and it was one the Romans achieved with a consistency that was probably unmatched in the ancient world and was unexcelled in Europe for more than a thousand years. Soldiers who are content with their pay (as Christ suggested to the legionaries of Palestine) are less likely to rob or practice extortion, activities that distract them from their duties and sow discontent among occupied peoples. The legionaries of the empire were long-service soldiers who received pensions after retirement (although only about half survived to collect) as long as they received the honorable discharge, the *honesta missio*.[28] A soldier who extended his twenty-year career to twenty-four could receive the *emeriti misso*.[29] Some soldiers with valuable specialist knowledge received extra pay; others, the *immunes*, received no extra pay but were excused from camp fatigue. The specialists included surveyors, pioneers, armorers, and priests.[30]

The Imperial Roman Army promoted on merit (itself a slippery standard for armies), but social status continued to count. Most Roman centurions did not come up from the ranks but were "commissioned" directly from civilian life or sometimes after service in the Praetorian Guard. Roman centurions in the empire were more than combat leaders; better educated and from a higher social class than most legionaries, they often served as magistrates and diplomats in the regions where they were stationed.[31]

Roman Military Strategy

Roman military strategy evolved over time, adapting to the outside pressures imposed by a gallery of adversaries, to the size of the republic and empire, and to a growing sophistication in strategic ideas. Roman military strategy may be divided into three main periods. The first was one of slow growth and the gathering of alliances that lasted through the Second Punic War. The second was a period of more rapid expansion, of conquest over allegiance or even hegemony that persisted through the birth of the empire. The last was the imperial period, which, with the exception of the conquest of Britain and some eastern expansion, was characterized mostly by defense and policing. Roman imperial defense was not passive, however, and it involved frequent punitive or preventive campaigns and large-scale counterattacks to restore and strengthen the borders.

The empire of the Romans was one of the largest and longest lasting in human history, especially when one considers that Roman holdings and hegemony were imperial in scale centuries before Rome officially changed from republic to empire. Historian Edward Luttwak ascribes this durability primarily to superior Roman strategy.[32] I have already argued that Roman culture also played a part in Rome's reign of dominance and that the Romans did many things well on the level of tactics and organization. However, it is certainly the case that the Romans also became successful strategists. How did this happen? One of the reasons for the longevity of the Roman Empire was the sheer time and effort it took to acquire it and the strategic expertise the Romans gradually acquired to defend it over the centuries of rule. By the time the Romans owned a territory, they had marched the ground and contested with the indigenous people repeatedly. They had the measure of their empire, a consequence partly of the nature of transportation and warfare of the period. Thanks to the work of Aristotle and other early cartographers, the Romans had road maps and a fairly sophisticated idea of space-time. The famous Peutinger Map is a copy of a map of the *cursus publicus* and the forts and cities through which it passed.[33]

Rome's enormous empire was frequently in turmoil, and the army had to be capable of controlling, defending, and sometimes expanding it. The Romans' strategic problem was in developing economy of force and a force of economy given limited resources. The legions had to be prepared to perform a wide variety of tasks well, and they had to be stationed near where they might be needed. Although highly advanced by the standards of the time in terms of currency, trade, and manufacture, Rome was still, like all societies of the time, based on subsistence agriculture that was highly labor

intensive and climate dependent. Little significant technological improvement took place during the centuries of Roman dominance. The people of
the empire could generate only so much wealth and no more. Rome could
undertake a massive "surge" like that following Cannae, but such levels of
force could not be maintained in the long haul if the empire was to function.
Excessive taxes could starve the people, bankrupt small farmers (turning
them into dependent city dwellers), and incite all classes to revolt.

Beginning with Augustus, the empire reckoned that it could afford to
sustain about twenty-five legions (later increased to thirty) in the long term,
plus auxiliaries and not counting the ten-thousand-man Praetorian Guard,
who were mostly located in Rome, not on the frontier. On the other hand,
Rome had to preserve the empire intact enough to provide the agrarian and
human resources on which its defense relied. Over the centuries this led to
a number of expediencies. One of them, the preference for spilling a gallon
of sweat over expending an ounce of blood, was characteristic of both the
offensive and defensive phases of Roman strategic history.

Roman engineering extended beyond the battlefield or siege so that it
became a strategic resource. The Romans could no more afford to wall in
their entire holdings than they could guard each meter of the *limes* (limits).
In some places, most notably in northern Britain, the Romans did build
walls. In others they contented themselves with watchtowers linked by signals and backed by mobile forces (which could make use of the Roman road
system and the Roman legion's ability to construct ships and convert itself
into a marine corps on command). The 50,000 miles of paved roads the
Romans built (of 250,000 total miles of Roman roads) had an enormous
impact on the mobility of the legion, more than tripling the amount of distance a legion could cover in a day's march from eight miles to twenty-five.[34]
Later, as the resources of the empire declined, the *limes* became very porous
and almost nonexistent, although habit and fear preserved the shadow of the
empire for a time.

The Romans' center of gravity, the main source of their strength, was
neither their army nor their apparatus of government, but the idea of Rome,
a heroic dream of order. As long as that persisted, the empire survived, but
once the Romans lost the ability to guard their own limits effectively, the
dream yielded to a rude awakening. Historians have surmised and specu-
lated on the cause for the decline and fall of the empire for more than two

hundred years, since Gibbon. For the purposes of this study, it might make sense to phrase the question by asking whether the army declined in effectiveness and in ethos, bringing the empire down with it, or whether declining imperial revenues and morale brought on a decline that encompassed the army. There is the further question of whether increased external pressure, perhaps brought on by climate change, was mostly to blame. Even in the contemporary world, when data and impressions are far more available and reliable, the causes and symptoms of national decline are not easy to identify, and causes are difficult to assign to specific cases.[35] The decline of civic militarism left the army without the formidable force multiplier that had enabled it to recover from Cannae and to extend the borders of empire to the ends of the earth, at least the parts the Romans felt worth having.

Can an army make up for deficiencies in the larger culture? Could the Roman army have saved the empire, given greater professional capacities? We will probably never know for certain, although this need not prevent us from speculating![36] It may be that what the army finally lacked was not just greater proficiency as a war-fighting organization (in fact, in this sense the army continued to perform reasonably well), but a more expansive and enlightened sense of its civic role. The army's repeated maladroit political interventions might be seen as a crude attempt to fulfill this role, although in the process it became an abettor or accomplice of disorder rather than a stabilizing force. Perhaps by aligning itself with the Senate instead of with a series of usurpers and temporary emperors the army might have fulfilled its implied pledge of *SPQR* and had a more salubrious effect on Roman civilization. On its side, the Senate might have lessened its own marginalization if it had aligned itself more closely with the army—if, for example, more men of senatorial rank had served as officers during the late empire.[37]

Roman Military Ethics

In an earlier section of this chapter I discussed the elements of Roman culture that influenced the army's war-fighting ability and the nature of Roman military professionalism. In this section I discuss the ethos and ideology of the army itself. The Roman system of discipline was strict, but it was the culture of *virtus*, soldierly pride, and unit esprit de corps that kept the army together and fighting. Esprit de corps was extremely important. The names, numbers, and standards of the legions attracted intense loyalty. Roman tactics demanded a high degree of flexible unit cohesion as well as effective command and control. Roman soldiers literally worshipped gods with names such as Honos, Disciplina, and Virtus. *Disciplina* and *virtus* are complementary or perhaps conflicting ideals, standing respectively for the soldier's need to obey orders but also to display aggressiveness whenever possible, even in excess or defiance of orders.[38] One result of this paradox was that centurions engaged in actual fighting much more often than we would consider usual for officers. The fact that centurions were often killed in higher percentages than their men mirrors the higher rate of officer deaths in some modern conflicts, particularly in elite units, in which the standards for leadership are high. Modern officers are often killed when they move about under fire in order to exercise command. The centurions' tendency to fight hand-to-hand may simply reflect the leadership demands of close-quarters battle as well as the expectations shaped by Roman military culture. The need for sheer aggression in the kind of sustained, close-in, hand-to-hand fighting in which the legion specialized perhaps made inevitable and necessary the tendency of centurions to fight as well as lead or direct.

Unlike some other armies that have practiced public forms of religion, the army of the Romans was eclectic and even tolerant in the matter of religious belief.[39] Although the pantheon of Jupiter, the other Olympians, and the lesser Greco-Roman deities constituted a state religion, its observance did not rule out other religious affiliations and practices. Roman imperial soldiers had their pick of a variety of cults and deities from around the empire. One of the favorites was Mithraism, an import from Persia. Mithras was a champion who combined virtue, strength, and the remorse of one who kills. Ordered to kill the first living creature, a bull, by the god of the sun through his emissary the raven, he did so loyally but reluctantly. Rites of Mithras included submission to extremes of heat.[40] Mithraism was a simple faith of endurance that made no intellectual demands. It could be compared with some later fraternities, such as the Freemasons, who have arguably given soldiers an additional basis for affiliation and comradeship.

The Roman army practiced an ethics of restraint as well as an ethos of war fighting. In fact, ancient Roman law forms the basis of much ethical thought and practice related to armed conflict even today.[41] The early Romans sometimes fought wars of extermination, as in the final war against Carthage, but their inclusive practices of citizenship and treaties made some clemency practical. The dead make poor citizens or allies. By the second century of the empire an even more humane approach to war and conquest appeared to be emerging. This is reflected in some of the triumphal arches of the period, which display an unwonted sympathy for the adversaries of Rome.[42] The rise of Christianity may have been humanizing, but it was not necessarily enervating. Modern historians generally do not agree with Gibbon that Christianity weakened the Roman fighting spirit. In fact, as early as the Battle of the Milvian Bridge, fought by Constantine in 312 CE to defeat a rival would-be emperor, Christianity appears to have provided the kind of spiritual force multiplier that the Romans had sought and found from a variety of sources during their history. Constantine's vision of the cross, ecstatic conversion, and victory prepared the way for centuries of Christian soldiers to come.

Roman Military Leadership

Despite the militant and hierarchical nature of Roman society, and even when its tradition of civic militarism was in full operation, leadership in the Roman army could be surprisingly challenging. New officers and centurions would have had to overcome their lack of formal military education, embarking on a steep learning curve in order to acquire the knowledge necessary to lead effectively, and to work very hard to establish credibility among the tough veterans and youngsters of a century or cohort. Polybius lists three ways to learn tactics (sometimes translated as generalship): study of history, study of scientific treatises, and experience in the field.[43] Roman officers did have recourse to harsh disciplinary measures. Entire legions could be dishonored and even literally decimated for misconduct. The wooden staff centurions carried was not merely symbolic; like the bundled sticks and ax head called *fasces* carried by the escorts (*lictors*) who accompanied senatorial and magisterial officials, it could be used to administer a corrective blow. For cases of cowardice in the face of the enemy, the penalty could be summary death. Finally, the considerable inducements offered to a legionary—the pay, pension, and promise of citizenship—could all be withdrawn if a soldier was deemed unfit to serve with the eagles.

For all of their *disciplina*, Roman soldiers could be restive and vocal. A Roman officer, a general especially, needed to be a man of words as well as actions. He would be expected to answer questions and even taunts, to speak to his soldiers before battle, and to be able to account for his actions to superiors and to the information-hungry Roman Senate and military bureaucracy. Fortunately, his education had prepared him to do so. Roman education developed and systematized the educational practices of the Greeks. In typically pragmatic fashion, Roman education focused on the skills a Roman citizen needed. The focus was on rhetoric, the responsible and convincing use of language to argue and to persuade. These practices were well established in the days of the republic, as exemplified by Cicero's *De Officiis* (On duties). Quintilian gave them full expression in his *Institutes of Oratory* (95 CE), which lays out in detail the education of young Roman males. The Roman system of education followed the armies as they built and settled the empire.[44] It ensured that at least some soldiers were literate, and it helped to define an officer corps that was carefully schooled in the use of language, both written and spoken. The practice of *imitatio* instilled a respect for style and brevity, and that of *actio* the need for the speaker to employ gestures, voice modulation, and facial expressions to complement and drive home the meaning of spoken words. This training would equip the Roman citizen to serve in the Senate or judiciary, and in the alternating civic and military postings and duties that characterized many Roman careers, it also gave him the facility with language necessary for a military leader and administrator. Rhetoric was sometimes criticized for being shallow and artificial, but in its ideal form (as described by Quintilian) it was based on broad knowledge and ethical awareness. Practice in persuasion and argumentation based in historical study could be an exercise in the sound decision making required of military leaders.

Among Roman military leaders are a number of exemplary military professionals who deserve admiration and even emulation. Julius Caesar undoubtedly heads this list. Caesar led by example and by precept. A descendant of one of the patrician families that claimed to trace their lineage to the gods, he was imbued with the cultural and ethical values of traditional republican Rome. His versatility extended to different types of combat operations ranging from pitched battles to sieges, amphibious operations, and counterinsurgency. Despite the fact that his substantial military service began when he was in middle age, Caesar made himself a soldier's general. He mastered both the humble details and patois of the soldier's occupation and the higher levels of professional planning and execution. Perhaps a great man as well as a great soldier, Caesar was wise and just enough to hold together the lands he won by the sword and spade. One historian says that Caesar was as much explorer as conqueror.[45] He may be considered one in a line of soldier-anthropologists stretching back to Ulysses. Caesar is also instructive of the importance of language to the military leader. His speeches and the military *Commentaries* themselves are models of the military professional's need to communicate effectively and expressively.

Caesar is perhaps the only Roman general to be popularly ranked among the foremost military commanders of history, but Rome's military culture, traditions, and institutions produced numerous officers who were nearly as great, as well as a multitude of competent and committed military leaders. Among the other great generals were the already mentioned Marius, Fabius Maximus, and Scipio Africanus. The long period of warfare in late republican Rome saw the rise of highly competent commanders who could attract soldiers to their armies.[46] The second-century emperors Trajan, Hadrian, and Marcus Aurelius combined to varying degrees the roles of soldier, strategist, and public administrator. Later emperors adapted the army to respond rapidly to threats and incursions. The Romans followed their practice of learning from enemies by becoming more cavalry-centric, and they maximized a strength of their own by increasing the use of torsion field artillery. Some (e.g., Gibbon) have viewed the rise of cavalry and artillery as a sign of overall military decadence, but in a sense the Romans were following a tradition of preserving manpower in terms of strength and numbers. Properly used, the cavalry could conserve the lives and energies of the infantry, and by expending torsion strength the Romans also limited their own exposure to danger and saved muscle strength by sending a catapult ball or *carroballista* bolt instead of a man.

Thanks to the writer Tacitus we have a detailed if selective and admiring narrative of the career of the Imperial Roman officer Agricola.[47] Young Agricola was educated "in all the liberal arts" and served a military apprenticeship in Britain. Tacitus praises Agricola's character and leadership abilities. Agricola took over a demoralized Roman legion, and after rebuilding it he modestly "let it appear that he had found in the legion the loyalty he had created." He refused to hold grudges or play favorites. Agricola showed considerable understanding and restraint in dealing with subject peoples. He was not content with merely putting down a rebellion, but would go on to discover and root out the causes of discontent that had caused it. He arranged for the sons of the "leading men" of captured provinces to receive a Roman-style education similar to his own. As a tactical leader he was active and observant. He demonstrated the benefit of his knowledge of rhetoric by delivering rousing speeches when necessary, as before the battle at Mons Graupius, a mountain of now disputed location in Britain. On this occasion Agricola praised his soldiers, calling them his comrades, but he also pointed out that the consequences of defeat so far from home or aid would be severe, so the legionaries might as well commit themselves to courage and victory or risk losing all the land and honor they had gained so far in the campaign.

The Roman Military Legacy

Was there a Roman profession of arms? The Romans certainly produced many soldiers like Agricola with a strong right to be called professionals. The generations of experienced, well-trained, and often well-educated imperators, legates, tribunes, centurions, and even ordinary legionaries (those long-service privates of empire and the cadre of men who returned to the eagles at every opportunity in republican times) were professional soldiers in character, outlook, and attainments. Many of them were professional in the broad sense, making strong contributions to the advancement of their culture and of civilization. With them came roads, books, and baths; light after dark; and the ability to cross boundaries that were previously and afterward hostile and impassable without an army. Roman soldiers remembered, wrote, built, and preserved. While they kept order, the work, commerce, and arts of civilization could continue and develop. Thomas Burns writes in his study *Rome and the Barbarians, 100 B.C. to A.D. 400* that the centers of Roman civilization were "irrepressible agents of change," both disseminating Roman culture and ideology and absorbing some aspects of the indigenous culture, and that "the Roman army often led the way" in securing and sustaining these foci.[48] Roman soldiers could be the tools of tyrants, some of them mad and very bad, and "the eagles" could be corrupted by power, especially during the intervals between acknowledged rulers. The character of soldiers throughout history has lain largely in the hands of their leadership. Even a fairly decent specimen of good soldier can be turned into a thug if he is employed as one. For the Roman soldiers, with their *sacramentum* to the general and their growing default role in emperor selection, the character of the leader may have been more important than for most. The best of Roman military professionalism was a combination of lethal competence and civic-mindedness. In the later empire this link became attenuated and lost. Fewer full-status citizens served as legionaries, and fewer of the upper classes as officers. The army lost many of its civic functions and became more narrowly military at the level of organizations and operations. Constantine completed the process of military specialization by separating civil and military commands.[49]

In a sense the Romans fell victim to their own inclusive form of citizenship. By outsourcing their army to a mix of second-class foreign citizens and confederates, or *foederati*, they surrendered self-respect, civic pride, and civilian control. The seeds of decline may have been planted even while Rome's military strength appeared to be at its height. The imperial legions depicted on Trajan's triumphal column sometimes appear to be standing in reserve while barbarian auxiliary troops fight the battle.[50] This practice may have made sense militarily and politically, but one can see that it also may have had an adverse effect on Roman fighting spirit. Civic militarism, in decline since even before the end of the republic, increasingly gave way to a civic/military divide. Another change in late empire military policy was the division of the army into the *limitanei*, who guarded the frontier, and the *comitatenses*, who were supposed to act as a mobile reserve.[51] The *comitanenses* were usually billeted in civilian households. This arrangement made sense in that, stationed in the empire's usually safe interior, they did not need the protection of a fort; however, the civilian billeting may have adversely affected the training and esprit de corps of those units intended to do the heaviest fighting. The allegiance of the army was transferred to the new breed of bad-boy, undereducated, often foreign generals who had little acquaintance with Rome and less appreciation of the ideals it had once represented. These men could become emperor, usually briefly and often with disastrous consequences. The wolf that had nurtured Rome since it suckled the legendary Romulus and Remus eventually turned on its master. (People shouldn't keep wild animals as pets!) The propensity of one component of the Roman army for maladroit involvement in politics has entered the English language through the word "praetorianism."

The problem still with us is to combine professional and citizen, to create professional military forces that maintain strong connections with civil authority and society. To paraphrase George Washington, even the most committed military professional should never set aside the citizen. Rome's legacy is civic militarism that functions at a professional level; its warning is the loss of the *civitas* and the triumph of *milites*.

LATE ANTIQUITY

Pagan Warriors and Barbaric Christians

T he civilizations of Greece and Rome may be said to have lived and died by the sword. After the fall of Rome, and with the arguable exception of the Byzantine Empire, more than one thousand years would pass before anyone could match the Roman army in terms of organization, standardization, and permanence. The armies of late antiquity (sometimes still called the Dark Ages, and which I will define as a period of about six hundred years after the fall of the Western empire) could not match the army of Imperial Rome on its strong points. However, we would be wrong to pass over this period as lacking in interest for a study of military professionalism. In fact, the decline of order in Western Europe that followed the fall of the Roman Empire saw a period of constant military activity and widespread interest in military matters. This was an era of almost incessant warfare affecting large areas and numbers of people. The soldier was involved in such developments in military knowledge as the use of the stirrup to enable heavy cavalry. The stirrup gave the rider a much more secure seat in the saddle, allowing him to strike harder with his sword or mace, and eventually led to the development of heavy armored cavalry who charged with the lance. In larger terms the soldier was at once an enemy of order, a repository of some remnants of ancient order, and a means by which order began to be restored to the chaotic political and military situation that followed the fall of Rome. The soldier of this period was a contradictory (even postmodern) mixture of the pious and the murderous, the faithful and the treacherous, the skillful—even innovative— and the maladroit and undependable. These were men who might commit Macbeth-like murders of relatives and entire rival families but would never violate an oath, who lost battles through carelessness but might fight and die to the last man for a lost cause. In terms of knowledge, ethos, and their transmission these men are difficult to categorize but fascinating to contemplate, embodying as they do so many of the paradoxes that are inherent in the military profession.

Roman military institutions survived the fall of the Western empire in the fifth century to a surprising degree. The Roman army lived on in the Eastern empire, which under Justinian I pursued a series of campaigns to retrieve the lands of the Western empire. The Byzantine army had the organization of its Western forebear but lacked the old Roman commitment to decisive battle and to the military virtues that enabled hard-won victory.[1] More surprisingly, Roman military institutions continued in the old lands of the fallen Western empire as well. Bernard Bachrach says of the military organizations of the Merovingian dynasty, which was dominant in Gaul for nearly two hundred years after the fall of the Western empire, that they "reflect more *Romania* than *Germania*."[2] Roman military units survived, with membership perhaps handed down as family legacies. Especially once the dominant Western armies adopted heavy cavalry as the principal arm, with infantry remaining present on the battlefield but getting little attention from rulers or chroniclers, the Western debt to the Romans became mostly nominal and imaginary. Even so, it is not necessarily to be discounted. Through Vegetius in particular the Romans remained a remote but inspiring ideal of discipline, organization, and general military excellence.

The survival of Roman military institutions after the fall of the empire is perhaps not so surprising when one recalls that the later Roman army had been recruited from among the same barbarian tribes that were in the process of dismantling and supplanting the empire. Still, long before the fall, the Roman army had ceased to resemble the classical form it had assumed in the late republic and through about 200 CE, not only in personnel but also in tactics, organization, and ethos. Greek soldiers had gone to *The Iliad* to recapture an ancient ideal of military heroism. In remembering Rome, the soldiers of late antiquity recalled both the army as it had been when the empire fell and also the army Vegetius nostalgically wrote about and preserved. In both instances what counted most was likely not the means of war but a poetics of military virtue transmitted across the generations.

The Byzantine Empire

The Byzantine Empire lasted from the division of the empire under Diocletian in 285 CE until the final fall of Constantinople in 1453. Byzantine military institutions were highly derivative of those of the later Roman army. They employed large numbers of cavalry and heavy infantry, along with individual and crew-served missile weapons, but the Byzantines were also innovators and adapters. They became adept at the feigned retreat followed by a prepared ambush, and they made good use of "war wagons" that could be formed in a circle to create a mobile defensive sanctuary.[3] If the Byzantines lacked the aggressiveness and *virtus* of their Western Roman forebears, according to Edward Luttwak they inherited two Roman practices that promoted their success and survival: taxation and training. The first practice ensured sufficient revenue to finance standing armies and to permit their expansion for war. The second ensured that "Byzantine soldiers went into battle with *learned* combat skills."[4] The Byzantines also produced a library of military books, including at least one classic, the *Strategikon* (attributed to the Byzantine emperor Maurice [582–602]), and one general of the first rank, Belisarius. The Byzantines not only held their empire for more than a thousand years, they also expanded it, reclaiming for a time the lost Roman lands in North Africa and Italy, including the city of Rome itself.

These victories, accomplished by the great Belisarius, illustrate a weakness in the Byzantine military system. Driven by the economical turn of mind of imperial bureaucrats such as John the Cappadocian and by a fear of large armies imparted to them by the Roman example, the Byzantines tended to prefer small armies, sending Belisarius on his legendary reconquest of North Africa with only 18,000 men, and to Sicily with 7,500.[5] In part because the empire was so sparing of manpower, the conquests of Belisarius were the exception. Byzantine war-fighting methods, as discussed in the highly influential *Strategikon*, stressed the use of the ambush, raid, and other hit-and-run methods over decisive battle. Like the other premodern military professionals discussed above, the Byzantines developed a doctrine of sorts, or at least a common understanding of the nature, practice, and purpose of warfare. Luttwak refers to a Byzantine "operational code."[6] In general (although with exceptions) this code aimed at limited forces and objectives. It might be described as more a formula for avoiding defeat than one for attaining victory.

Byzantine culture was mindful of itself as the remnant of a venerable, even outdated ideal of Mediterranean classical civilization, and it was conservative and fatalistic. From its founding by the Roman emperor Constantine, the Byzantine capital of Constantinople was decorated with aged artifacts of Hellenic civilization.[7] Byzantine Christianity could be bellicose, but it accepted decline as part of the natural order of things. Byzantine fatalism was confirmed by the rise of Islam and the repeated battering at Constantinople that culminated with the leveling of its walls by the ultra-heavy artillery of the young sultan and cannon enthusiast Mehmed II. The last soldiers of the Byzantine Empire died fighting alongside their soldier-emperor Constantine XI.

In a sense, however, the Byzantine Empire was well served by its army, which is in some ways a better model of military professionalism than that of the Romans. The Byzantine military made do in a society that considered the army to be one of life's many regrettable necessities rather than a crown jewel. The Byzantine armed forces were thus relegated to a more disinterested professional role than the one the Imperial Roman army filled. They never engaged in the kind of destabilizing political activism the Roman army practiced. Finally diminished by a broken system of taxation, as well as declining population and revenue, the army did not desert its civilization. By standing in the breach it helped enable the eleventh-hour dissemination of the classical learning that the Byzantine Empire had held in stewardship for more than a thousand years, and thus enabled the Renaissance.[8]

The Vikings

For more than two hundred years, beginning in the late eighth century, Vikings from Norway, Sweden, and Denmark sailed and raided in large numbers from their homes in the north. The name "Viking" comes from an Old Norse word for "plunderer."[9] They went as far as the Mediterranean, Greenland, Iceland, and even the New World, but they struck hardest and most often in Ireland, the north of France, and England. Given their reputation as wild berserkers and raiders, it might seem almost perverse to consider the Vikings in a discussion of military professionalism, but their example is worthy of respectful consideration. First, the Vikings' reputation has come in for a degree of revisionism, emphasizing their role as traders. The Vikings were colonizers as well as armed merchant seamen, most significantly in France, where the Viking Rollo founded the province called Normandy. In military terms they practiced early forms of power projection and amphibious warfare. They were not the first to do so—in fact, amphibious warfare is probably the earliest form of naval warfare—but the Vikings were especially ambitious, aggressive, and successful. Their swift longboats combined seaworthiness with a shallow draft, permitting them to cross bodies of open water and then to operate in rivers and intracoastal waterways, attacking inland targets directly from the water with minimum warning. Their tactics may be said to presage those of the World War II special operations commandos or perhaps to have been an early form of "operational maneuver from the sea," a modern concept that calls for amphibious forces to bypass landing areas and strike objectives inland. In modern times this is achieved mostly by the use of aircraft. The Vikings approximated this idea by using boats that combined the function of amphibious vessels and landing craft.

The Norse legend of *Beowulf*, a product of the warrior culture that spawned the Viking phenomenon, is a military classic that contains even more of the fantastical than does *The Iliad*. Beowulf fights not men but monsters and a dragon, yet his story is also an inquiry into the nature of heroism, of the experience of individual and group combat, and of leadership and the limits of force.[10] Although much of the poem is concerned with the physical details of action and fighting, considerable space is allotted to the thoughts of the combatants. *Beowulf* is concerned with such questions as why some go forward and others hold back or retreat, and why some groups of fighters stay together while others come apart at the first sign of real danger. The one soldier who remains by King Beowulf's side in his terrible final battle with the dragon is Wiglaf, a young man having his first experience of battle. At first even he hangs back, but thoughts of kinship and his own lineage press him forward when the rest of the fighters flee from the dragon's rage and uncanny fire. For the old king, wounded, discouraged, and seemingly deserted, the memory of past exploits is what heartens him. Unlike even the monstrous Grendel, the dragon is unnamed. He is simply a force, perhaps death itself. Beowulf kills the dragon with Wiglaf in close support. Afterward Wiglaf carries Beowulf from the scene of battle and rushes to bring some of the dragon's treasure out of the cave so that Beowulf can see it before he dies. Reputation, kinship, fear, and courage all meet in the poem. Beowulf's story, more than the dragon's riches, will be his legacy.

The Franks, Charles Martel, and Poitiers

The Franks were Germanic tribesmen whom the Romans settled in Gaul to fend off raids by other Germans. After the fall of Rome, the Franks were united politically through a series of military campaigns, dynastic weddings, and political maneuvers on the part of Clovis, who at about the age of sixteen inherited a minor kingdom and a band of armed followers numbering roughly five hundred. Charles Martel reunited and expanded the kingdom created by Clovis and his Merovingian dynasty, and was the grandfather of the most illustrious Frankish king, Charles the Great, Charlemagne.

The Franks' tactics evolved from a kind of decadent Romanism to a proto-chivalric approach complete with heavy cavalry and a nascent feudal-style economy that concentrated enough wealth in a few hands to support the cavalryman's needs for arms and armor, forage, and expensive mounts. At the Battle of Poitiers, in west-central France, the Franks used a solid shield wall of heavy infantry. Although the Franks appear to have had a reputation for undisciplined flight, on this occasion they stayed together and won the day, no doubt aided by the sense of fighting in a common cause against a foreign, non-Christian enemy in a battle with much bigger implications than those of routine intramural Frankish warfare. Victor Davis Hanson, following the few contemporary commentators on the battle, lays great emphasis on the solidity of the shield wall. Most Frankish combat seems to have taken place at close range, allowing the infantry formation to be maintained, but the Franks could not have killed the estimated ten thousand Muslims who died in the battle just by standing in formation and jabbing.[11] Nor is it likely that these casualties could have resulted from a pursuit by infantrymen weighed down with seventy pounds of arms and armor. The Frankish shield wall was supposed to have been flexible enough to permit the use of a wedge formation, giving it at least a limited offensive capability.[12] Like the Romans, and partly from them, the Franks had developed kill techniques to make their infantry lethal as well as impenetrable. The Franks may have derived their name from the *francisca*, the heavy ax that could be thrown with devastating effect at short range. The Franks also used the *angon*, a heavy spear similar in form and function to the Roman *pilum*. The *angon* had a barbed head that functioned like the *pilum*'s weakened shaft to make it stick in an opponent's shield. It also had a metal shaft like the *pilum*, making it difficult to hack off from a shield.[13] A Frankish method was to step on the *angon* once it had embedded itself in an opponent's shield, then strike downward to the head with the *francisca* or to the body with a second spear.[14]

Charlemagne

The Byzantine Empire represented an effort to preserve the dream and regain some of the corporeal reality of the Roman Empire; Charlemagne's Holy Roman Empire was an attempt to fuse the old idea of Rome with the developing independent culture of Western Europe. The highly militarized empire of Charlemagne was also the height of Western civilization during the period of late antiquity. It is notable that it originated in Gaul, the most settled and civilized Roman territory outside Italy, where Roman institutions, language, and ideas were well established.

The grandson of Charles Martel ruled a large, expanding, ethnically diverse empire from 768 to his death in 814, having been crowned emperor in 800 by a grateful Pope Leo III after Charlemagne's military intervened on the pope's behalf. Charlemagne's long reign saw important developments in the profession of arms. Although his empire barely outlived him, some of these changes had effects on Western military professionalism for centuries, and his empire set the pattern for the greater stability of the Middle Ages. Charlemagne's army was recruited through an early feudal system of vassalage and military obligation. Its backbone was a corps of heavily armored knights, their number perhaps rarely exceeding five thousand.[15] Charlemagne fought almost constantly, but his campaigns were usually of defense or expansion outside the existing empire. Internally his lands enjoyed a period of peace that was remarkable for late antiquity. These elements added up to the rehabilitation of the soldier from the status of warrior to a symbol of service and loyalty.

If the Arthurian stories represent the legendary origins of the knight as retro-Roman *miles*, the reign of Charlemagne constitutes the knight's historical beginning. (Latin for "soldier," the word *miles* came in the Middle Ages to specifically denote a heavily armored horseman, or knight.) The Carolingian knight has his own legend, expressed in the *Song of Roland*, in which abject, even pathological treachery is played against selfless loyalty to monarch and comrades: the reality of much soldiering in late antiquity versus a new ideal. Based on the retelling of a historical episode in 778, the poem probably reached its final form in the eleventh century, but it captures the attitudes and problems of soldiering in late antiquity. Perhaps most of all it shows the debt of medieval chivalry to the Carolingian profession of arms. As a soldier, Roland is brave but sometimes improvident. His

ORIGINS OF FEALTY. This depiction of *The Song of Roland* shows the various stages of the story, including the punishment of the traitor Ganelon and the emperor Charlemagne mustering his army for counterattack. *"Eight stages of The Song of Roland in one picture"/Wikimedia Public Domain*

guilelessness and simplicity blind him to the fact that Ganelon has betrayed him, although he recognizes this at the end. Roland's friend Oliver is the better tactician who makes decisions based more on reason than on pride. Against his advice, Roland delays sounding his horn, Oliphant, until it is too late to summon help. Both Roland and Oliver die in the rear guard of Charlemagne's army and are avenged by a combined force of Germans and detachments from the various regions of France.

As translator Dorothy Sayers points out, the gest of Roland represented an ideal of conduct for the people of late antiquity and the Middle Ages.[16] Along with the courage of Roland and the good sense of Oliver, the leadership of Charlemagne is one of the themes of the poem. The king is an experienced campaigner who is known to sometimes sleep in his armor, but he has not been hardened to the losses of his army. He swoons and weeps when he hears of the death of Roland and the rest of the rear guard, but he wakes at dawn the next day to marshal the army, assigning an order of march and commanders for the ten columns that make up his pan-European force. Soldiering was an intensely personal matter in late antiquity. Individual reputations were all-important. Even inanimate objects, swords especially, were given names: Durendal for Roland's and Hauteclaire for Oliver's. Swords were often passed down from father to son as both reminders and instruments of a family's tradition of military service.

The relatively secure economic base of Charlemagne and his army allowed them to remain a standing force, and constant campaigning gave them a high degree of proficiency at war fighting. Their tactical center of gravity was the armored cavalry, although this arm had not quite evolved into the form it would take in the Middle Ages. Lances were held high and often thrown rather than held couched under the arm for maximum shock effect. Archaeological finds indicate that most heavy cavalry still rode without stirrups.[17] The elite of the armored cavalry were the paladins, the twelve peers who had their literary origins in the companions of Roland, and who in Charlemagne's court combined civic and military functions. Charlemagne's armies also possessed heavy infantry of the kind that had fought at Poitiers as well as light forms of both infantry and cavalry who could be armed with bows or with weapons more suited to close combat, depending on the adversary.[18] Along with commanding military service from his vassals, Charlemagne was able to issue orders that resulted in their being properly armed and supplied. (Documents yet survive that give detailed instructions for types of arms and weapons to be carried to muster.) Charlemagne could command fields of crops to be set aside for the army's subsistence. On the level of strategy, he favored multiple lines of attack that seem to presage the operations of separate corps by Charlemagne's admirer and imitator Napoleon.

The Professional Ethos of Late Antiquity

The ethos of the warrior of late antiquity has been compared with that of the Mafia or similar criminal gangs. The comparison is not entirely inapt. Both share the narrow, exclusionary concern with property, heredity, and kinship.

Both are expressed in primitive symbolism and ritual, through blood feuds and bloodier punishments for acts of betrayal (which might amount to little more than a tactical error in choosing sides). Most important, the final arbiter of loyalty and service would seem to be money or some other tangible and exchangeable form of wealth: land or cash. Soldiers in late antiquity routinely practiced extortion and outright theft. However, the comparison or equation of soldiers with gangsters excludes the fact that the men-at-arms of late antiquity represented the police as well as the criminal element of their day. A rapacious, out-of-control magnate like Count Leudast of Tours could eventually be brought to account by a combination of social forces. In the words of historian Bernard Bachrach, Leudast's untrustworthiness as a vassal was compounded by his abuse and robbing "of the people he was charged to protect." Stripped of his countship and expelled from Tours, he was able to use the Church of Saint Hilary as a base from which to continue his criminal career, taking advantage of the sixth-century respect for sanctuary. Expelled from the church, he seems to have been on the verge of regaining the favor of the Frankish king Chilperic, but Chilperic's queen had had enough of Leudast, and she sent her soldiers to subdue and arrest him, leading to his torture and execution.[19] In the end, it required all of the pieces of the chessboard, from king to bishop to queen to knight, to restrain a titled and likely psychopathic renegade.

Soldiers were among those who preserved some remnants of Roman culture in the form of its military organization, and they were also in the vanguard of positive social change, contributing to the development of greater orderliness and civilization. The paradoxes of the military profession in late antiquity are given expression in the literature and legends of the time. This is perhaps most notable in the tales of Camelot, which depict a society struggling to retain and revive civilized works and attitudes amid social and political disintegration. The Round Table itself is a fitting image for the professional stature of the knights who conferred around it with their king. Interestingly, the militarily formidable knight Lancelot helps to bring about the end of Camelot and the reign of its just king through his ungoverned passion for Guinevere. The moral and spiritual qualities of Galahad prove to be more dependable and enduring, and it is he who finds the Grail. In this story we see another manifestation of the idea that the complete soldier is one who is more than fighting man or warrior.

The military profession of late antiquity was influenced by the surviving remnants of early Christian pacifism. Very early Christians did not fight as soldiers. The Christian tradition of just war began with Augustine in the fourth century, and its general intent and effect were permissive. With the conversion of Roman emperors starting with Constantine, the Church had acquired an earthly kingdom that had to be defended. Augustine combined a rather pessimistic view of human nature (sometimes called "original sin") with some practical ideas about how to control (as opposed to eliminate) human sinfulness. Augustine saw war as sometimes not only permissible but even desirable, as a redress of sin, as expressive of God's desire to punish the wicked. But for war to fulfill this redemptive role the Christian kings of earth had to abide by the rules of *jus ad bellum* and *jus in bello*, of just cause and means. A just war was one a legitimate ruler waged against a tyrant or usurper. It was conducted with restraint toward women, children, clergy, prisoners, and other noncombatants. The Christian idea that killing was an act bad in itself lived on, so for a time even soldiers who had engaged in legitimate acts of war in a just cause were expected to do penance. The penitential of the Venerable Bede required that returning soldiers fast for forty days.[20] Soldiers who served a tyrant, fought in an unjust cause, or harmed the innocent were required to perform much heavier penance; killing for an unjust cause or of a protected person could be considered tantamount to murder. In a sense, as Philippe Contamine points out, the later advent of chivalry was a continuation of the limits and penitence that the Church tried to impose during late antiquity. The greater orderliness of medieval society as compared with that of late antiquity was in part the result of chivalry's greater success, and this was due to the fact that chivalry was seen as an aspect of military professionalism rather than as a theological standard imposed from without by the clergy.

The First Knights

The practice in late antiquity of lords rewarding loyal soldiers with land contributed to the rise of a knightly class. The first knights were paid warriors who served a lord, usually residing in his household and with little social or economic autonomy. In a sense these men were pure paid professionals, and they lacked the corporate sense and ethical dimension of members of a profession. Their law was the lord they served. Many of the more successful men-at-arms rose from retainers to landlords who could equip themselves in the latest armor and weapons and afford the mounts bred and trained to carry them in battle. These wealthier, more independent knights grew beyond their military role, a trend that would be visible through the Middle Ages and beyond. The prestige and qualifications for knighthood rose, and the numbers of knights declined. By the early modern period, knighthood would become the reward for distinguished military service rather than the basis for a military career. Eventually knighthood would lose its necessary military connection, becoming an honor bestowed on the basis of civil service as often as service in a military capacity. The bestowing of once purely military honors in recognition of civil achievements would not be limited to knighthood, and it would continue to be a source of resentment on the part of some soldiers. But "imitation is the sincerest form of flattery," and the use of military honors in civil society is an indication of the special cachet of awards tendered for service in war. In the short term, the conversion of chivalry from a set of practical military skills to a moral code would be the gift of late antiquity to the Middle Ages.

THE MIDDLE AGES

Chivalry and Christianity

The periodization of Western history has undergone considerable reconsideration in the past few decades. For this study, I will take it that late antiquity ends and the Middle Ages begin at about 1000 CE. Europe still subsisted on the food produced by small plots farmed by families tied to the land legally or by necessity. These tiny farms were joined together in varying numbers under local landlords, who were likely to owe tribute and service to a remote magnate or king. Europe was still Christian, and all of Christendom was putatively presided over by a pope. Even if it was not as dark as historians once believed, late antiquity had been a time of disorder and privation. The coming of the millennium saw improving conditions, perhaps assisted by climate change and by a respite in the disasters of plague and of the Muslim and Viking invasions that had buffeted Europe, partially undoing periods of recovery such as the reign of Charlemagne. The greatest blessing came in the form of relative political stability. By 1000 Europe had been united into somewhat larger, more capable political units that could provide more security and opportunity for peaceful pursuits. Farming and trade increased. The population grew. Life was better.

Much of this political unification had been achieved at the point of the sword. The small armies of early late antiquity had merged and grown under the more powerful monarchs and in response to invasion. Medieval armies contained large numbers of foot soldiers, but the cavalry was assuming a role of probably unprecedented importance and decisiveness on the campaign and in battle. The growing wealth of Europe, particularly among the landowning classes, had created conditions for soldiers of sufficient means to mount themselves on expensively bred stallions and to fight encased in armor and wielding a variety of weapons. This panoply gave the horseman considerable advantage over a foot soldier, who would be wearing less armor and carrying fewer weapons, both because he could not afford them and because he had no horse to share his load. The mounted knight was not invulnerable, but he could move fast and strike downward; his destrier with its bulk, iron-shod hooves, and frightened fury constituted a formidable weapon in itself. Given the choice and the means, this was surely the preferred way to soldier in the Middle Ages. The means were limited to a few, but the relatively underdeveloped military organization and emphasis on social privilege of the period meant that those with monetary means were also those with the privilege of choosing how they fought. A soldier selected his military branch based on his income. For a time, at least, riding a horse into battle could also be a means of social and economic advancement. The man-at-arms who could afford to equip himself as a horseman could command better pay, the possibility of more prize money, and ransom. He might even lay claim to a spurious pedigree, although that claim might not go unchallenged. The popularity of armored cavalry among the well-to-do created the conditions for the medieval knight. It was all-important, both for prestige and survival, that the knight should keep his seat on the horse. From this necessity arose chivalry, an art of horse riding that evolved into a warrior's standard of conduct and eventually into a code of morals and manners and a powerful myth that still has the ability to attract and fascinate today.

The knight was the military professional of his time. He may be said to have shared this title with others—mercenaries, castle guards, and the knight's own retainers—but it was he who was the main repository of military knowledge, especially of the dominant beliefs of the medieval military world. Even so, some may question his right to professional status. The standards and centers for learning were too sketchy and scattered, and the mechanisms of institutional memory, let alone those for assessment and development, were too unsystematic to constitute the apparatus of a profession.[1] Granting all of that, if one considers the historical essentials of professionalism the knight has a fighting claim to the title of military professional. His learning was limited by the scope of medieval knowledge and education, but by the standards of the time most knights were well educated. What he knew he knew well, and he perhaps had a greater understanding about some aspects of war than many of his better-credentialed descendants. The chivalric ethos often went unobserved and was imperfect in itself, tainted by class arrogance, but it was a potent belief that was enriched over the years by deeds and words, by imagery and memory, and we would be wrong to think that many knights did not subscribe to it with great sincerity and often to their betterment. As one of the dominant ideas of the Middle Ages, chivalry represented a means of moral leadership through which the knight exercised a hold on the imagination and aspirations of his time, along with considerable economic, political, and military power. Many knights kept to their code and continued to practice their profession in battle after battle and campaign after campaign. They endured privation and the demands of close-quarters combat, dressed in armor that was shiveringly cold in winter and like an oven in summer. The experience of "war cruel and sharp" must have been disillusioning or brutalizing for some young knights. The truly committed professionals among them (perhaps always a minority in any time) kept ranks and kept the faith. It is noteworthy that they did so with few of the controls used to keep modern soldiers in check. We should not be surprised at the brutality of medieval warfare. War is always brutal, and these were violent times. In the relatively well-ordered kingdom of fourteenth-century England, for example, the possibility of death by homicide was much greater than it was anywhere on the globe in the twentieth century.[2] The knight both contributed to the violence of the age and, through his chivalric code and preferred means of fighting, helped to contain the violence. Chivalry was not the only influence on the restraint in war, but any restraint shown in the conduct of military operations had to come from knights operating in an atmosphere of considerable latitude.

Myth and Reality

The eminent historian Sir Charles Oman is largely responsible for forming the traditional perception of medieval warfare and warriors, particularly in his *The Art of War in the Middle Ages* (1885).[3] Written in the midst of the nineteenth-century "chivalric revival," Oman's work is in some ways a historian's debunking of a largely literary myth, but he shared some of the same misconceptions about medieval warfare as such literary and artistic figures as Sir Walter Scott and Howard Pyle. Oman did a great service to history by helping to revive informed interest in the Middle Ages, but his views on the warfare of the period tend to be dismissive and simplistic. Oman stresses the supremacy of heavy cavalry, and he has a low opinion of the discipline, tactical and strategic sense, and staying power of all but a few medieval armies. Partly through his influence, for years the professional study of military history tended to pass over the period in embarrassed silence, as if during this time, which encompassed both late antiquity and the Middle

Ages—say, from 500 to 1500 CE—the profession of arms was static and even regressive, awaiting the developments of the Renaissance and the Age of Reason, the symbiotic rise of nation-states and national armies to bring order to what had been a millennium of unseemly brawls. Knights might have been brave, so this interpretation goes, but their capabilities were severely limited by an individualistic approach to battle, by motives that were often quixotic, and by a general ignorance that encompassed nearly any military subject above the level of horsemanship and weapons handling.

Modern scholarship has largely supplanted this Monty Python–esque picture of the medieval warrior with a richer, more complex, and more accurate view. The revision of the history of medieval warfare began with the work of historians R. C. Smail and J. F. Verbruggen, respectively, in *Crusading Warfare, 1097–1193* (1956) and *The Art of Warfare in Western Europe during the Middle Ages* (1954, but first translated into English in 1977). This revision has been continued by Philippe Contamine in *War in the Middle Ages* (1980, trans. 1984) and by J. O. Prestwich, Maurice Keen, and John France in various works.[4] The medieval knight has gained new respect for his abilities as a war fighter. Along the way, the concept of feudalism, including its dimension of landed military obligation, has been called into question. Money, it turns out, may have been a more important motive and compensation for medieval soldiers than was a debt owed for land use. The idea of chivalry also has come in for revision, although it has not been removed from the historian's vocabulary.

In the pages that follow I discuss the professional credentials of medieval soldiers, of knights in particular, with respect to the categories of knowledge, belief, transmission, and compensations introduced earlier. In the process I hope to demonstrate that these men were indeed professionals. At least some knights mastered a demanding profession without the apparatus that is considered a necessary feature or means of professionalism in our own time. These men in mail and plate, or sometimes in plain russet coat, cap, and bow, may have some unexpected knowledge to impart about military service and its relation to the larger society.

Knowledge
The knowledge possessed by medieval soldiers, indeed by all people during the Middle Ages, had to remain afloat in a sea of ignorance. There were few maps or books. People were superstitious and largely illiterate. Some never

went beyond the visible horizon, either in fact or imagination. The world for most might have resembled the inscrutable and two-dimensional universe Edwin Abbot depicts in the mathematical classic *Flatland* (1884). The knowledge medieval soldiers possessed must be placed in this context and considered relative to the objectives for which they fought rather than by an absolute or modern standard. On the other hand, what knowledge medieval folk possessed could be especially intimate and intense. A person, whether peasant or noble, could know the small tract, few possessions, and small human community of his domain with great thoroughness. Learned people could still hope to have a grasp of virtually all existing knowledge. Lacking printed records, some scholars trained themselves, in an art now mostly lost, to prodigious feats of memorization.[5]

Knights were expected to possess a certain level of education and were in the vanguard of the increase in standards of literacy and education during the Middle Ages. One advantage that soldiers of this time possessed was the high social status of the military occupation and of knighthood in particular. Knighthood could be a means of social mobility for the less advantaged and a way for the well born to demonstrate their fitness to rule, whether over a vassalage or a kingdom. Knighthood was itself an education. It could put an ambitious young soldier or rural gentleman into contact with a wider social circle that might include scholars, high-ranking clergymen, and aristocrats.[6] He would probably come to imitate their speech and manners. A young man who aspired to be a knight might go to a clergyman to be tutored.[7] The great English universities of Oxford and Cambridge were founded to educate clergy, but some students ended up as knights, and by the 1430s the universities were educating for secular careers.[8] The Inns of Court provided a general education to the sons of the lower aristocracy as well as a specifically legal grounding, and some of these young men also went on to knighthood. The English upper classes were bilingual, and some knights knew Latin.

Knightly education was more than a by-product of religious or legal institutions; it was itself one of the key elements of the culture of the Middle Ages. The writer Peter Alfonsi (died ca. 1140) listed seven knightly skills: riding, swimming, archery, boxing, hawking, chess, and poetry writing.[9] Viewed in utilitarian terms, the first five are concerned with war and the chase, but chess and poetry might seem to be connected to, respectively, the development of a spatial, strategic outlook and to honing and enriching the knight's use of language. A knight was expected to be informed on three "matters": France, Rome, and Britain.[10] The matter of France was also referred to as the "romances of adventure," and that of Rome as the "romances of antiquity." The matter of Britain dealt with the Arthurian legends, which forged a link to post-Roman Britain and played an enormous part in the development of the concept and code of chivalry. To a degree, these matters were international. Historian Juliet Barker notes with some surprise the number of French knights killed at Agincourt who had Arthurian names.[11] Many rulers possessed privately written books called "mirrors of princes" that included advice on the conduct of war, and members of the aristocracy read copies of them. Some knights had extensive libraries, at least by the standards of the times.[12] In the fifteenth century Sir John Fastolf had a library of nineteen books, which included a copy of Vegetius' *De Re Militari*, the favorite military classic in medieval times. Not all of the military writing medieval soldiers possessed and consumed was ancient. The Middle Ages produced a military literature of its own, some of it written by knights.[13] Two works that served as "handbooks for the knightly classes" were Honoré Bonet's *Le Arbre des Batailles* (The Tree of Battles) and *The Book of Arms and of Chivalry* by Christine de Pizan.[14] Another was Ramon Llull's thirteenth-century *Llibre de l'Ordre de Cavalleria*. Llull was both a knight and an important philosopher who, while not neglecting the knight's role as a fighter, also saw him as a bulwark of social order who should be prepared to serve as a "royal official."[15]

Medieval society was highly militarized but not very well organized, so military training was extensive but unsystematic. The development of new knowledge was impeded in part by a strong conservatism shared, almost in the form of a conspiracy, by the clergy and nobility. The small numbers of books and schools limited the resources for education and for retaining and spreading knowledge. For knights, however, there were exceptions. With their garrisons, resident knights and squires, opportunities for gaming and training, and even their collections of books, the large castles of the great lords functioned as professional education centers for knights and other men at arms.[16] The military religious orders also served as repositories of military knowledge. The Templars composed a book that included sections on cavalry tactics, *The Rule of the Templars*, probably written in the thirteenth century and still surviving. *The Rule of the Templars* merits detailed consideration for several reasons: (1) it gives us an idea of the cavalry tactics of the Templars; (2) it demonstrates historical continuities in cavalry tactics that extend at least as far back as the Byzantine Empire and forward into the twentieth century; and (3) combined with their record in battle, the *Règle* (Rule) indicates a degree of discipline and orderliness in the Templars' operations that supports their right to the title of military professionals.[17]

Most knights did not have the opportunity to serve or train in a great castle or to join a military religious order. For them, training was more haphazard and individual. This does not mean that it was inadequate or even that it might not have been excellent. The apprenticeship model of military training conducted in the Middle Ages as a progression from page to squire to knight likely served its society well, at least as evidenced by its long survival.[18] In the periods of frequent warfare that characterized the Middle Ages, there were many knights with campaigning and combat experience who were capable of imparting their knowledge to younger squires and other subordinates. The term "knight master" is as old a term as "school master."[19] Knightly training conducted by a master was probably a combination of example, demonstration, and explanation. Other forms of training that were widely available were the tournament and the hunt. Medieval tournaments were viewed as military training and were extremely realistic as such. In a sense they filled a role similar to that of the live-fire exercises infantry and combined-arms units conduct today. Both are preplanned, even "canned" or ritualized, forms of warfare that do not allow for much in the way of change, surprise, or the exercise of initiative; but both are excellent training in weapons handling, techniques, and minor tactics. Both involve wearing full equipment and are an introduction to and partial inoculation against some of the sights and sensations of combat.

Like the joust, hunting offered an opportunity to practice the all-important skill of horsemanship, "chivalry" in its literal sense, since members of the knightly class normally hunted on horseback. Hunting also involved weapons handling and field skills, setting up camps, and field cookery and hygiene. Perhaps the best system of training, then and now, was to take part in the actual experience of arms. This was a time of frequent war on a small scale and of regular large-scale campaigns. The types of operation were also varied. They included the pitched battle, the raid or ambush, the long ride of plunder called the *chevauchée*, the siege, and naval and amphibious warfare.

Few knights missed out on at least some firsthand knowledge of warfare. Many, by choice or by chance, experienced a number of campaigns and a variety of service, in some cases extending over long lifetimes, which did not always end violently. A uniquely well-documented example is Sir Thomas Gray of Heton.[20] In a military career of forty-four years, Sir Thomas endured wounds and capture and participated in open battles, sieges (as defender and attacker), ambushes, and long, arduous rides even into his sixties. He killed men and in one case was thought to have been killed in action himself, but he died of natural causes in 1344.

Belief

Two related but distinct categories of belief defined the medieval knight: Christianity and chivalry. To understand what these ideas meant to him is to understand the knight. The Middle Ages was a time of faith, and more than the soldiers of any other era, the knight as a representative figure of his age may be said to have been defined by what he believed. In a sense, faith and belief rushed in to fill a void created by the limited knowledge, scant organizational abilities, and minimal resources of soldiers of these times. The military ethos of late antiquity had seen a conflict of seemingly irreconcilable opposites. By the Middle Ages soldiers had partially fused these opposites, delineating an ethical code in narrative, through precept, and in practice.

Christianity and chivalry had in common that both could function as means of restraint while also remaining force multipliers. In fact, chivalry as understood at the time could be an inducement to atrocity as well as a restraining influence. Chivalry undoubtedly had a moderating influence on knights' conduct toward members of their own class, ladies especially. Some wars, designated *bellum romanum*, were fought according to rules of restraint in the Roman legal tradition; others, *bellum hostile*, were to the death. The chivalric code put considerable stress on riches and social status, to the degree that the lives of the well born and well-to-do were considered simply worth more than those of the poor, whether combatants or noncombatants. Sometimes knights committed and were praised for acts of clemency toward even their social inferiors. At other times the depredations visited on farms and farmers seem to have been celebrated as consistent with chivalry. Chess may have been more than a form of war game or courtly pastime. It instructed the knight in a strict social hierarchy in which the monarch is worth more than all other pieces combined, and any capital piece, including the knight, outvalues a handful of the plentiful pawns. Some writers on medieval warfare regard the frequency of the *chevauchée* as evidence of the irrelevance of chivalry.[21] But both were realities in medieval warfare that the knight would not have seen as irreconcilable. The *chevauchée* was a rough test of the king's right to preeminence and rule and of the nobility's claims to prowess as protectors.

Chivalry as a form of belief would have been impossible without a degree of literacy and learning on the part of knights.[22] It was the *chansons*, *romans*, and other narrative and instructive writing that largely preserved and passed on chivalric values. Christine de Pizan's *Book of Deeds of Arms and of Chivalry* devotes considerable space to details of such ethical matters as prisoners, ransom, treaties, and reprisal. Modern research on the cognitive advantage of narrative suggests another, perhaps unintended benefit of the medieval knight's fondness for stories of chivalry. Stories gave the knight part of his edge, along with his horse and armor. The knight also had a position to maintain in civil society as well as on the battlefield. The praise given to the Arthurian Sir Gawain for the "verbal dexterity with which he steers himself through awkward situations" is an indication of one of the benefits of knightly education.[23]

Medieval Christianity had a strong but ambiguous influence on the military profession of the time. In the first thousand years of its existence the Church moved from pacifism, through a period of qualified and grudging support for some instances of warfare, to a position almost of partnership with the military profession. Essentially, for reasons perhaps combining the moral and the political, the servants of the Church wanted to be able to tame and control the practice of warfare, including regulating how, where, and when knights fought. The controls the Church imposed consisted of a mixture of the restrictive and the permissive or even imperative. Restrictive controls included the impositions of what were called the Peace of God, the Truce of God, and Peace of the Prince.[24] The Peace of God (*Paix Dei*) originated in the ninth century and was an effort to protect noncombatants, who had been referred to as *togati* and *inermis* in Roman and early medieval writing.[25] The later Truce of God attempted to limit combat to Monday, Tuesday, and Wednesday, with the justification that the other days of the week were in some way sacred in the life of Christ or the origin of the Eucharist. The Peace of the Prince was an effort to designate war-making authority as the province of "princes" or kings alone rather than extending the *droit de guerre* to lesser nobility.[26] Somewhat in accord with the tradition of just war developed by Christian theologians beginning with Augustine, the medieval peace campaigns sought to limit and legitimize armed conflict rather than to eliminate it. According to Udo Heyn, neither the restrictions on warfare imposed by the official Church nor the legalistic tradition of the just war had as great an influence on knightly conduct and the practice of warfare as did the chivalric code.[27] Just war doctrine actually came to absorb the chivalric code, so we may say that the restraints on warfare that came to exist in later times, culminating in the Geneva and other international accords, owe as much if not more to soldiers as to clergymen and lawyers on the levels of both theory and practice.

The most notable examples of Christianity serving to encourage and unleash military operations were the Crusades. The Muslims in the Holy Land were the *summa culpabilis*, the most odious enemy in a combative world. In a sense the clergy encouraged the Crusades out of a motive similar to what led them to call for the Truce of God and other restraints. The Crusades were a means to distract knights from brigandage and from fighting among themselves. It cannot be doubted, however, that many of the clerics who promoted the Crusades and the knights who fought in them were motivated by a sincere desire to claim the lands that they (along with Jews and Muslims) considered holy. The Crusades were unquestionably savage, inefficient, and unsuccessful. As with most wars, they also involved a paradoxical exchange of cultural ideas as well as of acts of violence and atrocities. The Crusades involved long-range strategic movements and the maintenance of deployed forces on a scale that was probably unique in the Middle Ages and not seen since the fall of the Roman Empire. Knight-Crusaders may have been motivated by a mix of familial obligation, a desire to prove their individual worth, or *probitas*, and worthiness for their social position. The Crusades also may be said to have played a role in the development of a growing national consciousness and the ability of proto-state kingdoms to organize and mobilize resources.[28]

War Fighting

We now turn from what the knight knew and believed to the practice of war on campaign and in battle. What strategies, tactics, and techniques did medieval armies and the knights who led them employ? How were logistics managed? In keeping with the approach of the previous chapters in this work, I will also reserve space for the specific area of leadership, which like war itself is recognizable across time as well as strongly historically and culturally coded, requiring an effort at understanding across a remove of dusty centuries.

Medieval knights may have seen war as a way of life, almost as an end in itself, but military campaigns had objectives, and military commanders dedicated planning, preparation, counsel, and command to arrive at the best means to achieve those objectives.[29] Even the infamous *chevauchée* was not just a joy ride. The objective might be merely booty, or even the shaming of a rival ruler through the unrequited depredations of his peasants' crops and countryside; but such a march would have to reckon with the possible presence of an enemy army, with fortifications, and with any natural obstacles. Medieval commanders made up for the absence of maps or a formal intelligence service by relying on hired or impressed guides, traitors, merchants, and others whose trades required them to know the physical and human terrain of a region.[30] Knights understood the importance of reconnoitering enemy dispositions.[31] The campaign often had the objective, or at least an option (a "sequel" in modern military language), of bringing an enemy to battle. There were impediments to battle. It could be challenging to bring an enemy to the field under even reasonably favorable terms. A numerically inferior force, such as that of Henry V during the Agincourt campaign, would try to avoid battle, and (as the French found again at Agincourt as they had at Crécy) even a battle undertaken with considerable advantages in numbers, position, or physical condition could end badly. Still, medieval commanders understood that pitched battle could be more decisive than a long ride or siege. In general, medieval armies were neither battle hungry nor battle averse.[32] The short campaigning system usually imposed by the seasons, logistical challenges, and limits of military obligations might impel a commander to seek battle as the only means to gain the desired objective in the time allotted.

Medieval armies survived and profited by pillage, but medieval logistics was not just a matter of living off the countryside. A medieval army would at least have to set out with a food supply. In a large and well-organized force such as the armies led by the English king Edward III, this was not left to the individual but was ordered, paid for, stored, and shipped according to decree and based on estimates of consumption.[33] Sometimes soldiers were paid while on campaign and expected to purchase their own rations from sutlers who followed the march.[34] An even greater challenge was maintaining an adequate supply of arrows. When English armies adopted longbows, arrows were standardized and mass-produced. The cutting, carving, and fletching of arrows were specialized skills. An army archer was expected to be able to shoot ten arrows in a minute, a rate of expenditure that required an enormous supply and frequent resupply, even if some arrows could be recovered. Arrows crossing the English Channel or any other body of water had to be shipped in watertight casks.[35] Another logistical issue was medical care. Medieval soldiers received fairly good medical care, although as in so many other aspects of medieval life, much could depend on social rank.[36] There was no knowledge of germs, but wounds were cleaned effectively with wine or honey.[37] The removal of arrows or other projectiles from the body required specialized care; for example, Henry V was subjected to the extraction of an arrow from his face by an intricately designed system of wedges and pliers.[38]

Medieval military personnel administration might be divided into three areas: musters and review, contracts and pay, and heraldry. Accounting for the soldiers of most medieval armies was a fairly simple matter because they were small and short-lived. However, as the feudal system gave way to contracts, as medieval armies became larger in size and of greater duration, and as the competence and ambitions of the proto-nation-states increased, the problems of military personnel administration increased also. The experience of England in the fifteenth century illustrates some of the administrative challenges faced by armies of the time. England maintained an army in France from about 1420 to 1440.[39] Close attention to the musters of an army was necessary to maintain the force and to ensure accurate numbers for pay. In order to make sure units were maintained at or near their intended strength, the Crown developed a bureaucracy separate from the military command. Challenges to accountability included illiteracy and underdeveloped medieval ideas about "authority and efficiency."[40] By 1439, however, desertion had become not only a breach of contract but a criminal offense as well. A military contract at this time was typically in the form of an indenture, under which a written contract would be jaggedly torn in half, with the indentured person's half to be presented at the end of a campaign and matched with the half retained by the contractor. Heralds conducted a kind of higher-level military administration. The institution of heraldry combined recordkeeping, symbolism, and narrative. Heralds kept track of the families and individuals who had rights to the title of knighthood and to specific coats of arms. Disputes over these rights were decided and recorded by the courts of chivalry, and the surviving written records contain illuminating accounts of medieval soldiers' military service, including records for both knights and squires. Not all squires were adolescents on the path to knighthood. Career squires formed a substratum in the military hierarchy. Heralds were supposed to observe battles in order to decide the victors and to note exemplary individual conduct, adding to the function of personnel administrator those of international arbiter, field historian, and awards branch.

Cavalry Tactics and Cohesion

Although the point has sometimes been overstated, it is nevertheless true that the armored cavalryman was militarily dominant for most of the Middle Ages. The Battle of Hastings in 1066, at which a Norman army equipped with heavy cavalry defeated a Saxon infantry force and went on to subjugate the rest of England, is often cited as the beginning of the knight's acknowledged reign. This reign was social as well as purely military in that the status of the knight had been rising from simple warrior to greater prominence and prosperity, and knights came to constitute a kind of bourgeoisie of property owners. Even the knight's military reputation may have been inflated by his own self-promoting mythos and by a misinterpretation of the true lessons of the pivotal Battle of Hastings (which might be merely that infantry must not break ranks in the presence of enemy cavalry). Still, the knight's social stature would not have increased as it did, nor his claims to military dominance been accepted by so many for so long, had his military capabilities not been the subject of regular demonstration.

How did the knight perform and behave in battle? Some of the individual advantages he enjoyed have already been discussed. He was on a horse, heavily armed and armored. He was also likely to be physically strong, well fed and well trained, and to have the mental advantages of a somewhat superior education that included games and narrative. Another advantage that knights enjoyed, one that encompassed their nonnoble sergeants, squires, and even other retainers, was an enormous amount of cohesion. In effect this was a social cohesion of shared values and a common, committed approach to warfare that translated into tactical cohesion on the field. The *Règle* of the Templars gives an account of knightly tactics that is authenticated by some contemporary accounts of battle and by historical continuities in cavalry tactical doctrine.[41] The most distinctive maneuver of armored cavalry was the charge. The *Règle* describes a charge that could combine mass and flexibility. The three hundred knights typically constituting the Templars could charge all at once, backed up by a second and even a third echelon of mounted sergeants, squires, and replacement horses for the knights who needed them (only knights possessed replacement mounts under Templar regulations). Each group of ten knights came under a leader and a banner that provided the tactical center of each group, a rallying point, and a means to signal change of direction. To deploy and launch such a charge, and to support, repeat, and regroup, with voice commands often nearly impossible to hear through helmets and the thunder of hooves, would have required a balance of aggressiveness, responsiveness, initiative, and alertness in a very fluid situation. The charge could be conducted against enemy infantry, cavalry, or mixed forces. The Templars and other Crusaders learned to adapt the maneuver against highly asymmetric forces like the Saracens. That the reign of the armored knights survived well into the ages of crossbow, longbow, and shoulder-fired gunpowder weapon is another testament to their adaptability and determination.

Castles and Sieges

Along with the armored knight, castles were the defining and distinctive aspect of medieval warfare. In strategic terms, castles represented a kingdom's complex defense in depth. Medieval rulers were less likely than the Romans to build walls or to otherwise establish definite territorial boundaries. Since medieval society was less centralized and threats could come from any direction, medieval defense at the levels of kingdom and fiefdom was anchored in castles that offered all-around defense and protection from assault or sudden onslaught over a significantly limited area.[42] A castle could not protect the crops or villages of the peasants, although it might offer them a refuge, as could a walled city or even a sturdily built church, some of which appear to have been constructed with defense in mind. Castles were designed with increasing ingenuity during the medieval period. Early castles were built of logs and would have served only to delay a determined attacker of sufficient numbers. Later castles of stone made good use of terrain and included clever means of protecting vulnerable points such as the entrances and corners, as well as diabolical devices to deliver arrows, burning liquid, and stones onto attackers who drew too near. If a castle could be taken, much of the wealth of the neighborhood came with it, and the hold of the local lord and his more distant liege over the territory was at least severely diminished. The strategic significance of a castle depended on the ability and willingness of its garrison to hold out and to pose a threat to an attacker entering the lands around it. A castle could keep an invading army occupied with an investment and a siege while reinforcements could be gathered from another part of the kingdom. An enterprising castle lord might "sally forth" to attack an invading or besieging enemy force.

The techniques of fortification and siege craft that were developed and employed during the Middle Ages perhaps represent the best refutation of any lingering stereotype of the medieval military profession as stagnant, or of the knight as an empty-headed horseman skilled only in individual combat. The defensive contrivances of medieval castles clearly indicate that fighting men as well as masons and engineers participated in their design. Only a soldier, most likely a knight, would have been able to suggest the design of some of the spiral staircases in castles that favored the swing of a defender's sword over that of an attacker advancing upward. The design of a castle not only could facilitate close fighting and the bringing of missiles to bear; it also evolved to enable command and control. H. W. Koch notes that the "keep-gatehouse" design was the "culminating point of the medieval castle builder's art."[43] It made the gatehouse of the second interior castle wall the bastion of a defense and the command post for the master of the castle. From here he could oversee the defense of the interior and order the employment of defensive devices such as lowering the portcullis to trap attackers in the lower part of the keep, where they could be wiped out through the use of traps and "murder holes." Like the conduct of a skillful defense, the design of a castle required a kind of "other side of the wall" leap of imagination, even of empathy.

The defender of a castle enjoyed enormous advantages. Because of this, soldiers of the Middle Ages exercised considerable thought and ingenuity in perfecting the tactics, techniques, and stratagems of the siege. Some medieval siege techniques were inherited from the Romans. Medieval armies sometimes had torsion artillery on the Roman model. In addition to authoring *The Book of Deeds of Arms and of Chivalry*, Christine de Pizan wrote a manual for attacking and defending fortified places that was a virtual translation of work by Vegetius.[44] Post-Roman siege machinery included the traction trebuchet developed in the sixth century and the improved counterweight trebuchet developed in the twelfth century, which was less labor-intensive than the earlier version, relying on a weight of earth or stone to propel a projectile. Until the advent of cannon artillery, it was the best means to breach or damage the walls and fighting positions of the stone fortresses that were common in Europe and the Middle East by that time.[45] In addition to damaging the castle itself, siege weapons could be used to provide fire support during an assault and while the forces were engaged. This must have called for considerable accuracy and even a degree of coordination.

Like the design and defense of a medieval castle or other fortified position (such as a walled city), the attack on a castle required judgment and insight. The attacker had a choice of offensive tactics to employ, and the choice might be influenced by the larger, strategic situation.[46] An attacking force that was strong in combat power but short on time might have to employ a more costly but potentially faster full-on assault. A weaker force or one with more time (due to a better supply situation or less risk of a relieving army) might settle in for a long siege. Such a siege might come down to a simple question of who could last the longest before being undone by starvation or disease, but medieval commanders also tried to defer their own "culminating point" or hasten that of an enemy by various means. A garrison might expel some of the noncombatants from a fortress in order to preserve their own food supply. On the other hand, an attacker might admit or even drive peasants from the surrounding country into a castle's outworks, adding to the problems and range of decisions weighing on a defending commander and perhaps creating more mouths to feed. Both sides often engaged in forms of psychological warfare. An attacking force could remind the garrison and residents of the fate of defenders who held out for too long and then fell to angry besiegers. The defenders might loudly speculate about the conduct of the besieging soldiers' wives in their absence.[47]

Battle: Agincourt

The causes, strategy, tactics, and outcome of the 1415 campaign of the Hundred Years' War that led up to the Battle of Agincourt illustrate some of the professional challenges medieval soldiers faced and their different ways of meeting them. The Battle of Agincourt was a victory for an English army that was dispirited, physically worn out, and outnumbered by four to one. The campaign had begun out of a typically medieval desire on the part of the young English king Henry V to win both glory and profit. The campaign had gone well for the English for a time, but gathering French forces put them on the run until they were forced to turn and give battle on 25 October 1415. The English chose constricted terrain hemmed in by woods on both sides that favored their inferior numbers. Even so, they formed up in just one line—a single "battle"—instead of the usual three in order to anchor their flanks, where they posted strong groups of archers. They planted the long stakes that they had cut and been carrying on Henry's orders. Both sides said prayers on the morning of the battle, with perhaps greater feeling on the side of the outnumbered English. The French were drawn up in a much denser formation on the northern side of the field. The English hoped that the French would attack them, as they had at Crécy in 1346, but the French (perhaps also thinking of Crécy) would not be drawn. At eleven o'clock in the morning the English advanced to bow range (about three hundred yards) and shot arrows toward the French. This missile attack probably caused few casualties, but it achieved its purpose in goading some of the French mounted knights to advance, followed by a group of dismounted men-at-arms and archers. Some of the riders got into the English formation, which stood fast. Many Frenchmen were impaled on the stakes that the English archers had planted unevenly among them. The archers had no doubt cursed the extra burden, but now the stakes saved many of their lives. The stakes functioned more like land mines than obstacles, presenting a lethal surprise to a man on horseback but allowing men on foot to move among them. The French cavalry did not get through. Turning about and in retreat, pursued by the arrows of the English, they rode down some of their own foot soldiers and archers behind them. The infantry, however, continued its advance. The French infantrymen were channeled into the center by the flurry of arrows that continued to come from the flanks, and by the time they got to the English line they were packed so tightly that they could barely use their weapons. The French directed their attack at the men-at-arms rather than the bowmen, but once the melee began, the bowmen dropped their bows and picked up mallets, axes, and swords—any weapon available to join in the fight. The scene that followed was a hell of carnage, the bodies stacked, some said, as high as a man. The French, bunched together in a tight mass and weighted down with armor, could barely resist, and the English, many of whom had given themselves up for dead at the start of the day but now perhaps seeing survival, riches from ransom and booty, even victory in their grasp, went into a frenzy of killing. John Keegan remarks that the English were responding to the "violent anger that comes with release from danger."[48] They also knew that their only chance of survival was to whittle down the odds, so they killed as many of the French as they could, eventually taking prisoners among the survivors. The third French line, still unengaged, hesitated to charge, and the remnants of the first two lines retreated outside arrow range. Probably because he feared a counterattack, Henry ordered the killing of all French prisoners. The counterattack never came. Whether Henry's order to kill the prisoners was justifiable has been hotly debated, as has the degree to which it was actually carried out.[49] The surviving French quit the field, and the combatants, heralds, and history agreed that the English had won a remarkable victory.

Agincourt has been depicted as a miracle, as a demonstration of one nation's superiority over another, and as won by the highly effective longbow that the English knights had adopted from the Welsh more than a century before and trained their peasantry to use, even proscribing other forms of diversion. Agincourt was an extraordinary victory, but it was neither a miracle nor the triumph of a single weapon. Part of the reason for the English victory lay in the differences in the two societies, one highly feudal and the other (thanks partly to the Magna Carta) slightly more egalitarian and meritocratic.

An argument also can be made that the English military profession had more successfully synthesized the military developments of the time. English military leadership was superior, beginning in the person of the foremost English soldier of the time. Henry V was both the commander on the field and the monarch of a united English nation. His England exercised hegemonic power on the island of Britain that he hoped to extend across

THE APT PUPIL. Henry V was the product of an aristocratic culture and educational system that imparted military knowledge and values. Here, he receives from Thomas Hoccleve *The Regiment of Princes,* an instructional work for rulers with advice on how to lead in war. © *The British Library Board, Arundel 38, f.37.*

the channel and into France. Like some of the Greek and Roman soldiers we have already discussed, Henry V was the product of a society that possessed powerful machinery with which to impart military knowledge and a martial ethos. He was one of the most apt pupils of an educational culture that sought to develop military and political leadership abilities. One of the "mirrors of princes" had been written especially for him by Thomas Hoccleve, clerk of the privy seal.[50] Henry had been schooled in arms, including the crossbow and longbow, had been knighted, and had passed the "Feat of Arms," a test combining mounted and unmounted combat that was a kind of "capstone" exercise for knightly training.[51] Henry had also gained hard experience and been wounded in a war in Wales.

The Hundred Years' War had brought on the development of a group of men in Britain who followed the profession of arms.[52] The frequent royally mandated warfare and fairly efficient finances of the English kingdom had made war honorable. Men who wanted to follow a military career could do so in the service of a king, as the Church and chivalry prescribed. There were opportunities for knights and for the English middle class. Like the Greek hoplites and rowers in their day, skill in the longbow gave these yeomen an important tactical role and a marketable military skill. Most English longbowmen were sufficiently well-to-do to meet the income qualifications to vote for Parliament.[53] They were not feudal levies, but men who were paid through indenture. The army of landed archers was no rabble of reluctant peasants pressed into service. They constituted a disciplined force held together by both regular remuneration and competent leadership.

Although the longbow in the hands of trained soldiers represented a potentially effective and even decisive instrument of war, this potential could be realized only if the soldiers were maneuvered and positioned effectively and if they were able to keep up a steady fire and hold their ground against onslaughts of opposing infantry and cavalry. The English knightly class made an investment to ensure that the English archers were protected and well led. At Agincourt one of Henry's most experienced knights, Sir Thomas Erpingham, was assigned to command the archers.[54] He was assisted by other knights who helped inspect the archers and by centenars, captains who commanded groups of one hundred (and who were perhaps the historical basis for Shakespeare's Welsh captains Gower and Fluellen in the history-based play about Henry V). Sir Thomas, his knights, and the centenars were functioning as proto–infantry officers. The archers them-selves showed some of the versatility and self-sufficiency of modern infantry, combining missile attack and close-quarters combat, firing their flights of arrows and engaging in hand-to-hand combat as the situation required.

As a commander, Henry had been outgeneraled before the battle, but his mistakes were redeemed by the fighting qualities of his army, by his own actions on the battlefield, and by French shortcomings and mistakes.[55] Henry showed that he could be decisive. He listened to advice. He was charismatic, exhorting, leading in person, and visiting men on guard, but also insisting on strict discipline. Henry is an example of the enduring nature of some of the essentials of good military leadership. The "antiquated feudal structure" of the French army, Hibbert notes, made "pay unthinkable, co-operation difficult to ensure and effective discipline impossible to enforce."[56] With the French king Charles VI mad and the dauphin sickly and only nineteen, the command of the French army was left to a coterie of squabbling nobles with no acknowledged senior. The French were strong in numbers, but their crit-ical vulnerabilities were poor command and control and the constricted ter-rain, which Henry, perhaps through a mixture of calculation and instinct, laid out his forces and conducted his battle in such a way as to exploit. Henry saw the enemy and the terrain in all of their dimensions. The French were too preoccupied and had too many preconceptions to see the situation as clearly as he did, and they lost.

Agincourt is a reminder of the enduring lesson of military history that, to quote military historian Geoffrey Parker, "success is never final."[57] One might also echo the reminder repeated to the victorious commander in the course of a Roman triumph that "glory is fleeting." Within a few years of his victory, Henry died young. A couple of decades later, Joan of Arc and the new siege artillery reduced the English forts in France and ended forever the claims of the English Crown to French territory. Henry's son, crowned Henry VI at nine months, went on to be deposed, reinstated, and eventu-ally murdered in the Tower of London. His death led to the Wars of the Roses, a series of bitter dynastic struggles that ended the lines of many of the English noble families who were ably represented at Agincourt. It is well for professional soldiers to remember (and to remind others) that even the most brilliant, well-earned victory may be undone in a short time by events and perhaps by fate.

Leadership

As the foregoing discussion of Agincourt indicates, military leaders in the Middle Ages faced many challenges and enjoyed certain advantages. State resources and competency were limited, often resulting in small armies, uneven training, and shortened campaigns.[58] Commanders had few means of command and control and usually little in the way of a staff or even a definite chain of command. For advice, planning, and the dissemination of orders, a king might have a council of experienced knights and perhaps a lawyer to help resolve disputes.[59] Such a council might present a variety of courses of action for the leader's decision, as the chronicler Jean Froissart describes.[60] In battle a knight might rally men to his banner through a combination of personal display, exhortation, and example. With limited means of command and control, a military leader might find himself in a dilemma between leading from the front and being in a position to supervise and direct.[61] Although medieval soldiers recognized the value of experience and ability, social rank often determined who was in command. As the example of the French at Agincourt indicates, the enormous social gulf that often existed between leaders and led could prove an impediment to leadership. Knights came from or were associated with the social class that took it as a right to issue orders to commoners and peasants, a right the lower classes generally accepted. If this entitlement translated into "noblesse oblige"—the instinct for responsibility and even for sacrifice among the knightly class—it could serve as an advantage. Many years after the Middle Ages, the philosopher Kenneth Burke would note the importance of the "glamour" of class distinctions to military discipline, even in the twentieth century.[62] In the Middle Ages this glamour was upheld by heraldic symbols and in effect by the entire organization of society, by its most deeply held secular and religious values. On the other hand, if the differences in class were expressed in arrogance, mutual avoidance, and dislike, they could prevent the exercise of effective leadership.

It should be remembered that most knights were part-time professionals. When not on campaign, serving their mandated period of service with a castle garrison, jousting, or engaged in training other knights or knight candidates, they were likely to employ their time as the owners and managers of agricultural estates. This experience would have been helpful to knights in giving them knowledge of logistics and of the livestock, crops, draft animals, and horses on which a medieval army depended for subsistence and transport. Time on the farm would also put them into contact with the peasants and farmers who formed the rank and file of an army, whether as feudal levies or paid bands. This contact would have been especially valuable for a knight riding off to war at the head of a local contingent. Whoever was in charge, town and village contingents demonstrated considerable built-in cohesion based on years of acquaintance.

The knightly ethos is often viewed as highly individualistic and conducive to neither military discipline nor self-restraint, but for members of a certain class, one defined by income and descent, knighthood was a social obligation as well as a path to self-aggrandizement. Those with a prescribed minimum income were required by law to equip themselves and serve as knights. Wealthy men were expected to provide an armed entourage in service to the king. If they were incapable or unwilling, a "scutage" fee could sometimes be substituted for service. The standard feudal obligation for a knight was forty days per year.[63] A knight who served forty days annually, and who rode, hunted, and perhaps tilted and jousted in between, had a good chance of keeping his military skills fairly well honed. If he read and reflected or even wrote in his off-duty periods, as the culture to an extent encouraged him to do, he might also develop the tactical and strategic sense that leadership in medieval warfare often required, along with some self-consciousness about his role as a military professional.

King Richard I of England, "the Lionheart," is generally accorded the title of the greatest medieval military commander. Richard is sometimes portrayed as a simple warrior, but he was much more complex than that. A devotee of Vegetius, as was his father, Henry II, Richard also left behind some of his own writings.[64] Known for spending as little time as possible in the country of which he was at least nominal king, he had scathing things to say about most of his kingdom, and about London in particular. Although his writings sometimes betray a sense of humor, Richard appears to have been an unpleasant person, given to frightening rages and becoming murderous when thwarted. He was the archetypal Crusader, almost a one-man army. In his campaigns he held together forces in the tens of thousands by personality and example, showing ability also as a strategist and alliance maker, as demonstrated in his correspondence with Egypt's first sultan, Saladin. His reign as king was entirely occupied by military campaigns and by efforts to raise money to finance them. Because he was an expert with the crossbow, it is perhaps fitting that Richard was killed by a crossbow arrow while recklessly exposing himself during a siege he had undertaken in order to obtain a treasure of Roman gold. He was one of those soldiers and commanders who seem driven by psychological need to fight and conquer, and he organized his time and considerable abilities to unremittingly belligerent ends. Richard is less an example to be held up for military professionals than a cautionary tale of someone who got so good at fighting that he could do nothing else.

His design of the castle Château Gaillard may be Richard's masterpiece. The château was expertly sited to control the key strategic Seine River near Rouen and to dominate the surrounding valley tactically. It incorporated some of the best of the Middle Eastern fortifications that Richard and other Crusaders had seen at Jerusalem, Constantinople, and elsewhere, along with some of his own innovations. It is a paradox of fortifications that a fortress must in effect leave itself vulnerable at some point if it is to be effective at protecting key terrain and allowing the garrison to pose an active threat. The fortress is a prize in itself for its symbolic import and for the riches and captives it may contain, but as a war-fighting structure it can strike out only if it can also be assailed. A completely impregnable fortress would have to be inert, capable neither of being supported nor of giving support. Château Gaillard came under a determined and skillful assault by another reader of Vegetius, Philip Augustus of France, in August 1203.[65] The castle was sited on steeply sloping ground on all sides except to the south, where more level ground offered access to the outer ward, a separate outwork connected to the middle ward by a causeway crossing a ditch. The middle ward encompassed the inner ward and keep within. Taking the castle involved three separate battles. The vulnerable outer ward fell when miners dug underneath its walls, replaced some of the stone with timber, and then burned the timber, toppling sections of the walls to make way for an assault. It proved very difficult to cross the gap between the outer and middle wards, but some besiegers noticed an unbarred window above the chapel latrine, and a small group used this to gain access to the middle ward, where they raised a clamor to give the impression of larger numbers. The defenders tried to smoke the attacking party out of their toehold, but the smoke blew backward and the defenders retreated to the inner keep. The château was a formidable structure, but a combination of mining and the blows of an enormous catapult, named Cabulus (medieval Latin for "horse") by Philip, brought down a section of wall, forcing the garrison of 20 surviving knights and 120 men-at-arms to surrender on 6 March 1204 after their attempt at escape failed.

The Medieval Military Revolutions

The mounted man-at-arms was king of most battlefields until well into the fourteenth century. The military revolutions of the Middle Ages that changed this were largely technical and tactical, developments Clifford Rogers describes as the "infantry revolution" and the "artillery revolution."[66] Infantry was quite effective in battle as early as Bannockburn (1314), given certain advantages of terrain. Later in the century, the use of the longbow and of the pike or halberd in close formation allowed the infantry to be consistently successful in an offensive role against cavalry in open, fairly equal terrain. The infantry revolution would be significant in professional terms because it created the conditions for the reigning military elite and professionals of the time—the knights and mounted men-at-arms—to assume roles involving greater leadership and command. As we have seen, by the time of Agincourt, knights were sometimes assigned to take charge of large formations of infantry.[67] As the importance, decisiveness, and lethality of infantry grew, victory increasingly came to depend on foot soldiers, and victory itself became more important as battles grew larger and bloodier. Infantry is both more susceptible to and more reliant on command than cavalry. It may be said that armies in this period gained in professionalism to the extent that they embraced this fact. The English knightly class quickly realized the importance of the infantry and its need for direction. The French were not as adaptable, and the consequences to the professionalism of their army would be evident throughout the period of the ancien régime.[68]

Like the infantry revolution, the artillery revolution created both the need and the opportunity for more professional knowledge. Although cannon artillery had appeared in Europe in the years 1320–40, it would not be until the 1430s that it would have an important impact on warfare.[69] In the intervening century the use of artillery would be gradually subjected to an approach that was less mystical and more scientific. This demystification would make usable knowledge of artillery more available and comprehensible to those outside the small guilds that for a time possessed the only knowledge available on the subject. The scientific and mathematical expertise necessary for the improvement and employment of artillery became part of the overall body of knowledge required of an increasing number of those in the profession of arms.[70]

Were Knights Professionals?

In some senses medieval knights do not fit into the professional category. Although increasingly they were paid rather than serving out of feudal obligation, knighthood itself was not so much a form of occupation as a way of life and a position in society. Many knights treated knighthood as an avocation, something to be done for its own sake and not for the sake of making a living. As I have suggested, however, the remuneration motive poses a paradox for professionals. In his disinterested dedication to knighthood and chivalry, the knight may be said to do more modern professionals one better. If the knight treated knighthood as an avocation, however, or as a game to be pursued for the love of the game, this could also limit his professionalism. The knight was likely to love riding, combat (especially individual combat with other knights), and in some cases the feeling of power and superiority that came from being the one on horseback riding ahead of (or down on) bipedal social inferiors. Some knights clearly did not love taking orders, waiting, yielding glory to anyone, or entertaining any suggestion that they might abase themselves to hold low-class villeins in the slightest regard. Added to these drawbacks were the lack of a professional apparatus or organization and the unorganized and sometimes threadbare means of education and training. However, many knights showed themselves able to rise well above these limitations, performing feats of arms that merit both study and admiration. In his role as a war fighter, the proof of the military professional's credentials are in the battle and campaign, in which the knight often performed bravely, competently, and even brilliantly. The knight's broad societal role may be seen as an aspect of his professionalism rather than as a detriment. In his self-perception, in the eyes of much of his society, and perhaps in reality, the knight carried forward, advanced, and bequeathed some of the most important values of his time. In the final analysis I must agree with medieval historian and World War II British Army tank officer R. Allen Brown that "medieval soldiers were as professional as during any age."[71]

The Legacy

I think no braver gentleman,
More active-valiant or more valiant-young
More daring or more bold, is now alive,
To grace this latter age with noble deeds.
        —SHAKESPEARE, *Henry IV* (part 1) v, I.

The knight should be assessed against the background of his time and in light of his legacy. He embodied the beliefs and aspirations of his society and was the symbol of his age both for his contemporaries and for moderns. It is possible to be cynical about him, but it is also fair and truthful to regard the knight in his better moments and based on what he valued as opposed to what he could sometimes achieve. What is quintessential about the medieval knight, the military professional of his day? Perhaps it is the primacy of his belief. In modern war a soldier may find himself or herself thrown back on character, on the strength of commitment to privately held beliefs that are outside the range of authority or supervision. Medieval society first equipped the knight with a rich tradition of secular and religious belief but then sent him mostly on his own to follow them as he would, without the comfort or control that modern institutions and supervisory practices provide. In this setting and against this background the knight keeps his honor and more. He still stands as a symbol for honor itself, for embattled honor especially. Chivalry remains a compelling, even if inevitably quixotic idea, and perhaps for no one more than the soldier.

Another legacy of the knight lies in the fact that he evolved from a pure fighting man into a landowner with military obligations. The evolved knight was expected to protect his vassals if they were threatened and to lead a local contingent or assigned element of an army on campaign and in battle. His motives combined feudal obligation, pay, and a desire to win glory and fulfill his identity as a knight. As local landowners knights often administered justice. In England, Andrew Ayton notes, "by the end of the twelfth century knights were training themselves in the arts of local government."[72] This "diversification of function" contributed to civil state formation. Their education and administrative skills, along with the tradition of leadership and moral authority derived from their military service, made knights ideal civil servants as well as fighting professionals. The diversity of the knightly role is perhaps the knight's most enduring example. He is a reminder that the only complete soldier is the one who is all of that and more at the same time.

THE EARLY MODERN PERIOD

The Army and the State

The late Middle Ages and the Renaissance were times of accelerating change. The size and competency of kingdoms grew. Transactions in cash increased, replacing civil and military feudal obligations of service. There was a revival of secular literature and education along with a gradually growing body of scientific and technical knowledge available for teaching and application. All of these changes had their effects on the practice of warfare and the profession of arms. As in other times, the profession of arms was in the vanguard of much important change: participating in the growing power of states, embracing (even to a deleterious degree) the European cash economy, and adopting both the products of science and a new scientific approach to military matters. If we consider this period as lasting from 1350 to 1650, the following characterizations can be said to apply. Armies grew in size, with substantial cadres of standing forces and larger mercenary contract forces. The development of gunpowder first doomed the medieval castle as a viable fortification, at least in areas of high-intensity conflict where artillery was available and employed, and then created a more important role for the infantry when foot soldiers were armed with smaller gunpowder weapons. Cavalry, including armored cavalry, remained important, but it assumed a place in the trinity of horse/foot/guns, losing some of its social and military exceptionalism. The invention of movable type and an expansion in the number of schools and universities provided the means to extend more formal knowledge to a wider audience, including more members of the knightly or officer class. The last century of this period comprises what is sometimes referred to as the "military revolution," which in effect confirmed the developments of the previous two hundred years. During the years 1350–1650 the causes for war in Europe shifted from the dynastic to the religious and back again. The soldierly ethos also underwent changes, partly in reaction to the causes and masters served by soldiers. The eclipse of chivalry—and perhaps even more the end of a united Christendom with the advent of the Reformation—eliminated the common martial codes and

religious allegiance that had united most of the military professionals in
Europe, removing two (albeit limited and imperfect) impediments to war's
brutality. Wars among Christians during the Reformation could be initiated
or intensified by confessional differences, sometimes introducing a note of
viciousness that in its own way was more repellant than the brutality of
medieval warfare. The period saw the beginnings of true national standing
armies but also the widespread use of individual mercenaries and large mercenary contract forces, which were often as unprincipled in their conduct of
war as the conditions of their service were unscrupulously pecuniary. But
this was also the era of attempts at statutory controls over the conduct of
war. A new generation of political philosophers, military theorists, soldiers,
and ethicists took up where Augustine and Aquinas had left off, building
an unprecedented consensus whose influence is still highly significant today.
The century of the military revolution saw some of the first standing military academies; greater knowledge on the part of more soldiers in the areas
of gunnery, drill, organization, and logistics; and the revival of some social
and chivalric ideas, along with a new code of national service. For a study of
military professionalism, the most important event may be the birth of the
modern figure of the state-commissioned officer.

The matter of a "military revolution" in early modern Europe has occupied military historians since Michael Roberts' famous and seminal lecture
in 1955. Roberts' original thesis was that in the years 1560–1660, advances
in tactics—in particular, the adoption of linear formations capable of greater
firepower—had impelled major changes in the practice and societal impact
of war.[1] Since Roberts' original work, the matter of the military revolution
has been debated and subjected to many efforts at revision and even outright
dismissal. It has sometimes been championed by the same people who have
seemed its most skeptical critics. One of the great virtues of Roberts' thesis
is that it has produced so much engaged and interesting writing in the field
of military history. The list of those who have participated in this debate is
long and distinguished and includes Geoffrey Parker, Jeremy Black, Gunther Rothenberg, David Eltis, and Clifford Rogers.[2] Some have argued that
the revolution occurred later, some earlier, and some that it occupied a much
longer period of time but was revolutionary nevertheless, if irregularly or
intermittently.[3] Other writers have argued that no revolution occurred, only
a centuries-long succession of evolutionary changes. The idea of the military

revolution has spurred some of the best writing on early modern military history, and it has also been extended into other periods, perhaps especially the age of Napoleon and the twentieth century.[4]

The Renaissance Revolutions

Three main developments occurred in the century and a half leading up to the start of the early modern military revolution in 1560 that had significant impacts on the development of military professionalism; two were technical, one was social. Like so much else that happened in this period, the focus of these developments was in Italy, specifically in the military campaigns that took place on the Italian peninsula between 1494 and 1529. France's invasion of Italy in 1494 led by Charles VIII inaugurated a new era of aggressive international politics in Europe.[5] From this point, nearly continuously until 1815, European rulers would attempt to expand their own holdings, revenues, and prestige at the expense of their neighbors and of the residents of the newly discovered lands abroad. The army that invaded Italy was well equipped with movable cannon artillery that could be used on the battlefield and was also extremely efficient against the standing masonry fortresses of the time. Aside from its immediately apparent effectiveness on the battlefield and in reducing castles, the development of useful and mobile artillery had two longer-term consequences.

The first consequence of the more effective, mobile, and employable artillery was the "artillery fortress revolution."[6] The new style of fortress was developed in response to a combination of the more successful artillery and the advent of international warfare on a large scale, in Italy especially. The new fortress had low, thick, sloping walls that were protected by a glacis and thus were much more resistant to breaching than the old higher and thinner walls. The new style also involved bastions: outworks designed to direct fire on any force that was close to the base of the walls or attempting to exploit a breach. A siege of this style of fortress usually took months, and most fortresses surrendered because food and supplies had run out and the possibility of a relief force arriving seemed slim.

The other consequence of better gunpowder, better gunpowder weapons, and a greater understanding of the dynamics of trajectory and penetration was "the infantry firepower revolution"—the development of more effective infantry weapons and their more successful employment by volley and relay.

Although sometimes identified with Maurice of Nassau in the early seventeenth century, the increase in infantry firepower began in the early 1500s with the adoption of the harquebus. Combined with developments in volley fire, the harquebus gave the infantry enormous potential killing power that could be used either offensively or defensively.

These three developments in Renaissance warfare all had an impact on military professionalism during this period, and they were timed to contribute to greater advancements in the period of the military revolution that followed in the years 1560–1660. France's invasion of Italy and its portent of a new era in European politics initiated a historical process by which the concept of national service would become the raison d'être of the military professional. The development of the artillery fortress revolutionized two areas of professional knowledge: fortress design and siege craft. The greatest fortress designer of the age, Vauban (one of a new breed of engineering officer), was also an innovator and expert practitioner in siege craft. The development of greater firepower on the part of the infantry posed questions for soldiers of the time. How could they maximize the potential of powerful but slow, inaccurate, and often unreliable weapons? How could they develop units and formations that would be resistant to rout and breakdown in the face of enemy fire? These were matters of tactical knowledge and its dissemination, but they were also matters of morale and of morals, of soldierly belief and how it would be instilled.

The military profession in 1560, and for much of the period of the military revolution, faced challenges but also had opportunities. Technical developments, especially in fortress design, tended to bloody stagnation. A complex tactical picture for the infantry involved mixes of pike and shot in a fine balance between offense and defense, firepower and shock action. Perhaps worst of all was the absence of a postchivalric soldierly ethos. The polar motives of sixteenth-century soldiering were God and money, the one leading toward fanaticism and the other toward amorality. Knowledge is the mechanism of a profession, but belief is at its heart, giving to a profession its vital moral component. In the sixteenth and early seventeenth centuries the mind, heart, and soul of the soldier were essentially up for grabs. By 1660, in the course of the military revolution, this ethical challenge, along with the challenge of new knowledge, had been met and largely mastered, at least for a time.

The Revolution in Professionalism

At the start of the military revolution the military professional faced challenges of both knowledge and belief. The amount of knowledge required of soldiers had increased considerably because of technical advances. These technical advances were not simple expedients handed to soldiers and their commanders; they represented problems to be worked out and potential to be realized. Technical developments in Europe at this time tended to proceed slowly but to disseminate relatively quickly, so a soldier could count on a technical advantage lasting for only a short time. In addition to technical or tactical changes, a further change occurred during this period in the size and range of armies. The greater resources of nation-states made bigger armies (just) possible. The greater ambitions of states made bigger armies necessary and sent them on campaigns of longer distance and duration. The new scale of warfare stretched states' financial and manpower resources to the breaking point and placed much greater logistical demands on armies. Not only did armies have to provide food and a degree of shelter for men and animals, they also had to feed the new and proliferating weapons with powder and shot. Artillery weapons, the massive siege cannon in particular, were an added impediment to movement. The demands of supply had to contend with the still-primitive infrastructure of roads and bridges in early modern Europe.[7]

As I have said, the challenge to find a meaningful system of belief, or ethos, among soldiers of the sixteenth and early seventeenth centuries was even more severe than the challenge of knowledge. During this period the regard in which the soldier was held was at an all-time low, and not without good reason.[8] Whereas soldierly belief once had been partly a means of restraint, in the forms of Christianity and chivalry, the soldier of the early modern period was more typically driven to excess by ideology than restrained or humanized, as a consideration of the French wars of religion, the Dutch war for independence, and the Thirty Years' War perhaps best demonstrates. Those who were not motivated by religious belief were commonly attracted by money, perhaps combined with a desire for danger and excitement, and by little else. Commanders and high-ranking officers profited from contracts, bribes, and large-scale booty. Lower-ranking individuals sought loot and expected ransom in return for acts of forbearance. In a sense none of this was new, but the absence of any higher aspirations or motives than adventure and gain, paired with religious divisions and large armies with powerful weapons, had placed soldiering as an honorable profession in danger of extinction even at the birth of the political modern era in Europe, and with implications for the world.

Three elements may be said to have come to the moral rescue of the military profession in this period. The first was a revival of the Stoicism of the ancients in the form of a creed that came to be known as Neostoicism. In this the soldiers of the time received considerable help from outside the profession of arms. The second element was a kind of resuscitation of the still-surviving elements of chivalry and the Renaissance aristocratic code of honor that succeeded it. The third was a code of national service, of raison d'état, that gave soldiers their secular God.[9]

The Knowledge Revolution

The increase in knowledge among soldiers in the years 1560–1660 took place in the context of the late Renaissance and the early years of the Age of Reason. Max Weber refers to the "disenchantment" of the world as taking place between the Renaissance and the late eighteenth century.[10] The seventeenth century was perhaps the tipping point at which science and magic seemed to be in roughly equal balance, with science in the ascendant. This was a period of growing confidence about the ability to perceive order in the universe. It was a great age for measurement, from the mapping of the solar system undertaken by Tycho Brahe and Johannes Kepler to the proliferation of clocks to measure time, to the development of maps, compasses, and telescopes. Galileo himself invented a compass for military purposes, and the first use of a telescope in war followed closely on its invention in the early 1600s.[11] Measurement means numbers, and the spread of numeracy was important to soldiers who were charged with designing and mustering the complex formations and firing systems that were being developed to maximize the effect of the new weapons. For this reason, not officers alone, but also members of the emerging class of noncommissioned officers had to be able to handle numbers.[12] Under the influence of such Renaissance classicists and reformers as Machiavelli, European soldiers had been prepared to adopt Roman methods of order, drill, and discipline. The advent of gunpowder weapons forced soldiers to adapt the Roman methods instead. Once used to provide fresh manpower in the front rank, relays now maintained firepower. In addition, the advent of cannon artillery gave the combined-arms tactics of Alexander and the imperial legions new scope and importance. The requirements for greater knowledge on the part of soldiers were answered in this period by developments in the essential subdivisions of professional military knowledge, which I have grouped in this chapter under the headings "Combat" and "War Fighting." Under "Combat" I discuss techniques, tactics, and leadership; under "War Fighting" I address strategy, logistics, and administration.

Combat: Techniques, Tactics, and Leadership

Little written record exists of how combat techniques, the individual skills that a soldier must possess in order to function, were developed, instilled, and practiced in the Middle Ages and through the sixteenth century. Even the redoubtable Swiss seem to have relied on example, word of mouth, and a kind of osmosis to ensure that men knew their jobs.[13] It was not until the early 1600s that drill manuals started to appear, and this is also when instruction in technique began to take a more systematic form than it had in the past, perhaps since the days of Rome or Byzantium. Manuals included instructions on the highly complex firing of the musket, but also on the handling of the pike, which could be planted firmly, thrust, or even thrown.[14] Yet even with the advent of drill manuals and more regular training supervised by officers, it took additional time to develop a standardized language of command.[15] Indeed, by 1660 not all armies had developed regular training or commands in drill. The army of Cardinal Richelieu seems to have continued to rely on informal instruction in arms by older soldiers,[16] but this period also saw the beginnings and spread of a body of written professional knowledge of military technique.

Like instruction in technique, regular instruction in tactics became much more widespread during the period of the professional revolution than it had been previously. This has been attributed largely to the innovation and example of the Dutch, and in particular to the spread of reforms initiated by Maurice of Nassau. Maurice favored smaller and less dense formations than the large blocks of infantry most armies used, as in the Spanish *tercio*, a regiment drawn up in a solid block of musketeers and pikemen. The new units were designed to make more use of firepower by masking the fire of fewer musketeers in the rear ranks, and to be more flexible and maneuverable. The smaller, more articulated formations required a higher percentage of unit leaders in the form of officers and noncommissioned officers.[17] They also

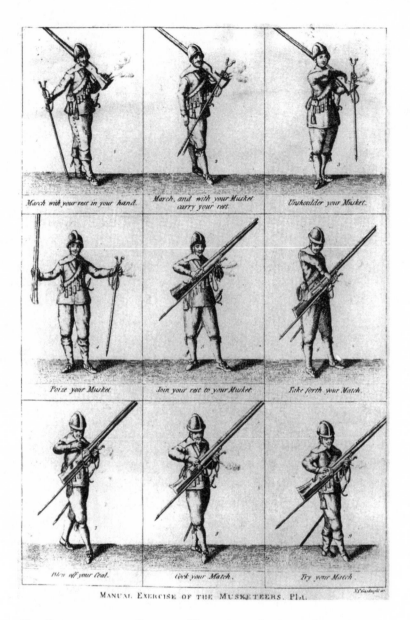

March with your rest in your hand.   March, and with your Musket carry your rest.   Unshoulder your Musket.

Poize your Musket.   Join your rest to your Musket.   Take forth your Match.

Blow off your Coal.   Cock your Match.   Try your Match.

MANUAL EXERCISE OF THE MUSKETEERS. Pl. 1.

THE SCHOOL OF THE SOLDIER. The early modern period saw the development of military manuals with detailed instruction on training and tactics. Here, a soldier goes through the manual of arms to prepare the matchlock for firing. *"Manual Exercise of the Musketeers, pl. 1,"* by Francis Grose/Wikimedia Public Domain required more drill to perform the movements of which they were theoretically capable. Maurice's reforms were greatly admired and imitated, and his army became the school for a generation of progressive soldiers (and for the philosopher Descartes, who accompanied Maurice's army, although in what capacity is still debated). The inclusion of a higher percentage of individuals with leadership responsibilities, although undertaken with the goal of more effective drill movements, paid additional dividends in terms of command and control, discipline, and the development and spread of general professional knowledge. It has been argued (e.g., by Geoffrey Parker) that the "revolutionary" development of smaller units was not the clear and unequivocal improvement that Roberts and other supporters of the revolution thesis would have it.[18] In fact, the choice between larger and smaller units remained a contest between stability and shock effect, on the one hand, and flexibility and efficient firepower, on the other. Still, as Raimondo Montecuccoli, the brilliant imperial general, observes in his classic *Sulle Battaglie* (Concerning Battle), "small units remain preferable."[19]

Seventeenth-century tactics, at least on the open field, were based on drill, and this drill increasingly required knowledge and regular training (which is, after all, a means of disseminating knowledge) to perform. The development of gunpowder weapons also gave added incentive to the coordination of combined arms. The cooperation of arms was taught and practiced at the small-unit level within the infantry. The evolution of smaller units created the conditions for pike and shot to work together more closely. Rather than operating in separate units, pike and shot were part of the same battalion.[20] The fact that cavalry needed firepower support for a charge to be successful was well established by the beginning of this period, but reforms in the seventeenth century (led by King Gustavus Adolphus of Sweden) had units of musketeers mixed in with cavalry for an even closer form of cooperation. Gustavus was also responsible for efforts to make the artillery lighter and more maneuverable, and therefore more tactically responsive and easily integrated into a combined-arms team. That his efforts and those of others along the same lines were not entirely successful is due in part to limitations in metallurgy and design. The smaller guns and carriages were disproportionately heavy compared with the weight of the shot they delivered, and they tended to overheat quickly. Truly effective and maneuverable light artillery would have to wait until the eighteenth century.

Advances in the art of leadership had impetus from several directions during this period, and these are amply demonstrated by examples of leadership in action. By 1660 the majority of military leaders of commissioned rank continued to come from the nobility or upper classes. The prevalence of the nobility in the officer ranks would become even more pronounced in the next century, but by the end of the military revolution the ties between birth and military rank had become more flexible than previously. Even a highborn leader had to acquire a growing body of technical and broadly professional knowledge. The composition of the new armies gave scope and opportunity for leadership. In an era of infantry-dominated but combined-arms-capable forces, a more sophisticated approach to leadership was required. Commanders now had to rely more on large numbers of soldiers from diverse social origins for victory and less on compact bodies of mounted aristocrats at their backs, men who were usually more self-sufficient in terms of their need for material and motivational support. A defeated cavalryman could seek refuge in flight or, especially if noble, secure capture, but a defeated infantryman or gunner had nowhere to go and no horse to take him there. He knew that defeat could mean quick death or the prolonged demise of harsh captivity and neglected wounds. We perhaps cannot blame him if his valor was sometimes as "precarious" as James Wolfe described it in the eighteenth century.[21] Such soldiers as these needed more care and reassurance, and the paternalistic traditions of military leadership, seen in somewhat nascent form at Agincourt, for example, underwent development as a result. By the end of the military revolution these traditions were established, inscribed in texts, and embodied by numerous members of a diverse military profession. On the battlefield, restraint and self-control could be as important as dash and aggression, or even more so. Although some of this was characteristic of infantry combat going back to the Middle Ages, the more sophisticated maneuvers, formations, and firing systems of the early modern period put an even greater emphasis on control and self-control and also on accurate calculation. The choice of leadership style depended partly on the situation and the spirit and abilities of the troops under command, and an officer or leader now needed more performances in his repertoire. The causes for which men fought were changing as well, and this also placed greater demands on the leader. The new nation-states had to substitute national loyalties for local feudal or civic ties, even for religion.

The older ties could still be very strong, and they would in effect be renewed by the extension of nationalism via imperialism, which brought tribal and other local loyalties into conflict with the claims to allegiance the colonizing nations demanded.

War Fighting: Strategy, Logistics, and Administration

At the highest level of strategy, sometimes called grand strategy, where the military instrument meets the goals it is sent forth to achieve, the period of the professional revolution created significant changes in conditions and practices. Whether one completely agrees with Sir George Clark's observation that before the period of the military revolution, wars were "collision[s] of communities" rather than acts conducted in pursuit of a policy, it does appear that these wars were often general expressions of antipathy: religious, personal, or hereditary.[22] Armies often sought to demean or punish. Cities often were besieged based on their wealth or prestige value rather than their strategic significance.[23] These motives did not disappear during the century of 1560–1660, but they were often modified or overshadowed by reasons of state.[24] The main exponent of the new approach to grand strategy was probably a statesman, not a soldier—Cardinal Richelieu of France. The raison d'état Richelieu propounded guided his country's involvement in the Thirty Years' War and became in effect the model for a war that turned out to be less a collision over religion and more a matter of policy pursued through force.

On the level of military strategy, Raimondo Montecuccoli (1609–80) is a pivotal figure. He was both a leading general of the period and the author of books on military matters that were perhaps the best and most important written between those of Machiavelli and Clausewitz.[25] His writings, his later writings in particular, constitute the most successful attempt up to that time to compile a theory and axioms about the higher levels of warfare. Montecuccoli's writings are broadly professional in the sense that they are based on a combination of learning, experience, and reflection.[26] Montecuccoli is actually more than a strategist because he often addresses the nature of war and its place in human society. He goes beyond the pursuit of narrow expertise to the true professional's desire to understand the value and import of his vocation. For a century and a half Montecuccoli was a favorite of soldiers, especially of thoughtful and intellectual soldiers such as Frederick the Great and Gerhard Scharnhorst. Montecuccoli addresses the question of how battles are to be fought and won in *Sulle Battaglie*, but in his later writings he discusses when to fight and the larger question of how to defeat an enemy in the course of a war or campaign. He understood the dichotomy between attrition and annihilation that Hans Delbrück later expanded upon and strategists still discuss. Can one hope to overwhelm and destroy an enemy in a short time, or does one plan for a "long slog" of small successes and incremental progress? Montecuccoli's discussion of this question is more nuanced than those of many others who have written since his time as if the choice were simply an "either-or" question (with most writers preferring the former, decisive course). For Montecuccoli, both decisive battle and gradual wear and tear on the enemy could be elements of victory, courses of action to be undertaken judiciously based on an assessment of relative strengths and one's own objectives. Montecuccoli advanced both the systematic study of military strategy and the practice of strategy based on avowed principles.

The strategic advances of the military revolution could not have taken place without advances in the fields of administration and logistics. In the area of administration, armies became more systematic in such matters as musters and recordkeeping. On a larger scale, the important administrative advance was in the development of the state commission army. A discussion of advances in logistics is necessary before addressing this development in greater detail.

During the military revolution the growth of army size, combined with campaigns that took armies far from bases or friendly territory, made it imperative that armies develop systems of logistics that were more sophisticated and on a larger scale than those of the past. In 1560 most armies simply paid their soldiers (when possible) and allowed them to find, buy, or steal what they required to live. Since pay was often in arrears, if it was paid at all, theft and plunder by soldiers were common expedients.[27] Armies could quickly become almost impossible to restrain or control. Their military usefulness would be eroded by desertion, by the absence of many soldiers who were nominally members of the army but off in search of loot, and by the overall climate of indiscipline brought on by these practices. In effect, the mercenary spirit of their commanders filtered down to their men, although even such nonmercenary commanders as Gustavus and Maurice experienced similar difficulties.[28] Armies could be nearly self-sustaining as long as they stayed in lands that were well supplied with food, which usually meant moving constantly because large armies could quickly eat their way through even a rich countryside. Such armies also became nearly self-justifying, existing only to feed and enrich themselves by preying on the countryside. In response to these challenges armies began to develop systems of logistics: munitions magazines, acquisition through payment rather than theft, and means of transporting and preparing food, especially bread.

The Spanish Road, which linked Spain to its Dutch possessions during their long war for independence, is an example of advanced seventeenth-century logistics. Geoffrey Parker describes the road in "The Treaty of Lyon (1601) and the Spanish Road" as follows: "Between 1567 and 1620, almost 100,000 troops traveled from Milan to reinforce the Spanish army in the Low Countries along the itinerary that contemporaries came to call 'le chemin des espagnols': the Spanish Road. Countless couriers carrying messages and orders travelled the same route, as did convoys of carts and mules carrying gold and silver coins."[29]

The history of the Spanish Road illustrates the mutual dependency of strategy and logistics and their basis in diplomacy. Without the overland route, Spain would never have been able to sustain its northern empire or pursue its eighty-year war to keep the Netherlands under Spanish control. By weakening Spain's claim to use of the road, the Treaty of Lyon not only ensured that Spain would lose the Netherlands but also signaled the decline of Spain as an empire. Although the empire the road upheld and represented fell, the road itself represents advances in engineering, organization, and cartography, as well as strategic vision maintained and adapted over time.[30]

Standing armies had been in existence since the Middle Ages, but the early modern period saw the development of a new type of standing army, one that is still the model for national armies today (albeit one challenged by the military organizations of nonstate entities and states' increased reliance on contract military units): the state commission army.[31] State commission armies gradually replaced the mercenary armies on which states had come to rely since the decline of vassalage and the feudal system. Originally hired by kings and the higher nobility, by the sixteenth century many mercenary armies were raised by military entrepreneurs, some of them operating on a large scale and creating what have been termed "aggregate mercenary armies." The eclipse of the entrepreneurs had several causes, some of them illustrated by the career and death of Albrecht von Wallenstein, but its effect was to promote greater professionalism. The state commission army first required greater knowledge than had been needed previously. Not all of this knowledge was in the possession of members of the profession of arms. States developed military bureaucracies staffed by individuals who specialized in the administrative tasks needed to keep an army in the field and to sustain and develop it over time, but the uniformed military profession expanded its competencies to include administrative functions that formerly had been left to civil clerks and administrators. The officer's commission attached his authority directly to that of the monarch or state. This tended to legitimize his authority, to make him directly accountable, and (perhaps most important) to place state loyalty in a position to at least rival such competing considerations as profit, religious belief, and personal honor.

A Revolution in Belief

The emergence of new branches of knowledge and types of cognition helped to create a new type of soldier, but the revolution in belief was equally significant and probably even more necessary to the continued development of the military undertaking as a profession. In the fifteenth and sixteenth centuries, soldiers had developed practices of tactical moral leadership for the battlefield, but a larger ethos for war fighting was still lacking. Most of the century from 1560 to 1660 was marked by a lack of restraint or constraint in warfare that makes it stand out even among the bloody pages of military history. The reasons advanced for this include the religious causes involved, the rootless and often unpaid nature of the combatants, and the growing scale of warfare, in which the size of armies and affected populations confounded efforts to impose control or to provide security.[32] By the end of the seventeenth century a more restrained, "limited" form of warfare had been introduced, one that would dominate most European warfare through the 1700s. The explanations for this change are numerous. Some historians cite pragmatic reasons such as economic interests and reciprocity as the most significant.[33] Others stress the sense of moral revulsion or outrage many in Europe undoubtedly felt at such atrocities as the sack of Magdeburg in the Thirty Years' War. The hopes of sixteenth-century pacifists such as Erasmus and Thomas More had been dashed by an era of frequent warfare, but the seventeenth century also saw the appearance of literature by Hugo Grotius and others calling for controls on war.[34] An important although sometimes overlooked aspect of this changing picture was the change in soldierly ethos and ideology during this period. These changes certainly reflected developments in the larger society, but they were not the passive or inevitable consequence of societal trends. Broadly speaking, soldiers as much as others began to recognize that the pursuit of warfare unrestrained threatened everyone and everything.[35] The profession of arms developed and adopted a strong professional ethos that guided acts of commission as well as acts of omission, of the conduct of warfare and of the soldier's place in society.

As I have already stated, three developments in the soldierly ethos in the sixteenth and seventeenth centuries were key in reforming the conduct and reputations of European soldiery: the revival of the concepts of chivalry and honor, the advent of Neostoicism, and the rise of an ideal of national service.

The Chivalric Revival and the Ethos of National Service

The resurgence of chivalric ideals in early modern armies involved a remilitarization of the aristocracy and their values. This development is one of those aspects of the professional revolution that is interesting in that it challenges some of the assumptions social scientists (and some historians) have made concerning the nature of professionalism. I will argue that the early modern officer corps was rescued from marginalization and a perhaps permanent moral downfall by developments that might seem to some a process of "de-professionalization." This process involved the supplanting of the putatively professional, mercenary, or careerist soldiers by an infusion of aristocrats. The return of the aristocrat to preeminence in the military profession and in positions of military leadership came about through a revival of chivalric ideals. It also created an officer corps prepared by their ownership of land and their membership in the aristocratic social class to undertake the wider social responsibilities of national service and loyalty to the sovereign. By the mid-eighteenth century this dominance of aristocrats arguably had become destructive to professionalism, especially in France, where the greatest and most unqualified insistence on an officer's aristocratic lineage reigned and intensified.[36] Aristocrats, with their sense of entitlement and insistence on privilege, could be obtuse and difficult to manage. But for the period under consideration, the return of the aristocracy and the ameliorating effect of aristocratic ideals had a beneficial effect on military professionalism and the practice of warfare. The concept of national service, it might be argued, also came to be fetishized, perhaps especially in the late nineteenth and early twentieth centuries and in countries that evolved autocratic forms of government.[37] For soldiers of the seventeenth century, however, it provided salvation from the Scylla and Charybdis of mercenary amorality and religious extremism.

The seventeenth-century trend of placing aristocrats in positions of command, thereby reviving chivalric ideas and perhaps making armies more biddable to royal command, began with the Spanish army in Flanders. Fernando González de León explains that for reasons combining the practical and the moral, the seventeenth-century Spanish army was increasingly officered and commanded by men of traditional aristocratic background who were also distinguished by a notably chivalric attitude toward war.[38] The court-commissioned painting by Diego Velázquez depicting the surrender of Breda to the noble Spanish commander Ambroglio Spinola in 1625 is a vivid representation of this trend. In addition to picturing the Spanish army as a disciplined force, with pikes held upright in formation, the painting has Spinola adopting a gracious attitude as he accepts the surrender of the Dutch city. Other intimations of the value attached to chivalrous ideals in the Spanish army of this period may be seen in Edmond Rostand's historical drama *Cyrano de Bergerac*. Cyrano himself is a poor but intensely honorable Gascoigne aristocrat in the French army. His beloved Roxanne pays tribute to their Spanish adversaries after she succeeds in crossing the Spanish lines, calling them "the most polished gentlemen / In the world."[39] In a later scene a Spanish officer salutes the courage of the Gascoigne cadets, uncovering his head and asking, "Who are these men who are so fond of death?"[40]

In his article González describes the price of the "professionalism" instilled in the Spanish army in Flanders by "*soldados platicos*" (perfect soldiers) such as the Duke of Alba who were successful in promoting discipline and combat readiness, but whose militant outlook, religious bigotry, and "hard-knocks" rejection of any restraint on warfare led to the war in the Netherlands descending into a brutal and stalemated struggle between increasingly implacable enemies.[41] This began to change with Alba's recall in 1573, and major changes followed the appointment of a new captain general in 1578. "A key to the campaign success of Alexander Farnese, Prince (and later Duke) of Parma," González claims, " . . . was his ability to soften and modulate Alba's terror policy."[42] This new moderation was linked to the changing social composition of the officer corps of the Army of Flanders.

The officers of the "school of Alba" found themselves replaced by a generation of aristocratic officers who were determined to see the war pursued
and perceived in the terms of chivalry. The new officers were not uninterested in success, but they were also concerned with honor and ethics as
opposed to an unalleviated emphasis on the principle of military necessity.
González writes that they achieved a "well-balanced synthesis of chivalry
and professionalism."[43] It could be argued that this balance deserted them
at Rocroi when an exaggerated fastidiousness about exploiting any unfair
advantage probably contributed to the Spaniards' defeat and expulsion from
Flanders. As González points out, this loss must be placed alongside the
horrific and ineffectual massacres perpetrated under Alba and his ilk.[44] For
political and logistical reasons the Spanish defeat in Flanders may have been
inevitable, but the actions of the "school of Parma" ensured honorable defeat
and helped to save the emergent European military profession from a moral
debacle from which it might never have recovered.

The English and British experience of the chivalric revival and emerging ethos of state service was both particular to the history of Britain's Three
Kingdoms and characteristic of the military professional revolution that was
making an impact all over Europe and beyond. By the late sixteenth century
the English nobility had largely lost its military function and English society had become significantly demilitarized.[45] A few expeditions (such as that
led by Leicester in 1585) and opportunities for service with foreign armies
fighting on the Continent gave some Englishmen (and a larger proportion
of Scots and Irishmen) the occasion to experience military life, and in some
cases to pursue careers as soldiers. The situation began to change in 1638
when civil wars at home prompted a "military migration" of experienced
British soldiers returning to serve with the armies being raised throughout
the kingdoms. Many of these veterans had served with the Dutch or Swed-
ish and therefore had been directly exposed to the reforms of the military
revolution.[46] The two main contenders in the civil wars, the Royalists and
the Parliamentarians, approached the matter of military leadership and professionalism somewhat differently. Although the social status of Royalist
officers declined as the war wore on—and even committed Royalists were
forced to admit that such status alone did not confer military aptitude—class
continued to matter. In consequence the Royalist army remained under the
control of "peers and gentry," and about one-quarter of Royalist officers had

received higher education.[47] The Parliamentarians, on the other hand, were increasingly uninterested in lineage, perhaps in keeping with their efforts to undermine the monarchy. According to Ian Gentles, it was in the New Model Army (formed by Parliament in 1645) that "respect for social hierarchy [was] most decisively overturned."[48] There were commonalities between the two sides too. In both armies, ideas of chivalry influenced the behavior of the rank and file as well as officers. Both sides also adopted articles of war that were usually observed.[49]

In matters of belief the greatest differences between Royalist and Parliamentarian soldiers and armies might be classed as ideological. Religious belief was important on both sides, but more so for the Parliamentarians, for whom it was not only a powerful morale booster but also an incitement to atrocities.[50] Even more problematic may have been the New Model Army's involvement in politics, which in some ways recalls that of the Roman Praetorian Guard and army of imperial times. In keeping with their more egalitarian approach to officer selection, the New Model Army's General Council represented an experiment in "military democracy."[51] Eventually the New Model Army arrogated for itself a political function that went beyond the conduct of its own affairs. The army became a radical, armed debating society, and its influence was most important in bringing about the execution of Charles I. The army also found itself in a political role in 1655 when Oliver Cromwell, weary of dissension, divided England and Wales into eleven military districts, each run by a senior army officer, the "major generals" of ill fame.[52] These men may have been effective soldiers and combat leaders, but as civic administrators they were heavy-handed and oppressive.

By the time of the Restoration in 1660, the people, governments, and soldiers of the British kingdoms were prepared to adopt a model of military professionalism that was apolitical, nonconfessional, and in some ways a reaction to the careerism, amounting to militarism and praetorianism, of the New Model Army. The rejection of the New Model Army pattern of egalitarianism, political engagement, and religious zeal was perhaps inevitable (despite its military effectiveness) given the restoration of a Stuart king to the throne. But the pattern of a standing army was one of those problems that basically had been resolved (at least temporarily) by the conflict. As John Morrill notes, "Although eighteenth-century governments enormously expanded the size of the British army, the British navy, and the bureaucracies of war, all the foundations had been laid in the 1640s and the 1650s."[53]

The broad outlines of how to man, supply, and pay for military forces had been established. So too had the beliefs and values that would guide the British Army into the present day. Control over military matters would have a constitutional basis. The army itself would cultivate an aura of aristocratic amateurism (but not amateurishness) in reaction to the careerism (often combined with radical political ambitions) of the mercenary soldiers of obscure origin who had largely led the New Model Army.[54] Officers would ideally be connected to the land and wealth of the nation by ties of kinship and ownership. Some at least would have sufficient education and ability to act as diplomats and civil and colonial administrators. John Churchill, Duke of Marlborough, is perhaps the model of the Restoration general. He was an experienced professional soldier from the middle gentry who had the wit and manners to move among (and to manage) the nobility while remaining as neutral as the circumstances allowed in political matters. He combined charisma with practiced attentiveness both to his men and to detail in a manner that was in some ways reminiscent of Cromwell (without his political agenda or religious rigidity), but that Charles I and many of his Cavalier generals did not display.[55] Although Marlborough had little formal education, he was a reader of Shakespeare, that frequent writer on military themes, whose plays often suggest an ethical basis and practical utility for military and chivalric virtues.[56] Marlborough's contemporary General George Monck, 1st Duke of Albemarle, instructed his officers to cease holding meetings to discuss "civil things." Monck had been trained in Holland, where, he observed, "soldiers received and observed commands, but gave none."[57]

The challenge to the French military during this period was not to revive military and chivalric ideals but to ensure that such ideals could be made consistent with efficient management and command and control, and could be subordinated to state authority. In France, the country where chivalry had originated, military ideals never lost their cachet or aristocratic associations, and chivalric ideals retained their individualistic and exclusionary character to a degree and for a duration that was probably destructive of military effectiveness. For most of the seventeenth century, proprietorship and corruption interfered with effective administration and logistics, and a fetishistic insistence on class distinctions impeded the exercise of leadership for as long as the monarchy lasted. David Parrot points out the low and late impact of military revolution ideas and practices in the French army.[58]

Colin Jones argues that many needed reforms and advances in professionalism did not take place until well into the personal reign of Louis XIV, which began in 1651.[59] Victories such as the one at Rocroi over the redoubtable Spanish suggest that the French were attaining a degree of professionalism before then.[60] Cardinal Richelieu and his immediate successor, Cardinal Mazarin, had worked hard to make the army an instrument of state policy, and French aristocrats had fought bravely, and in some cases brilliantly (as in the case of the duc d'Enghien, "the Great Conde," at Rocroi), if on their own terms.[61] Some outward signs of professionalization were dubious improvements in human or ethical terms or with respect to civil-military relations. The bourgeois minister of war François Michel Le Tellier Louvois was responsible not only for reforms in provisioning, pay, and promotion but also for many of the war crimes the French army committed during Louis XIV's reign. Improvements in discipline tended to dehumanize the soldier (and restrictions on plunder kept him poor).[62] The army enjoyed a period of numerical superiority and success under the *grand siècle* reign of Louis XIV, but in the end the French monarchy and army failed to legitimize their claims to authority either in moral or in practical terms. The government insisted on absolutism but did not have much to show for it in the way of prosperity or success. The French army acquired more of the trappings of professionalism without becoming very effective. Among the officer corps, although some of the worst extremes of malfeasance, misfeasance, and nonfeasance were removed, professionalism continued to be defined in terms of rank and prestige rather than service. In 1789 French officers who were concerned with their own interests joined a revolution against the monarchy they were sworn to protect.

Neostoicism and Constantia

Of nearly equal importance to the development of military professionalism as the revival of chivalry and upper-class involvement in the military profession was the seventeenth-century rebirth of Stoicism, a phenomenon often referred to as Neostoicism. The principal author of Neostoicism was Justus Lipsius, a Dutch Protestant academic who often found himself threatened by the changes in military fortunes and political-religious ascendency that swept his country during its long struggle for independence from Spain. Lipsius was understandably frightened and put to flight by these events, and one suspects that his philosophy of personal constancy in the face of unsettling change was partly a personal antidote to the times. His thinking was also based on extensive scholarship on ancient Roman military practices, and it made an important contribution to the emerging ethos of early modern military professionals.[63]

Lipsius' philosophy was an adaptation of the ideas of the Roman statesman Seneca to the conditions of early modern Europe. Lipsius saw the need for a realistic acceptance of unpleasant realities and a willingness to work to preserve order in a time of conflict and chaos. In keeping with its classical origins, Lipsius' approach was secular, and it was therefore a corrective to the confessional zeal that characterized his time and contributed to a lack of restraint in warfare. Lipsius drew on the philosophical Stoicism of Seneca, but he was also strongly interested in Roman military theory and history and their applications to modern times. His most famous work on this subject, *De Militia Romana libri quinque, commentarius ad Polybium* (1595–96), was highly influential, as was his lecturing. One of his students at the University of Leiden was Maurice of Nassau, who set about putting his teacher's ideas into practice. These men and their followers viewed the discipline of the Romans not merely as a path to military efficiency but also as part of a moral reawakening, in effect led by soldiers, and by officers in particular, and communicated to all of society. The purpose of drill was not only tactical; it was also intended to instill purposeful habits in both those who commanded and those who obeyed, habits of mind and behavior that would form the basis of real virtue.

Lipsius was not the only writer of the time who preached along these lines. He was part of a rationalist undertaking that also included writers such as Michel de Montaigne. Others wrote in his spirit on military subjects. In some of these writings one may perceive an ethical trickle-down effect, as the traits once thought necessary to commanders are commended to ordinary soldiers as well.[64]

Although the chivalric revival and Neostoicism are sometimes treated as manifestations of the same movement, they are really separate, if related, phenomena.[65] The origins of the former can be traced to Hapsburg and aristocratic Spain, the latter to their adversaries, the bourgeois Dutch. At least in the later seventeenth and eighteenth centuries, the aristocrat's reclaiming of his ancestral martial territory had the larger impact, although Neostoicism may have contributed to this by helping to provide the well-read or at least well-informed aristocrat and bourgeois alike with a modern, intellectual justification for civilized soldiering. The predominance of aristocrats in the officer ranks continued to intensify well into the eighteenth century. This was a complex phenomenon that played out differently depending on the country and decade, but in general terms it served to ensure a fairly uniform ethos of restraint for the century following the military revolution and beyond.[66] Neostoicism, but especially neochivalry, created a pan-European officer corps whose members would fight with restraint and even on occasion question their orders on moral grounds.[67]

Tutelage and Learning

How were the professional knowledge and belief being developed during the early modern period formulated and communicated? Writing obviously played an important part, as did universities like the one at Leiden where Lipsius taught. The presence of aristocrats of ancient and martial lineage in the officer ranks maintained the importance of "fireside tales of heroic deeds," as well as of traditions of landed leadership and a cult of physical courage developed through hazardous sport.[68] Other fora or media for knowledge and belief included military schools, the standing units being established by the new state commission armies, and a pan-European military culture that had soldiers of many nations serving together, then parting ways to return to their native countries or to seek out other military employment that might find them on opposite sides from erstwhile comrades.[69] The freewheeling style of seventeenth-century soldiering meant that military knowledge, always inherently exchangeable, was figuratively part of the debris on every battlefield. Opposing armies always learn from each other, but in the early modern period this could take place in ways that modern soldiers would find surprising. The period of continental captivity of young Prince Rupert, who had been tutored in the military art by another future civil war general, Jacob Astley, was one of "systematic military study and discussions with senior Imperialist commanders."[70] Before an important decision or engagement, generals might convene councils of war, and these often served the role of field tutorials or seminars, enlivened by the fact that many of the participants would be fairly well read and experienced in the art of war. The open exchange of ideas within military units and communities perhaps reached its height in the New Model Army, in which conversation ranged far beyond military subjects. However, in most armies and campaigns its principal function was to enhance professional knowledge, supplementing the emerging methods made possible by a growing professional literature, the advent of military schools on the model of the one established at Siegen by Maurice, and the ability of state commission armies with bureaucracies and permanent units to institutionalize training and education. Standing national armies also donned uniforms. This trend began as a pragmatic effort to standardize clothing and improve recognition on the battlefield, but uniforms quickly became a means of imparting a sense of belonging and shared belief, and they eventually embodied a cryptic language, imparting information about the rank, unit membership, specialization, service, and individual achievements of the soldier.

The acquisition and transition of knowledge during this period were influenced by the "economy of knowledge" of the time, both in form and in content. As Erik Lund notes, armies relied on nonmilitary knowledge to move, eat, and provide themselves with shelter.[71] Officers might require knowledge of roads, machines, animals, crops, clothes, and politics, along with the ability to recognize and navigate the subtleties and indicators of social status. The need for broad knowledge on the part of military leaders was not new, but in the early modern period much knowledge was acquired in a hands-on manner that was in some ways peculiar to the times. Although science and formal education were on the rise, professional scientists and educators were few, with the result that those with the desire for knowledge conducted their own experiments and measurements, often using instruments they had made themselves. As Lund points out, these practices were followed in the military realm, so war became a "science of practical experimentation," and officers "speculative thinkers grounded in empiricism."[72]

This empirical or scientific approach to military knowledge (and innovation) was a departure from the past. It had not existed in the Middle Ages, when the deep conservatism of the ruling classes had slowed change and impeded a critical approach to military matters. Even during the Renaissance the approach to military knowledge had been more literary than empirical, and it had been closely tied to classical sources. In the later part of this period, Isaac Newton would characterize the intellectual history of his time as a victory of reason over sense. T. S. Eliot would later refer to a "disassociation of sensibility" in the later seventeenth century, a kind of crisis of belief expressed as a separation of mind and heart. Knowledge became less rooted in the past and more systematic and verifiable. The scientific methods soldiers developed during the period of the military revolution would be spread and institutionalized by those of later times, and they are still in use today.

The Legacy

The military culture of the early modern period was extraordinarily rich and dynamic. Knowledge grew and beliefs evolved, and their dissemination took place on a tapestry of methods that were formal and informal, traditional and modern, and of polyglot written and spoken language. The legacy of the period is the ability of soldiers of the time to reach out and reform themselves, increasing their knowledge and developing a professional ethos that bears considerable resemblance to that of many soldiers today. The period is an example of combining the old and the new, of looking to the past for examples but also seeking new knowledge. It constitutes a lesson in how historical and scientific perspectives can be combined. Such a synthesis offers exciting possibilities for today's soldiers as both the historical record and the ledger of scientific knowledge increase daily. Soldiers should cultivate this Janus-like ability to view, if through a glass and darkly, the past and present together for keys to the future.

THE EIGHTEENTH CENTURY

Soldiers of the Enlightenment

The eighteenth century is generally seen as a period of relatively slow development and limited objectives in warfare. This might suggest an era of decadence or limited contribution on the part of the military profession. The mercenary professionalism of the sixteenth and seventeenth centuries had seen a degree of upward mobility in the officer ranks. With the advent of the state commission army, the officer ranks became more closely tied to the social hierarchy and perceived legitimate sources of authority. Access to the officer ranks became limited to the upper 2 percent socioeconomic stratum of the population, tending to create an unambitious officer corps uninterested in change. This conservatism mirrored the overall mood of the ancien régime, and not only at the top. People and nations were tired of the turmoil and overheated confessional struggles of an earlier time. The civil leadership and populations of the later seventeenth and eighteenth centuries seemed in this sense to have been well served by their military profession. Indeed, the soldiers of this period were probably more successful than those of any other in keeping from opening wide the Pandora's box of armed conflict. Eighteenth-century European officers, to a remarkably universal degree, subscribed to a code of honor and restraint. They contributed to the relative stability and growing prosperity of Europe by conducting war in accordance with this code. The members of the profession of arms were active participants in the Enlightenment, pursuing their own profession in a manner that was consistent with and that contributed to the rationalist spirit of the age. Standing units, family tradition, and an explosion of books on military matters after 1750 added to the spread of some new ideas on the military profession and its place in society.[1] Few would deny that the soldiers of this period were brave men. The warfare of the period may have been limited, but the experience of battle was as horrific as in any period of history.

Even before the French and American Revolutions, changes in the classic, limited, and linear picture of eighteenth-century warfare had begun to appear. Some of this change originated from within the military profession—from the many educated and intelligent officers who wrote books, revised training manuals, and trained their men in innovative tactics. Some officers and civilians also saw a changed social role for military forces, and as in the previous century they referred to antiquity for positive examples, calling for a return to the Roman idea of the citizen-soldier. These changes were most discussed in France following that country's humiliating defeat in the Seven Years' War; they were given wings by the revolutions of 1776 and 1789 and a brilliant if Icarus-like practitioner in Napoleon Bonaparte. In this period we also see the beginnings of an American military tradition, one that was derived from European antecedents but under the influence of American conditions and culture would develop into something new and in turn significantly influential. The U.S. military would eventually extend both its operations and its influence around the globe.

A number of paradoxes beset the military profession and warfare of this period. Like those of the Middle Ages, the soldiers and warfare of the eighteenth century hold a strong place in the modern popular imagination. The picture of battles in orderly but suicidal formations, fought by the duped, captive, severely disciplined dregs of society in elaborate uniforms and led by haughty and unfeeling officers, has some truth but more of cartoon-like simplicity. One of the sometimes overlooked features of the period is the number of not only great but also unlikely professional soldiers. Men like Marlborough, Frederick II, Wolfe, and Washington are indicative of the individualism and variety of personality and methods that can accompany great skills as military organizer, strategist, tactician, and leader.

Eighteenth-Century Warfare, Limited?

Warfare of the eighteenth century was frequent. No decade of the century passed without the involvement of some European countries in large-scale warfare. Wars could be costly and widespread in terms of geography. Still, warfare was subject to a number of limitations (perhaps reminiscent of those of Greek hoplite warfare), some imposed by the circumstances of the time, others self-imposed, and some perhaps a mixture in that limitations that might have been overcome were willingly tolerated and observed by statesmen and by soldiers. The limitations might be further divided into ends and means, with monarchs having most to do with the former and soldiers sharing responsibility for the latter. The military revolution of the previous century had made armies more capable and ambitious military operations more achievable, but ultimately the revolution could not transcend certain limits, and in a sense it even had been responsible for some of the self-imposed limitations of the warfare of the age. The resources and competencies of states had increased considerably since the Middle Ages and Renaissance, but Europe was still an agrarian economy with a small surplus where people and news moved at the speed of a horse or man. To maintain an army consumed most of the resources of the national budget; to increase an army for wartime and put it in the field often put a country in debt; to hazard an army in battle involved a risk that might pay off or might mean ruin. The causes of war in this period were most often dynastic or territorial. Wars were fought to secure a succession that was favorable to some reigning monarch or to claim a disputed area or colony for its economic advantages. This was the pattern of three major continental wars of the period: the War of the Spanish Succession (1701–14), the War of the Austrian Succession (1740–48), and the Seven Years' War (1756–63), which began as the French and Indian War in America in 1754. Even the American Revolutionary War (1775–83), although it involved ideological issues, was fought by the British to retain a valuable colony.

European countries, Britain in particular, fought colonial wars with native peoples, in India especially; and naval and amphibious operations were assuming a new importance. As Jeremy Black points out, European military superiority in this period was far from absolute and was based more on superior command and control than on better weapons.[2] The age of the overextended Spanish and Holy Roman Empires was essentially over, and the age of international ideologies had not yet arrived, so the Continent was dominated by an unequal balance of compact and fairly stable if underresourced nation-states ruled by hereditary monarchies. This homogeneity may have contributed to limitations both in ends and in means, since monarchs might be hesitant to topple their fellow royals, some of them related by blood or marriage, and officers saw themselves to a degree as members of an international European military guild who by virtue of class had more in common with their fellow officers of other countries than they did with soldiers in the ranks.

Even if ambitious plans were contemplated (the English general Marlborough wanted to march on Paris in the War of the Spanish Succession), slow-moving armies could accomplish only so much in a short campaigning season. The shortness of the season was dictated by the effect of winter weather on the health of the troops, on the food supply, and on the navigability of frozen waterways and snow-covered roads. Armies lived on bread, although the use of root vegetables for food (pioneered by Frederick II of Prussia) later helped to free them from their bakeries and bread magazines. During the campaigning season, armies with their baggage could rarely manage more than ten miles a day. Eighteenth-century Europe produced limited surplus food, but in a rich country armies could stay fed by moving continually.[3] Agriculturally rich areas tended also to be those most hemmed in with fortifications, however, which in the time of Vauban had resumed their castle-like status both in numbers and in their ability to withstand siege and assault. Operations were further limited by a sparse European road system that gave few options for movement. On the tactical level, battles were limited by daylight just as they were strategically limited by the seasons. Smoky and very noisy battlefields made command and control difficult even in close formations. Battles were often bloody (casualties of 25 percent were not unheard of) and sometimes even tactically decisive, granting to one side or other overwhelming victory, as at Blenheim or Leuthen, but because of the battering even the victors sustained and the strategic constraints discussed above, a battle would rarely decide a war. Pursuit after victory was limited by fears of flight and desertion. The risks of battle posed a professional dilemma that soldiers have faced before and since, although perhaps not quite in the stark terms posed in the years 1650–1815 that Russell Weigley calls "the Age of Battles."[4] In a sense, winning battles is the acme of professional skill, especially if one allows that victory in war often has more to do with nonmilitary factors. Battles also admit, however, the chance, imponderable elements in war, elements that have the potential to negate careful preparation, even superior training and tactics. For the military professional the battlefield is the ultimate test, but it is also the place where the concept of the soldier's occupation as a profession that is capable of delivering predictable or probable outcomes breaks down.

Professional Influences and Antecedents

The officers of the eighteenth century presided over an international status quo that was punctuated and upset, although also in some ways sustained, by periodic conflict. If, as Clausewitz was later to claim, war may be compared to commerce, the conflicts of the period might be compared to a fluctuating free market in an international economy of military force and the other manifestations of national power. Soldiers assumed the burden of this often-violent equilibrium, and they did so with style as well as fortitude, expressing their thoughts with the wit and polished prose characteristic of the age of John Dryden, Voltaire, Samuel Johnson, and Thomas Jefferson. In some ways the eighteenth-century officer was an extension and descendant of the medieval knight. Both groups drew from privileged, relatively well-educated social classes in societies where civil rank and military rank were strongly linked. Both subscribed to codes of behavior that were largely international: the chivalric code of the medieval knight and the eighteenth-century officer's code of honor. In fact, the "multinational" nature of "postmodern" military professionalism was presaged by the premodern soldiers of the medieval and early modern periods. The eighteenth-century profession in some ways reached back past the early modern period for examples. It eschewed both the mercenary model and the Neostoical ideal that had arisen in reaction to it, opting for a more individualistic ethos of personal honor and an emphasis on family descent.

A number of cultural and institutional factors, however, distinguished the military professional of the eighteenth century from the knight. Between the Middle Ages and the Enlightenment stood the Reformation, the Age of Reason, and the "knowledge revolution" of the seventeenth century. Never again would orthodoxy be so free from the gaze of inquiry, or mere sense so able to rule out reason. The cognitive world of the soldier had changed along with that of the rest of Europe and the world. The profession of war had been thrown into contact with the humanities since their rebirth in the Renaissance. To this revived learning were added the emphases on empirical knowledge and reason of the seventeenth century. Into the eighteenth century, ideas about human liberty and enlightenment entered the discourse of educated people. The nature, settings, and media of discourse changed as well as the content. The eighteenth century saw the first regularly published newspapers and magazines. In England the expiration of the Printing Act in 1695 opened the way for freer communication of the news. In 1702 the first daily newspaper in England, the *Daily Courant*, began publication. Magazines such as the *Tatler* and *Spectator* followed. These publications often carried news on military operations. In fact the word "magazine," first adopted by *Blackwood's Magazine*, derives from the military term for a storehouse of supplies (or, in the case of *Blackwood's*, of information). Later, journals specializing in military matters began to appear. Perhaps the purest example of the spirit of the Enlightenment in military writing is the work of Denis Diderot and the other Encyclopedists, whose work was meant to be a compendium of all useful knowledge. The articles on military matters may seem incongruous, but they reflect the still-surviving perception of the military profession as something of an international guild and the Enlightenment ideal of the free exchange of knowledge.

The increased number of schools and the growth of universities meant that more officers and even some enlisted men had formal education, although the members of the top aristocracy were more often educated at home by tutors, some of whom were ex-officers or among "the unemployed university graduates who thronged Europe."[5] Officers could continue their professional and general education by reading and through discussion. Conversation was an art both cultivated and prized in this period, and it was facilitated by the existence of standing units and of officers' messes; by the growth of cafés, coffeehouses, and salons (some of which specialized in military matters, especially in France and in Prussia); and by the fact that French was the common language of the European upper class. Some public eating and drinking establishments developed into members-only clubs, and some of these were explicitly military in character. In order to fulfill his social obligations, the officer was expected to speak wittily and well in both French and his native language, to know the news of the day, and to be able to dance.[6] The wealthy, well-born officer who neglected his duties in favor of participating in "society" is a military stereotype of the period. This picture also has an element of truth, but the wide sociability open to many officers in the eighteenth century could provide opportunities for the exchange of professional knowledge. The pursuit of pleasure could help to create connections between military and civil society and to provide stimulus and relief from the narrowness of garrison life. In a sense it is to this period that the modern officer owes whatever remains of the communal lifestyle and organized comradeship of the officers club, officers call, mess night, and the seasonal dinner or dance. The military writings of the period are informed and enlivened by officers' sociability and acquaintance with news and ideas.

Military Writing by Soldiers

The eighteenth century saw an increase not only in published military literature but also in books written by serving or retired officers themselves, including some of the famous senior commanders of the day. The genres of military writing were established by this time. Military books by officers might be divided into training manuals, or "instructions"; memoirs; and histories of campaigns (often expanding on personal experience, like the work of the uniformed field historian of today). Some of these works combined an element of theory along with the narrative and detail. They often served the function of adding depth and detail to military regulations. A novelty of the period was the memoir written by a literate "enlisted man" (a term not yet in use). The historian Edward Gibbon credited his own service in the militia with giving him a feel for tactics and military formations that was useful to him as a historian of the Roman Empire.[7] In addition to books, military men wrote letters and "memorials" (memoranda), some of which made their way into print. The most illustrious of the military authors was Frederick the Great, whose "Military Instructions" were initially given limited circulation so that they did not give aid to enemies. Eventually a copy of the document was found on a captured general, translated, and published. Written in 1747, when Frederick was only thirty-five, the book is an impressive indication of his proverbial hard work and dedication to his role as the nation's first soldier. Given his reputation for unfeeling arrogance, the work is also notable for its humanity, for Frederick's openness to the ideas of others, and for the affection he expresses for his soldiers, particularly for the Prussian infantry. Frederick says that general officers should visit their men in camp in order to inquire about their needs and that they should be protective of soldiers' lives. He also advises asking selected subordinates for their ideas, and if their suggestions are good, to mention this frequently in public. As we shall see later in this chapter, Frederick may not always have lived by the advice he gave, but since he was writing for a limited audience of perhaps fifty senior Prussian officers, there is good reason to think that he was at least sincere. Much of the book is taken up with tactics and maneuvers, and it illustrates that Frederick's ideas changed on these subjects. In 1747 he was still advocating the attack at shoulder arms and without firing. By 1758 he was insisting that the infantry must gain superiority of fire before launching an attack, and in 1768 he wrote, "Battles are won by superiority of fire."[8]

Another high-ranking officer-writer, one Frederick admired, was the Dresden-born marshal of France, Maurice de Saxe. In good Enlightenment fashion, de Saxe set out to replace unthinking custom with principles and theory. He was a highly successful commander who in his book *Reveries on the Art of War* seems to be advancing some radical and even impractical ideas for the sake of argument. His work has the virtue of being dialogic rather than dogmatic. He writes that experts should not be offended by the assurance with which he makes his points; instead they should refute him, as "that is the fruit that I expect from this work."[9] His advocacy of the pike is reactionary although also indicative of the debate between shock action and firepower that occupied French military circles in particular. On the other hand, some of his ideas express a justifiable impatience with the unexamined military practices of the time. He is in favor of more practical uniforms and of better integration of arms. Before the end of the century, light infantry units in particular would adopt uniforms more conducive to ease of movement, and the adoption of the division as a permanent combined-arms formation would make effective mutual support among arms more practical.

General Wolfe's Instruction to Young Officers, written by Major General James Wolfe, the victor of Quebec, was published posthumously by J. Millan in 1768.[10] The work is actually a collection of writings by General Wolfe covering a broad range of military subjects from drill to discipline, guard duty, training exercises, embarkation, and orders for combat operations. As the title of the collection indicates, however, much of it concerns what we would term today "leadership" (a word not coined until the next century). Wolfe himself sets a fairly good example in this regard, both by the attention to detail and duty that his writings exemplify and by their tone. Wolfe was a disciplinarian with high expectations, but he praises and encourages as much as he scolds or finds fault, and one senses a conscious effort to do so, even to leave some criticism unsaid. Wolfe wants officers who are not only efficient but who also take an informed, enlightened interest in their duties. He tries to make the routine matters of guard duty, drill, training, and housekeeping appear interesting and important, even to imbue them with a moral significance in the manner of Polybius.

Other officer-writers included the Prussian-officer-turned-American-drillmaster Friedrich Wilhelm von Steuben; his commander in chief, George Washington; and the Welshman Henry Lloyd. Von Steuben's drill manual contains details of individual and unit drill movements, notes on tactics, and a separate section on the duties of soldiers from regimental commander to private. Washington wrote an account of his service in the French and Indian War as adjutant of the colony of Virginia and on campaign with Edward Braddock. Both von Steuben and Washington were officers who wrote books based on the knowledge and narrative of their service. Henry Lloyd was something else: a true military intellectual in the tradition of Montecuccoli.[11] Lloyd had the advantage of an Oxford University education and had been a student at the Jesuit Roman College in Venice. As a writer he also may have benefited from being forced to live a rather itinerant, hand-to-mouth existence. Both middle-class and Welsh, Lloyd was an outsider who found it hard to secure regular employment in the status-conscious national armies of eighteenth-century Europe. Although his busy military career spanned four decades, he likely made his living by his pen as much as by his sword. Lloyd was an iconoclast like the later proselytizers for sea and air power Alfred Mahan and Billy Mitchell. Such men, frustrated with traditional thinking and perhaps in their careers as well, tend to overstate both the problem and the solution. The warfare of his time was too slow and indecisive for Lloyd. On the tactical level, somewhat like Maurice de Saxe and some other writers, including Jean Charles, Chevalier Folard, Lloyd wanted tactics that would emphasize shock and flexibility. Unfortunately, as historian Patrick Speelman notes, Lloyd's tactics sacrificed too much firepower for the sake of shock and concentration of combat power.[12] At the higher level of warfare, Lloyd's conclusions were sounder and more significant. His writings anticipated and influenced Napoleon's conduct of campaign at what came to be known as the operational level of war, a middle ground between strategy and tactics. Even more important, Lloyd wrote insightfully about the relationship between the character of societies and how they waged war. Lloyd saw that a radical change in the practice of warfare such as he thought necessary could not be undertaken on a merely military level but would have to be accompanied by social change. Perhaps sensitized on this point by the disappointment of his own military ambitions, he thought the indecisiveness of the warfare of his time was the fault of a social hierarchy that did not reward merit. Lloyd died suddenly and unexpectedly in 1783. His writings were generally neglected—or, if read, unacknowledged—in his own time and in the tumult and change of the Napoleonic period that followed close on his death. His work saw a revival in later years and into our own time. He is a prime example of the military intellectual who combines wide experience of war, dedication to the profession of arms despite discouragements, and a determined, sustained effort to write and to reflect on his profession.

Pierre Choderlos de Laclos was a French officer whose career spanned the ancien régime, the French Revolution, and the rise of Napoleon. Laclos was the author of *Dangerous Liaisons* (1782) and other literary works and was responsible for innovative work in the field of artillery. As both a keen and critical observer of the manners and morals of his time and a military innovator (he is credited with the invention of a modern shell), he demonstrates that the Enlightenment soldier's sociability might complement his engagement with his profession.

The number and prominence of officers writing on military subjects in the eighteenth century (and ever since) raises the question of why officers write. Certainly many were (and are) motivated by the desire to share their knowledge and ideas. Writing could also be a vehicle to professional recognition and advancement. For some (the dedicated and intelligent regimental soldier Wolfe comes to mind) it may have been the desire of a good mind for exercise, for relief from the boredom and routine of life in camp and even on campaign. It could also be a form of mental discipline, forcing the writer to bring order to his thoughts for his own sake as much as for that of the readers. (De Saxe begins his work by saying it was written "to amuse and instruct myself.") Whether memoir, instruction, or history, the works also stand as monuments to their writers and to the soldiers with whom they served. As the addled British colonel observes in *The Bridge on the River Kwai*, a soldier usually has little tangible to show for a career. Even the building that they perform is usually of an expedient and temporary nature. The nature of their profession is distinguished as much as anything by its evanescence and reliance on the acts of the moment. This is why soldiers place so much store in pieces of ribbon, decorative metal, and stone memorials, and it is surely part of the reason why they write.

Military Careers

By the eighteenth century the military profession had assumed many of the attributes of a career. National and private military academies existed in most European countries, with Prussian officers the most likely to be academy trained. In general the academies dedicated to training officers for the technical arms of artillery and engineers had the best reputations.[13] The question of what academy curriculum is best suited to producing a combat arms or line officer is still debated today, but the fact that about one-third of Prussian officers shared the formative experience of an academy education may have contributed to the considerable cohesion and dedication noted among the Prussian officer corps. Commissions and promotion were determined by varying combinations of social class, purchase, and merit. The French military aristocracy fought back against the encroachments of the sometimes wealthier bourgeoisie into the officer ranks, eventually (in 1782) causing an ordinance to be passed requiring all officers to demonstrate four quarterings of nobility—that is, four generations of noble descent on both sides of the family. Prussian officers were also expected to document their noble lineage. The nonnobles who had been overlooked or tacitly permitted wartime officer status for the Seven Years' War were purged from the army afterward by Frederick. The British were a more mercantile nation with fewer titled aristocrats and a somewhat more flexible social system. Their purchase system favored the well-to-do, but certain spaces in the regiments were reserved for officers promoted on merit and seniority. In all armies, commanders, especially at the higher levels, tended to be moneyed members of the upper aristocracy. Their seconds in command and staff officers, who handled the routine details of pay, supply, inspections, and training, were likely to be men of more modest income and somewhat lower social position but of long and faithful service. Most of even the highest-born officers were not mere aristocratic dilettantes. It would be fair to say that the more efficient officer corps of Europe, which would include the English and Prussians, had achieved a fusion of social rank and professional competence. At the various ranks they tended to have served for periods that were as long or longer than those of their modern counterparts.[14]

Societies were willing to make moral and tangible investments in this type of military leadership, providing inducement for the aristocracy to serve and bestowing titles and occasionally fortunes on successful soldiers from relatively modest beginnings. In an era when private income could rival state revenue, wealthy officers sometimes spent huge sums to make up shortfalls in government funding, both to meet basic needs and to ensure that their men were turned out in a fashion worthy of their commanding officers. Generals were expected to maintain a certain level of hospitality, inviting their juniors to join them in the big tent and at the head table for an occasional lavish meal. Failure to uphold this practice with what was considered sufficient largesse would excite unfavorable comment. At the start of the period, some form of proprietary system at the level of the company and regiment was common, but this was largely replaced in the course of the century by more centralized means of pay and supply. This reform removed opportunities for corruption and neglect of soldiers' needs, but it also replaced a patriarchy with a bureaucracy and sacrificed responsiveness and flexibility for efficiency.

The growth of military bureaucracies in effect created an alternative military career path: a military profession (as opposed to a profession of arms) of bureaucrats in the employment of a central government. This was not entirely new, but the expanded wealth and ambitions of nations gave these officials a power and reach that the civilian servants of the Crown had likely not had in previous times. In the Middle Ages, royal officials were involved in army affairs mostly over matters of supply, muster, and review. The rising cabinets and bureaucracies (significantly, named for the furniture of their offices) that began to appear in the early modern period sometimes encroached on activities traditionally reserved for the profession of arms. Arthur Wellesley, 1st Duke of Wellington, would later famously write to his own War Department that the need to answer correspondence from "gentlemen quill-driving in your lordship's office" was keeping him from "the serious business of campaigning." The tension between armed and unarmed, or uniformed and nonuniformed, military professionals continues to this day.[15]

Historians have discussed and debated the role of warfare in building the modern state for decades.[16] As has already been indicated, warfare could put internal stresses on the state that might threaten its existence. These stresses arguably convinced the Dutch (after the casualties of the Dutch contingent at Malplaquet in 1709) and the Swedes (beginning with Poltava in the same year and confirmed by the death of Charles XII at a siege in 1718) to eschew the practice of warfare, and were at least partly responsible for putting an end to the French monarchy. The state apparatuses that were initially devised to recruit, supply, and provide standardization to national armies were also national civil bureaucracies in embryo. The enhanced competency and means of control governments enjoyed could be a mixed blessing for the population, especially since countries with limited resources or alliances could be tempted to adopt autocratic means in order to support and employ their military establishments efficiently. Monarchs' impatience with the slowness and military inexpertise of parliaments was perhaps understandable.[17] The eighteenth century saw some true soldier-kings, hereditary monarchs who also commanded their national armies in the field. The major and most illustrious examples are Charles XII of Sweden and Frederick the Great of Prussia. The Battle of Dettingen (1743) was the last occasion of a British monarch being present on a battlefield.

Organization and Training

The new organizational abilities of governments and armies in the eighteenth century could have mixed results. Improvements in organization, standardization, and discipline could also deprive the soldier of a degree of his individuality, initiative, even his humanity. Conditions on the battlefield impelled a certain amount of this deprivation. Perhaps as in no time before or since, the weapons and tactics of the time required subordination of the individual to the group. The infantryman especially was frequently less an individual fighter than a single note in a fugue of firepower. Officers and men were tied together in mutual dependence and at close quarters. Close-order formations, uniforms, and the growing trend toward housing soldiers in barracks put an emphasis on drill, housekeeping, and adherence to minutiae of various kinds. Like other institutions of enlightenment—the new hospitals, asylums, schools, and prisons—barracks could be crowded and unhealthy. However, discipline also helped to raise standards of conduct, instilling habits of hygiene and behavior and even self-respect and independence among soldiers recruited from the rural peasantry and urban poor, and it reduced in number and scale the depredations soldiers visited on civilians.

Given the increasingly strict controls on soldiers' conduct and living arrangements, the bloodiness of battle, and the paltry remuneration (with a much reduced chance for booty relative to previous centuries), why would men join the army as privates? Recruitment techniques were certainly unscrupulous and did not cavil even at kidnapping. Indeed, army recruiters are a frequent target of satire in contemporary literature. George Farquhar's

The Recruiting Officer (1706); Voltaire's *Candide* (1759); and the nineteenth-century novel of the eighteenth-century *Barry Lyndon* (1844) by William Makepeace Thackeray all depict dishonest recruiters and gullible recruits. Prussia and other countries had systems of military induction but relied on volunteers as well. The British Army had no draft and no institutionalized practice of forcible recruitment like the navy's press gang, so it was largely dependent on voluntary recruiting. Some of the reasons for enlisting are the enduring ones: the lures of travel and escape, of variety and self-development, the appeals of patriotism, and an interest in matters military. The men of this time were neither the first nor the last to be curious about what it would be like to be in a battle. The army could be an alternative to rural drudgery. Europe had a number of rootless, unemployed or underemployed men, some educated "beyond their station," who might see military service as an alternative to pointlessness and penury. The newly adopted uniforms had their attractions as well. Not only were they flattering (if impractical), but they also imitated the dress of the aristocracy. The well-to-do man wore a wig for public appearance, while soldiers whitened and dressed their own hair for parade. Soldiering had enough residue of knightly status at this point to be viewed as a form of social promotion. The "glamour of class distinctions" was at work here too. A private would not be a guest at an aristocratic wedding, but he might form part of the guard. A well-educated recruit might reasonably expect to advance to noncommissioned officer rank with its better pay, privileges, and pleasures of authority. The stereotype of the eighteenth-century enlisted man as a renegade from the lowest level of society drilled into an automaton-like state of submission is mostly unfair and inaccurate. Even with the close formations, eighteenth-century battles were not mere exercises in mindless drill. Like the battles of any time, they made demands on individual skill, leadership, and fortitude, and the men who fought them had joined up with a mixture of motives, some of them certainly understandable, especially given the conditions of life at the time. The cynical Frederick once averred that if they thought about it, none of his men would remain in the ranks, but he may have been unacquainted with the realities of life for ordinary people. Military service provided clothing, pay, food, and opportunities for wider experience and associations unavailable to most. It filled a gap in eighteenth-century society, offering employment and purpose to young men, rich and poor, who were not content to stay home.

A surprising aspect of eighteenth-century basic training of new soldiers was that it emphasized the individual to a greater extent, it would appear, than does most modern entry-level military training. Whereas modern military training often begins with shock and awe and proceeds to greater familiarity and informality, eighteenth-century training often started with indulgence but moved to greater exactness as the officers and noncommissioned officers came to expect higher standards from a trained soldier than from an untrained man who lacked both martial skills and attitude. A new recruit who made an error would be remonstrated with only mildly, but the same mistake from a trained man could invite a serious rebuke or even a blow.

It is tempting to speculate about the reasons for the different approaches to basic training. Modern training is sometimes said to be aimed at making recruits think of themselves less as individuals and more as members of a unit. Once the initial harsh training has helped to enforce group identification, the treatment can become less severe and more accepting. Modern training is intended for a recruit who may have a well-developed, if not exaggerated, sense of himself or herself as an individual. In the eighteenth century a recruit was more likely to be the product of the slow rhythms and strict hierarchy of traditional society that were not so far removed from the medieval. His sense of self might not be so highly developed as in a modern recruit, and his patterns of learning were undoubtedly different. (This distinction might be kept in mind by members of the armies of developed countries charged with training recruits from underdeveloped regions.) The close-order drill that still occupies a considerable amount of entry-level training in the American armed forces and in other modern armies is intended to develop a corporate spirit. In the eighteenth century, close-order drill was the basis of tactics. The soldier was expected to remember and execute drill movements on the battlefield, not merely on the parade ground. This may help to account for the careful way soldiers of this period were introduced to drill and for the severity that could be meted out to trained soldiers who failed to execute movements properly.

Corporal punishment was a feature of virtually every army of the time, but it was also prevalent throughout society. Schoolmasters, employers, and parents beat or otherwise physically chastised their charges and children. Some crimes that were punishable by death in civil law incurred flogging or other lesser penalties in the army and navy, mostly because a trained soldier was more valuable than one of Europe's many criminals and vagrants, but also perhaps because officers and other ruling-class men felt a paternalistic regard for their soldiers that they did not feel for lower-class civilians. This period saw the revival of the practice of bestowing individual decorations to reward superior performance; for example, the Prussian Pour le Mérite (the "Blue Max") instituted by Frederick II and the American Order of Military Merit (the "Purple Heart") created by George Washington.

Advanced, large-unit training in the eighteenth century faced a number of challenges. For recruiting purposes and sometimes to enhance their use as civil police, even soldiers housed in barracks were rarely together in numbers larger than a battalion. In the British Army, where soldiers were billeted in inns and other public, civilian establishments, the challenges to large-unit training were heightened.[18] Peacetime armies were on a stringent budget; even live-fire training might be limited to only a couple of rounds per year, and the expense of moving units long distances to congregate for training might be prohibitive. Many officers of the time recognized that the lack of large-unit training had serious consequences for their own professional development and for overall combat readiness. Efforts were made to conduct annual and predeployment training camps. About one-third of all British battalions headed overseas had the benefit of training camp, and the difference between those who did and those who did not was notable. The battalions decimated at Pennsylvania's Monongahela River under General Braddock had not had the benefit of this training, and their lack of cohesion and tactical flexibility might be attributed in part to this fact.[19] The Prussian army under Frederick II annually capped off its summer training regimen with large-scale maneuvers conducted in early fall.[20] Although Frederick could be dismissive about the value of these exercises (as he appears to have been, at one time or another, about nearly everything), they were imitated and admired, and they almost certainly contributed to the excellence of the Prussian army. Officers could try to compensate for a lack of actual experience in handling large units by reading, writing, and discussion, but the absence of formal, advanced training or war games for officers (both would be innovations of the nineteenth century) limited the value of study and theory.

The important tactical maneuver units for the horse, foot, and guns were respectively the squadron, the battalion, and the battery. Smaller units were either primarily administrative rather than tactical in nature (e.g., the infantry company) or were too small to operate independently on the battlefield. Larger formations might be improvised but did not exist in permanent form until late in the century when first the French and then others began to adopt the permanent division.

The Tactical Problem

The slow progress in weapons technology during this period, if there was any at all (the British Army, for example, used essentially the same Land Pattern, or "Brown Bess," musket during the War of the Spanish Succession and against Napoleon a hundred years later), combined with the spirit of the age and the methods for exchange of ideas, gave soldiers the opportunity to perfect methods to maximize the potential of the available weaponry. The range of innovation may have been limited, but such as it was it fell within the province of soldiers, and it was given encouragement by the spirit of inquiry that was one aspect of the Enlightenment. During this period, armies consisted of three main and balanced arms of cavalry, infantry, and artillery—or horse, foot, and guns, as those of the period would have said. The military professionals of each arm fine-tuned this balance in different ways. On an organizational level, the various arms subdivided or specialized to meet different tactical needs. Each of the branches eventually broke down according to "weight," from light to heavy. "Weight" in its military sense was partly literal, since a fully equipped heavy cavalryman with his horse, weapons, and protective equipment would have greater mass than his light-cavalry brethren with his smaller mount and lighter equipage. But weight is also an "effects" term; more significant than the literal weight was the shock or firepower effect that a unit could be expected to deliver and the generally slower speed of the heavy units.

The combat arms, individually and in concert, addressed the problem of movement and combat power. The relationship between these two elements was complex. For the cavalry, the ability to move rapidly could translate into the ability to deliver combat power and to run down and scatter an enemy unit; but the lighter, swifter cavalry were also unarmored and more vulnerable. Speed could be self-destructive if a cavalry unit launched itself at an enemy formation at the wrong time or from the wrong direction. It could meet withering fire or an unexpected willingness to withstand a charge and strike back at horses and riders. For the infantry, movement and shock effect had to be weighed against the ability to deliver fire. The Prussians and English came to favor firepower, while the Russians and French continued to regard shock action—the charge—as the most formidable element in the infantry repertoire, and they were quicker to resort to the bayonet. The artillery benefited the most from technical advances during this period. Powder charges, gun carriages, and gun barrels grew lighter, and aiming systems improved, the screw replacing the wedge as a means of elevating or depressing the barrel. In the early years of the century, artillery usually remained where it was emplaced throughout a day of battle. Later, lighter horse-drawn artillery could be moved to exploit a changing tactical situation. The artillery developed different types of ammunition for different ranges and targets. Canister and grapeshot were antipersonnel ammunition for shorter ranges. Round shot was used for longer ranges and for material targets such as walls and fortifications. The development of lighter charges, barrels, and carriages tended to increase the standard weights of shot.

The balance among the arms varied and evolved. All armies retained large forces of cavalry that might be used in tactical, police, command-and-control, logistical, and reconnaissance roles, according to the needs of the situation and the preferences of the commander. Some armies, including the Austrians and later the Americans, relied heavily on artillery for firepower. Others, the Prussians and to a degree the British, counted on their infantry to deliver a steady stream of fire. Each arm faced the organizational and tactical challenge of maximizing its own effectiveness and being able to engage in combined-arms battle. The gunpowder revolution and the refinement of muzzle-loaded smoothbore infantry and artillery weapons had made possible an unprecedented ability to focus combat power on the battlefield. But firepower was still very much a manpower-intensive, limited-range affair, so the concentration of force on the battlefield was a fragile and transitory matter, a question of speed and timing enabled by sound judgment and often calling for fearless leadership.

Eighteenth-century war fighting placed a great premium on forbearance.[21] The conventions of war imposed restraints that military professionals were expected to observe and enforce. Perhaps even more important, the tactics often favored the side that committed last, held fire until the last moment, or delayed the charge—withholding the fragile military instrument, often under fire and taking casualties—until the favorable moment arrived when one's forces were prepared and in the best position and the enemy had overextended, prematurely committed itself, or overreacted to the threat of attack. On the open fields where they fought—in conspicuous uniforms, lacking (except for the heavy cavalry cuirassiers) protective equipment, and forced to stand or to sit upright in the saddle to move, load, shoot, or strike—combat units on eighteenth-century battlefields were lethal but extremely vulnerable. A well-timed, accurate volley or salvo could decimate a battalion. The legendary incident of the French officer inviting the British guards to fire first may have been part bravado and a gallant gesture, but it also made tactical sense, because a few yards of range could make all the difference in a volley of musket fire. Infantry could be held back on the reverse slope of high ground to preserve it during the artillery duel and bombardment that preceded many battles. The cavalry could pin down enemy forces without charging, forcing infantry units to form a square, which made a dense, vulnerable target for artillery. Artillery fire on the battlefield was mostly done by line of sight. Ideally the guns had to be positioned where they were in range of the enemy, were not masked by friendly troops, and could enjoy a certain standoff distance relative to advancing enemy units, enabling them to get off multiple salvos for self-defense. Artillery could also benefit from protective terrain, firing in defilade from behind a slight rise to give it cover, even shooting from the open and then moving quickly to a protected area.

Infantry Firing Systems

Since the sixteenth century, infantry units armed with muskets had been trained to fire by volley or relay and on command. By the start of the eighteenth century infantry firearms had improved considerably. Both the large, powerful, but very cumbersome musket and the lighter harquebus fired using a matchlock system that was slow, subject to misfire, and susceptible to wet weather. The lighted "matches," actually smoldering lengths of rope, also made a unit of musketeers very visible during operations at night. By 1700 most European infantrymen were armed with the lighter musket originally called the fusil and issued to specialty troops guarding the artillery trains (since matches posed an obvious danger around the guns' powder supply). The lighter fusil was still a formidable weapon of about .45 caliber, the flintlock firing system was more reliable, and the infantry by 1700 had a socket bayonet that would not prevent firing as had the earlier plug bayonets. The socket bayonets and improved rate of fire had first reduced the proportion of pikes and then eliminated the pike as a weapon. (Despite Maurice de Saxe's recommendation, the pike never returned, although a shortened pike continued in use as a badge of office and rank-alignment tool for noncommissioned officers.)

The methods to control infantry evolved along with their weapons. The slow fire of the early muskets necessitated deep ranks with many files to sustain a steady fire. The ranks were reduced from nine or ten in the sixteenth century to five or six in the seventeenth, to three or four by 1700, reflecting a changed rate of fire from one round every three minutes for the old musket to five rounds in two minutes for the fusil.[22] By the War of the Spanish Succession the British had adopted a system of firing by platoons that was easier to control than the earlier system (still used by the French) of firing by the ranks of a battalion. The platoon firing system placed a heavier burden of presence of mind and leadership on the company-grade officers and noncommissioned officers, but it created more firepower and was more flexible and responsive. British units and others adopting the system could fire by entire battalions, sections (pairings of platoons), or individual platoons to deliver either shattering bursts of fire, a series of blows, or a sustained curtain of fire. The volley of an entire battalion might be reserved as a final blow to halt a charge. After the first volleys it seems to have been common to resort to individual, or "general," fire. The British developed a drill movement known as "locking" to stagger the ranks and permit firing by multiple ranks at once.[23] The platoon system also permitted a form of marching fire in which units moved ahead by bounds between bouts of firing, providing covering fire for adjacent platoons and maintaining pressure on the enemy line. All of this called for considerable cohesion, effective small-unit leadership, and quick thinking. Even the simple act of fixing the bayonet was fraught with potential consequences.[24] Although the musket could be fired with a fixed socket bayonet, it was more difficult to load in that condition, and a bayonet on the end of a musket barrel added weight to the weapon that could affect aim, contributing to the "musket droop" that occurred when tired men had difficulty holding the weapon level.

Beginning in the seventeenth century, specialty units of grenadiers were formed to use hand grenades. Sometimes these were individual companies within battalions, but grenadiers were also formed into battalions, at first on a task basis but later permanently. Eventually its limited range and unreliability resulted in the grenade's being virtually abandoned. Perhaps this was hastened by the replacement of the matchlock with the flintlock, since infantry soldiers armed with the flintlock no longer carried the matches also needed to light the grenade.[25] After losing their distinctive weapon (although they retained their distinctive tall headgear, which was both impressive in appearance and did not get in the way of an overhand throw, as the three-cornered hat was prone to do), the grenadiers became elite and assault troops. There seem to have been different criteria by which they were selected, with some units choosing for sheer size and others for strength, soldierly qualities, or veteran status. Their being assigned some of the most dangerous missions, in sieges in particular, could lead to an early version of the "selection-destruction" cycle noted in twentieth-century special forces units. De Saxe complains about the demands for grenadiers on the part of commanders who viewed them as a sort of military panacea.

Changes in Tactics and Organization

The military historian Hew Strachan describes an "eighteenth century revolution in tactics" consisting of four elements: the development of light infantry, the use of the column on the battlefield, improvement in artillery, and the adoption of the permanent division organization.[26] All of these tactical developments had an influence on the military professionalism of the period, with implications for the future. Light infantry troops for irregular warfare had traditionally been recruited from among huntsmen (*jaeger*) and the inhabitants of rugged, semicivilized areas like the Scottish highlands and Croatia. By the middle of the century their usefulness and potential had been demonstrated in North America. By the time of the American Revolution, the French and British were adopting light infantry not only because of its tactical usefulness but also because it embodied a new form of training and discipline that stressed "kindness and emulation" and produced better soldiers with more motivation and initiative.[27] The British raised a local unit, the 60th Royal Americans, and used some of their own units to practice the new ideas, which required a different form of leadership than the hands-on, drill-centric form practiced by traditional eighteenth-century infantry officers. An officer of a light infantry unit often could not see or issue verbal commands to his soldiers in action. He had to rely more on training, trust, and individual motivation and judgment than on compulsion or exhortation to perform a tactical mission. This approach had an influence on the rest of the army, especially when joined with the new ideas of citizenship and liberty that were emerging even before the revolutions in America and France.

The adoption of the column for use on the battlefield was in some ways an expression of the continuing French fascination with massing troops, even at the expense of firepower. But the column could have its uses on the battlefield, with one unquestioned advantage being superior mobility. After the Comte de Guibert developed a system of quickly deploying troops from line into column and back again, the commander of a battalion had another set of options to consider.[28] A column could deploy or a line could reform to column to the left, to the right, or in the center. Even in this fairly simple maneuver a number of factors would have to be considered, including the terrain, the dispositions of the enemy, the placement and movement of adjacent friendly units, and the overall plan of attack. The movement would have been best executed just outside enemy musket range, since the troops would have been vulnerable and unable to return fire while executing. On the other hand, a unit that changed formation prematurely could also find itself at a disadvantage, sacrificing firepower or mobility at the wrong time. In effect there were two types of columns: a marching column with a narrow front organized primarily for movement, and a shallower tactical column that was actually a line about ten ranks deep. Another option was the French *ordre mixte*, which combined battalions in line formation with others in tactical column. The tactical column had some advantages in maneuverability and ease of control over the line. It sacrificed firepower for an alleged advantage in shock in a tradeoff that is difficult to gauge. The column would also concentrate a higher number of men for a collision or showdown between units of infantry. The greater number of men per square yard must have had a psychological effect on both those in a column and those facing one in line, and if an encounter came to a melee, the soldiers charging from a column would outnumber those of a line, giving encouragement to both the aggressive and the timorous and creating opportunities for soldiers to individually outflank and encircle opponents who were distracted by others advancing at their front.

Improvements in artillery derived from a combination of technical and conceptual factors that together influenced both the tactical conduct of battle and the nature of military professionalism. The discovery in the 1730s that smaller amounts of powder could be used for weight of shot than had previously been the practice allowed for lighter barrels and carriages. The work of French artillery inspector general Jean-Baptiste Vaquette de Gribeauval in France on standardization, and Frederick's introduction of true horse artillery, with the crew and all components of a battery either mounted or horse-drawn, contributed to the increased effectiveness of guns on the battlefield.[29] The increased importance of their arms gave gunners more prestige. Gunners had been civilian contractors in the Middle Ages. By the seventeenth century they were uniformed officers but of a lower social class than the infantry and cavalry officers. Gunners were promoted more slowly and were looked down on as technicians by officers who engaged in direct combat. The changes in artillery made it more tactically decisive and created the spectacle of artillery units ranging around the battlefield rather than remaining stationary during a battle. The officers of the new artillery had to be tacticians and combat leaders as well as technicians. These new roles had an effect on the nature of military professionalism, creating greater regard for competence and loosening the monopoly of the upper classes on military leadership.

A similar development can be seen among army engineers. Uniformed engineering officers had existed in seventeenth-century armies, but during the eighteenth century they developed greater autonomy, emerging as separate corps of often academy-trained officers commanding specialist engineer units. Engineering officers such as Lafayette came to see themselves as figures of the Enlightenment.[30] Like artillery officers, many engineers had to overcome their bourgeois status in armies dominated by aristocratic officers, but engineering officers in their separate battalions came to symbolize the fusion of leadership abilities with education and technical knowledge, a fusion that would in effect set the standard for officer education and cognition. In the Middle Ages the military profession had been largely a question of faith and belief; in the Renaissance it had been a literary subject with classical roots; and in the seventeenth century it had been a matter of empiricism that was pursued individually and anecdotally. By the late eighteenth century the military profession was starting to be seen as an institutionalized branch of engineering, a trend that would continue in succeeding centuries and, in a perhaps fetishized form, into the contemporary high-technological era.

Another development (one Strachan discusses) was the introduction of the permanent division organization.[31] The division perhaps had an antecedent in the "battles" into which medieval armies were often divided, and even in the auxiliary-reinforced legion of the Romans. Eighteenth-century divisions were provisional and experimental, but by the mid-1790s the division as a permanent combined-arms force capable of independent maneuver had been accepted in France, and it soon spread. The new organization simplified the army chain of command just as the change from the manipular to the cohortal structure had for the Roman legion. The division gave armies the ability to divide on the march and reunite on the battlefield, to cover large areas and then concentrate to meet an enemy threat or focus an attack, and to deploy and rearrange themselves on the battlefield without the need for the commanding general to exercise command and control over individual battalions, or for subordinate generals to lead ad hoc units thrown together for a particular engagement. In professional terms the division called for a permanent staff of officers who were trained in various functional areas to support the commander.[32] This was another trend that had the effect of downplaying heroic display and simple "follow-me" troop-leading skills and of promoting skill and diligence as credentials for military professionalism.

Leadership: Officers and Noncommissioned Officers

Writing about the warfare of the eighteenth century, historian Christopher Duffy warns that the past is an "alien landscape" that we can only partially understand.[33] Still, a study of this period indicates for him the existence of "enduring principles of leadership."[34] By the eighteenth century the figure of the "good officer" had emerged in a form that is recognizable to us in modern terms. The officer was usually a person of some social status and education who chose to make his living in the profession of arms despite other, safer or easier, options, although sometimes under considerable familial or social inducements. His motives were a mixture of patriotism, professional

pride, and a desire for advancement in the hierarchy with the greater material rewards and marks of honor that came with it. The good officer was a
leader, someone who by instinct and training followed the precepts that
later would be laid down by military historian Douglas Southall Freeman:
"Know your stuff. Be a man. Look after your men."[35]

Although officers were still concerned with personal honor and heroic
displays on the battlefield, changes in social organization and military
methods had required them to master a growing body of knowledge and
to be attentive to many small details—so many, in fact, that a middle class
of military leader, the noncommissioned officer, had developed to assist
them. By the eighteenth century, sergeants and corporals were assigned to
units according to standard tables of organization. Their roles were fairly
clearly defined, although they varied somewhat among armies. From this
century on, the culture and competence of an army depended to a considerable degree on its noncommissioned officers—not only on their experience,
caliber, and conduct but also on how they were employed and perceived by
the officer ranks, and even by the numbers of them allotted and available.
A number of cultural and organizational factors would determine how noncommissioned officers were utilized.

In a sense, noncommissioned officers symbolize the desire of officers to
delegate certain responsibilities they believe do not require their attention,
or that they believe noncommissioned officers, who almost invariably come
up from the ranks, are better equipped to handle. The authority delegated
to noncommissioned officers is a measure of the officer's recognition that
he or she needs extra eyes, ears, and hands to disseminate information and
accomplish necessary tasks. Noncommissioned officers can have a humanizing influence on a military organization if they act as a buffer and interme-
diary between the demands of the officers and the needs of the soldiers, but
if officers either abdicate their responsibilities to noncommissioned officers
or depend on them too much, this can lead to inefficiency and brutality.

The British tended to rely heavily on their noncommissioned officers,
especially for training, a practice the Prussian von Steuben criticized but
that was perhaps in keeping with the games-playing British officer culture
of amateurism.[36] The hardworking Prussian officer drilled his own troops.
He was also more likely to berate or strike a soldier than his British coun-
terpart. The Austrians assigned only six noncommissioned officers per

company, which, combined with a less than diligent officer corps, meant they were overworked and often ineffective.[37]

Commanders and Armies

This chapter so far has addressed mostly generalizations about eighteenth-century European military professionalism. In the next few pages I will focus on some notable senior commanders and the armies they led. Armies and their commanders reflect and influence one another. In each example that follows, I mean to illustrate both a particular approach to the profession of arms and a more general problem of military professionalism. Eighteenth-century writers sometimes refer to the profession of arms as "the devouring profession."[38] Running throughout the stories of some of the great commanders of this period, people who seemed most equal to war's demands, is much of the sad and the tragic, as if the "devouring" aspects of war resist all of our attempts to rationalize or professionalize a vocation that is in fact different from all others.

John Churchill, Duke of Marlborough

I discussed the earlier career of John Churchill, later Duke of Marlborough, in chapter 4. By the early eighteenth century, after years of obscurely serving a series of monarchs, his star was on the rise. The accession in 1702 of the Whig Queen Anne, his wife's friend and their patron, ensured the favor of the political leadership, and the beginning of a war with France over the disputed Spanish succession in the same year guaranteed a suitable arena for his talents. Marlborough is an attractive figure in many ways. As a boy he had enthusiastically begged for an ensign's commission after seeing a review of English troops. Very handsome and something of a rogue in his early years, he fell madly in love with and married a beautiful and spirited but demanding woman. Throughout his life he would remain devoted to his wife, Sarah, to the point of uxoriousness. Their separations for his campaigns weighed on him, especially as he grew older and the War of the Spanish Succession dragged on for more than a decade. His kindness to subordinates and reluctance to administer even a mild rebuke were proverbial.[39]

Marlborough was also the senior member of one of the closest and most successful partnerships in military history. The young Prince Eugène of Savoy had converted himself from an unprepossessing young man into one of the most respected commanders in Europe. Hard physical exercise and diligent study had paid off in some astonishing successes on the battlefield.[40] When Marlborough and Eugène united against the prince's erstwhile master, Louis XIV, they made an almost unbeatable team. Unlike Louis, who had rejected Eugène's military services, Marlborough was able to see past the prince's appearance to perceive the courage and character beneath. The two men knew that they could count on each other. Their relationship and combined talents regularly defeated the formidable French.

Finally, Marlborough was conscientious in his attention to the needs and welfare of his soldiers, was a diligent campaigner, and was personally fearless. During the early years of the war, Marlborough managed restive allies and with Sarah's help kept his finger on the political situation at home. He and his quartermaster-general, Colonel William Cadogen, became self-taught logisticians and outdid the better-organized French in providing material support for their multinational army.[41] His English troops and Dutch, Imperial, and other allies won a series of brilliant victories over a French army that was previously thought to be the master of the battlefield and indeed of Europe. Blenheim, Oudenarde, Ramillies, and finally Malplaquet were all British victories, but Malplaquet in 1709 was a nearly Pyrrhic one, with the victors sustaining heavy casualties to drive the French out of well-placed entrenchments and the burden of losses falling disproportionately on the Dutch, once the leader in the resistance to Louis XIV's France but now a junior partner in the struggle between France and England. The bloodiest day in European history until Borodino in 1812, Malplaquet was an unnecessary battle fought using Marlburian tactics that had become (as Jeremy Black puts it) "stereotyped," with an outcome that frayed the Dutch alliance, weakened support for the war in Britain, and encouraged the French to fight on for better terms.[42]

Marlborough's declining abilities on the political, strategic, and tactical levels show the cost of constant campaigning and perhaps the growing indifference to losses—the "battle habit"—that can overtake even a kindly and sympathetic combat leader at the senior level. Marlborough retired with honors to oversee the building of Blenheim Palace, a gift from the grateful nation. In the distinguished Masterpiece Theater television series *The First Churchills* he remarks that it did him good to see walls going up after seeing so many come down. The paintings at Blenheim stress the peace secured by the Treaty of Utrecht in 1713, but the illustrations of the battle at

Marlborough House, another of the duke's residences, do not omit the ugly, unheroic scenes of what the poet Robert Southey would ironically title the "famous victory": the dead stripped of their clothes, the horses and riders drowning in panic in the Danube, victorious soldiers callously clubbing the defeated with the butts of their muskets. Marlborough was grateful for the honors bestowed on him, but he was always embarrassed by the magnificence of the palace. His life at Blenheim was marred by quarrels among his beloved Sarah and their daughters that he was unable to ameliorate. He suffered several strokes and died, perhaps too good a man to really enjoy the fruits of his victories.

Frederick II

Frederick II, the son and heir of Frederick I of Prussia, was born to be a soldier-king, although for the first years of his life into young manhood he seemed an unlikely candidate for that title. Young Frederick was sensitive and artistic, with a fondness for things French. When he attempted to desert his country and his father's court, with its boozy, uncouth, pipe-smoking atmosphere, he was arrested and put into prison, king's son or no. A friend and fellow deserter, an army lieutenant, was beheaded for desertion before Frederick's eyes in the courtyard of the prison. Frederick was eventually rehabilitated and at least ostensibly reconciled with his father, among other things agreeing to a marriage that never amounted to more than a formality. When Frederick I died, the younger Frederick inherited an efficient showpiece army that had rarely fought. Frederick had ambitions, and it made sense to him to put the instrument his father had created to work, maybe even as a way of getting back at the man who had killed his friend by subjecting the old king's beloved soldiers to the test of war. Frederick's first efforts at war were inauspicious. He ran away from his first battle (at Mollwitz in 1740), having erroneously been informed that the day was lost. Frederick eventually converted his well-drilled army into an effective combined-arms combat force. He audaciously took on much larger enemies and won. He may have been saved in the end by the Prussian military mystique when an admirer came to the throne of Russia, heading off a coalition that might have crushed the upstart nation of Prussia, the latest in a series of small European countries (Sweden, the Netherlands, and Prussia) that had stolen marches on their larger and wealthier adversaries. Prussia was unique

THE SOLDIER-KING. Frederick the Great casts a critical eye on the terrain of Silesia. His uniform is the same as that of the young officer riding respectfully behind him. *"Friedrich der Große vor Schweidnitz" by Emil Hünten/Wikimedia Public Domain*

in consolidating and retaining its position with the help of a coalition and eventual unification of German states.

It is possible to both admire and be appalled by the army that Frederick and his father created.[43] The Prussian officers dedicated their lives to the service in return for a unique prestige in Prussian society and among their fellow officers throughout Europe. Paradoxically, Frederick's tendency to unreasonableness and his habit of testily relieving officers on the spot may have contributed to the cohesiveness of the Prussian officers, uniting them in mutual protection against his moods.[44] Despite stereotypes, the Prussian officers of this period appear to have gone about their duties with a high degree of common sense. As a result, at its best the Prussian army was brilliant at the basics. The emphasis was on rapidity of movement. Drill periods were short but exacting.[45] Formal movements such as the "oblique order," a favorite Prussian tactical method of attacking in echelon, were employed but not viewed as panaceas. If pedantry set into Prussian military thinking, it came later, after Frederick's death and during the long period of peace that followed. On the other hand, Prussian recruitment, discipline, and policy appear to have gone their adversaries one better for brutality and unscrupulousness. In nearly all armies of the period, recruits were duped and soldiers were beaten. All monarchs were opportunistic and often untrustworthy as allies and in adhering to treaties; Frederick and Prussia just went further.

Frederick himself is a rather disheartening example of great gifts and limited affections. The composer, flute player, and patron of such Enlightenment luminaries as Voltaire could also speak and act with astonishing callousness, as if his early denial of his own feelings had led him to discount those of others. Perhaps from his early brush with failure and bad advice at Mollwitz, Frederick came to trust his own opinions to an excessive degree. His arrogance and contempt could impair his military judgment, as in his cavalier decision to impress troops captured en masse without even bothering to integrate them into Prussian units. (Most of them promptly deserted.) He was perhaps right not to concern himself with minor details like the exact shade of Prussian blue uniforms, but wrong to neglect the quality of infantry muskets. He tended to look down on officers from the engineers and artillery as socially inferior, but when he disagreed with these men he often displayed his own ignorance of technical matters.[46] The intelligent, sensitive person within sometimes emerged in later years, maybe especially at reunions with old comrades, but Frederick's combination of arrogance, narrow-mindedness, and dedication to war was bad for him, and it was arguably even worse as a legacy for the Prussian and German state.[47]

James Wolfe

James Wolfe is a perhaps neglected figure in the development of British military professionalism. To the leadership abilities, heroism, and dedication of soldiers like Henry V and Marlborough he added a restless, inquiring mind, presaging intellectual, literarily inclined British officers from Captain Louis Nolan of Balaclava to Colonel T. E. Lawrence of Arabia, to Francis Yeats-Brown, author of *Lives of a Bengal Lancer*—figures who were often discontented with the constraints of military life and disconcerting to the military establishment. On one level, Wolfe was an intensely practical soldier. He was introduced to the complexity and human element of infantry firing as a teenage officer on European battlefields, describing himself in a letter as begging his men to hold fire until the enemy was within effective range. He became an innovator in such techniques as the double- and triple-shotting of muskets and the use of alternate fire, a refinement of the platoon-firing system that used the company organization instead of breaking down the battalion to create firing units.[48] Wolfe was impatient with the lack of professional education for officers, and he requested leave to tour Europe in order to learn more than garrison service in the British Army could teach him. He made his reputation at the siege of Louisburg and later returned to Canada to command the expedition against Quebec. There he encountered a strong French position; an even shorter campaigning season than in Europe, thanks to the Canadian climate; and difficult relations with his three main subordinates.

As a commander Wolfe could be moody and petulant, perhaps because he was sensitive to the fact that two of his three brigadiers considered him their social inferior. His Quebec campaign may not have been a model of speed and efficiency, but it did demonstrate the values of flexibility, persistence, and good training. After months of reconnaissance and aborted probing patrols, with winter approaching Wolfe finally found a landing from which his army could make an amphibious approach to the Plains of Abraham overlooking the city undetected and unopposed. When the French defenders sallied forth to meet them, months of musketry drill (and two balls per musket) allowed Wolfe's battalions to deliver one of the most perfect volleys in history, effectively ending the battle—and campaign—in a matter of minutes.

During the battle Wolfe was wounded repeatedly and in the end mortally. The painting of his death by Benjamin West is one of the icons of North American history. Wolfe was probably ill with tuberculosis, and on the day of battle he had premonitions of his death, which he expressed by reciting Thomas Gray's "Elegy Written in a Country Churchyard." Gray observes that the paths of glory lead but to the grave, and so they did in Wolfe's case. Still in his thirties, unmarried but with a fiancée back home, Wolfe had grown up in the army but in a way had not grown up at all. Sent off to war like Coriolanus while still a boy, and a precocious, sickly boy-general at his death, Wolfe is nevertheless an example of cerebral and courageous professional dedication.

Maria Theresa

Empress Maria Theresa of Austria was not a field commander, but she was an intelligent and humane monarch who took a personal interest in the affairs of her army. Her efforts at reform, and their limited success, might be called the "Austrian problem." Why couldn't the Austrian army win? Most particularly, why couldn't they beat the Prussians? The Austrian empire was a patchwork of different languages and cultures, and therein lay one of the answers. Maria Theresa was able to develop national institutions that held the empire together until its disintegration in 1918.[49] Her military reforms reflected the same intelligence and ability that she displayed in other areas, but battlefield success still eluded the Austrians. Maria Theresa's reforms included a streamlined high command, a free and rigorous military academy, and improvements in medical care and education for soldiers' families.[50] An officer or noncommissioned officer was forbidden to strike an enlisted soldier in her army.[51] Some might conclude that Maria Theresa's maternal influence was excessively humanizing, that war is a brutal business and requires brutal methods like those of Frederick. Another factor may have been the gemütlich (cozy and unhurried) culture of Austrian society, the people's lack of a "killer instinct." Much of the blame might be laid at the feet of Austrian officers and their lack of intellectual interest in their profession, as indicated in the paucity of writings by Austrian officers, and the fact that many of them appear not to have even read the army regulations.[52] Periodic Austrian military reforms (often after defeats) had to contend with an innate social and Roman Catholic religious conservatism and anti-intellectualism. It was this rather than the greater humanity of Austrian culture expressed by their empress that most hindered their efforts to achieve military excellence.

George Washington

George Washington combined the outlook of an Enlightenment gentleman and officer with the experience of a New World man. It might be said that he was a frustrated British regular officer who created his own army: the Continental Line of the United States. The new army was not merely a copy of the British or European model. Like the revolution itself, it took on some of the most advanced ideas that were then current on the Continent. In Washington and in his army, the Neostoic image of the officer as public servant was revived via the ideas of French eighteenth-century thinkers such as Rousseau and Montesquieu, and of soldiers like de Saxe and Guibert. Washington's early service as adjutant of Virginia and on campaign with the British gave him grounding in the military practice of the time and provided him with an idea of the social and tactical differences between Europe and America. He wrote and published an account of his service with General Braddock during the British officer's last battle and campaign. When war came again in 1776, Washington was given the chance to show what he could do, but perhaps most of all to learn and to grow—and his army along with him. The evolution of Washington and his army was not smooth, however. It involved an uneven synthesis of old and new, of liberty and discipline, honor and democracy, soldier and citizen. Although the citizens of the new republic at first held up the virtues of the citizen-soldier over those of the professional, many Americans were overawed by the trappings of officer rank that those seeking employment in the new American army displayed. Washington himself may have been attracted to the practice of soldiering to an extent because he so much looked the part, as early paintings of him indicate. It eventually became clear that the trappings did not necessarily indicate substance, and that even a good European-style officer might not be useful in the New World absent a degree of flexibility. People realized that military expertise could be bought and imported, but that America needed an indigenous officer corps to train and lead an army of citizens.[53] Soldierly pride and habits were required of anyone bearing arms—Continental Line or militia, officer or man—but the paradox of citizens subordinating themselves to military discipline in defense of liberty was a separate problem of American military professionalism to be resolved in the New World.[54] Although by experience and inclination Washington was something of an authoritarian, he came to realize that the conditions in the new nation called for a less autocratic style. Citizens enjoyed rights and deserved respect, more so than subjects. Washington was creative in shaping the distinct culture of his new army. At Valley Forge he had Joseph Addison's history drama *Cato* performed for all in the army as a reminder that the new American republic was also a return to ancient Roman republican virtue.

One of the ways change was manifested was by a new interpretation of the idea of soldierly honor. As David Hackett Fischer points out, three different versions of soldierly honor were on display among the Hessians, English, and American forces fighting in New York and New Jersey in 1776.[55] The Hessians were not the unprincipled mercenaries that they are sometimes portrayed as being, but they subscribed to a rather dated, even feudal idea of honor that involved personal enrichment as well as prowess. The English honor code was becoming tied to membership in the regiment, creating a corporate, dutiful corollary to the more individualistic and aristocratic code that had prevailed. The American code was arguably the most moral and inclusive. All three armies allowed privates as well as officers to share in the corporate honor of the military organization, but the American version was most concerned with individual rights. Charles Royster makes an interesting argument that American soldiers, especially the veterans of the Continental Line, adopted the soldierly ethos of their European counterparts as if they considered this their ideal, when in fact the ideals were freedom and liberty, and the discipline and subordination of the soldier were means to an end, perhaps even good in themselves, but not the greatest thing, and certainly not that for which they fought.[56] The different ethics of the armies were reflected in how they campaigned and were commanded. The Hessians were known for theft and for arrogance toward civilians. The social stratification of the English officer ranks usually meant that aristocratic senior officers like Charles Cornwallis set down completed plans as orders to be obeyed. Washington was learning to ask for advice and to hold councils of war.[57] When inspecting troops, he often asked the soldier before him how long he had agreed to serve. If the answer was "for the war" (in other words, for the duration), Washington would reply, "I perceive that you are a gentleman, sir, and I am very pleased to make your acquaintance," thus putting into effect Voltaire's dictum that he who serves his country well has no need of ancestors. In addition, the Americans' treatment of prisoners was generally more humane than that of the British and Hessians. They were also less likely to plunder, perhaps partly because they were operating in their own country, albeit often far from home and under conditions of considerable want. Finally, the American soldier's dedication to the civic ideals of freedom and liberty under law would be enshrined in the constitutional oath of enlistment, first introduced in 1789.

Washington's greatest and most enduring accomplishment as a military professional may be his handling of the disbandment of the American army after the war, at a time when restive elements in the officer ranks were spoiling for political authority. His own assumption of political power was not as a man on horseback but as an elected civilian who had laid aside his uniform. The American practice of the relationship between civil and military authority arguably became the pluralistic model for the rest of American society and social institutions.[58] By precept and example, Washington established a tradition of military professionalism, ethics, and citizenship among American soldiers that would continue to serve it well, although the American military culture would be beset by more challenges and change than perhaps any other.

The Naval Officer

This work is mostly concerned with the military professionals who lead armies on land, but in this and subsequent chapters I devote some space to what in the eighteenth century was a fairly recent development: the naval profession and naval officers. Much could certainly be said about the men who commanded, sailed, and fought on board the warships of antiquity and the Middle Ages. I have omitted doing so partly to maintain focus, but also because in those times the role of navies was usually limited and subordinate to that of armies, and because the commanders of combatant navies and warships were usually transplanted army officers.

Naval battles themselves began as fights between groups of land soldiers embarked on ships; thus the techniques and tactics of naval battles in ancient and medieval times closely resembled those of the land. Sophisticated early navies like that of the classical Athenians developed specialized

weapons and tactics, but in general early naval warfare was an amateurish business conducted by men who were much more used to fighting on
solid ground. In Europe naval warfare began to become more professional
and specialized in the early modern period. This was accomplished most
successfully by Britain. The British naval officer corps achieved a fusion of
nautical and military knowledge. A logical path of training and promotion
was established, in part by the seventeenth-century diarist and Admiralty
official Samuel Pepys. A young man could sign on as a "gentleman" or "First
Class" volunteer and advance to midshipman rank by age fifteen.[59] By the
time he was commissioned a lieutenant he was expected to be a competent
sailor and fighter. Uniforms were adopted for British Royal Navy officers
in the mid-eighteenth century.[60] By about this time the British Navy in
particular had developed a considerable amount of expertise in amphibious
operations, and certain naval officers (and some of their army brethren) had
come to specialize in the methods of power projection ashore.[61] Warships
also conducted patrols, convoys, and blockades. Battles were usually fought
line-astern to maximize the firepower of cannons that were mounted to
fire broadsides. Navies developed detailed fighting instructions to guide the
actions of commanders in battle.[62] Naval officers were drawn from a similar
class and generally adhered to the same codes of personal and professional
honor and duty as their army counterparts.

The Legacy

During the eighteenth century the ranks, careers, regulation, and organization of officers and other soldiers assumed a roughly modern form. Soldiers
served in national armies, advancing through a hierarchy as their abilities
and fortunes permitted, subject to orders and reassignment from a centralized command and bureaucracy. The organizational capacity of governments had created the conditions for armies comprised of standing units of
infantry, cavalry, artillery, and engineers that became objects of loyalty and
esprit de corps, and these units acquired their symbology and infrastructure
of flags and badges, messes and barracks. Regiments were often connected
to a geographical region, sometimes aiding cohesion and making them a
permanent part of the national life across class lines. Armies became self-
replicating national institutions, symbols and upholders of order and authority, and the nature of the soldier's professional ethos assumed a familiar

shape. As in previous times, the social gulf between officers and other ranks could be both enabler and impediment. The fact that officers were often the social superiors of military bureaucrats could have the effect of holding officers above the bureaucracy in some matters. The profession of arms maintained some independence from the unarmed military professionals, in effect imposing a rough balance among the subsets of the military profession. Personal honor and duty to the service were also in a kind of balance, with duty in the ascendant and honor morphing from an individualistic code to one that was more corporate, national, or even broadly moral.

War at this time was still, to borrow a phrase from Winston Churchill, "cruel and magnificent."[63] The eighteenth-century military profession had style as well as substance. Their code of conduct, restraint, and steadiness under fire held these often unwashed but scented men in lace cuffs and buckled shoes at their posts through some of the bloodiest battles in history. Added to this are traditions of literacy and sociability that have left behind artifacts and examples for the modern soldier to peruse and ponder, even to imitate, singly and in company. Christopher Duffy, a prolific writer on eighteenth-century warfare, wrote that he considered the soldiers of the day very good company. So they are, and they are instructive as well as usually congenial companions for latter-day soldiers and civilians.

7

NAPOLEON AND THE NINETEENTH CENTURY
Revolution, Reaction, and Expansion

The developments in military professionalism and the broad contributions of military professionals during the years of Napoleon's ascendency and immediately thereafter are complex and more than typically paradoxical. His dramatic career engendered a new respect for the art of war as an arena of human genius and an arbiter of the fate of nations and of supranational movements. This period saw the birth of famous and still existing military academies such as Sandhurst in England and West Point in the United States. The experience of the Napoleonic Wars produced two of the great classics of Western military thought: Clausewitz's *On War* and Baron Antoine-Henri Jomini's *The Art of War*. The adoption of permanent organizations at the levels of division and corps created a requirement for officers qualified to serve on staffs and distinguished that most professional level of war, the operational middle ground between the tactical and the strategic. On the other hand, Napoleon's career of conquest, along with some of his heartless self-promoting pronouncements, set a poor example for soldiers to follow. *On War* and *The Art of War* are mostly silent on ethical matters beyond the need for strong character in a commander. The apolitical nature of the soldier's role began to verge on the amoral. Admiration for the military commander sometimes appeared to be based on a kind of aesthetic appreciation. The formalism of the eighteenth century was replaced by a romantic conception of the genius of the military commander as a Prometheus figure who broke rules and brought on change through decisive battle.

During the Napoleonic period, as in the aftermath of the Seven Years' War, those who lost most dramatically were also those who learned most from the experience. Prussia's defeats at Jena and Auerstadt in 1806 were a rude awakening from a sleep of presumptive military superiority. To meet the challenge of Napoleon and to restore their self-respect, the Prussian state and army instituted major reforms. Some of these were rescinded after Waterloo, but enough remained to create a Prussian war machine that was the largest and best led in Europe. The professional acme of these developments was undoubtedly the Prussian General Staff. This organization was remarkably successful in institutionalizing military excellence, most particularly at the operational level.[1] Unfortunately, it also cultivated a narrow, even politically naïve, and strategically obtuse form of professionalism that would make it a danger to a united, powerful German state by encouraging its belligerent tendencies and prickly national paranoia. Ultimately this most "professional" of institutions would become a danger to humankind, prorogued to rise again as the servant of a mad tyrant. The German model would transform itself into a cautionary tale of excessive nationalism and deficient conscience, of narrow know-how rather than broad understanding or humanity.

The nineteenth century saw significant changes in weaponry as well as in other forms of military-related technology, organization, and officer education. Muskets and cannons acquired rifled barrels and breech-loading mechanisms, increasing their accuracy, rate, and range of fire. The railroad and telegraph were pressed into military service. After 1815, armies reverted to the small volunteer formations of the previous century, but conscription and reserve establishments were well-established means of augmenting manpower. The increased size, lethality, and range of armies all created a need for more formal professional education, and the period also saw the spread of military academies for officer cadets along with advanced staff and war colleges for middle-ranking officers. Naval forces arguably acquired their Clausewitz in the person of Alfred Thayer Mahan, a serving U.S. Navy officer and one of the first on the staff of the new Naval War College. In the latter part of the century, as in the time of Frederick the Great, German military practices spread, although sometimes more in form than in content. For a time, Germanic-style uniforms were all the rage. The general staff idea was adopted by most of the major armies, which now included some of those in Asia, especially in Japan. Many European soldiers experienced colonial service. Some were involved in exploration or scientific discovery and wrote of their experiences.

The nineteenth century also saw the start of international written accords and organizations dedicated to limiting the destruction and suffering caused by war. Eventually the conventions established at The Hague and Geneva and the standards imposed by the Red Cross would become aspects of the military professional ethos. In a sense these written standards were more explicit, universal, and enforceable versions of the soldier's chivalric and honor codes of the past. Although the mostly civilian drafters of the new codes, perhaps unfortunately, made scant reference to those of the past, as in the past it would be soldiers who would have to adopt, apply, and adapt those standards of conduct. Under the influence of the legal conventions, war would lose some of its propensity for casual, ad hoc, or individual violence. Nevertheless, some of these humanitarian improvements would be overcome by the range and destructive power of new weapons and by the power of ideology to dehumanize victim and assailant at once.

Napoleon

In the popular imagination, Napoleon is likely still *the* model for exceptional ability in a senior military commander. His reputation among soldiers and historians is nearly as high, although naturally more nuanced; it is also quite varied. In professional military terms, Napoleon's reputation is probably highest and most secure in his mastery of the operational art, the middle level of war fighting between strategy and tactics, which he may even be said to have invented. Napoleon benefited from some of the military developments of the latter eighteenth century (some of which I discussed in the previous chapter) and from the political and social upheavals of his time, which he did not create but upon which he cleverly capitalized.

An essential ingredient of Napoleon's successes was the French Revolution itself and the changes it wrought in the French army. Between 1789 and 1794 the army was transformed into the kind of national military force that Montesquieu and other Enlightenment writers had long espoused. The early revolutionary movement, like early Christianity, contained elements of pacifism, or at least it tended toward a view of itself as a force for peace.[2] This idea was soon overcome by external threats, and eventually it gave way to a militant and aggressive revolutionary ideology. The national mobilization of 1793 termed the *levée en masse* created enormous resources for the army and established a precedent of unlimited demands placed on France in service of the revolution. The army grew in size, its leadership became far more representative of the population of France, and it embraced a revolutionary ideology that the rest of the nation shared. Many of the officers of the revolutionary army had been noncommissioned officers in the ancien régime, and they soon gained experience in war and in command. The cost of the transformation from an army of royalty to one of popular ideology was high for some officers; more than eighty French generals were executed between 1793 and 1794.[3]

Napoleon is most famous as a fighter of battles—in fact the large, decisive, set-piece battle has been termed "Napoleonic" ever since his time—but he is even more distinguished as a conductor of campaigns. His most famous victories were culminations of campaigns during which he had shaped the decisive battle for victory. For these campaigns he employed a new level of organization, the permanent corps, officially adopted in 1799.[4] The corps was a collection of divisions under a lieutenant general. The improved infrastructure and economy of Europe created the conditions for better maneuverability, and the corps gave Napoleon a means to divide his army for maneuver and selectively reunite it on the battlefield. If Napoleon was strong relative to the enemy, he could employ the *maneuver sur les derrières*, pinning down or distracting his adversary with one or more corps while conducting a flanking attack with the others. If he did not have sufficient forces for this maneuver he might occupy a central position, allowing converging enemy forces to come to him and then lashing out with all or part of his army, defeating the enemy units piecemeal before they had time to unite.

Napoleon was brilliant as a leader as well as a war fighter. Not only did he understand the spirit of the revolution, he also shared enough of it to be plausible as its spokesperson. He was brave enough not to hesitate when the needs of the situation called for conspicuous personal courage under fire, as when he carried the colors at Lodi. If Napoleon sincerely believed in anything other than his own destiny, he seems to have had a genuine admiration for what he called the *feu sacre*, the "sacred fire" that drove the soldier on to victory. His feats of memorization about his soldiers' deeds and accomplishments may have been fueled by that admiration. Even his callousness could be considered as expressing an understanding of the fact that the soldier's service is inseparable from suffering and death. Soldiering, especially in a time of frequent warfare, is not so much a career as the conditional surrender of a personal future.

Although he liked to be compared with Charlemagne, Napoleon was perhaps nearer to Alexander. Both were conquerors, military innovators, and opportunists who built short-lived empires that undeniably, and at great cost, provided the means to disseminate some of the advanced ideas of their times. The Hellenism that Alexander propagated flourished in some of the places where it was planted. The same perhaps can be said of the revolutionary spirit and ideas that Napoleon continued (even if cynically) to espouse. In the decades after his fall, a political reaction set in against "liberty, equality, and fraternity," in part because of the means that had been used to spread them. The political violence of the Reign of Terror that had gripped revolutionary France and the unrestrained military force of Napoleon's campaigns gave revolution, even liberalism, a bad name. By the 1830s and 1840s revolutionary concepts were reawakening. Napoleon was important not just for what he represented but also for how others reacted to him. The virulent nationalism that he awakened in Spain, Russia, and especially in Germany would prove enduring, and it would trouble the peace of Europe into the next century.

In *The Cognitive Challenge of War, Prussia, 1806*, Peter Paret engages in a tour de force on the reaction of the Prussian state to its military defeat by Napoleon.[5] Paret points out that Prussia engaged in a society-wide examination of the implications of the defeat and subjugation. Literary works such as Friedrich Schiller's *Wallenstein* and pictorial art such as Caspar Friedrich's *Chasseur in the Snow* posed questions about war, military service, and their relationship to the individual and the state. *Wallenstein* depicts the historical Thirty Years' War military commander, but he is clearly a stand-in for Napoleon. Prussia undertook societal and even psychological changes in order to reclaim its self-respect and its position in the European political arena. For educated Prussians the internationalist spirit and sympathies of the Enlightenment and its revolutionary stepchild became a thing of the past. In philosophy, Hegelian embeddedness took the place of Kantian autonomy; in politics, nationalism took hold, perhaps among soldiers especially. Germany was not unique in embracing the nationalist creed, but as in the time of Frederick the Great, its adherence to its own interests was narrower than the average, fueled by a sense of the wrongs done to it and by vulnerability that had been sensitized by Napoleon's rough handling.

Like the French after their defeat in the Seven Years' War, the Prussian military's response to its loss of *amour propre* was to reflect and reform. In fact, the Prussian army had attempted to begin reform before its defeat. The brilliant military theorist Gerhard von Scharnhorst started the Academy for Young Infantry and Cavalry Officers in 1801. One of his pupils was Carl von Clausewitz. Paret describes the students of the school as a general staff in embryo. The academy helped at least to develop some of the intellectual capital that would be called upon once the reforming movement began in earnest. Scharnhorst headed the Committee on Military Reform that was created in 1806. Thirteen percent of all general officers were cashiered along with a smaller proportion of more junior officers. The country adopted a militia system and issued simplified manuals for infantry and cavalry. Discipline was made less punitive. Other changes included the creation of permanent brigades (which were intended to be cadre divisions), new supply battalions to replace the old system of civilian contractors, and the establishment of a war college.[6] A positive influence of the larger culture on German officer education at this time was the concept of *bildung*, which involved the cultivation of character and intellect through study and reflection.[7] The process of *bildung* was not so much a matter of curriculum as of narrative, and the bildungsroman became an important genre of the novel starting with Johann Wolfgang von Goethe's *The Sorrows of Young Werther* (1774) and *Wilhelm Meister's Apprenticeship* (1795). In some ways a reformulation of some earlier ideas of Stoicism, chivalry, and Neostoicism, *bildung* as part of officer education aimed to create qualities that were useful in a militarily instrumentalist way while also seeking to develop an individual who was ethically and socially exemplary in a broader sense.

The military developments of the Napoleonic period would have an abiding impact on the profession of arms. Napoleon's opponents were forced to adopt some of the reforms that had made him successful in order to produce forces capable of defeating him. Some of these had social implications, perhaps especially the expanded social base of the officer ranks. The hold of the aristocracy over those ranks was loosened but not ended, and European armies, that of France included, went back to the old exclusivity when peace permitted them to do so. The political-ideological-military fervor awakened by the French revolutionary army slept after Napoleon's defeat, but it had been shown to be a potent morale builder and force multiplier, and it would crop up again in the twentieth century. The corps organization was available now whenever armies grew to sufficient size to warrant it. Like the division, the corps demanded a staff of specialist officers trained in "the operational art." The acknowledged experts in this area came from the various general staffs that had grown and developed in the war years and remained at least in skeletal form in peacetime. Napoleon himself had not always exercised effective command and control; his good and bad examples indicated a need to develop a cadre of officers who understood war at the ground level but would be enough above the fray to conduct high-level and sustained planning and to provide strategic direction. The leading general staff in Europe for more than a century was that of the Prussian and later (after unification in 1871) German army.

Jomini, Clausewitz, Tolstoy, and Vigny

Napoleon's career inspired two highly influential military writers whose work continues to be read and to exert a sometimes unseen influence on the military profession: Antoine-Henri Jomini and Carl von Clausewitz. Jomini was a Swiss soldier for hire who was an admirer of Napoleon but who took an approach to warfare that in a sense went back to the eighteenth century. Jomini believed in certain immutable principles of war. His list of guiding principles (e.g., "mass" and "the offensive") survives in various altered forms today. The more profound and enduring writer is unquestionably Clausewitz; few would deny him his place as the premier theorist of war. Clausewitz's debt to the intellectual currents of his day is sometimes mentioned as if it were a deficit, but his broad reading and exposure to those currents (with the help of his high-born and intellectual wife, Marie) gave his work depth and richness it could not possess if it had been produced by a less cultivated mind. Thanks perhaps to the influence of Hegelian thought in his time, Clausewitz presents a complex, dialectical picture of war. His commander is no mere follower of rules or historical precedents. Clausewitzian ideas such as "friction" and the "remarkable trinity" are more inducements to doubt and thought than they are rules.[8] Friction is the tendency of military operations to go awry as a result of violence, losses, and fear. The trinity represents the contesting influences of reason, chance, and the passions that are involved in warfare. Clausewitz makes use of history, but he is doubtful that history establishes didactic or immutable lessons or principles.[9] In war, even more than in most areas of human endeavor, every rule has its opposite. The greater or more sensible course may be the lesser; it depends on the context, or it may even be more accurate to simply say that it just depends. Only a mind that is both innately equipped and sufficiently prepared will be able to tell the difference between the best course and its counterfeit. For Clausewitz, genius in war is not solely a matter of intellect but also a question of courage and character. In the manner of *bildung* and reminiscent of the Stoics, for him a mastery of the art of war involves self-knowledge and self-command.

Another literary legacy of the Napoleonic era is Leo Tolstoy's great work *War and Peace.* In earlier sections of this book I discussed how works of imaginative literature have helped to express and shape the perceptions of war among professional soldiers. Tolstoy was too young to have any personal memory of the Napoleonic Wars, but he served as a Russian officer in the Crimea at the siege of Sevastopol, and his fictional depictions of battle are perhaps the most vivid and memorable ever written. He also records the words and thoughts of intelligent soldiers such as Prince Andrei, who quickly becomes disillusioned with war and with efforts to conceal its murderous reality behind a veneer of glamour and courteous ritual but who nevertheless continues to serve until his death. Tolstoy's villain is the self-important Napoleon; his heroes are the humble soldiers such as Captain Tushin, who commands an indomitable battery and, summoned to headquarters, modestly thinks he is going to be reprimanded for some slight omission rather than commended for his leadership.

French officer and writer Alfred de Vigny is much less well known today than Tolstoy. Like Tolstoy, Vigny was an aristocratic officer who lived too late to see service during the Napoleonic Wars but who makes an imaginative effort to conceive them in a literary work that draws on his own service. Vigny served for thirteen years in the French army starting after the first fall and exile of Napoleon and into the reign of the restored Bourbon monarchy. His work is difficult to classify, perhaps contributing to his neglect by critics and readers, including his fellow soldiers. His best-known work is a collection of vignettes and reflections titled *Grandeur et Servitude Militaire.*[10] Vigny describes the personal cost of military life, even in peacetime, as a submission to control and discipline, a dedication to routine and detail that may be numbing and stultifying. Although not a combat veteran, he writes empathetically on the guilt about killing that soldiers may experience. Vigny's resignation from the French peacetime army perhaps came when the servitude came clearly to outweigh the grandeur, at least in his own case.

Armies as Institutions

The final defeat of Napoleon at Waterloo on 18 June 1815 put an end to large-scale warfare on the European continent for more than forty years. As in the wake of the Thirty Years' War, the participants were tired of war and had had enough of grand causes. The period after 1815 and the Congress of Vienna was one of conservatism. The tensions that had brought on the French Revolution and the rise of Napoleon had not been eliminated, but the violent means used to bring about change had created a desire for stability, even if that meant a return to the antiquated and discredited social organization of the previous century. With the upstart Napoleon in lifetime exile, hereditary monarchs and their aristocratic supporters were restored to power. Armies came to be seen and to see themselves increasingly as guardians of order and the status quo, a role that in a time of relative peace could seem to take precedence over their war-fighting function, at least on the peaceable continent of Europe. The major European countries developed in this period what were in effect two armies. One was a home establishment of military schools, installations, and units that were engaged in training, ceremonial functions, and aid to the civil authority in times of unrest (which peaked in the years 1832 and 1848); the other was a colonial army that secured, policed, and expanded an overseas empire. The home organizations could serve as recruiting and training centers for the overseas forces and, especially in times of heightened tension and conflict, might themselves deploy overseas.

Some countries maintained completely separate establishments for colonial service, the largest being the British Indian Army, which was placed under Crown control rather than the supervision of the East India Company after the mutiny of some Indian army units in 1857. Officers of the colonial establishment tended to be less wealthy and well connected than their home counterparts, but they often had the opportunity to become highly accomplished as war fighters and in other roles. Not only did they fight frequently, usually against asymmetrical adversaries, they also had to cultivate the non-war-fighting skills that have been required of soldier-colonizers since the Roman Empire and before. Soldiers were among the first on the scene in a newly acquired colony, and they had to be versatile, acting as administrators, builders, linguists, and even practical anthropologists. European officers serving with locally recruited colonial forces often explored ways to exploit local martial traditions and to accommodate indigenous family structures and religious practices.[11]

The nineteenth century was in some ways the great age of both professions and bureaucracies. By mid-century the education, credentialing, functions, and advancement of the members of professions had become largely standardized. Professional associations existed to establish and enforce criteria for entry and advancement, and universities regularly published journals and hosted conferences and conventions to disseminate the knowledge and ethos required of members of a profession. The speed of transportation and communication increased radically in mid-century thanks to the railroad and telegraph. This facilitated the spread of professional knowledge by circulating ideas from the centers of learning, and it brought professionals together in cities and at universities for meetings and consultations. The rate of travel was still slow enough that professionals maintained a considerable measure of autonomy, both by necessity and by virtue of their documented credentials. The lone doctor or town lawyer was a fixture of European and American life. Professionals came in for a reverence that could be exaggerated in relation to their actual abilities, their prestige upheld by the conservatism and social stratification of the age. The doctor, the professor, the family lawyer always knew best, even if his knowledge was sometimes shallow and out of date and his mental faculties unimpressive. Charles Dickens, Mark Twain, and other writers frequently satirized self-important mid-century doctors, teachers, and lawyers.[12]

The military profession is more inherently corporate than the law or medicine, but nineteenth-century military officers also possessed considerable autonomy, especially on campaigns and in the colonies, and they enjoyed some of the same prestige as members of other professions, reinforced by the nationalism and class-consciousness of the time, since officership still carried a unique neochivalric social cachet. The military academies in Europe and America grew in size and influence during this century and played an important role in implanting esprit de corps, common ideas, and values. (Although as the experiences of the American and the later Austro-Hungarian armies make obvious, there are limits to how much an academy education can overcome regional or sectarian differences.) Army regiments had been in continuous existence by mid-century, in some cases for two hundred years, and had acquired unique traditions and proud (if sometimes richly embellished) histories. Paintings, silver, and trophies commemorating their histories adorned their barracks, messes, and headquarters, and the colors of a regiment, still sometimes carried into battle, had acquired almost mystical significance. Were the officers of this time significantly more professional than those of previous centuries (as most social scientists writing on the subject believe), or did they merely have the tangible trappings of professionalism: the recorded formal schooling, membership in professional associations, and subscriptions to professional journals? It can probably at least be said that professional knowledge and beliefs were more uniformly disseminated among military professionals than they had been in the past. The army was also in general a steadier and more regular means of employment than it had been in previous centuries. Armies consisted of standing units, and those units, at least the more celebrated and venerable, were permanent in a sense probably not seen since the Roman Empire, their existence justified not merely by their war-making capacities but also by their role as symbols of order and hierarchy in the post-Napoleonic European world. The flip side of this uniformity and durability may have been a certain self-regarding and self-perpetuating professional solipsism. Unlike the incompetent physician or lawyer, whose limitations could be unmasked in the surgery or courtroom, an inept, unintelligent officer in the nineteenth century might be able to spend peacetime years basking in the regard of his countrymen and secure in an illusory sense of professional competence. Indeed, an entire officer body and its doctrine might be shown to be inept and irrelevant by the test of war or the tide of change, as we shall see. The institutionalization of armies perhaps did not constitute militarism in itself, but it helped to establish the basis for crypto-militarism in some countries and a prevailing, official militarism in others, along with a reification of military symbols and determinedly separate military values that could drive psychology and policy in disastrous directions.

Along with the rise of professions, nineteenth-century governments and other social institutions were becoming increasingly bureaucratized.[13] Bureaucracies enhanced the competence of armies and gave civilian professionals the means of imposing military policy. As a result, armies generally became more responsive to civilian control during this period, but there were exceptions, most notably in Germany, where a strong general staff gave the uniformed military a powerful instrument for shaping policy as well as strategy. Walter Goerlitz says that the German General Staff acquired a "nimbus of invincibility."[14] With the fall of Bismarck and the collapse of Germany's treaty with Russia and an essentially defensive strategy, the dedicated, detailed offensive planning of the general staff took on an air of inevitability and self-fulfillment.

Chaplains, Lawyers, and Physicians

Armies had been accompanied by priests, lawyers, and medical doctors for centuries by the 1800s, but the nineteenth century saw the rise of uniformed military officers with professional training and credentials in these areas. In a manner reminiscent of the rise of the military engineer and artilleryman, by the nineteenth century members of the clerical, legal, and medical professions were in military uniform and pursuing careers as army and navy officers. A significant difference in the case of doctors and clergymen was that they usually did not bear arms; in fact, regulations often prohibited them from doing so. The entrance of these professionals had the overall effect of raising the level of education in the officer ranks and introducing professional perspectives into the officer corps that could complement or compete with the outlook of the combat arms officers. The uniformed ministers, doctors, and lawyers developed specialist knowledge of armed conflict and its effects within their own areas of expertise. Chaplains came to function as counselors and were sometimes looked to as possessing ethical knowledge. Medical officers developed knowledge of trauma surgery and of the psychological impact of war and combat. They also learned about the regional illnesses in the places where they were stationed, perhaps most famously in the case of Walter Reed and his battle against yellow fever in Cuba in the late nineteenth century. In addition to expertise in their own national codes of military law, army and navy judge advocates might be consulted on the international law of war, including the growing body of written guidelines for combatants.

The Military Academies

Only a small minority of European officers were academy trained in the eighteenth century, and in the twentieth century the means of commissioning nonacademy graduates (in America and during the world wars especially) grew in numbers and favor, so the nineteenth century may be considered the golden age of the military academy. In many armies, academies had a large share in officer accessions, and academy graduates often monopolized senior officer positions. This was in keeping with the tenure of nineteenth-century professionalism, which expected lifelong commitment beginning with an early apprenticeship. The three greatest, still-existing military academies—West Point, Sandhurst, and St. Cyr in France—were all founded early in the century. The organization and routine of nineteenth-century military academies essentially mirrored those of the army garrisons of the day. In that sense, cadets were well equipped to assume the responsibilities of the officer on duty: to drill their men; to inspect their living quarters, messing arrangements, persons, weapons, and equipment; and to sit in judgment on them in the case of infractions. The routines of garrison life may have been appropriate to train enlisted followers, but the same routines in an academy setting might actually suppress the future officer's capacities for initiative and adaptability.[15] The military academies of the day approached this paradox in different ways. West Point and Sandhurst present an interesting contrast in the different ways they addressed what may be the essential challenge of military academies, which is to develop an orderly system that also enhances future officers' adaptability to change and conflict.

West Point had little order or established curriculum until the arrival in 1817 of Sylvanus Thayer, who as superintendent instituted a system of discipline, drill, and daily classroom recitation that survived into the next century and still exerts an influence today. The cadets evolved an unofficial code of honor and a rough-and-tumble means of enforcement that were eventually appropriated and tamed by the administration.[16] Under Thayer's leadership the academy evolved into the nation's premier engineering school. Top graduates such as Robert E. Lee were commissioned in the Corps of Engineers, and West Point alumni faced considerable temptation to accept lucrative civilian jobs with the railroad and other industries. Some, like George McClellan, resigned their commissions to do so but returned to military service in the Civil War. Their engineering education allowed many West Point officers to take part in erecting the infrastructure of westward expansion, again particularly in the building of the railroad. In essence West Point evolved a particularly rigorous academic and military regime that made incessant demands on the cadets, placing them under close scrutiny, forcing them to respond to frequent evaluations, and ensuring through the honor code that they were not resorting to shortcuts or deception in order to make the grade. Some West Point graduates, McClellan among them, imbued with orderly habits of mind through the academy's curriculum and daily routine, were probably better engineers than war fighters.

Interest and involvement in military officer training in nineteenth-century America went beyond the Regular Army. The state military colleges that became popular in the antebellum period imitated the West Point model. In general, these institutions did not produce officers for the Regular Army. Southern military colleges such as the Virginia Military Institute (founded 1839) and the Citadel (founded 1842) eventually supplied officers for the Confederate army; in fact they may have been founded in anticipation of the secession that was already looming.[17] The U.S. Navy acquired its own training ground for officers at Annapolis, Maryland, in 1842; the site was designated the U.S. Naval Academy in 1850. If the state military colleges and high schools were mostly a Southern phenomenon, perhaps it was because they represented an expression of the idea of a Southern cavalier military aristocracy. In both North and South, by the 1850s volunteer militias had begun to replace the less efficient local militias. These organizations would aid in the spread of military knowledge and serve as cadres for the tremendous war to come.[18]

Great Britain had acquired a military academy at Woolwich in 1741 that began as a school for artillerymen but eventually expanded to train officers for the other technical branches of engineers and signalmen. Sandhurst was created to train officers for the infantry and cavalry. In general these British institutions were less academic than West Point and its American imitators. Their emphasis was on sport and military training. General education and character development were thought to have been accomplished at home or in a "public" boarding school. Somewhat more freedom and self-policing were allowed than at academies like West Point. There was no equivalent of the strict honor code of West Point and the other American academies, but the cadets enforced an unwritten code of conduct. Nineteenth-century Sandhurst periodically erupted in riots between companies that sometimes resulted in serious injuries and even deaths. Gilbert and Sullivan lampooned mid-Victorian army officers in their operetta *Pirates of Penzance*. The Major General of the play admits, "My military knowledge, though I'm plucky and adventury, has only just come down to the beginning of the century."

As even a satire acknowledges, Sandhurst graduates possessed the dash and esprit de corps that were important credentials for the officers of the Victorian army.

General Staffs and War Colleges

In the eighteenth century Prussia had led the other European nations in providing an academy education for officer cadets. In the nineteenth century it was the first country to adopt advanced education for competitively selected middle-ranking officers and to use the War College experience to train and screen officers for the general staff. The curriculum at the War College evolved into a rigorous three-year course of study in operational methods culminating in a staff ride led by the chief of the general staff. After the ride a small percentage of the graduates would be selected to serve as general staff officers, rotating between duty with units in the field and at the army headquarters in Berlin. The course of instruction at the War College stressed historical study, and one famous chief of staff, Count Alfred von Schlieffen, wrote a monograph on the Carthaginian victory at Cannae. The Cannae-style victory was to become a near obsession with Schlieffen and other Prussian General Staff officers. The plan for victory over the French inspired by Cannae that bears his name, and that was finally executed in modified form in 1914, has sometimes been labeled a work of genius, but in fact it was a remarkable piece of professional myopia and unexamined assumptions at many levels, as we shall see.[19] What the German army in the era of the general staff did it did well, but German officers seemed to be collectively blind to the fact that they frequently were doing the wrong thing well.

One of the useful things the Prussians did well, and that they may even claim to have invented, was the war game. The Prussian war game evolved from chess, or more directly from elaborate derivatives of chess played in the eighteenth century on a much larger board of up to 3,600 squares. A young artillery officer and his father changed the playing surface from blank squares to a map, making the game a less abstract and more realistic simulation of war. The chief of staff at the time, Baron Karl von Müffling, on seeing a game played is supposed to have exclaimed, "It is not a game at all! It's training for war! It is of value to the whole Army!"[20] The general staff adopted the *Kriegsspiel* as a tool for training and planning, and the practice of war gaming trickled down to the lower echelons of the Prussian army, where tactical games were often played on sand tables to reproduce terrain; eventually it spread to the armies of other countries, becoming an established aspect of professional education and operational planning.

Other armies also adopted the Germans' general staff idea, although the selectivity, rigor, and prestige of the original version, eventually named the Great General Staff, probably remained unique. Academically and militarily selective and demanding, the German General Staff sought to create a professional elite, one that may have been inspired by the Guardians of Plato's ideal Republic, and it shared with other oligarchies a tendency to become insular and conformist. An anonymous British memoirist who served in the German army in the early years of the twentieth century wrote that some general staff officers seemed to have been reduced by the rigors of their training to a state of permanent mental exhaustion and depression that sometimes led to drug addiction.[21] Despite the pitfalls, the evolution of general staffs from the largely clerical servants of command to intellectually elite repositories of military expertise in the half century following the fall of Napoleon was a pivotal change in the nature of military professionalism. Military operations would increasingly depend on large staffs of officers with specialist training, and at a slightly greater remove on civilian bureaucracies. In fact, these two groups would come to intermingle and resemble one another, expanding but also perhaps diluting military professionalism and its provenance.

The Wars: Technological Change, Tactical Adaptation, Strategic Impact

Starting in mid-century, large-scale conflict and technological changes tested the adaptability of nineteenth-century military institutions and the profession. Military professionals faced challenges in three major conflicts: the Crimean War, the American Civil War, and the Franco-Prussian War. Each conflict introduced new weapons and other new technologies, creating the need for changes in tactics and approaches to strategy. Together they saw the last of the close infantry formations that had evolved from the Middle Ages through the age of Napoleon, and the beginnings of greater dispersion at the tactical and operational levels. Strategy is always the slowest level of warfare to change, but the expanded battlefield brought on by increased weaponry ranges and the railroad did have an impact at the strategic level of war. The military profession would have to adapt to these changes and to the altered geopolitical map of Europe and of the globe. The developments of this period presaged the even greater technological advances of the twentieth century that would revolutionize warfare at all levels and across the spectrum of conflict.

The Crimean War

Since Tennyson's poem "The Charge of the Light Brigade," along with the 1936 and 1968 feature films of the same name and such historical works as Cecil Woodham-Smith's *The Reason Why* (1953), the Crimean War (1854–56) has gone down in popular memory as a historical parody of military incompetence. The British are remembered as blundering into an unnecessary war for which they were unprepared and that was then pursued by doddering relics of the Napoleonic period and arrogant, inexperienced, almost comically stupid upper-class twits in uniform, with James Brudenell, Lord Cardigan, commander of the Light Brigade at Balaclava, their standard-bearer.[22] Like most caricatures, this picture is not entirely inaccurate, but it omits important details and context. Although they appear inefficient and reactionary in the light of modern sensibilities, British military institutions had served the nation well in the past. Even in the lampooned Crimean War, the navy performed competently, with the British demonstrating their usual flair for amphibious operations, and the army fought on through setbacks and disasters, advanced inland, and participated in the eventual capture of Sevastopol. The British suffered from the usual ossification of military practices that accompanies a long period of peace, and from the necessity of fielding and feeding a large army at the end of very long lines of supply (although extensive use of the new canned food greatly aided in this). The armed forces also had to endure the increased oversight provided by embedded correspondents such as William Howard Russell, who could file stories directly to *The Times* in London by telegraph. The photography of Roger Fenton also helped to bring home a new reality of war, one grubbier and less splendid than the garish depictions of violent combat at Blenheim House. It is interesting to speculate whether Marlborough's and Wellington's reputations would have been quite as high if they had labored under such scrutiny.

Young Count Leo Tolstoy, an officer in the Russian army who served in the Crimea, wrote a series of dispatches from besieged Sevastopol that earned him his early literary reputation. The junior officers he depicts manning the batteries on the redoubts were no doubt the models for Captain Tushin of *War and Peace*. Tolstoy's writing shows a professional's eye for the equipment and technicalities of war, the words and actions of the men, and the meaning and application of abstractions such as fear and courage. He notes the effect on soldiers of long-term exposure to danger: the diminishing physical and psychic energies husbanded by evolving instincts for survival. Tolstoy noticed too that the Russians were technically inferior to their enemies in having muskets rather than rifles and in the shorter range of their artillery. He was moved and perhaps a little mystified by the stoic acceptance of prolonged fighting at a disadvantage that even ordinary peasant soldiers displayed. For a time he apparently considered founding an unofficial army journal that would "truthfully express the spirit of the Russian army."[23]

The best-known (if generally misunderstood) episode of the war was the Battle of Balaclava and the famous charge of the Light Brigade. Perhaps even more than Agincourt a matter of British national legend, the battle and the charge were the result of British forces around Sevastopol heading off a Russian advance that threatened to raise the siege. The dilatory and vaguely worded orders from the elderly Field Marshall FitzRoy Somerset, 1st Baron Raglan; the insistence and impetuousness of the bright but inexperienced Captain Louis Nolan; and the literalness and cryptic, inexpressive communications between the socially estranged commanders George Bingham, Earl of Lucan, and Lord Cardigan added up to a disaster. Extraordinary though the circumstances may have been, the event helped to crystallize what was wrong—and right—with the British Army. The class distinctions and code of conduct that had perhaps once reinforced the discipline, esprit, and effectiveness of the British Army, reified by Waterloo and stubbornly supported by Wellington, had been allowed to run riot in peacetime and the absence of national danger. The army had come to be not only a reflection but indeed an exaggeration of the British class system, a plaything of wealthy men who felt entitled to despise the less aristocratic officers even when the latter were more professionally accomplished.

Cardigan had certainly bought and "birthed" his way to command of the Light Brigade. His poor judgment and presumptuousness had involved him in frequent scandals during the course of his military career, but they did not prevent his pocketbook and pedigree from having the final vote in his promotion and assignment to a coveted command. The purchase of officer commissions, which had been intended to make their ranks more legitimate and reliable, ended up often having the opposite effect. Super-rich officers like Cardigan felt they were above the standards of professional qualification and advancement, even above the power of political authority if it dared presume to hinder their ambitions. Wealth and property might give officers an investment in the nation, but great wealth plus arrogance might actually impede an officer's sense of civic and professional responsibility. Given Cardigan's contempt for officers who had served in India, an attitude many of his fellow aristocratic officers shared, one might wonder whether even the talented and high-born Wellington would have prospered in the insular environment of the mid-century British Army.[24] Sandhurst, like Wellington the progeny of the Napoleonic Wars, had been allowed to languish, as had the Staff College, and few officers attended either during this period. On the other hand (and as Tennyson suggests in his paean to the Light Brigade), the extraordinary cohesiveness and costly tactical success of the Light Brigade indicated that British units could perform well even in a highly adverse situation brought on by inept leadership. The British regimental system was something to be retained and reinforced. Eventually, British reformers would undertake changes that considered the lessons of the Crimea, Balaclava, and the charge, and permitted the British Army and military profession to play a large part in the expansion and consolidation of the empire for the next half century.

The leadership failures of the Crimea campaign, the disclosure of the inadequacy of British forces for the combination of a major war and routine imperial policing, and the rise of a militant and aggressive Prussian-German state gave impetus to the reformers.[25] Secretary of State for War Jonathan Peel led a commission in 1858 that identified some deficiencies but brought about little immediate change, although efforts were made to revive the Staff College and Sandhurst. Edward Cardwell, secretary of state for war under Prime Minister William E. Gladstone, was more effective, in part because by 1870 the threat posed by Prussia had become much more evident. As a result of the Cardwell Reforms, corporal punishment was curtailed and then proscribed, enlistments were made shorter, and the purchase of commissions was abolished.[26] The army was increased in size; it acquired a reserve component and a system of regimental home depots for domestic and deploying battalions, and it was withdrawn from many of the small imperial garrisons that had dispersed its strength. From the experience of the Crimean War the British developed an effective and forward-deployed imperial force based on the regiment. Lines of command, finance, supply, and political oversight were simplified and strengthened.[27] The question of whether the army could be competitive in a major war on the Continent against an enemy that might be more able than the somewhat hapless Russians would be a subject of doubt, debate, and anxiety for more than fifty years.

The Civil War

The American Civil War preserved the world's oldest and largest democracy while also leaving intact racial and regional divisions that still affect both public and private life in the United States. It remains America's costliest war in terms of casualties. The core of the antebellum American military profession consisted of the regular officers of the Army and Navy, with those of the Army nearly all graduates of West Point. The wartime record of the profession is mixed. On the one hand, officers on both sides get high marks for courage and leadership. The regulars of the prewar establishment mustered and trained enormous armies in a short time and with few existing facilities, creating formidable fighting forces on both sides that sometimes ran in battle but remained in the field and fought on until the exhausted South surrendered to an almost equally depleted Union. To lead these forces effectively required courage, command presence, an eye for terrain, and an instinct for enemy vulnerabilities. The number of generals in the United States grew from four in the prewar Regular Army to about a thousand on both sides by the end of the war.[28] This group of men from diverse backgrounds ran the spectrum of competence, but the best of them demonstrated an ability to learn and to adapt to the challenges of a kind of war that was new to them and in some ways new in the annals of conflict. Some of these men became famous; others who were less well known not only met the demands of the day but also set examples and established standards that had a positive influence on the American military profession ever after. One such was George Thomas, a studious, painstaking West Pointer who fought in the less-publicized western theater and earned the nickname "the Rock of Chickamauga." Thomas pioneered combined arms and developed a mobile command post that was imitated for years afterward.[29] Officers of the time may deserve more credit than they usually receive for adapting to technological change. Ulysses S. Grant and other senior officers made frequent and innovative use of the telegraph, even employing it as an early form of "instant messaging." The use of trains to aid maneuver and provide logistical support was pioneered in the Civil War, with West Pointer Herman Haupt creating the Union's plan for railway use. Officers on both sides are sometimes faulted for failing to take into account the increased firepower of the rifled musket. Brent Nosworthy argues that this increase has been overrated and that toward the end of the war tacticians had switched from a preference for pitched battle to a tendency toward long lines of adversaries in continuous contact (presaging the trench lines of World War I).[30]

For a time, attacks by infantry in close formations succeeded often enough to make them appear feasible, and the lack of command-and-control resources at the tactical level and of time for advanced training or the development of doctrine on the part of armies that were quickly raised and committed to combat permitted few alternatives. Both armies inherited tactical manuals that were European in origin and already becoming outdated. Deference to European methods was typical of a time when America was still finding its own cultural and intellectual identity. Added to this was the fact that European armies had more recent experience of conventional conflict. Still, the results were costly. Improvements were extemporized in the field and were eventually codified in new American tactical instructions. Another success both armies achieved is that they usually fought honorably and with restraint. There were exceptions, mostly in the records of irregular forces such as Quantrill's Raiders, but civilian deaths were remarkably few. Even Sherman's March to the Sea, although still infamous in the South, was conducted in a disciplined way. In a sense the march through Georgia bears some resemblance to the medieval *chevauchée*. Sherman wanted the civilian South to feel the "hard hand of war" and to put the lie to the claims of Confederate newspapers and home-front enthusiasts that the South was winning. On the other hand, and unlike a medieval commander, Sherman did not seek this goal by allowing murder or pillage for gain.

Alongside the successes of the American military profession are a number of shortcomings the war exposed. Going into the war, much of the strategic thinking of military professionals appears to have been confused and pedantic. A Jominian obsession with interior and exterior lines may have impeded Union strategic thought.[31] A principal exponent of the

THE MAN FOR THE JOB. Ulysses S. Grant wanted to be a math teacher and was never promoted past captain in the antebellum Regular Army. In the Civil War he developed a war-winning strategy as he cultivated an understanding of the moral issues at stake in the struggle. *Library of Congress*

importance of interior lines was General Henry "Old Brains" Halleck, an intellectual who had perhaps too well absorbed the professional thinking of his time. Abraham Lincoln's struggle to find a competent and successful commander for the Army of the Potomac illustrates the paradox of American military professionalism at the time. Many American officers had gained valuable experience in the Mexican War and western frontier, but the scale of the Civil War was something beyond their imagining. The commander of large forces faced many challenges. Although many American regular officers had studied the Napoleonic Wars, there was no systematic instruction for senior officers on the operational art. Command and control in battle was so difficult that some commanders seem to have given up on it entirely. General George B. McClellan would retire to his tent at the beginning of a battle to pray for victory and await the outcome. The more militant South was eventually beaten by the North, which had less in the way of martial tradition, and the professionals Robert E. Lee, a career soldier with thirty years of continuous service, and former U.S. secretary of war and fellow West Pointer Jefferson Davis were bested by the onetime militia officer Abraham Lincoln and ex–Regular Army captain Ulysses S. Grant, who claimed never to have studied tactics. The adaptive, pragmatic mind had proven superior to professional service and stature. There were other elements of victory, of course, but one was surely that Grant and Lincoln learned their lessons better than did Lee and Davis.

Lee represented the zenith of antebellum military professionalism, and his strengths and weaknesses were in some ways characteristic of the American military professionals of that time. A superb tactician and leader of men, Lee was less adept at both the operational and strategic levels. His natural aggressiveness as much as his dedication to the idea of the decisive Napoleonic battle got away from him, as at Gettysburg, and it may have blinded him to the option of the Confederacy pursuing a more Fabian approach, as the forces under General Joseph E. Johnston had in Tennessee.[32] In his personal dignity and uprightness, in his devotion to duty and concern for others, Lee exemplified the terms of honor of his time. His desertion of the Union for the lesser cause of the Confederacy is understandable in the context of the time, but it highlights the failure of the prewar military academy and officer corps to develop sufficient cohesion to overcome regional rifts. Secession had long been anticipated, and the assumption that Southern officers would leave the army if it came had never been challenged, their oath to the Constitution notwithstanding.[33] Divisions in the country were neither strictly North/South nor Blue/Gray. McClellan and a coterie of conservative officers favored more modest war objectives that would have left slavery intact. McClellan's uniformed politicking and unseemly bid for the presidency probably represent the nearest to praetorianism that the United States had come since the end of the Revolution. The uniformed soldier who perhaps best understood the war in its moral dimensions was not a West Pointer but a professor and graduate of Bowdoin College in Maine. Joshua Chamberlain was an amateur who rose to the rank of major general in the course of a wartime career that was distinguished by brilliant and fearless combat leadership, and by humanity and magnanimity in both adversity and victory. After the war, Chamberlain wanted to write a history of V Corps, the organization to which his own 20th Maine and subsequent commands belonged. Eventually, when he was in his eighties, he settled for writing an account of the final weeks of the war, culminating in his selection by General Grant to receive the Confederate surrender on 12 April at Appomattox, and his famous rendering of honors to the defeated Southerners. Chamberlain is Lincolnesque in combining a conciliatory stance toward the Confederacy balanced with an appreciation for the moral import of the Union cause and the issue of slavery.

Not only did the amateurs best the professionals in the Civil War, the nonmilitary factors of population and productivity were decisive as well. Again the knight had been shown to be just one piece in the bloody game. The professional legacy of the Civil War was a complex mixture of valuable lessons, misperceptions, and denial. Some European officers and even some Americans considered it too much of an exception for lessons or imitation. The elder Helmuth Graf von Moltke is alleged to have dismissed it as a clash of armed mobs, which has suggested to some that he perhaps lost interest after the First Battle of Bull Run. Change did occur rapidly after 1865. The Civil War was the last stand of the muzzle-loader; within a few years all advanced armies had adopted breech-loading rifles and artillery.

For a time Lee and the Confederates were the favored professional model from the Civil War. British officer education was especially enamored of Andrew Jackson's Shenandoah campaign, in part because of the very popular Jackson biography by the British officer George Francis Henderson, who taught at Sandhurst and the Staff College.[34] British major general J. F. C. Fuller rated Grant over Lee in his joint biography of the two generals, but the example of Lee and his officers tended to reinforce the aristocratic image beloved of European officers into the twentieth century and in some ways still at the heart of officership even in democratic countries. More officers on the side of the South fit the Cavalier model. The less colorful and less conspicuously upper-class officers on the Union side, typified by the unostentatious Ulysses S. Grant, more resembled the Roundhead commanders, who had been an anomaly among the royalty-serving officers of Britain and elsewhere in Europe. Lee's preference for the set-piece battle rather than economic or attritional warfare also reinforced the preferred interpretation of the Napoleonic legacy.[35]

The Franco-Prussian War

The Franco-Prussian War ended the Second French Empire and united the German Empire, also known as the Second Reich. The political implications of these developments would be considerable and even catastrophic. France, stung by defeat and by the loss of both imperial status and significant territory, would be bent on revenge until hostilities were recommenced in 1914. If defeat was unkind to the French, robbing them of a sense of proportion and stirring in them mostly unearned feelings of outraged innocence, victory was worse for the Germans, who, guided by an unstable monarch, would give free rein to a mixture of pride and paranoia in foreign policy. On the level of military professionalism, the war had a number of important consequences. The popularity of French military fashion and practice ended, and German style and methods became the thing. Armies hastened to create their own version of the general staff, and they adopted various forms of conscription and the reserve system that had given the Germans an advantage in trained manpower. In Europe, Britain would be the exception and would continue to rely on both a small volunteer active army and reserve and, like Athens in its day, on its fleet to provide security, although by the 1870s the protective naval wall was more of steel than of wood.

Historian Michael Howard views the victory of the Prussians over the French as being a result of the former's greater ability to adapt to "industrial changes and scientific discoveries."[36] An important aspect of these changes was the improvement in weapons and resultant increase in firepower. In fact, both armies went to war without a sufficient understanding of how much the increase in infantry firepower called for changes in tactics. Both sides began the war using close formations for charging infantry and expecting the cavalry to play a decisive offensive role on the battlefield, as it had to varying degrees since the time of Alexander. The Prussians, but not the French, by 1870 had realized the potential for the new breech-loading and rifled artillery. The Prussians' operational-level edge was in their employment of the railroad and the telegraph. There are a number of reasons why the Prussians were in a position to grasp this advantage. The first was that an examination of the map by the topographical experts on the general staff had revealed the potential impact of the railroad. The railroads could give the Prussians, especially acting in concert with the other German states, the ability to mobilize and attack quickly, taking advantage of a central location as Frederick and Napoleon had done, but now speeded by the new technology. The Prussians fought brief, victorious wars with the Danes in 1864 and the Austrians in 1866, and this experience had been valuable as training and practice. The regular French army had plentiful combat experience, but most of it had been away from Europe in France's overseas Asian and African empire against non-European foes. It had taught them nothing about the problems of mobilizing on their own borders and little more about the capabilities of an enemy army equipped with modern weapons in large-scale combat.

Both sides at least had access to the same or similar technology. Perhaps the most important and essential advantages the Prussians enjoyed over the French were more intellectual and cognitive than purely technical. As in the period after Frederick in the eighteenth century, the Prussian army had undergone a degree of decline in the years after Napoleon, with the aging officer corps and diminished sense of urgency in training that come with a long period of peace. However, the Prussian monarch in the years leading up to unification in 1871 was a soldier-king who took an active and informed interest in the army and the officer corps in particular throughout his reign. William I saw the army as playing a key role in state formation, both by challenging other claimants to European military dominance and by acting as a symbol of unity and leadership.[37] William shared the narrowness of his milieu, but in military matters he was committed and knowledgeable. In 1862, over the objections of liberals, parliamentarians, and even some officers such as Minister of War General Eduard von Bonin, Otto von Bismarck finally secured for him the three-year mandatory service and larger establishment that William considered vital.

The Prussian military profession also enjoyed the advantage of its own unique prestige, and it attracted some of the brightest as well as the highborn. Some of these men became distinguished military historians and theoreticians as well as proficient commanders and staff officers. One of the most brilliant officers of this period was the Danish-born Helmuth Graf von Moltke, who served as army chief of staff from 1858 to 1888. Once he had somewhat reluctantly settled on a military career (he had hoped to become a university professor), Moltke transferred from the Danish to the Prussian service. As staff officer and chief of staff, Moltke helped to revive the intellectual and humanistic tradition of Scharnhorst and Clausewitz, whose works he is credited with reintroducing to the officers of his time. Moltke is remembered as having read the minimum number of military books while at the War College, preferring works on geography, language, and literature.[38] Under Moltke's leadership the general staff grew in importance and assumed an independent influence on operations. The general staff also took control of the War College, thereby putting itself in a position to dictate how its own members would be selected and trained. Officers of the caliber and education of Moltke ensured that the Prussian army was a learning organization that was in a position to act on what it learned. The Germans went into their war with France with some understanding of the importance of the telegraph as a means of communication, but when they realized early in the conflict that the allocated means did not match the demand for telegraph communication, they quickly provided additional resources.[39] The classically educated general staff officers perhaps had recalled the military advantages of the Roman road system in appreciating the importance of railways. Prussian railways close to the frontiers were constructed with military use as the primary consideration. Moltke and his officers grasped the significance of the railroad for offense and for defense as a means of supply and troop transport. Moltke even saw that the placement of rail lines could take precedence over the siting of fortresses, so vital was the railroad to modern warfare.[40]

The increased authority and autonomy of the general staff, along with their international reputation for near infallibility after the Franco-Prussian victory, perpetuated a powerful force multiplier for the armed forces of a

Germany united in 1871. Some of the drawbacks of so potent a weapon being placed in the hands of an ambitious and even reckless new empire have already been noted. Although he was a devotee of Clausewitz who grasped many of the ideas of *On War*, Moltke passed on to his successors almost a complete reversal of Clausewitz's central idea that war was politics pursued by other means. Moltke insisted that military officers alone should determine military strategy, with minimum input from civilian ministers. This was held to be true especially in time of war, but also during preparations for war. His belief was in part a reflection of Moltke's great faith in the abilities of the general staff officer.[41] With their lengthy and rigorous training, great prestige, and record of success, it may be easy to see why he placed such confidence in the abilities of these Neoplatonic state guardians. The government ministers in frock coats did not have the same intensive preparation, nor did they possess the same shared methodology or corporate sense. The officers, even the cultivated ones like Moltke, inhabited the limited physical and mental horizons of field army, War College, and general staff headquarters, and their perspective would remain continental and almost purely military. This limited perspective would be reinforced by the history of the Second Reich. Germany came late to colonialism and an investment in sea power. When the time came for general staff officers to think in terms of combined operations or larger national objectives, their elaborate schooling failed them. Thanks to the structure of Prussian and German society and the traditions forged by monarchs like Frederick and William, the German army would also remain deeply unfriendly to democratic ideas as well as conditioned to obey the orders of one man—the head of state—who was always to some degree a soldier.

Although the perceptions of German officers were somewhat blinkered (while they could still be penetrating and even brilliant), officers of the Second French Empire were often ignorant and even illiterate.[42] They had no organized intellectual elite like the Prussian General Staff with the ability and authority to plan and to solve problems. As a group they had difficulty understanding the challenges and opportunities posed by the new technology and the danger posed by a focused professional organization like the Prussian army and its general staff, although Prussia's victory over Austria in 1866 alerted some among the French to the danger they faced. Recognizing that the use of reserve forces had been important in that outcome, the French attempted to revive and replace the old Garde Nationale of prerevolutionary origin with a Garde Mobile.[43] The reforms resulted in an increase in numbers on paper, but the French did not allocate sufficient time or resources to train and equip the reserve forces. The French did acquire a breech-loading rifle, the *chassepot*, that was superior to the German Dreyse needle gun. The newer weapon used a rubber washer to contain propellant gases, increasing the range considerably and reducing the effect of escaped gases on the shooter. The French also fielded a rapid-firing, multibarrel gun, the *mitrailleuse*. Between these technological advances and their record of military achievement, the French were able to convince themselves that they could win a war against a Prussian alliance that both sides saw as inevitable. They were mistaken.

An outstanding exception to the incuriousness and anti-intellectualism of the French officer corps was Colonel Ardant du Picq, a veteran of the Crimea and Syria, who was killed in action on 15 August 1870 while serving in command of an infantry regiment. His book, *Battle Studies*, compiled posthumously from notes and an outline, begins with a review of ancient and recent military history. [44] But du Picq is mostly concerned with the problems of command and cohesion resulting from the increased range and accuracy in firepower on the part of the infantry and artillery. Greater ranges and lethality would call for greater dispersion, expanding the battlefield and stretching the distances over which men would have to communicate—to give, relay, and receive commands. The new weapons would also place units under fire earlier in an advance, and at close ranges units would be subjected to unprecedented amounts of fire, so the exposure to fire would be greater in both duration and intensity. The battlefield was becoming a more confusing and terrifying place, a place combining prolonged exposure to fear and fire mixed with sudden surprises and death from afar and unseen. To the certainty of facing a deadly foe were added multiple uncertainties, because the enemy could now strike long before revealing himself, and even the forces on one's own side would be out of sight, widely dispersed and going to ground, difficult to control, and offering none of the moral support of visible comrades.

Du Picq believed that soldiers in all times had been able to endure only a certain amount of terror before breaking, and that under exposure to modern firepower, units would melt away unless tactics were adapted. More than tactics, the means of unit cohesion would have to change; the bonds among men must be made more flexible to prevent them from breaking. The pressures on each individual are greater in modern warfare, and this calls for training that realistically anticipates the demands of combat. Du Picq was also concerned that the martial spirit of his countrymen was unequal to that of the Prussians, and the Franco-Prussian War perhaps proved that his doubts were justified. Du Picq foresaw a need to reevaluate not tactics and training alone but the ethos of the soldier itself, stressing individual initiative and a kind of moral self-sufficiency. He left behind a succinct, memorable admonition: "To verify, observe better. To demonstrate, try out and describe better. To organize, distribute better, bearing in mind that cohesion means discipline."[45] Like Montesquieu and the other Enlightenment reformers, and the Prussians reacting to Napoleon, du Picq called for military reform, but also for a change in social ethos and organization.

The Colonial Military Experience

The British and the French were the major colonizers and colonial soldiers during the nineteenth century. The British were largely consolidating, policing, and maintaining their holdings in India and Asia. The French were carving out their North African empire, and both countries, along with the Germans and Belgians, were making a grab for land in sub-Saharan Africa in the latter part of the century. Unlike their predecessors of the eighteenth century, nineteenth-century colonial soldiers began to enjoy a marked technological advantage over local forces in the form of breech-loading rifles and artillery and, eventually, fast-firing, fully automatic weapons: machine guns. They also generally had better organization, discipline, and logistics, although this could be a critical challenge in remote areas and across rugged, inhospitable terrain. In general, nineteenth-century colonial soldiers were masters of the battlefield and of the campaign. The larger, more complex matter of developing stable, secure, and reasonably productive colonies was more elusive, requiring soldiers and civic administrators to acquire a complex mix of skills and to institutionalize them through doctrine and education.[46] This challenge would be more fully addressed in the twentieth century, although even before World War II the European colonial empires were starting to come under a wave of cultural and political self-consciousness among the colonized peoples that no amount of military professionalism could likely have defeated or redirected. It must also be said that the colonial empires have had a long, rich afterlife in which their militaries have played an important role. This can be seen in the organization and service cultures of existing military institutions in the former colonies; in the numbers of seconded individuals, deployed units, and permanent outposts of former empire found in ex-colonies; and in the role of European militaries in training and educating Third World military officers.

Among the most impressive accomplishments of colonizing soldiers of this period was the creation of cross-cultural military organizations such as the British Gurkhas and the French Spahis. The rank and file of these units was made up of natives of the colonized regions. Senior officers were Europeans, but locals did occupy some officer and the noncommissioned officer positions. The training, organization, cultures, and calendars of these units required a degree of knowledge and sensitivity on the part of their European officers. For pragmatic reasons, European officers were expected to master the language of the country and to respect its customs and religion. The cultures of these hybrid military organizations were often a dynamic fusion of imported and home-grown beliefs and practices. Most colonized countries had indigenous military traditions, and wise European officers made use of these rather than merely supplanting them with European practice.[47] The Europeans contributed organization, weapons, and tactics; the local cultures provided martial traditions, religious beliefs, and social and familial ties that could contribute to fighting spirit and unit cohesion. The local soldiers also often brought formidable individual fighting skills such as the deadly use of the Gurkha *khukuri*, a knife made for throat cutting and decapitating. In addition to such cross-cultural military units were other units comprised entirely of Europeans that specialized in colonial operations and rarely served in Europe. Some of the colonial units have survived into the present day; a Gurkha brigade still serves in the British Army, and the French Foreign Legion survives as a colorful and militarily effective anachronism.

The home military educational establishments tended to ignore the colonial experience. Napoleon, Frederick, Jomini, and to an extent Lee and Jackson continued to be the exemplars and teachers.[48] As a result, some soldiers arrived at their colonial station with little knowledge of the local climate, hazards to health, and tactical conditions; they were, as Rudyard Kipling says, "frequent deceased." The military academies' neglect of the survivors' hard-won knowledge deprived the services of much of the institutional memory that might have been of benefit to future generations. Fortunately, some of the colonial soldiers wrote books, and these helped to preserve a record of the colonial military experience and to educate soldiers who were fighting in colonial or counterinsurgency wars.

From the standpoint of professional education, British colonel Charles Edward Callwell's *Small Wars: Their Principles and Practice* (1896) was one of the best on the subject. Callwell's book is based on wide reading and on his own extensive service. Most of *Small Wars* is concerned with tactics, which Callwell categorizes by types of terrain, arms of the service, and the nature of the adversary. He also gives advice on supply, intelligence, and communications. Callwell is most concerned with removing impediments to battle, since his experience and reading had taught him that regular forces almost always have a tactical advantage over locals, even if the latter possess modern organization and equipment. Callwell shows insight into the psychology of indigenous fighters and of the colonial troops operating in a strange country. His well-informed and concise analysis of fighting methods in small wars has continued to have an influence that is not always recognized. When some U.S. Marine Corps officers assembled at Quantico, Virginia, in the late 1930s to write a guidebook based on their service in the Caribbean, they titled the work *Small Wars Manual*, and it owes a considerable (although unacknowledged) debt to its eponymous ancestor.[49]

America after the Civil War

While European armies were subduing and policing their overseas colonial empires, the U.S. Army was engaged in similar activities on the American western frontier. The open, symmetrical battles of the Civil War had perhaps been poor preparation for this role. In the West the army gained experience of counterinsurgency that would be useful when the United States acquired its own overseas empire as a result of the Spanish-American War in 1898, and later when U.S. forces in the twentieth century were deployed in Central America and the Caribbean to enforce stability and to protect U.S. economic interests. The American Indian Wars themselves were bloody and brutal on both sides. Native Americans and American soldiers had completely different ideas about how war should be conducted, and outrage on both sides over departures from these ideas often brought on mutual escalation. The two sides learned from each other, and often what they learned was the brand of atrocity favored by the other side. Some Native American tribes saw no crime in the torture of captives and mutilation of the dead. Army soldiers sometimes responded in kind. The opening of the West translated quickly to the dispossession and extermination of the previous owners. Some soldiers saw themselves as Indian hunters. The period bred tough, even brutal campaigners such as George Armstrong Custer and Nelson A. Miles who saw the Native Americans as quarry, but the Army also protected Native Americans and their treaty rights from efforts to exploit or infringe on them, fulfilling a role that might be described today as peacekeeping; and some officers acquired the same quasi-anthropological, juridical, and negotiating skills as other colonial soldiers.

The role of the Army officer as explorer and cultural expert perhaps began with the Corps of Discovery led by Captain Meriwether Lewis and Lieutenant William Clark from 1804 to 1806. As a junior officer in the antebellum Army of the West, George Thomas collected samples of plants and animals that he shared with eastern botanists and zoologists. He even wrote a dictionary of a Native American language that ethnologists still value.[50] Lieutenant John C. Frémont became known as "the Pathfinder" in the 1840s. Other officers explored the new lands too, often traveling with civilian scientists, scholars, and artists.[51] This was especially the case for expeditions conducted by officers, like Frémont, of the Corps of Topographical Engineers. The corps and the antebellum Smithsonian Institution maintained a close relationship through the institution's assistant secretary, Spencer Baird, the son-in-law of an army colonel. Among the most accomplished officer-naturalists was James W. Albert, a graduate of both Princeton University and West Point, who continued his naturalist studies and writings after retiring as a result of wounds suffered toward the end of the Civil War.[52]

In addition to gaining experience in combat, peacekeeping, and exploration, the U.S. Army of the later nineteenth century underwent a professional renaissance at the doctrinal level and in the area of advanced professional education. Intellectual officers such as Emory Upton and Arthur Wagner led an effective reform movement. Wanting to ensure that the hard-won lessons of the Civil War would not be lost, Upton wrote a drill manual in 1867 that called for a departure from the tactics of close-order formations that had been the Army's written doctrine. The manual was adopted for the Army by a board headed by Ulysses S. Grant, and it went into several editions.[53] The essence of Uptonian infantry tactics was the single, extended line of breechloader-armed riflemen. Upton also worked on "assimilated" tactics that created common commands and formations for the infantry, artillery, and cavalry. This and some of his later work contributed to an early stage in the development of the combined-arms techniques that would revolutionize warfare in the twentieth century and finally provide a solution to the dilemma posed by the successive increases in firepower. On orders from Army commander William T. Sherman, Upton embarked on a grand tour to assess military institutions around the world, with particular emphasis on the recently victorious German army. He became an admirer of the German General Staff, arguing against civilian control and in favor of greater military autonomy on the German model. His writing, perhaps most notably the posthumously published *Military Policy of the United States*, influenced the thinking of American officers for years to come. Some of Upton's readers would continue to cherish the hope that the uniformed military could achieve greater autonomy. This idea would culminate in the unification debates of the post–World War II period when senior officers of the Army who had been raised on Upton's writings would reimagine a united military organization with greater independence from civilian control.

One solid accomplishment of Upton and the other progressive officers of his day was the institution of advanced education for officers. This began with the School for Infantry and Cavalry (its name is reminiscent of that of the school the young Clausewitz attended early in the century), founded in 1881, which evolved into the Command and General Staff College. It was established at Fort Leavenworth, Kansas, which became the center of professional education for the U.S. Army. The School for Infantry and Cavalry began as a rather pedestrian institution for lieutenants, combining instruction in minor tactics and garrison routines with a remedial program in reading and writing.[54] The haphazard conception of the dour, by now aged, and perhaps war-burdened brain of William T. Sherman, the school curriculum was in effect a concession to mediocrity. It languished but began to see improvement in 1886 with the arrival of a new commandant and a young instructor named Arthur Wagner, who would go on to play a significant role in the reform of the Army over the coming decades. Wagner was a follower of Upton, but he showed a greater sense of the need to adapt European ideas to the New World, and even for America to develop its own military institutions without deference to Europe. In his first book, *The Campaign of Koniggratz*, written as a lieutenant, he puts the Prussian military reputation in perspective, pointing out errors in tactics that might have been avoided by the adoption of practices developed in the Civil War, and also noting the small geographical scale of the Franco-Prussian War, fought, Wagner says, over a space about half the size of Kansas![55] The schools at Leavenworth followed the German example in adopting war gaming and tactical exercises, sometimes over the objections of conservatives who preached that only war could be a school for war. The Army also embraced training for accurate marksmanship with contests, prizes, badges, and even extra pay for proficient marksmen. The period after the Civil War also saw a large increase in the number of military journals such as the *Journal of the Military Service Institution* and the *Journal of the Cavalry Association* that relieved some of the personal and professional isolation many Army officers stationed at small posts throughout the West experienced.

Considering the appeal and circulation of Upton's ideas, it is interesting to speculate why America never had to face, then or since, any realistic concerns over an assumption of power by its military. It is tempting to point to a Constitution that limits soldiers' ability to assume power short of an actual coup d'état, and to a constitutional oath that strengthens what is perhaps a deep cultural and psychological attachment to the authority of the civil government over the armed forces. The subjection of soldiers to civil authority is perhaps a limit to the complete fulfillment of the kind of autonomy that distinguishes an acknowledged profession, but all professions face limits on their exercise of autonomy. Physicians do not determine national healthcare policy. Neither lawyers (unless they are also legislators) nor even judges make the law. Soldiers may decide how but not when or whether armed force is to be applied, although this is no simple formula.

The Spanish-American War and the Philippines

Like the Crimean War, the Spanish-American War revealed both the capabilities and the limitations of a strong nation projecting military power against the periphery of another nation inferior in economic and military power. Both wars were undertaken by the eventual victors for questionable causes in climates of popular hysteria; both ultimately advanced the overseas strategic ambitions of at least some victorious national policy makers and opinion shapers; and both contributed to effective military reform.

When the United States decided to invade Cuba in 1898, it found itself unable to invade even the neighboring outpost of a dying empire without raising a large volunteer force to supplement the small Regular Army. The U.S. Navy, on the other hand, having benefited from a professional and technological revival over the previous couple of decades, was the master of the seas. Whenever Spanish naval forces came out to give battle, either in the Caribbean or in Manila Bay off the coast of the Philippines, the Americans were one-sided victors. On land and in the transition from sea to land the contest was more equal. Amphibious operations in Cuba were fortunately unopposed, since even light resistance could have caused serious problems for the amateurish landing arrangements. On land, the American weapons were often inferior to those of the Spanish, who had the benefit of some of the latest German technology in the form of Mauser rifles and Krupp artillery. Reminiscent of the Napoleonic Wars veterans in the Crimea, some senior American officers were aging Civil War holdovers who were notably past their prime. It made no difference in the outcome. The Americans were clearly cast in the role of victors. The Spanish, with no hope of support from home or from the Cubans, were fighting a forlorn rearguard action on behalf of an empire that had outlasted the gold that once sustained it. Spanish forces fought for a time and then surrendered both in Cuba and in the Philippines. In Spain the defeat set off a generation of self-examination on the part of a group of young writers called "The Generation of '98."

For America, the war resulted in the instant acquisition of an overseas colonial empire, along with the revelation that its own Army was insufficient for the task of securing, policing, or protecting the new territories. The United States needed a bigger, better Army in order to play the role of world power for which it appeared to be grooming itself. Stephen Crane, already famous for his novel *The Red Badge of Courage* (1895), experienced war for the first time in Cuba and had high praise for the fighting qualities of the American regular, but there simply were not enough of them. In a short time the size of the Army was doubled. Conceptually as well as in numbers, the Army had to adapt and expand. An opportunity to do so arose out of challenges in the Philippines. Some Filipinos considered the Americans simply another, equally unwelcome colonial power like the Spanish and wanted them gone immediately. The American government was paternalistically unconvinced that the Philippines were ready for self-rule after nearly four hundred years of colonial domination, and anyway wanted to secure the strategic advantages of a base in the western Pacific. The difference in views quickly led to war in the archipelago. The war between the Filipino insurgents and the American armed forces, like the American Indian Wars, was often brutal on both sides, with the indigenous population paying the price of being in the way and having nowhere to go. Eventually, the American military command and the isolated units of soldiers and Marines evolved a policy of "attraction" that emphasized the benefits of a continuing American presence rather than the consequences of noncooperation.

Historian John M. Gates notes that the American military, led by General Arthur MacArthur, whose son would one day fulfill his promise to return to the Philippines after being ejected by the Japanese, was more committed to the policy of attraction than was the appointed political leadership on the islands.[56] William Howard Taft combined a patronizing attitude toward the Filipinos with a preference for repressive tactics against the insurgents. Eventually the Army's policy won favor and succeeded, with the aristocratic and humane MacArthur in the role of a latter-day Duke of Parma. The Philippine Insurrection was the first of a series of large-scale counterinsurgencies that would form an important backdrop to the twentieth-century experience of the American military profession. Although the world wars went on to define doctrine and expectation, the U.S. armed forces continue to find themselves involved in counterinsurgency, requiring rapid adaptation and the renewal of old institutional knowledge.

Navies and Navalism

The nineteenth century saw the most significant developments in naval technology certainly up to that time, and perhaps in all of history. The long reign of the sailing vessel came to an end. Steam power was being used to supplement sail by mid-century; steam became steadily more efficient, and before the end of the century it had replaced sails altogether on warships. Vessel hulls went from wood to iron to steel by the 1870s. Rifled breech-loading guns replaced muzzle-loaders, and shells replaced solid shot and grapeshot.

Conservative navy officers, seeing their hard-won knowledge being rendered irrelevant, and distrusting (with some justification) the dependability and sustainability of steam especially, resisted change for a time, but as a new generation of officers entered the naval services, men raised with the mid-century belief in the capabilities of the machine—and as the technology improved—navies that could afford to do so changed rapidly and often to keep pace with developments. Those who were less economically endowed, like the Spanish, and forced to stay with last year's technology learned that they were bound for defeat if they hazarded their ships in battle. The new navies were dependent on coal and coaling stations (which gave an additional incentive to colonial expansion), but they were much less vulnerable to the elements and were able to come and go reliably and on schedule in all but the worst weather. No longer would blockading fleets be wrecked by keeping too close to coastlines; nor would ships have to refuse battle because of an enemy's wind advantage, or have their progress halted by unfavorable or nonexistent winds. The improved maneuverability and protection of the new vessels and the increased range of their weapons overturned Nelson's dictum that a ship was a fool to fight a fort. Masonry coastal forts like those built to protect the American Eastern Seaboard were rendered obsolete. Almost coincidentally with the increase in the war-fighting potential of navies, the prestige of a naval career in Europe and in America also rose. The conspicuous service in naval uniform of a number of members of the European royalty added an extra cachet.[57]

With their strict hierarchies of space (the wardroom and "officers' country"), naval vessels would continue to lend themselves to sharp distinctions in rank, especially between officers and enlisted men. Steam power and steel hulls also meant that the naval officer was now less a technical sailor and more a combat leader and war fighter, because the propulsion of steam vessels was left to a separate, lower class of engineering officers. Officers no longer had to master the complexities of extensive sails and rigging or to be as mindful of the vagaries of the sea, but could now devote more of their attention to weapons and tactics. Steam even contributed to a brief revival of the ram, since steam power in effect recaptures the control that is possible with an oared galley. (Rams are obviously impractical on sailing vessels.) For the rest of the century, however, and until the ascendency of the carrier aircraft and the deck-launched missile, the naval officer's primary obsession would be with gunnery. At the strategic level, fleets and navies became more reliably subject to command (the use of the telegraph of course aided in this) and therefore more effective as armed proponents of state policy. Navies were now more in the category of *ultima ratio regis*, and earthly rulers no longer had to share them with Neptune's wind and tide.

In addition to technological advancements, increased capability, and a change in naval professional identity (and partly in response to them), navies developed conceptually, doctrinally, and in the area of professional education. The late-nineteenth-century prophets of sea power were Alfred Thayer Mahan and Julian Corbett. Mahan was a serving U.S. Navy officer with no great fondness for the sea when he began writing. His books were based on historical research, but their main purpose was not so much to give a historical account as to present an argument for the unacknowledged importance of sea power. Mahan also developed a particular approach to naval strategy that essentially went against America's long dedication to the *guerre de course*: the naval war of small engagements, of patrolling frigates rather than battling ships of the line. The time appeared right for Mahan's ideas. America now had not just trade routes and coastlines, but also an overseas empire to protect. In addition to viewing the sea as consisting of routes linking destinations, Mahan also saw it as a "great common," an expansive space for maneuver and struggle that was neither limited by the fragility, weather dependency, and narrow communications range and resources of the old sailing vessels, nor hemmed by the boundaries, terrain, cities, and forts of the land. Mahan was all in favor of big ships in fleets to ensure—and if necessary enforce—freedom of the seas. Theodore Roosevelt, then Secretary of the Navy, read Mahan's 1890 *The Influence of Sea Power upon History* over the course of a weekend at Sagamore Hill in Oyster Bay. He corresponded with the author and never again was out from under Mahan's influence—nor was the U.S. Navy. A later Secretary of the Navy once wrote that on entering Navy Headquarters in Washington he had the sense of entering a "religious world" where "Neptune was God, Mahan his prophet, and the U.S. Navy was the one true church."[58]

Mahan may have oversold his ideas; nevertheless, he constructed a strong narrative of historical progress that was almost Marxian in its sweeping scope and ability to win converts. He developed an idea of sea power that was based in history yet still seemed appropriate and timely given the new capabilities of steam navies with armor plate and powerful weapons. Indeed, underlying Mahan's claims for sea power, a historical theory that might be called "navalism," was a concept of national destiny. For Mahan, maritime nations Britain and America were destined by geography and national character to dominate the globe. Mahan's ideas represented a significant development in the intellectual history of the naval profession. His writing legitimized historical study as a means to develop ideas about naval policy and maritime strategy. His idea of the "great common" also moved the thinking of naval officers from a mostly linear outlook to a more fully two-dimensional perspective. As we shall see, however, even this enlarged view would soon fall behind the times.

The Englishman Julian Corbett, whose writing is less sweeping and captivating than that of Mahan, was more alert to detail, exceptions, and change. Unlike Mahan, Corbett saw the value in smaller vessels and supporting operations, such as the amphibious landing, which Mahan tended to see as distractions. He was also quicker than Mahan to recognize that emerging technologies such as the self-propelled torpedo and the submarine presented threats and competition to the capital ships. The submarine literally added another dimension to the cognitive space required of naval officers, who for the first time had to consider the ocean deep as a tactical domain, not just a place of mystery and fate.

Together, the writings of Mahan and Corbett gave naval officers a sense of calling and intellectual respectability. This was furthered by the advent of advanced professional education for naval officers. In 1885 the Naval War College opened in Newport, Rhode Island, under Commodore Stephen B. Luce, a Civil War veteran who had pushed for the establishment of such a school. On the faculty were Mahan (his fame as a writer still in the future) and Army lieutenant Tasker Bliss, who would head the Army War College when it was founded in 1901.[59] The Naval War College not only educated students in naval war fighting, but from early on it also helped to develop tactics and strategic plans (to include some of those for the Spanish-American War) through war gaming and research.

"The Martial Spirit"

By the end of the nineteenth century a combination of politics, culture, technology, and ideology was creating an enthusiasm for military matters

and even for the prospect of war that likely astonishes us today. The griev-
ances and aggrieved pride of France, Germany, and Japan; the territorial
ambitions of these nations and of the United States; and the broad, jealously
guarded holdings and prestige of the British Empire had all encouraged the
idea that war was a necessary means to ensure their own advancement and
to thwart that of their rivals. The growth of cities, literacy, and print media
(the newspaper and other forms of popular press) had provided the means to
fan patriotic enthusiasm and sway the population for a national cause. The
new technology had provided opportunities for spectacle: the launching of
impressive warships and the demonstration of new and powerful weapons.
Coronations, inaugurations, royal weddings, and state funerals were among
the premier forms of public spectacle, competing with sports and the stage
in a time before film or radio. Nationalism, imperialism, militarism, and
navalism, combined with a long period of peace in Europe, contributed to
the martial spirit of the age.[60]

Life for many had become rather grim and static after a century of postwar reaction and industrialization, and the pageantry of nationalism and
the promise of change, or at least a break in the monotony, made the idea
of war attractive. Starting to have an influence on popular thought too were
contemporary philosophical ideas. Those of Darwin and of Nietzsche in
particular were distorted to serve bellicose ends.[61] The urge for war was not
limited to nationalists or the political right wing. Some on the left saw war
as a necessary quick fix, a way to purge and punish society for its crimes
and inequities. Perhaps the most militant and militaristic of the leading
Communists was Friedrich Engels, a Prussian army veteran and self-taught
strategist whose preference for a military solution to the class struggle may
have been fueled by a desire to put his considerable military knowledge into
practice.[62] His hope for societal change through open class warfare was
unfulfilled in his lifetime, but it was a dream that lasted into the twentieth
century.

Not all soldiers or sailors embraced the nationalistic, militaristic, or
navalistic creeds that were abroad in the nineteenth century. Some adopted
or entertained socialist ideas, even manning the revolutionary barricades in
1848 or during the Paris Commune in 1871. Soldiers of all ages have had the
benefit of experiences that tend to make them skeptical of slogans or simple formulas for complex situations. The elder Moltke warned the German

Reichstag that a European war might last as long as seven or even thirty years, adding, "Woe betide him who sets Europe ablaze."[63] President Grant, in his memoirs, is highly critical of the Mexican War. In 1871, as commander of the British Staff College, Edward Hamley wrote in opposition to the narrow nationalism that was dominant in his own time and country.[64] Later, U.S. Marine major general Smedley Butler wrote a book recanting his own soldiering in support of American economic interests in the Caribbean. Some soldiers undoubtedly saw nationalism and its stepchildren as giving greater justification and scope for the exercise of their profession. Bigger armies and war would offer opportunities for advancement and a chance for some men to emerge from the obscurity of service in a small peacetime army to exercise command in combat and show off their abilities on a large public stage. Whether soldiers adopted the xenophobic or belligerent tendencies of the age or not, as prevalent ideas they would influence how soldiers fought, along with the causes and casualties of the wars in the coming century.

Japan

The opening of an initially reluctant Japan through the intervention of a small American naval squadron under the command of Commodore Matthew C. Perry in 1854 began the process of Japan's modernization and entry onto the world stage. The Japanese armed forces were quick to see the superiority of Western military technology and methods. They employed European military officers as instructors, bought modern weapons, and adopted conscription and a German-style general staff. The Japanese had a potent military tradition that they were able to adapt to a modern force. In modernized Japan every man became a samurai, the figure that for centuries had been Japan's cultural ideal. This proved to be dangerously intoxicating. The original Bushido code of the feudal military had possessed considerable elements of humanity and compassion, but the humane and poetic side of the code was largely lost as it was simplified for use in an aggressively nationalistic conscript army.[65] The new Japanese army owed direct loyalty to the emperor. Every military command was to be considered an imperial edict. The simplified version of Bushido and the cult of obedience to the emperor for whom all one's military superiors spoke as if ex cathedra mixed all too well with the militarism and authoritarianism that were growing in Europe. The concept was given added kick by the racism that had grown out of the European colonizing experience, the presumption of European and Caucasian superiority that the proud Japanese, and others, would find so galling and provocative. In the coming century, the ethics and tactics of the Japanese army would devolve into greater and greater intransigence and unreality, until Japan's armed forces would almost come to seem a force bent on self-immolation rather than on victory or even honorable defeat.

The Nineteenth-Century Laws of War

The nineteenth century saw the origin of efforts to write international law that would regulate the conduct of states, armies, and soldiers engaged in armed conflict. It also saw the founding of international organizations, most notably the Red Cross, whose mission was to limit the suffering caused by war, and sometimes to rebuke those who overstepped the bounds of acceptable belligerent behavior. Some people involved in these efforts hoped to abolish war entirely, or at least to radically limit the occasions of armed conflict. The peace movement had to compete with the nationalistic and belligerent tendencies of the era that have already been noted, and it must be said that it failed.[66] The more modest goal of restraining combatants from excessive violence and caring for those who suffered because of war was partially achieved, but perhaps at the cost of giving up the broadly pacifist and internationalist aspirations of the idealists. National Red Cross movements formed in effect separate, supporting branches of their countries' military establishments.

The nineteenth-century effort to compose written rules for the conduct of war began with the Lieber Code written in America during the Civil War. Although named and known for Francis Lieber, the Harvard legal scholar to whom Lincoln turned for a written code of conduct in war, General Henry Halleck assisted in drafting and implementing the code. President Lincoln signed it as General Order 100 in April 1863, and Halleck became Army chief of staff in 1864.[67] The code served as a model for codes of military conduct worldwide for years to come. Another significant written code was the first Geneva Convention of 1864. Inspired by Henri Dunant's memoir of the Battle of Solferino, the focus of the first convention was on care for the wounded.

The neglect of medical aid on the battlefield noted by Dunant and many others before him was the result of several factors. An army that had fought a battle was often on the move, either in pursuit or retreat, so by tactical necessity the soldiers on both sides had to simply leave their comrades on the field and perhaps hope that others would care for them.[68] The number of casualties after a large battle like Solferino simply overwhelmed the logistical and medical services of the armies in a premechanized and "pretherapeutic" era. Further, such casualties required evacuation and treatment at exactly the time of maximum physical and psychic exhaustion on the part of the combatants. The limited ability of medical science to alleviate pain and to treat certain types of wounds was another disincentive to rapid evacuation and treatment. Gunshot wounds to the abdomen, for example, if not immediately or quickly fatal, routinely resulted in terminal peritonitis. Finally, among military professionals the spectacle of wounded on the battlefield had come to be seen as part of a sublime landscape that included also the dead, wrecked and abandoned equipment, churned roads, and expended projectiles. If, as Shakespeare's Henry Percy Hotspur said, "dry with rage and extreme toil," they noted these sights at all, it was characteristic to do so in a spirit of elegy rather than of humanitarian activism. On the night after Waterloo, the intelligent and humane Captain Cavalié Mercer noted with pity the cries of the wounded, but it does not appear to have occurred to him to go to their aid.[69] It took the civilian banker Dunant to see clearly both the situation and the possibility of a solution. Soldiers did play a prominent role in the early international Red Cross organization, which was another direct result of the 1864 meeting in Geneva.[70] Swiss general Guillame-Henri Dufour, who served as an engineer under Napoleon, was on the Committee of Five that first put some of Dunant's ideas into practice. Dutch captain Charles van de Velde was one of the first Red Cross delegates to operate in the combat zone.

The Legacy

The nineteenth century is the period during which social scientists and many military historians credit the military occupation as fully graduating to the level of a profession. The institutions of the military were by now well established, complete with advanced education and a publishing industry devoted to military subjects. Like professional education, assignment and advancement were regularized and relatively free of the influences of birth and personal favoritism. Military professionals of this period dedicated lengthy careers to service that might combine prolonged absence from home with the dangers of adverse climate and exotic disease, added to the risks of combat and of capture by enemies with no tradition or means for humane captivity. They carved out and held overseas and frontier empires for governments to whom they remained subordinate and loyal over long distances that were geographical and to varying degrees cultural. For more than three decades after Waterloo, Europe itself was free of major combat operations, and even later in the century they were few and of limited extent and duration. The military profession of the nineteenth century also existed in a period of unprecedented and perhaps unequaled regard for professions in general. Military and naval officers were acknowledged as members of their professions, and they had credentials and affiliations that were similar to the members of other professions. When the time came for combat, for the most part they fought bravely, led from the front, and kept faith with their own codes of behavior.

The faithfulness of the military officers of this period became almost proverbial, if sentimentalized, in the work of contemporary writers Frederick Marryat (British naval officer and author of historical novels about the Royal Navy) and G. A. Henty (prolific writer, proselytizer for imperialism, and another British enthusiast for the Cavalier-like Confederacy). Soldiers benefited from the nineteenth-century "chivalric revival," which tended to enshrine the military occupation and to link modern soldiers to the traditions of knighthood. The novels of Alexander Dumas, himself the son of a general, depict French soldiers from the minor aristocracy as honorable and enterprising. The tradition of admiring literary works about officers and armies in the colonial enterprise continued into the next century with the work of A. W. Mason (who wrote *The Four Feathers* [1902]) and P. C. Wren (author of *Beau Geste* [1924] and its sequels). The Victorian poet and priest Gerard Manley Hopkins gives a more complex but still in its way reverent appraisal of the soldier in the octave of an unnamed sonnet (usually called "The Soldier" in published collections).

> *YES. Why do we áll, seeing of a soldier, bless him? Bless*
> *Our redcoats, our tars? Both these being, the greater part,*
> *But frail clay, nay but foul clay. Here it is: the heart,*
> *Since, proud, it calls the calling manly, gives a guess*
> *That, hopes that, makesbelieve, the men must be no less;*

It fancies, feigns, deems, dears the artist after his art;
And fain will find as sterling all as all is smart,
And scarlet wear the spirit of wár thére express.

The most famous literary exponent of the soldier in this period was unquestionably Nobel laureate Rudyard Kipling. Kipling is perhaps best known for his depictions of British privates and noncommissioned officers, but he also writes with insight about both junior and senior officers, and in a sense he depicts all ranks as members of a military profession by emphasizing their expertise, shared values, and reflections on the sometimes brutal business of the soldier. Kipling does not sentimentalize; in fact he has been accused (by George Orwell, himself something of a military enthusiast) of exaggerating the brutality of late Victorian military service.

Even if his scarlet, blue, or khaki coat concealed the "foul clay" of base habits and appetites, even criminal tendencies, the soldier was nevertheless a representative and revered figure in Europe, America, and elsewhere. Partly because they could manage such bestial soldiery as Kipling's Private Stanley Ortheris, nineteenth-century military officers secured a respectable and even honorable position in the public life of their time, as well as a place in the public and literary imagination. They played their part, and it might be said that they stayed in their lane. Civilians and members of a larger military profession outside the profession of arms were responsible for much of the advancements in knowledge, ethos, and organization, and they sometimes showed themselves to be more able strategists than the officers. Why? With all of their admirable qualities and accomplishments, what was lacking among the professional soldiers of this time? Certainly the fact that postgraduate military education was just beginning played a role in limiting officers' professional horizons. The conservatism of the age and the narrow segment of the population from which officers were typically drawn may also have had an influence. Officers could seem to embrace their own insularity. The most glaring example of this is likely the Dreyfus Affair in France (1894–1906), during which the officers of the French army closed ranks to resist public outrage over unfounded and even manufactured charges and conviction by court-martial for espionage against a Jewish captain of artillery. This cause célèbre brought into focus a degree of estrangement between much of French society and its military profession over issues of class, religion, and politics that would resurface in the twentieth century.

In his book *Little Wars*, H. G. Wells notes that the army officers who attempted the simple war game that he invented and describes in the book invariably had trouble grasping the rules. Wells concludes that British officers were generally less intelligent than their roles required ("the available heads . . . are too small").[71] Wells is not the first or last person to cast the slur of intellectual inferiority at soldiers, and at officers in particular. The younger sons of the upper and middle classes who joined the army tended to be less bookish and more athletic than their peers who entered the other traditional professions, as they likely have been in every age. This did not rule out many of them being very intelligent, and a few officers of each generation have been brilliantly intellectual and creative men like Scharnhorst, Clausewitz, Moltke, Upton, du Picq, and the young Winston Churchill. Aside from self-selection, however, the pursuit of the military profession can be limiting and even harmful to cerebral activity. The routines of garrison duty and the demands of campaigning can dull the mind and crowd out creativity with their petty detail, horrid scenes, and their physical and psychic toil and toll. The obverse of soldierly pride and esprit de corps can be distrust of people and even of ideas that do not come wrapped in a uniform. The military profession can also be a fatal one. Nolan and du Picq were both killed in action. Scharnhorst died of battle wounds. Clausewitz died on duty of cholera, perhaps (this is debated) before his great work was complete. Other soldiers may have been too worn-out, wounded, or traumatized to engage in the late-career reflection and writing that can help a profession to advance, or were killed before their potential could be known. This is a unique drawback to the military profession. Its most devoted practitioners may be called upon soonest to fulfill the soldier's ultimate duty.

THE TWENTIETH CENTURY

A World of Conflict

For the military profession in the twentieth century, the years leading up to World War I were the prelude to a tragedy. Despite the apparent advances in professionalism and some conflicts in the early years of the twentieth century that ought to have been more instructive, the military profession was generally ill-prepared for the challenges they faced. The mobilization and movement of large masses of men and material was planned and conducted successfully but was also quite inflexible at first, perhaps accelerating the headlong path to war in August 1914. Most important, the impact of the firepower of the new defensive weapons (rifles and machine guns) was not sufficiently taken into account and the capabilities of offensive weapons (artillery and the emerging weapons of tanks and airplanes) not fully exploited. As a result, it has become a cliché to call the first three years of the war a bloody stalemate. At sea, traditional naval forces mostly conducted a bloodless standoff, with the most important naval conflict being conducted by the submarines, their surface targets (including passenger vessels), and their hunters. World War I provided military experience to millions of men, among them writers who would create a body of war writing that was unprecedented in its volume and general level of artistic achievement. This constituted a new poetics of war and military experience that was both old and new, derivative of past accounts but often self-consciously different and "modern." The war also introduced a virulent nationalistic militarism, not solely but chiefly among the defeated nations in Europe.

The armies of Europe and America shrank considerably after 1918, most especially in Versailles-mandated Germany and the isolationist United States, but these armies had learned painful lessons from their war experience, and they continued to learn and innovate during the two decades before World War II. On land the major tactical innovation was the development of the combined-arms battle. This was not merely a matter of armored vehicles and airplanes. The high-frequency radio was needed to provide communications among fast-moving combined-arms forces that were dispersed along all three dimensions, and new organizations and procedures had to be developed for fire direction and command and control. At sea the use of aircraft carriers radically changed the nature of surface engagements, while both the submarine and antisubmarine technology and methods improved. The new air forces contributed to the development of new aircraft in cooperation with a growing industry and created doctrine and techniques for the tactical and strategic employment of air power. In the cash-short militaries of the 1920s and 1930s, many new ideas were developed in the classroom or in exercises of modest scale using mock-up equipment or "constructive" units that existed only on paper. Strategic ideas were discussed, and plans for war were made.

The 1930s were years of rearming and militarization. The established militant regimes of Japan and Italy conducted aggressive campaigns against vulnerable neighbors. The Nazis came to power in Germany in 1933 and threw off the Versailles limitations, organizing a new army based on the military doctrine developed during the previous decade and a half. The ideology of National Socialism, Nazism, came to strongly influence the German military ethos. When war came, countries that had maintained small peacetime professional militaries expanded to meet the needs of global war; conscription was practiced almost universally. Military professionals of the interwar years had shown themselves to be adept at innovation and adaptation, and when war approached they demonstrated competence in building much larger armies out of raw recruits. A combination of systematic, even scientific selection and assignment, realistic doctrine, and considerable advances in technology allowed the belligerents to field large, generally capable forces on air, land, and sea. The Germans, with their general staff and other military institutions and propensity revived and updated, fought well at the tactical and operational levels, but they were undone by strategic errors and limitations, and perhaps too by the wickedness of the ideology that had given them impetus. The Allies were good enough tactically, advanced impressively in operational art, and developed a war-winning strategy that, however unwittingly on the part of Britain and America, also set the stage for Soviet expansion and the Cold War. For the Allies, World War II introduced a generation of men to military service and infused democratic ideas into the areas of military recruitment, selection, and leadership. The autocratic, remote style of leadership had fallen into some disrepute in World War I, advances in transportation and communications technology enabled a more mobile style of command, and authoritarian methods struck many as inconsistent with a struggle of democracy against tyranny. The Allies were very successful in creating partnerships between academe and the military, with career professional officers usually in command of efforts like the British code-breaking center at Bletchley Park, with its university mathematicians, and the American atom bomb laboratory at Los Alamos, where many of the scientists were refugees from Hitler's rule. Then as now, totalitarianism could be an incentive to stern endeavor, but it often was a poor background for brilliance or creativity. The widespread use of bombers to attack enemy cities, culminating in the dropping of two atom bombs on Japan by the United States, was a vexed legacy, rolling back a trend toward fewer civilian deaths in war that had been going on for three hundred years.

In the second half of the century, wars had a greater tendency to be "asymmetrical," as the colonial empires that European countries had acquired in the eighteenth and nineteenth centuries became the scenes for wars of national liberation, sometimes inspired by communist ideology. These struggles usually began with terrorist or guerilla tactics, although the insurgents might switch to conventional methods if they felt strong enough to use them. The military profession was forced to acquire new knowledge in response to these developments. The guerilla fighter and commander, often lacking any of the outward signs of professional status, could present a challenge to the military professionals' claim to superior knowledge and proficiency in armed conflict. Although guerilla or insurgent warfare was not new in the twentieth century, it acquired new importance. Insurgency and counterinsurgency generated a whole genre of military writing, doctrine (sometimes complete with a matching counter-ideology), methods, and training. The century and millennium ended with the rise of terrorism as a tactic, and tribal and religious loyalties—a militant Islamic ideology in particular—became the adversary ideas for Western armies. The emergence of a belligerent Islam in effect renewed a conflict that had been fought throughout the Middle Ages and into early modernity. Among the questions that will continue to beset the military profession in the future is whether Islam is again to be the *summa culpabilis*.

Pre–World War I

The years of the century before World War I saw revelation and some reform. Wars in South Africa, the Far East, and the Balkans were precursors and premonitions of the Great War that would engulf all of Europe and much of the rest of the earth from 1914 to 1918. In the earlier conflicts, soldiers and armies were exposed to the impact of new technology on tactics. The advent of the magazine-fed rifle and the fully automatic machine gun had accelerated the trends toward increased firepower begun at mid-century with the adoption of rifled barrels and the later breechloaders. The general staffs and war colleges that had proliferated in the previous century gave many armies the intellectual capital and organization to adapt to the new realities. Considering the terrible power of the new weapons, the military professionals of the early twentieth century might even have made a greater effort to halt the drive to war, to question the assumption that large-scale war would come, an idea that seemed to possess many soldiers and civilians, followers and leaders alike. No such warning was effectively uttered, however, and the military profession of the day failed to change adequately or realistically, so the armies went to war in 1914 equipped with ideas based more on defiant wishful thinking than on reality.

The British experience of the Boer War was a neglected lesson in the effectiveness of modern small arms and artillery. Colonel G. F. R. Henderson, an officer on the staff of Lord Frederick Roberts, wrote impatiently of the failure of many of his fellow officers to acknowledge the revolutionary change in tactics brought on by accurate long-range small-arms fire.[1] Officers who thought as Henderson did were said to be suffering from "acute Transvaalitis." The tendency to dismiss the lessons of the South African war was strengthened by the experience and perceptions of the Russo-Japanese War of 1904–5.[2] Officer-observers from the major European armies and America noted with satisfaction that Japanese frontal attacks with fixed bayonets on Russian positions could succeed. These eventual results were so much in keeping with the prejudices and desire for professional reassurance on the part of the spectators that they largely ignored the huge casualties and the need for repeated attacks, often conducted in darkness to reduce the effect of the defenders' fire. The Japanese, peasant soldiers and ex-samurai alike, bore their losses with fatalism, but the psychic scars of those war losses may have been one of the influences that later pushed Japanese military thinking toward extreme intransigence. It was after this war, in 1908, that a law was passed forbidding Japanese soldiers to surrender. Japanese doctrine and writings increasingly express a callousness and suicidal readiness for death that would culminate in the later phases of World War II.

The Spanish-American War had seen victory brought on by the plentiful resources of the nation and by popular enthusiasm for the war, combined with considerable improvisation on the part of the War Department and the forces in the field. It had also revealed the inadequacy of the U.S. Army in terms of numbers and organization, especially in light of the newly acquired colonial empire that stretched from the Caribbean to the Pacific. As if to reinforce this point, America quickly became engaged in a counterinsurgency campaign in the Philippines, one of its new possessions, a struggle that ended up being longer and more costly than the conventional war through which America had obtained its new possessions. Although the Regular Army was reduced to its prewar strength immediately following Spain's surrender, the establishment was soon enlarged, as was that of the Navy. An Army War College was established in 1901, and a German-style general staff was created, although like other imitators it never possessed the prestige or Teutonic rigor of the original. Under the leadership of Secretary of War Elihu Root and Leonard Wood, the Army chief of staff (a new position that replaced the older, weaker position of commander in chief), the Regular Army acquired a sense of itself as a cadre for the larger national Army that would be required to fight a major war.[3]

The U.S. Army of the early twentieth century was a revitalized force. Victorious in Cuba and in the Philippines, expanded in size, and fired by the nationalistic and martial spirit of the time and by the contemporary creed of virility and strenuous living championed by Theodore Roosevelt, it was a spit-and-polish body of capable marksmen turned out in the smart but functional khaki uniforms of the day. Relieved of the unpopular and at least morally ambiguous necessity to police the West, it was eventually able to concentrate in some larger and less remote garrisons, facilitating both training and contact with the civilian population. The ties between the Regular Army and the expanding National Guard enhanced this trend. Regular officers such as Dwight D. Eisenhower and George C. Marshall had the opportunity to serve with the soldier-civilians of the National Guard as instructors and staff officers. The sense of themselves as custodians of military expertise and organization, who in wartime would conduct the expansion and integration of the national Army and oversee the allocation of national resources toward victory, became in some ways the defining aspect of American military professionalism, and foreign military officers took note.[4] The role of teacher became uppermost for American career professionals, even overshadowing that of combat leader. Neither Eisenhower nor Marshall, arguably the foremost American soldiers of the twentieth century, ever commanded a tactical unit in combat. Both developed much of their early professional reputations by their excellence as students and instructors at Army service schools. This stress on education had a tendency to intellectualize the American officer corps that would ebb and flow over the course of the century.

For America, the costs of entering the ranks of imperialist nations as a consequence of the war with Spain were more war and a bigger military establishment. Most historians see this period as representing a change in the national psyche along with the development of the material circumstances of power and empire. With the military's enlarged role and size came some of the militarism that was well established in Europe but new to America. Military officers acquired a greater role in the shaping of policy and sometimes debated on the nature and necessity of civilian control.[5]

World War I

In his essay "Men against Fire," historian Michael Howard dissects the reasons for the failure of armies to create tactics that were suitable to the technology of the time, and to the strategic situation in Western Europe in particular.[6] Some of these reasons have already been mentioned. They include the conservatism and fears of irrelevance on the part of the officer corps, the intellectual climate and "pretentious metaphysical vocabulary" spawned by ideas such as social Darwinism and certain interpretations of the philosophies of Henri Bergson and Friedrich Nietzsche, virulent nationalism, and a hypermasculine code of behavior. Suggested in some of the literature of the war was an unspoken desire on the part of the aristocracy to discipline and chastise an increasingly restive working class who could now be described (thanks to Karl Marx) as a proletariat, a motive that arguably was as old as Agamemnon and his use of the rescue of Helen and war with Troy as a pretext to assert his authority. This motive clearly backfired in both cases. Agamemnon's victory is a hollow one, and the Russian, German, and Austrian empires all fell as a consequence of the war and the sacrifices it imposed.

Even once the war began and the impact of the new weapons had been amply demonstrated, armies continued to cling to methods that had proved their costly ineffectiveness. Masses of artillery shells were expended to prepare for ground attacks, often with little effect on the field fortifications where defending troops took shelter. Offensives seemed always to be either on too wide a front to be adequately supported, or too narrow, making them vulnerable to counterattack. The technology of the time was against the decisiveness of the offense. The machine gun and bolt-action rifle were powerful defensive weapons but more difficult to employ in the offense because they required a stationary shooter, and transportation technology was just beginning to make an impact on the tactical battlefield. Artillery could be used in the offense, but it rarely had the precision or destructive power to be effective against troops sheltering in bunkers during a bombardment. The survivors could quickly emerge, shaken but still capable of functioning, to man their damaged defensive positions. The tank and the airplane began to come into their own, but they were hindered by mechanical limitations and problems of command and control in this era before reliable and portable radios. Gas and flame weapons were tried (first by the Germans, with their characteristic alacrity to embrace the frightful), but they too were not decisive. Gas was difficult to control and could be countered by masks, detection, and avoidance. Flame was most useful in confined spaces and could be used only at close range, even later in the century when tanks were outfitted with large flamethrowers. The hand grenade was another mostly offensive innovation—or revival—that gave attackers of trench lines and bunkers a small but significant weapon.

Exhaustion and political division on the losing side and improved tactics on the winning side finally broke the deadlock. The advances in nascent technologies would not fully come into play until World War II. Given that victory was largely won with weapons available in 1914, could the tactics that won the war have been developed sooner, perhaps even before 1914, so that when war came it might have been brought to a swifter, less costly conclusion? Perhaps if the admonitions of pragmatic soldiers like du Picq to "try out and describe better" had been followed, the needs for greater use of terrain, more flexible employment of supporting arms, a combination of fire and maneuver, and small units operating independently to exploit gaps and successes might have been anticipated. In fact, as Michael Howard points out, writings calling for the adoption of at least some of these methods had appeared before 1914, but they failed to bring about the development of significantly improved tactics. Howard seems to blame in part the conscript nature of armies for the delay, but the armies that won in 1918 were also conscript armies, many of them as new to their jobs as their older brothers had been in 1914, few of whom would have survived as combatants to see the war's end. The failure to adapt new tactics could be described in terms used by contemporary writers on adaptive leadership.[7] Given the experience of the early twentieth century, the need for change was apparent, but the work involved and the need to step out of established competencies proved too daunting for the military profession to undertake. They may be said to have treated the problem as "technical," calling for the enhancement of established methods, rather than "adaptive" and requiring a complete reconsideration of the tactical (and by extension the operational and strategic) problem.

Military professionals and soldiers at all times have had to endure hardships and danger, but conditions on the World War I western front were perhaps in a class of their own. The combination of prolonged danger, physical misery, and the enormous scale of concentrated firepower and casualties made heavy demands on individuals and units. For soldiers at the platoon, company, and battalion levels, service on the western front meant long stretches of time in the trenches performing routine tasks to improve fortifications and billets and to remain supplied with the bare necessities of food, water, ammunition, and construction materials. These tasks had to be performed around the clock, in all weathers, and often under the harassing fire of the enemy. In an assault, officers rushed forward with their troops. Leadership and command and control in no-man's-land were difficult and limited to a few of the individuals nearest to the person trying to give orders or otherwise exercise direction. Those who survived the assault might have only a few minutes to consolidate a defense of their new position before the almost inevitable bombardment and counterattack. Defenders had to endure days of bombardment while confined to airless bunkers and with the knowledge that the next shell might be the one to get through. After this, there would be a race to man their damaged positions before the first wave of attacking troops arrived. Even when the first wave was beaten back, successive waves would follow, with artillery support. Battles on the Somme, at Verdun, and at Ypres went on like this for months, with the chances of personal survival diminishing to almost a mathematical impossibility.

World War I expanded the domain of warfare, requiring military professionals to acquire or recruit specialist knowledge in a number of new fields. Technical and scientific knowledge, which had been institutionalized among the officers of the engineers and artillery in the eighteenth century, and which had roots in the gunpowder revolution and even as far back as the ancient Greeks, would gain in importance as an aspect of military professionalism. The military profession would be required to expand and adapt its base of knowledge and sometimes to outsource highly technical tasks to an alternative military profession of scientists, technicians, and manufacturers. The new knowledge was not limited to technology. The effect of fear and combat stress, an area in which professional soldiers had been the tacitly acknowledged experts, was now perhaps better understood by some psychiatrists than by officers in the combat arms themselves, even those with combat experience.[8] The profession of arms was both beset and enriched by these developments. Military officers sometimes had to defer to the conclusions of the specialists, but they also now had avenues they could explore to expand their own professional grasp of armed conflict and its methods, manifestations, and impact.

Another aspect of World War I that had an undoubted influence on the ethos and public perception of the profession of arms was the huge volume of literary works the war inspired. This was a more than literary phenomenon. As famously described by Paul Fussell in his seminal work, *The Great War and Modern Memory*, the war influenced the psyche of Europe for decades to come, and in some ways still does today.[9] By influencing the cultural context in which the military profession operates, the literature of World War I had both direct and indirect influences on military professionals, since of course many of them read Erich Maria Remarque's *All Quiet on the Western Front* (1929), Robert Graves' *Good-Bye to All That* (1929), and the poetry of Wilfred Owen. Not all World War I literature was antiwar, and even the writing of decorated infantry officer turned conscientious objector Siegfried Sassoon could be read as in essence extolling the warrior (although not war) by emphasizing the soldier's service and sacrifices. (Sassoon voluntarily

returned to the trenches after a period in Craiglockhart Hospital as a puta-
tive mental case. He was wounded on patrol in no-man's-land shortly before
the armistice.) In addition, the literature of World War I, as war literature has since *The Iliad* and *Beowulf*, provided examples of leadership and
expressions of the soldierly ethos. Both Graves and Sassoon belonged to
the 2nd Battalion, Royal Welch Fusiliers, and both men, perhaps Graves
in particular, were caught up in the intense regimental spirit of this prewar
regular infantry battalion; to a considerable degree they adopted the values
of the regular officers under whom they served. In his life and work, infantry officer and poet Wilfred Owen navigated the paradoxes of war and the
soldier until his death while leading his company a week before the armistice. Although Owen was a sensitive man who suffered some of the worst
the western front had to offer, he expressed gratitude at returning to active
service after his own period of exhaustion and convalescence at Craiglockhart. World War I also produced a number of nonfiction works that military professionals still read today, among them *Anatomy of Courage* (1945) by
British army and Royal Air Force physician Lord Moran (Charles Wilson),
and *Morale: A Study of Men and Courage* (1967) by officer and historian John
Baynes. These works address the leadership and personal attributes required
to sustain both the individual and the cohesive unit through heavy casualties
and intense, prolonged combat.

World War I represents both continuity and departure for the military
professional. After World War I, war could never again be seen as a part of
the normal pattern of political relationships, as a mere extension of policy.
As Russian strategist and games theorist Anatole Rapoport notes, war came
to be seen in more cataclysmic or eschatological terms, perhaps recapitu-
lating some of the ontological significance it had possessed in biblical or
prehistoric times.[10] These changes began to influence soldiers' perceptions
of themselves in complex ways. The military ideologies of the fascist countries at times seemed to nihilistically embrace their new role as universal
destroyer, but for most military professionals the increase in war's destructiveness (and potentially even greater destructiveness) was sobering and
challenging. The military mistakes of World War I and the flood of writing
that followed the war gave officers a new license to question conventional
wisdom and to bring a more critical approach to the military profession. The
seriousness with which some military professionals in the years between the

wars pursued innovation and adaptation is perhaps a sign of this chastened sense of responsibility. A generation of men who had served as junior officers in the Great War set themselves the task of improving military methods to make them less heedlessly wasteful of life. In some instances these men also sought to enhance the caliber of military advice given to presidents and other policy makers, and to instill in their fellow soldiers a greater sense of social responsibility. For a few soldier-intellectuals, the need for officers to reflect on and understand their social and ethical roles, even their ontological significance, acquired new immediacy.

The hierarchical social organizations that characterized most countries involved in World War I, including to an extent those of the United States, were reflected in an autocratic command style that was gradually impelled to change by the demands of war. In World War I even senior officers were often forbidden to question orders, being peremptorily ordered to "do as you're told."[11] Although the habit of obedience could be beneficial, it could also isolate the decision makers from reality and allow flawed plans and methods to go forward unquestioned.[12] The communications technology of the time exacerbated this tendency. All armies in World War I relied on wire communications. Telephone lines had to be laboriously laid, and once in place they had a tendency to tie a commander to his command post, especially if he depended on his telephone as a primary conduit of information. More traditional and flexible means of relaying information such as messengers and staff meetings fell into disuse, with sometimes comical but more often tragic results. A World War I cartoon shows a front-line officer in his dugout under heavy bombardment receiving a request on his field phone for an accounting of the number of tins of jam consumed by his company. According to legend, the chief of staff of the British Expeditionary Force, on a rare visit to the battlefield during the course of Third Ypres, is supposed to have burst into tears and blurted out, "Good God! Did we really send men to fight in that!"[13]

The social, affective, and physical isolation of the higher command from the soldiers and the battlefield not only resulted in costly tactical and strategic errors, but considered on a larger canvas it likely also contributed to the fall of the empires of Austria-Hungary, Russia, and Germany, and to the mutiny that tore through the French army in 1917 when soldiers lost all confidence in the civil and military leadership. Marshal Philippe Pétain suppressed the uprising ruthlessly and efficiently. Pétain would later lead the Vichy government in cooperation with the Nazis, having blamed the defeat of 1940 on the French people's addiction to pleasure. The unresponsive style of command that traditionalists practiced was something that many younger men came away from the war determined to avoid. Somewhat paradoxically, but also in keeping with the trend of "losers learn best," it was the soldiers of the authoritarian states, of Germany especially, who best learned the lessons of leadership from the front, combining constant interaction with subordinate commanders, mission-style orders, and allowance for initiative.

Finally, with the widespread use of powered submersibles and aircraft in World War I, military officers would henceforth be required to think in three full dimensions. The range of operations brought on by the new technology and the scale of global warfare might make the battle space very large indeed, calling for a more expansive cognitive range to match. The development of wireless communications would add a virtual dimension to warfare, one that existed outside the usual boundaries of space-time. These changes in the battle space were both irreversible and ever accelerating as new transportation and communications technologies were created and adapted to military use, and as the union of war and what would come to be called "information science" grew more intimate and important.

Between the Wars

Military historians Williamson Murray and Allan R. Millett have written extensively about the change and innovation that took place between the world wars.[14] The record of this innovation is often distinguished if uneven. It was generally undertaken with more commitment and success by the Germans and Russians (by now the Soviets) than by the armies of the Allies. The Germans had the sting of defeat, the lure of revenge, and (after 1933) a belligerent ideology to egg them on. For a time, the Soviets were also driven by ideology to consider war as the inevitable engine of necessary change. When Stalin found the Red Army's innovative spirit a threat to his own authority, however, he purged the officer corps of most of its best minds in 1937, although by that time the army had developed enough sound doctrine to prepare for war when it came, most critically against the German invaders starting in 1942. In the victorious nations, zest for war was at a low ebb after the trauma of World War I. Realistic military thought (not to mention national foreign relations policy) in the democracies had to contend with a deep distaste and denial on the subject of war.

The German and Soviet military professions made the greatest contributions during this period to the development of the art of war on land, in particular to the mobile combined-arms battle that came to be known as blitzkrieg. By the terms of the Treaty of Versailles the post–World War I German army was severely limited in size; it could have no more than 100,000 men, only 5,000 of whom could be officers. Under the direction of General Hans von Seekt, the Germans picked the best men and trained them for positions of responsibility above their nominal rank. Privates were prepared to assume the duties of noncommissioned officers, NCOs of officers, and officers of senior command and staff positions.[15] The officer ranks also became more meritocratic, so that a middle-class officer with a distinguished combat record such as Erwin Rommel could rise to heights that likely would have been impossible under the Kaiser. Another condition of Versailles was the abolition of the general staff, but the officer ranks contained many general staff veterans, and von Seekt set them the task of studying the past war and other military history in order to develop realistic doctrine. Although the Germans were forbidden tanks and planes, they grasped many of the implications of the new weapons based on their distilled experience of World War I, their observation of other countries' military maneuvers, and their imaginative professional thought.

The new style of mobile warfare that had been developed in the latter years of World War I required the development of new technologies for its potential to be realized; it also required a new approach to command and control. The Germans, with their development of storm trooper tactics as basis and background, were the first to recognize this fact and the first and most effective in putting it into practice.[16] Driven by defeat, as they had been in the years after 1806, they developed a system of mission orders that encouraged initiative and aggressiveness in junior leaders. Unfortunately, the same nationalist insularity that had overtaken Germany after the defeat by Napoleon was renewed with a vengeance in the years after 1918. The liberalizing tendencies of Wilhelmian Germany and of the Weimar Republic were swept away by the rise of Nazism and the sinister hold it exerted over the hearts of the German people. The small army of the Weimar period could not satisfy the militaristic tendencies of many German veterans and younger men, giving rise to the infamous *Freikorps*, volunteer military or paramilitary groups, and later to private and politicized armies, chiefly on the right, of which the Nazi paramilitary Sturmabteilung (SA) was the largest.

Most German officers did not trust or like the amateur political armies, but they saw Nazism as a defense against socialism and communism, which many believed had eroded soldiers' morale in the latter half of World War I. Many officers also somewhat paradoxically accepted the myth that the German army had never been defeated in battle but had been "stabbed in the back" by liberal and disloyal elements at home, with German Jews playing a leading role. The German officer corps was ready for Hitler in 1933, as was the rest of the nation. German professional myopia or amorality would prove to be not limited to military officers, as engineers, industrialists, lawyers, university professors, clergymen, and physicians demonstrated how much they were willing to compromise in return for personal security and the retention of their professional titles, prestige, and income. This was not unique to Germany; professional people in the occupied countries usually showed themselves to be just as willing to neglect their broader societal obligations. In France, at least, a segment of the officer corps would follow General Charles de Gaulle into exile rather than take the more comfortable route of remaining with Marshal Pétain and the right-wing Vichy government, and in Germany a group of officers would take near-suicidal risks in an attempt to overthrow the Nazi regime.

The fascist movements that came to prevail in Germany, Italy, and Spain existed in other European countries and the United States, but they were not strong enough to dominate political life unless given impetus and support by a successful outside (usually German) military intervention, as happened in Austria, France, Norway, and elsewhere, in Eastern Europe especially. Ironically, some of the advanced military ideas that found such a welcome in Germany had originated in the democratic countries but had not taken root there. The quasi pacifism expressed in (for example) the Kellogg-Briand Pact of 1928 (in which signatories renounced the use of armed force) tended against military preparedness.

Two men who had served as officers in the British Army in World War I provided much of the theoretical basis for the adaptation undertaken by officers in Germany: J. F. C. Fuller and B. H. Liddell-Hart. Fuller was a commander and proponent of tank forces. His work was visionary and backed by a thorough knowledge of military history; some of his historical writings are still read today. Liddell-Hart, an infantry captain in World War I, developed a strategy of the "indirect approach," which he may have sometimes overstated but which was a logical corrective to the World War I practice of battering attacks that emphasized numbers and firepower over maneuver and precision.

In France, Charles de Gaulle advocated for armored forces and was eventually rewarded with command of France's sole armored division; unfortunately it was not enough to stave off defeat in 1940. Interest in armored forces in America during the 1920s and 1930s remained largely vicarious and theoretical because the tiny size and constrained budgets of the period allowed the Army neither tanks nor the exercises for testing new tactics. The American military also had considerable numbers of men stationed or deployed overseas, especially in Asia and the Pacific. This gave American officers of the time such as Joseph Stilwell in China and Douglas MacArthur and Dwight Eisenhower in the Philippines a global outlook that would prove very valuable, but it did not lend itself to the concentration of resources for extensive planning and practice.

Late Colonialism

America was far from unique among the developed and victorious nations of the period in posting large numbers of soldiers overseas. Britain, France, Spain, the Netherlands, and other countries also retained overseas colonies after World War I. The colonial armies that had been created during the previous century also gained in experience and in competence. Airplanes, motor vehicles, and some of the fighting techniques developed in World War I gave modern armies a greater advantage than ever over indigenous forces and fighters. Imperial policing replaced imperial expansion, and the competition among states for colonial possessions declined in importance, so colonial armies, by now integrated into the countries they occupied, could focus on holding on to their own against any local unrest. This unrest, however, became more serious and ideological as colonized peoples became more politically self-aware and active. Improved technology could also enable excesses of force and sometimes atrocities, as happened at Amritsar, India, in 1919, when a platoon of Indian army troops under the command of a British officer and armed with bolt-action rifles shot down a thousand peaceful Indian protesters in a matter of minutes. The use of aircraft in colonial policing (termed "air control" by the British Royal Air Force) could be a force multiplier, but it required restraint and precise intelligence to apply effectively.[17] In short, powerful weapons and techniques could help colonial powers to retain control, but they had the potential to fray the relationship between the colonizers and indigenous people, as had the heavy-handed use of force in the American colonies more than a century before. With twentieth-century weapons, the Boston Massacre in 1770 could have been much bloodier with perhaps a more immediate effect on the mood of the colonies.

The late colonial period produced a significant amount of literature, much of it written by soldiers and military professionals. The memoirs of John Masters and Francis Yeats-Brown show career officers reflecting on their profession and seeking cross-cultural knowledge and personal fulfillment while they serve.[18] Professional treatises such as General Andrew Skeen's *Lessons in Imperial Rule* (1932) and the Marine Corps' *Small Wars Manual* (1940) also appeared. The iconoclastic Marine general Smedley Butler wrote *War Is a Racket* (1935), a book that was highly critical of the quasi-colonial American involvement in Central America and the Caribbean. T. E. Lawrence's *Seven Pillars of Wisdom* (1926), although written about events in World War I, is another example of the literature of colonial soldiering. Lawrence was an archaeologist before he became an officer, and his highly intellectual, individualistic, almost entrepreneurial approach to soldiering is brilliant and fascinating. Like Butler, Lawrence fell out with his political masters. For the colonial soldier the physical and affective distance between the area of operations and the centers of power was often an issue. It may also be that service on the outposts of empire can lead to the kind of eccentricity and egotism reflected in the character Kurtz in Joseph Conrad's novella of the colonial Congo, *Heart of Darkness*.

One of the more interesting and professionally significant episodes in the genre of Western officers abroad concerns the career of Joseph Stilwell, a West Point–trained infantry officer. In some ways Stilwell was a typical Regular Army officer of the first half of the twentieth century, but his extensive service in China placed him in the roles of diplomat, linguist, engineer, and intelligence operative. Highly critical of warlord Chiang Kai-shek and his corrupt nationalist regime, he tried to develop a Chinese army that would be disciplined and tactically proficient. Stilwell is nearly an American Lawrence of Arabia, albeit a regular officer who remained rooted to an old-fashioned code of behavior that would have been familiar to American officers of the Civil War period. Indeed, with his rough manners and plain uniform topped off by a battered felt campaign hat, Stilwell was something of a throwback to Grant and his contemporaries. Although his mission eventually failed, his career merits study as an example of versatility making do on scarce resources. Stilwell's death from cancer shortly after the war may have deprived history of a fascinating memoir.[19]

The Military Aviation Profession

Although the advances in ground warfare that took place in the twentieth century were dramatic and significant, the most revolutionary change was the arrival of a new domain of warfare in the air. The advent of military aviation at first gave birth to an aviation specialist subset of the army officer, and then to air force officers as members of separate services with distinctive uniforms and increasingly distinct doctrines and outlooks. The British were the first to establish a separate air force when the Royal Air Force was created in 1918. The United States began with an aviation component that was subordinate to the signal corps, then in 1919 created a separate air service. The Army Air Corps was created in 1926 and an air force general headquarters in 1933. These movements toward greater autonomy were in the right direction but not enough for most American military aviation professionals. They desired an air force that was a completely separate branch of the armed forces, on equal footing with the Army and Navy, a development that eventually occurred as part of the creation of the National Military Establishment (later the Department of Defense) in 1947.[20] Even today, however, not all military aviation professionals are members of separate air forces. Navies have separate air arms that fly off carriers to operate in support of the fleet and to project power ashore, and ground armies have retained some aviation assets for direct support.

The drive for a separate service on the part of military aviation professionals had war-fighting implications as well as an impact on the nature of military professionalism. Aviators tended to favor war-fighting methods that granted them greater autonomy. To align organization with mission, they preferred to use aircraft in a strategic or operational role rather than in a tactical mission such as close air support. Understandably, military aviators and other military aviation professionals wanted their career paths, credentials, and terms for advancement established by others who shared their knowledge, experience, and physical and conceptual perspectives. The military aviation professionals who were most favored in their own world tended to be those who flew the kinds of missions that air forces most wanted to fly: the heavy bomber pilots, who performed strategic bombing, and the fighter pilots, who established air superiority far above the fray at ground level. The U.S. Air Force would go through periods when one or the other of these groups was dominant among the senior leadership.[21]

The creation of autonomous air forces may be said to represent an acknowledgment of the vital and sometimes independent role of air power in twentieth-century war. The degree of independence to be exercised by air forces would continue to be one of the issues involved in framing the separate identity of the air force officer. This identity would be a complex combination of the traditional and the new, the ethereal and the technological, the earthbound and the high-flown. Like ground and naval officers, air force officers would be defined in part by their characteristic physical milieu. Air force officers would always tend to think in terms of distances and speeds that others found almost incomprehensible. At first, the operations of military aircraft were closely connected and subordinate to what was happening on the ground. Later, as technology improved, and as theory took to the air and began to envision the potential of military aviation (even in advance of its actual capabilities), aviation operations sometimes seemed to possess a separate existence. Like the cavalrymen of old, the nature of the pilot's calling could bring out poetry or hubris. He could come to see himself as above the fray and even become contemptuous of those who still insisted on crawling on the earth and plowing the seas. His limit and his salvation may have been the inescapably technological aspect of flight—the cockpit rather than the sky itself—insisting on a prosaic attention to the machine, curbing theory and reminding him of his limitations and mortality.

The twentieth-century literature of military aviation, the greater part of it written by pilots, occupies a respectable but often disregarded subset in the literature of the military profession. Writing by and about military aviators can often be seen as working out the various paradoxes of aviation, this liberating activity that was so often lethal, that seemed to grant new insight while lifting the pilot above ordinary human concerns and society.

If the pilot was the man of the future, what did this say about the future, and what was the pilot's responsibility, in a life that might be all too brief, to ensure the future of aviation in service to national and human goals? Even more than the sailor, the category of aviator seemed to transcend national boundaries; this could create difficulties for military aviators who wore their country's uniform, especially in time of war. Perhaps more than other officers, and especially in the early days, military aviators may feel that they have more in common with their civilian or foreign counterparts than with fellow military officers of their own country. The career of Charles Lindbergh, who became an international hero after his successful solo flight across the Atlantic in 1927, is a good example. In the 1930s Lindbergh was a frequent guest of the Nazi regime and the Luftwaffe, with whose pilots he felt a connection based mostly on the fellowship of aviation, although perhaps also on Lindbergh's naïve ideas about a common "Nordic" heritage. This relationship became highly embarrassing to Lindbergh when the United States went to war with Germany and some Americans accused him of Nazi sympathies. Perhaps in penitence, although surely also in a spirit of solidarity with his fellow American aviators, Lindbergh flew missions on U.S. aircraft in the Pacific during World War II and developed a technique to save fuel on long flights.[22]

The ethos of the armed aviation professional was also divided. To some early enthusiasts air power seemed to be a means to end wars quickly and therefore humanely. It certainly did help to tip the scales of warfare in favor of the offense, most demonstrably at the tactical level, although arguably at the operational and strategic levels as well. This prevented a repetition of the deadlock on the 1914–18 western front, but military aviation also significantly added to the terrors and horrors of war. Attacks by air forces on ground troops added a uniquely helpless and terrifying experience to the menu of the soldier's hardships. Even worse, air power expanded the range of the battlefield to encompass civilian populations far from the scenes of surface fighting.

In the words of David MacIsaac, airmen could sometimes seem to pass over this prospect with the "callous assumption" that victory through air power could be quick and easy.[23] MacIsaac's essay is a seminal and essential description of the development of air power theory and doctrine in the interwar years. While proselytizers such as Giulio Douhet, William

P. "Billy" Mitchell, and Alexander de Seversky could overstate the case for the decisiveness of aviation operations in war, they also encouraged interest and debate on the subject of military aviation.[24] The air forces of the world went on to develop doctrine for the use of air power in future wars. The earliest role of reconnaissance for military aircraft continued to be important, but combatant roles at the tactical, operational, and strategic levels gained in importance as the abilities of aircraft to move fast, carry large payloads, and fly greater distances improved over the course of the 1930s, when many of the fighter, ground attack, and heavy bomber aircraft used in World War II were developed (e.g., the British Spitfire, the German Messerschmitt 109, and the American B-17, or "Flying Fortress"). The tactical use of aircraft involved close support of units on the ground, a hallmark of the German blitzkrieg that was also pioneered by U.S. Marines in the Caribbean and Central America. At the operational level, air forces could "interdict" enemy targets that were not in direct contact with friendly ground forces but might be in a position to provide support and reinforcement. The strategic use of air forces was at once the most alluring, most defining, and most problematic use of air forces as envisioned and later as practiced when war came. The debate over the morality and effectiveness of strategic bombing in World War II goes on, and it was perhaps crystallized by the use of atomic bombs against an encircled but still belligerent Japan.

Planning for War

In addition to their various efforts to make their armed forces as ready as possible for the war that most of them believed was coming, military professionals in the interwar period conducted contingency planning, anticipating in detail where and how they expected to fight and hoped to win. These plans evolved over time in response to changes in government policy, military doctrine, and the international situation. Contingency planning reflected the doctrinal development and force planning that was taking place in various countries. The victors of World War I planned for a repeat of 1914 in Europe. The British would send a small (in fact slightly smaller than in 1914) expeditionary force to hold the flank on the English Channel while the Royal Navy controlled the Channel and the North Sea. The French would hold the line against another German invasion that would come principally through Belgium and Holland and run up against the impregnable Maginot Line. The futility of such a fixed defense in a new age of mobile warfare aside, these fortifications were facing the wrong way because the Germans were planning to upset expectations by attacking not along their 1914 route but through the "impassable" Ardennes, making use of both the Allies' misjudgment about the direction of the attack and their underestimation of the entirely new tempo, in effect a new space-time relation, brought about by the advances in tactics, technology, and the means of command and control.[25] The fascist countries of Italy, Japan, and Germany conducted what might be described as strategic shaping operations before the start of the world war in 1939, annexing and conquering nearby countries and territories and also conducting war by proxy—for example, in Spain. The armies of the totalitarian states gained valuable experience in these campaigns, although Italy's efforts at aggressive, militant imperialism in Ethiopia bordered on the inept, and for Japan mainland China would prove to be a bottomless pit of military manpower that would later be needed against the Americans.

"Color plans" (which included Orange, Red, Red-Orange, and eventually several Rainbow Plans) dominated American war planning between the world wars.[26] The plans began with a focus on Japan but then shifted to an emphasis on Germany. When war came, though, it began in the Pacific, not the Atlantic. The speed of the Japanese advances surprised the Americans as much as had the initial attack. In naval and amphibious warfare, as on the ground, the advantage had shifted in favor of the offense, largely because of the improvements in the airplane and its weaponry, and in command-and-control technology and methods. Starting in 1919 the Americans had the benefit of an established Joint Board and Joint Planning Committee, predecessors of the Joint Staff, to perform strategic planning. Much war planning in the United States was also conducted at the war-gaming center of the Naval War College in Newport, where students can still read the posted claim from a letter by Admiral Chester Nimitz that the college planners were able to anticipate all major wartime developments save the advent of the kamikaze. Historian Russell Weigley concedes that this hindsight claim to prescience may be exaggerated, but the success of the American Pacific campaign gives the statement considerable credibility.[27] Even with the Pacific campaign in full swing, the "Germany first" attitude of American planners persisted, partly in the form of the relative resources allocated and also reflected in the desire of the Americans, Army Chief of Staff George C. Marshall among them, to invade Europe as soon as possible. Their early experiences in North Africa and the advice of the British convinced them to delay, but the emphasis on Germany remained.

The caliber of planning by military professionals in this period was mixed. It showed an improvement over the planning for World War I, but it was also unduly influenced by the course of the earlier war. In fact, World War II may be seen as a resumption of World War I. That so many feared the coming of the second war was not enough to prevent it from happening. Others desired war, and they imposed their will in bringing on the conflict, but not, finally, on the outcome. The greatest planning error of World War II was the Axis decision to refight a war that had been lost once already. Perhaps the second greatest was the failure of the Allies to convince the aggressors of the wicked folly of this plan.

World War II

World War II continues to loom large in the historical memory, imagination, and thought of military professionals. For the Allies it was and is "the Good War": a just war fought successfully for clear goals. Many of the types of military operations still planned and conducted today—the combined-arms battle, amphibious operations, and airborne operations—were developed and conducted on a larger scale during World War II than at any time before or since. Military professionals on all sides of the conflict were invested with unprecedented power, and they became national heroes whose names still matter in history.

The 1930s were years of frequent, widespread conflict, providing the World War II belligerents with experience in person and by proxy. As in every age, the wrong lessons might be drawn from preliminary bouts. The operations of the Luftwaffe units of the Condor Legion provided the Germans with valuable experience but also may have given them an exaggerated idea of the effectiveness of striking civilian targets from the air. Republican Spain was defeated, but not Britain. The Japanese were also successful on the Asian mainland against the Chinese and later the British, emboldening them and setting the stage for their confrontation with the United States.

The technical advances of the decades between World War I and World War II created the conditions to restore the primacy of the offense at all levels of war. The challenge for military professionals was to make this potential a reality by developing new doctrine, tactics, techniques, and even patterns of thought. On the tactical level, a significant development was the advent of light automatic weapons that were capable of both concentrated firepower and rapid displacement. A single soldier could carry magazine- or belt-fed automatic weapons like the Browning Automatic Rifle (BAR) and the formidable German MG-34 and MG-42, and small vehicles like the American Jeep, British Bren Gun Carrier, and German *Kubelwagon* could transport these weapons rapidly and serve as mobile firing platforms. Tanks and other armored vehicles increased the speed and effectiveness of the offensive. Armies as well as companies might move faster on the battlefield and in the course of a campaign. (They did not always do so, as the slow Allied marches up the Italian peninsula and across France illustrate.) The combined-arms battle was made possible by weapons and transportation technology, but really was enabled by the wireless radio and the expertise of the army, air force, and naval officers and enlisted personnel who specialized in combined-arms fire control. Virtually all combat-arms officers played important parts in the orchestration of combined arms. Aviation, artillery, and naval officers were attached to maneuver units in order to provide dedicated technical expertise in fire support. Infantry officers might find themselves at an artillery or aviation headquarters, or even in spotter aircraft to provide liaison and identify targets. Officers in logistical and administrative support roles required some proficiency in combined arms for defense. As communications equipment became more sophisticated and important, the signals officers of previous generations became in effect radio officers, and a new branch of military operations—electronic warfare—was born.

The advent of radio communications and electronic warfare gave new impetus to a field of operations as old as the Trojan horse. Military deception operations played a significant part in World War II, requiring military professionals to acquire new forms of expertise and enhance their capacity for creative thought. Military deception is essentially the effort to convince enemy forces of something that is not true so that they will pursue a course of action to their own detriment. The Allies, the British and Americans especially, were better at military deception than were the Germans, who subscribed to a more classically orthodox Clausewitzian approach to the employment of force. The Germans counted on speed and violence of attack to overwhelm the ability of an opposing force to react. They worked hard to keep their own secrets, but they were less committed and successful in getting information from or deceiving their opponent. It may have been that the militaristic, methodical German turn of mind, along with an authoritarian system of government, rebelled at the messy, rather unmilitary idea of deception. The same can be said of the Japanese. The Allies used deception successfully in many if not most of their major offensives, from Midway to Sicily to Normandy. The practice of military deception requires the military planner to construct a narrative that is close enough to the facts to be believable but far enough from the truth to convince the enemy to get it wrong in a significant or decisive way. After the narrative and objective of military deception have been worked out, practical means have to be found to convey this narrative. In World War II this was often a combination of deceptive radio traffic, feints or demonstrations by actual units, and the use of artful mock-ups and other forms of misleading appearance.

Offensive methods became so effective in World War II that they were adapted for defense. Defending units employed nonlinear mobile defenses characterized by large reserves, counterattacks, and the (at least temporary) yielding of territory for tactical advantage. These methods put a high premium on training and rehearsal and on initiative, command and control, and cohesion. The officer conducting such a defense needed much more than doggedness leavened by a sense of when retreat was unavoidable. He required detailed knowledge of his battle area and its surroundings, the imagination to envision possible incursions and effective counterstrokes, the discipline to ensure that his command was prepared for a variety of possible situations and actions, and the adaptability and decisiveness to execute as necessary on the day of battle. The art of the counterattack was probably best practiced by the Germans, who were to have frequent need of it during defensive and delaying actions against the Soviets, British, and Americans later in the war, and whose systems of leadership and command stressed the essentials of initiative and small-unit cohesion, generally depending less on orders and indirect fire support than did those of the Allies.

Special Operations

Special operations were not new in the twentieth century. Raids, reconnaissance, and insurgent and counterinsurgency operations are as old as warfare;

indeed the raid may be its earliest form. Nor were elite units trained for special operations a World War II innovation. Grenadier, *jaeger*, and the other forms of light infantry units had been an important aspect of eighteenth-century warfare, and the colonial experience had spawned a new generation of special units. By the twentieth century most of those earlier elite units of grenadier and light infantry had largely lost their specialist functions. They might be considered generally superior to line units, although this presumed superiority tended to derive from the social connections of their officers and a kind of self-conscious esprit de corps rather than from any demonstrable special capabilities. By World War II, however, a combination of circumstances seemed to be calling for the creation of a new breed of special operations units. This was partly a result of advances in technology. The aircraft and parachute, the submersible, lightweight boats, portable radios, plastic explosives, underwater breathing equipment, and the submachine gun and silencers gave special operations units the means to strike quickly, lethally, and from a distance. Improvements in selection and training methods provided the means to identify those suited to special operations and to give them the physical endurance, military skills, and mindset to carry them out.

The global nature of World War II, perhaps especially for the Allies early on, created a demand for units that could move fast and far and strike hard. The war also saw an influx into the enlisted and officer ranks of individuals who did not have the experience and habits of a peacetime regular army, but who in some cases had skills and outlook that could be put to use in a special operations role. Mountain climber David Stirling gave up training for an Everest ascent, joined the British Army, and founded the unit that would develop into the modern Special Air Service (SAS). Skiers, many of them Europeans, filled the ranks of the U.S. Army's 10th Mountain Division. That unit would never be called on to ski into combat in World War II, but it demonstrated the importance of the physical fitness and small-unit cohesion that came of hard training in the mountains of Italy. Twentieth-century special units were often inspired by European and American armies' colonial experience. The British Commandos were named for the mounted Boer units the British had fought in South Africa at the turn of the century. The American Rangers were styled after the French and Indian War Rangers of Robert Rogers. Many elite organizations still in existence today, such as the Rangers, Green Berets, SAS, and Royal Marine commandos (there are no longer any Commandos in the British army), can trace their lineage to units formed in World War II.

In a way resembling the evolution of artillery and engineering officers in the eighteenth century, and of military aviation professionals in the twentieth, special operations military professionals eventually moved from the periphery toward the center of the profession of arms. Special operations officers were at first viewed with distrust by regular officers, who often saw them as undisciplined eccentrics and adventurers. Today a high percentage of the top officers in many armies have a special operations background, and some special operations capabilities have trickled down to regular units. Special operations themselves cover a broad spectrum ranging from the brief, violent airborne or amphibious raid to destroy a selected target to protracted, low-intensity counterinsurgency missions. The most difficult operations (based on distance to be traveled and remoteness from sources of support), however, are reserved for the small, highly selective, and assiduously trained special operations unit. The achievements of special operations groups have come to more nearly match their aspirations, escaping the "selection-destruction" cycle that was once thought to be characteristic of special operations units that saw very high casualty rates among carefully selected, highly trained, and therefore particularly valuable soldiers.

The development of amphibious operations in the mid-twentieth century created a military specialty that in a sense bridged special and conventional operations. Amphibious operations are as old as naval warfare—in fact they were likely the first naval operations—and most navies since ancient times had possessed marine detachments who served on warships and were capable of landing ashore. British Army, navy, and marine officers since the eighteenth century had practiced, conducted, and sometimes specialized in amphibious operations. After the British debacle at Gallipoli in 1915, however, many believed that amphibious operations on a large scale were a thing of the past. The defensive power of modern weapons made the traditional amphibious obstacles of sea and shoreline impassable, creating an ideal killing zone for modern, accurate, rapid-firing, low-trajectory weapons. Some of the same developments that shifted the advantage more in favor of the offense on land had a similar impact on amphibious operations. The ability to call in and control accurate supporting fire was extended to carrier aircraft and naval gunfire. When U.S. Marine Corps officers foresaw the possibility of a naval war in the Pacific that would require amphibious operations, they were forced to question the assumption that the problems and perils of such operations were insurmountable. In World War II some amphibious operations, like those conducted by the British Commandos and the American Marine Raiders, remained in the special operations category, but others conducted on a divisional, corps, or army scale mixed the features of special and conventional operations: special in range and intensity, but conventional in scale and in that the units conducting them were not subject to the same degree of selection or training as true special operations forces.

Airborne operations in World War II similarly blended conventional and special operations. Special forces conducted small-scale, often long-range and behind-the-lines airborne operations, but airborne operations were also conducted at the division level under conditions, on a scale, and by forces that blurred the distinction between special and conventional. Both airborne and amphibious pioneers had to overcome adverse "conventional wisdom." New equipment, techniques, and tactics had to be developed. The airborne and amphibious fighter had to be on intimate terms with all dimensions and all states of matter. Like the pilot, his flights and passages had to be grounded in an appreciation for some unpleasant facts and fearful odds. Airborne and amphibious warfare assumed symbolic as well as practical significance for the twentieth-century military profession. Preparation for these roles came to stand for a willingness to undergo the most rigorous training and to conduct the most dangerous military operations. The "airborne mystique" was to become an important part of the belief and a basis for morale in many armies. Soldiers who wear the distinctive wings of a paratrooper are acknowledged to have passed a significant test, a rite of passage resembling combat itself. Marines may occupy a similar place. In a sense airborne and marine units have gone the way of earlier elites in that their specialist function has assumed a position of lesser importance compared with the symbolic importance of their advanced training and self-selection.

The kamikaze phenomenon was both peculiarly Japanese and a kind of reductio ad absurdum of the special operations selection-destruction cycle. Still, it cannot be dismissed entirely as a mad symptom of national neurosis. The kamikazes presented a real, unexpected, and almost unanswerable threat to the American fleet in the Pacific. They appeared in the skies just in advance of guided-missile technology, and they might be said to have been a form of terrorism, one of several terrible genies that made their appearance in World War II and still haunt our lives.

On the strategic level, the expansion of military aviation was certainly the most significant development, adding a new literal dimension to warfare and radically changing how war was fought on both land and sea. For some, including the proselytizers like Mitchell and Douhet, it seemed at first that military aviation would completely rewrite the book of war. This was not to be, but military aviation had an undoubted influence on strategy. Aviation did not liberate warfare from the seas and terra firma, but it did add greater independence from the dimensions of the map. Like every new development in warfare, airplanes had their limitations and vulnerabilities. Planes need secure areas to launch and land. Aviation units are among the logistically neediest of combat forces, requiring huge quantities of fuel, replacement parts, and ordnance to function. One way to answer the threat posed by a plane is with another plane, the interceptor, which in World War II could be guided by radar.

Specialized antiaircraft artillery improved and became a separate branch of the ground forces. In addition, the advent of military aviation, along with the almost contemporaneous beginnings of modern meteorology, gave a new military significance to weather prediction, creating yet another specialist subset of military professionalism.

←——————————→

World War II probably constituted a military revolution, one perhaps unmatched since the seventeenth-century revolution described by Michael Roberts. Multiple technologies came into being and into active service, spawning new doctrines, areas of expertise, and whole new types of warfare. The military profession had to adapt and expand, although the impact of technological change was not as radical or complete as some proselytizers had predicted. The infantry still had an important role to play. By the start of World War II the infantry was being almost discounted in comparison with the new aviation and armored forces. This had led to a neglect of the infantry in terms of numbers, selection, and training, among the Allies especially, which required a reconsideration of priorities once the armies truly came to grips. Not enough replacements had been allowed for, too many of the high-caliber recruits had been siphoned into the new or technical arms, and units sometimes had to be trained in the field on tactics (such as those required for urban terrain) they should have learned and practiced before they were committed to combat. Infantry was hugely important in the decisive campaigns of the war on land. As ever, it was needed to take and secure ground, to attack and defend cities, to operate in terrain impassable to vehicles such as mountains and jungle, and to permit the close-up knowledge of terrain and enemy that had been a vital function of the infantry since the time of the Roman legions and before. The traditional dominance of infantry in the West has sometimes been challenged, as it was by heavy horsemen in the Middle Ages. In the twentieth century, increases in firepower and accelerating mobility seemed to put the infantry in the shade, but the World War I stereotype of suffering "PBI" (poor bloody infantry) was not nearly so accurate in World War II. The infantry now carried lightweight automatic weapons, grenade launchers, and rocket weapons such as the American bazooka and German *Panzerfaust*. Crew-served antitank weapons had been improved and made lighter so that the infantry had an effective answer to enemy armor. Specialized armored personnel carriers gave the infantry the same speed and mobility and some of the protection of tank forces. The use of parachute infantry meant that foot soldiers could be introduced into battle with the speed of an airplane, and amphibious infantry had the ability to conduct forcible entry across even a well-defended coastline.

Scientists, Scholars, and Soldiers

The tradition of scientific knowledge as the handmaiden of armed force, and of scientists as unarmed military professionals in partnership with members of the profession of arms, is at least as old as Archimedes. In the West especially it has never entirely been lost. Even in the dark days of late antiquity, technical military knowledge was preserved and expanded in the areas of siege craft, fortification, tactics, and organization.[28] Undeniably, however, the twentieth century saw something new in this regard. The practical impact and capabilities of science, which had been growing sporadically over the centuries, took wings in the twentieth. War would now be driven and decided by scientific knowledge and technological advancement as never before, and soldiers would struggle to keep up with the new developments, sometimes feeling it was the scientists and not themselves who were really in charge and whose professional knowledge and abilities counted most. The most obvious examples of this influence were in the areas of military technology already discussed: airplanes, armored vehicles, submersibles, radio, and a family of efficient new long-range, rapid-fire, and high-explosive weapons and ordnance. Early forms of sonar were implemented shortly after World War I, although sonar did not completely solve the problem of detecting enemy submarines, as some initially believed it would.[29] Radar was developed and fielded just in time to stave off Britain's defeat in the Battle of Britain.

In both world wars the contributions of science went beyond the development of new technology to arm the fighting forces. A sometimes overlooked development was the new field of operational research.[30] The British were especially quick to embrace this approach, and a partnership of officers and some of the most brilliant scientists of the day helped to win the Battle of Britain and to counter and defeat German submarine warfare in the Atlantic. Using probability statistics and computations to predict enemy movements, operational research survived the war in several settings, including the American Operations Research Office, and also in various "think tank" organizations such as the RAND Corporation. Some of the methods of operational research were subsumed into the mainstream military profession. Cadets majoring in math at West Point can still minor in operational research. The postwar partnership between academic and military professionals has been an exception to a tendency to standoffishness and sometimes antipathy between the two groups. A pattern of cooperation followed by disenchantment and rejection can be seen in the postwar career of the Alameda atom bomb project head, J. Robert Oppenheimer, whose leftist connections contributed to the revocation of his security clearance, and in the persecution and still-disputed death of gay Bletchley Park code breaker Alan Turing. The close partnership of science and the military in World War II perhaps represents a missed opportunity for the two professions to integrate more fully, even on a political or ethical level. In World War II the U.S. Army appears to have recognized the need to cultivate its own intellectual capital, since it formed the Army Special Training Program, under which high-IQ recruits were held back from being sent overseas and were instead enrolled in prestigious universities to continue their education and prepare them for assignments calling for particularly high intelligence. Unfortunately, the Army underestimated the number of infantry replacements that would be needed in Europe and the program was discontinued, with many of those enrolled being summarily sent into combat.[31]

Despite the miscalculations and missteps, for the military professions of the victorious Allied countries World War II was the finest hour. The "Good War" and the names, engagements, and even the equipment associated with it have a unique place in the popular imagination and in the institutional memory of the military professionals of today, defining an ideal of decisive conflict against an incontestably evil adversary. Like most if not all victories in war, this one owed much to the simple arithmetic of population and resources translating into combat power. Sometimes overlooked is the considerable openness that the Allied military displayed toward innovation and ideas from outside its own ranks. Like the scale of the war, this degree of openness, of cross-cultural connections between military and civilian professional knowledge, was unprecedented and is perhaps unmatched to this day. The existential threat of World War II undoubtedly helped to break down barriers, as did the range of conscription and mobilization of national resources. The cautionary example of military unmindfulness in World War I was another factor, leading the military professionals of World War II to restlessly seek creative solutions to problems in preference to formulae. Some of the best of the accumulated cultural and cognitive capital of the profession of arms came to be expressed in a generation of Allied officers who organized and led the armies, navies, and air forces to victory.

The ending of World War II gave the victorious militaries the task of occupying and, for a time, governing lands reclaimed from the Axis powers, and finally the home Axis countries themselves. As early as April 1942 the United States had opened a School of Military Government, and military government units followed close behind the combat units in Europe to assume control of recently captured territory.[32] Armies had had an institutionalized place in local governance since at least the time of the Romans, and many soldiers among the Allies could draw on recent experience in the colonies, but World War II posed special challenges. Allied armies of occupation were expected not just to govern but also to create national and local democratic structures with which to supplant themselves. (In fact, the

Marine Corps' *Small Wars Manual* includes instructions on conducting the transition from military to civic rule, although on a much smaller scale.)

Another unprecedented task British and American soldiers took on was the preservation and restoration of art treasures damaged by war or stolen by the Germans. Curators and academics in uniform for wartime did most of this work, but they had the support of career soldiers such as Eisenhower, who as a major had served on the World War I monuments commission in Europe.[33] By World War II, military establishments both Axis and Allied possessed official art and history programs of their own, with uniformed soldiers in the field creating art and working to capture and preserve the historical record. These undertakings assisted in the military profession's effort to preserve its own institutional memory and knowledge of war, although the art and history departments, staffed largely by reservists and temporary officers from the art world and academe, could also seem outside the mainstream military profession, their products disseminated but not necessarily widely read or appreciated.[34]

Citizen-Officers: Literature and Leadership in World War II

The literature of World War II illuminates many of the challenges Allied military officers faced in the conflict. The armed forces of the major belligerent nations expanded massively in the years leading up to and during World War II. Most conspicuous in this trend was the United States, which in the 1920s and 1930s had seen its military establishment cut back through the influence of pacifism, isolationism, and the scarcities of the Great Depression. In 1939 the U.S. Army, by far the largest branch, numbered fewer than 200,000 personnel. In 1940 an unprecedented peacetime draft began the process of expansion, and by 1945 the armed forces of America had grown to more than 8 million.

The industrial, transportation, infrastructure, and sheer manpower needs that this expansion imposed have been well quantified and studied. What has received less attention is the task of enormously increasing the existing officer corps and adapting it to the demands of an expanded, lavishly resourced, largely citizen army that had to ready itself for deployment, war, and combat on a very tight schedule. In other words, the nation not only needed to produce personnel who were trained to fight, drive, type, build, and fix things; it also needed to train a large body of commissioned leaders almost overnight. It needed to develop a professional leadership body within the larger body of skilled and semiskilled workers who made up the majority of the armed forces.

America and its Allies were quite successful in creating these new, mostly temporary officer corps. America and Britain were highly organized and generally disciplined societies that were capable of adapting to the hierarchical nature of the military. The new sciences of personnel administration and recordkeeping, punch-card technology, and the emerging field of intelligence and skills testing to classify and assign soldiers to suitable roles and training made mid-twentieth-century armed forces more efficient. The war had the support of people in and out of uniform, although the desire to serve or sacrifice varied widely. On the other hand, and unlike the German (and Soviet) armed forces, the Allies had no strong unifying ideology to use as an ethos or aspect of leadership. The disciplinary means of the armies of the United States and the United Kingdom were considerably less ferocious than those of the fascists or Communists.

Finally, many saw a paradox in a war fought for democracy and even in support of egalitarian ideas (World War II was sometimes referred to as the "People's War" in Britain) that was led by a separate, somewhat privileged caste of individuals, many if not most of them drawn from the upper socioeconomic levels of society.[35] As had happened before, arguably since *The Iliad*, some saw the war as a pretext used to reinforce the power and privileges of those already in charge and of a few newcomers who were absorbed and indoctrinated by the ruling elite. Thus, the question of officers' rights to give orders, to be obeyed, and to enjoy certain distinguishing signs and privileges became an issue for the Allied armies in World War II, one that is reflected in the literature of the war, most especially in the novel, often the big, epic novel. Aside from their historical or literary interest, these works illuminate a discussion of the nature of leadership, the role of an officer in a democracy, and the mission and legacy of an officer body.

The categories of leadership problems or dilemmas in World War II literature might be labeled as reward and punishment, mission or troops, and reserve versus regular. One of the problems of military leadership highlighted in the works of the American James Jones and the Englishman Evelyn Waugh is the uncertainty of reward and reputation. The problem of recognizing merit, correcting poor performance, and censuring crime or

serious error is a challenge in any organization, but it may have been especially difficult in the huge militaries created for World War II. Added to this
is the fragile nature of military reputation, which may result in a soldier's
status and promotion turning on a single episode. Officers may have only
one opportunity for command in combat and perhaps one episode in which
they have the opportunity to set themselves apart. Battalion commander
and career officer Lieutenant Colonel Gordon Tall seems to realize this in
Jones' *The Thin Red Line* (1962). An overage lieutenant colonel who says of
his long career that he has "eaten untold buckets of shit," Tall is maniacally
determined to have his battalion distinguish itself in combat. He pushes his
exhausted, waterless men toward the objective on Guadalcanal. He is successful, and may go on to the promotion and eventual star he desires, but it
is uncertain whether he has succeeded through real leadership or mere brutality, with implications for the prospect of his receiving other commands
and increased power and responsibility. Another officer in Tall's command
gains national notoriety and the Medal of Honor for an exhortation in combat that his men consider banal and an exploit they view as commonplace.

In Waugh's *Officers and Gentlemen* (1955), aristocratic officer Ivor Claire,
whom the narrator, Guy Crouchback, somewhat ambivalently admires for
his independence and self-possession, is accused of cowardice on Crete. It
remains ambiguous throughout the trilogy whether these accusations are
founded (he is never charged), although he at least appears to be making an
effort at self-redemption when he later joins a special operations unit in the
Far East. Claire's alleged desertion follows a conversation with Crouchback
on the nature of honor in a changing world. To Crouchback it appears that
Claire may be too ready to adapt to modern, pragmatic ideas. Unlike Claire,
Crouchback persists in staying with his men through a difficult and hazardous retreat and evacuation.

Another leadership problem the war novels of World War II explore
is the perennial question of which comes first, mission or men? An officer
must both care for his men and be willing to sacrifice them. As in the case
of Lieutenant Colonel Tall, at what point does toughness become brutality?
On the other hand, can empathy become enervating? How much suffering
and sacrifice does an officer have a right to expect of his men? It might not
be enough for an officer to share the sufferings of those whom he leads. In
Kurt Vonnegut's *Slaughterhouse-Five* (1969), a regimental commander who

has assigned himself the rollicking nickname "Wild Bill" suffers cheerfully and eventually dies after his capture. He tries gamely to the end to keep up the spirits of the men captured with him, but he can do nothing to aid them or to alleviate the harsh winter conditions. Brigadier General Frank Savage takes over a bomber group in the 1948 novel and 1949 feature film *Twelve O'Clock High.* Thinking to challenge his men and shame them to better efforts, General Savage makes an uncompromising speech that results in all of his pilots asking for transfer. On the other hand, when Savage eventually learns to empathize with his men, he breaks down and becomes ineffective.

British navy officer Nicholas Monsarrat fought a long war at sea that he renders into fiction in *The Cruel Sea* (1951). For him the hardening of heart that takes place in war is as much a virtue as a necessity. His Captain George Ericson steels himself to perform the necessary destruction of war, ignoring crew fatigue, any claims to sympathy on the part of the enemy, and even on one occasion merchant sailors exposed in the water to the collateral effects of his depth-charge attack. His relentless pursuit of the enemy is an act of character undertaken in order to attain a victory that is far from assured.

Ericson, unlike Tall, is a reserve officer who is called to active duty "for the duration." In some World War II novels, the two groups are distinguished from each other in a way that makes clear that the professionals of the Regular Army and Navy have been bettered by their temporary colleagues. In James Jones' *From Here to Eternity* (1951) the ambitious, self-involved, and sports-obsessed regular Captain Dana "Dynamite" Holmes is relieved and replaced by reserve officer Lieutenant Barney Ross. Ross demotes the non-commissioned officers in the company who have been favored for their skill at boxing and takes an interest in the more mundane matters of training and administration. In Herman Wouk's *The* Caine *Mutiny* (1951), Naval Academy graduate Captain Philip Queeg is depicted as tyrannical, sometimes unethical, often inept, and even cowardly, but reserve officer Barney Greenwald warns the other officers on the *Caine* against judging all regular officers based on their experience of Queeg. Queeg may be an example of a regular officer for whom the extraordinary demands, rapid promotion, and suddenly increased responsibility of war were simply too great. Major "Fido" Hound in *Officers and Gentlemen* is another regular officer who undergoes a personal disintegration. The orderly habits and routines of peacetime soldiering have perhaps ill-equipped him to deal with the dislocation and uncertainty of combat and retreat, while the (sometimes younger) reserve officer may have a more flexible perspective that allows him to adapt to change and setback. Regular officers like Queeg, Hound, and Waugh's Brigadier Ben Ritchie-Hook are sometimes depicted as personally and professionally limited, yet they come across as preferable to reserve officers like Don Keefer in *The Caine Mutiny* and Lieutenant de Souza in *Officers and Gentlemen*, who suffer from tenuous and even divided loyalties, perhaps influenced by the pacifist or leftist ideas that were current among British and American intellectuals of the 1930s.

Another regular officer determined to make the most of the opportunities of wartime is General Edward Cummings in Norman Mailer's *The Naked and the Dead* (1948). Cummings' egotism, partly the product of a lifetime of giving orders, leads him to exaggerate his own ability to control events in combat, and he is obtusely absent for the crisis and climax of the battle he had hoped would make his name. Cummings is representative of the senior officer who is distrusted not for his intellectual limitations but because he is perhaps too arrogantly brilliant, too comfortable and even careless with the seemingly godlike power of a commanding general in wartime.

It is a sign of the success of the United States and the United Kingdom in creating wartime officer corps that many novels of the period have at their center a junior officer hero—that is, someone who is actually heroic and not merely the protagonist. Interestingly, even if the writer had served as an enlisted man, as in the case of Norman Mailer, in his novel the protagonist is an officer. This may be partly because of class-consciousness or cachet, a device to increase sales, but it also comes through that many enlisted men admired their officers, particularly those closest to them. Wouk's Ensign Willie Keith and Mailer's Lieutenant Robert Hearn are both young officers who rise above inexperience and a slow start to become effective and principled leaders in crisis. Military officership in war creates a service and leadership elite that cuts across class and other surface similarities and affiliations. Keith and Thomas Keefer are alike in being literary intellectuals, but Keith has the character to succeed under stress while Keefer does not. Doug Roberts in Thomas Heggen's novel *Mr. Roberts* (2009) is a highly competent deck officer respected by enlisted men and officers and dedicated to the larger cause of the war. His repeated insistence on being transferred from a support ship to a combatant vessel results in his being killed in action, but he leaves behind a legacy of courage in the face of petty tyranny as well as of the enemy.

Some nonfiction memoirs also contain vivid and positive portraits of officers by their enlisted subordinates. Some of the best appear in Eugene Sledge's personal account of the Marines' Pacific campaign, *With the Old Breed* (1981). Sledge's book is dedicated both to the "old breed" and to "Capt. Andrew A. Haldane, beloved company commander of K/3/5." Haldane was a 1941 graduate of Bowdoin College (Joshua Chamberlain's alma mater) who was killed in action on Peleliu on 12 October 1944. Sledge describes a brief but inspiriting conversation with Haldane during a rainy hike from the rifle range and notes: "He had a rare combination of intelligence, courage, self-confidence, and compassion that commanded our respect and admiration."[36]

Another question raised by the large national armies and quickly raised officer corps of World War II was whether enlisted men expect their officers to be gentlemen or common men, men who look, talk, and think as they do. Sledge's description of another officer in K/3/5, Lieutenant Edward A. "Hillbilly" Jones, may be the best answer to that question: "An act of Congress may have made Hillbilly an officer, but he was born a gentleman. . . . Between this man and all the Marines I knew there existed a deep mutual respect and warm friendliness. He had that rare ability to be friendly and yet not familiar with enlisted men."[37]

The answer to the dilemma of an officer corps serving and defending a democracy may be this: that officers are expected to constitute an elite, but a service elite, one that is distinguished more by ability and fidelity than by privilege or distinctiveness of uniform, comforts, lifestyle, or lineage. If officers receive privileges, they are to be based on a corresponding assumption of greater responsibility and are intended to free the officer for the higher demands of his or her position, mentally and physically. The publication in 1950 of the Department of Defense manual *The Armed Forces Officer*, which attempts to justify and articulate the position and responsibilities of the officer in a democracy, was a direct consequence of the problems that arose with commissioned officer leadership in World War II.[38] Written by journalist, reserve officer, and combat historian S. L. A. Marshall, this extraordinary book involves an inspired discussion of the officer's roles as a leader and a member of the profession of arms, emphasizing his or her status as a servant and exemplar of democracy. The structure of the book is dialogic and inclusive, with a broad range of allusion based on Marshall's eclectic reading. Marshall emphasizes the officer's role as a member of the wider society. Officers must not be "intellectual eunuch[s]" who remain aloof from debate out of either an exaggerated sense of infallibility, a habit of obedience, or because they do not feel they have a right to express themselves on the policies they believe are their professional duty to enforce. Officers are instructed to address subordinates as they would their "intellectual and political peers from any walk of life." The officer is expected to be a gentleman, not an aristocrat: "Upon being commissioned in the Armed Forces of the United States, a man incurs a lasting obligation to cherish and protect his country and to develop within himself that capacity and reserve strength which will enable him to serve its arms and the welfare of his fellow Americans with increasing wisdom, diligence, and patriotic conviction."[39]

Marshall worked as a journalist for two decades before once again donning a uniform (he was a veteran of World War I) in 1942. He is an outstanding example of the journalist as military professional. Military correspondents emerged as a distinct subset of the journalist profession in the nineteenth century, but they can perhaps trace their lineage back to the heralds of medieval times and to classical soldier-writers like Aeschylus. By the twentieth century, military correspondents were making substantial contributions to the collective knowledge of armed conflict, in both the particular and the general. Famous soldiers such as Winston Churchill and distinguished men of letters such as Stephen Crane and Ernest Hemingway contributed to the canon of military journalism. Some journalists became experts in regions of conflict and types of military operations. Bernard Fall became an acknowledged expert on Vietnam and on counterinsurgency. His insistence on seeing the conflict at first hand led to his death while on patrol with U.S. Marines in February 1967.

The Professional Contribution

If World War II represents a pinnacle of professional military achievement, two officers who worked as partners throughout America's participation in the conflict may be seen as personifying that achievement. George C. Marshall and Dwight D. Eisenhower enjoyed successful prewar careers, each serving as an aide to a general (John Pershing and Douglas MacArthur respectively). Their talents also attracted the notice of General Fox Connor, who was an older mentor to both officers and conducted Eisenhower through a postgraduate tutorial on strategy when they were stationed together in Panama. Connor prepared his protégés for the individual roles they would play in the coming conflict and for their no less important professional partnership.[40] The two officers were very different in personality, and were never really friends, but with the personable Eisenhower in command of the coalition in Europe and the coldly logical Marshall providing the strategic direction from Washington, America had a superb partnership. For all their contrasting styles, the two shared what biographer Mark Perry refers to as a "visionary" conception of the war that was the product of a combination of hard study, intellect, and imagination. The grasp of the global situation, with its human and moral implications, that Marshall and Eisenhower had gained as soldiers they were able to put at the service of their own country and the rest of the world. Having helped to rescue civilization, they went on to restore and preserve it in the difficult, pivotal postwar era. Not the least of their accomplishments was that both men helped to inspire and encourage the writing and publication of the original 1950 edition of *The Armed Forces Officer*. Marshall retired from the Army and went on to be secretary of defense (briefly) and of state, and to create the concept for the plan of European recovery that bears his name. Eisenhower served two terms as president, the great intellectual gifts behind the winning smile likely unappreciated even by many of his most ardent supporters.

The role of the officer as scholar and teacher is conspicuous in the careers of both men. Both made their early reputations largely through performance at Army service schools. Echoing Grant and Moltke, Marshall once expressed regret that he had not been able to pursue an academic career. Like Robert E. Lee, Eisenhower served as a university president after he retired from the Army (although he would have preferred to teach history). Eisenhower wrote an excellent book on his World War II experience, *Crusade in Europe* (1948), which was self-consciously patterned on Grant's memoir in both tone and form. Like Grant, Eisenhower limited his account to matters of which he had personal knowledge. Eisenhower also imitated Grant's plain style, which biographer Geoffrey Perret says "demonstrates that simplicity is ever the heart of elegance and the hallmark of sincerity."[41]

THE OPERATIONAL ART. American generals in Europe after VE Day. Due
largely to a progressive system of officer education that encouraged problem
solving and creative thought, the small, underfunded prewar U.S. Army produced
senior commanders able to adapt to the demands of a global war. *National Archives
and Records Administration*

It was Marshall who was primarily responsible for educating the greatly
enlarged American officer corps of World War II. He did this by helping to
equip the Regular Army to fulfill its role as educators of the wartime force
and by emphasizing through precept and example that the military profession is an occupation calling for careful and creative thought as well as for
training and discipline.[42]

It is ironic that as officers both Marshall and Eisenhower had been conditioned to see themselves as purely military men, apart and even aloof from
political concerns and matters of policy. Inheritors of the Anglo-American
tradition of constitutional subordination of the military to civilian control,
and products of the spartan and largely separate U.S. Army of the early years
of the century, they were also dedicated students of the military profession.
Their studies, combined with great intelligence and benevolence, allowed

them to perform their roles in a broad sense, as servants of civilization as well as paid fighters in the service of their republic.[43]

The military profession of mid-century played an important role in the solution to the crisis of the times, but it was also a large part of the problem. The professional militaries of the Axis countries, including the much imitated and somewhat ambivalently admired German army, were willing tools of the repressive, aggressive regimes they served.[44] More than this, they came to embody the fascist and racist ideologies that had taken root in their countries. By the mid-1930s the militarism incipient in the nineteenth century had captured the military professions of the Axis powers, acting in a kind of partnership with the political, social, and racist ideas of fascism. There were crypto-fascist officers in the armies of the democracies as well, but in the course of the war the armies became more egalitarian and representative, and these changes were not all rolled back with the end of hostilities and the enormous wartime armies. In effect siding with the Allies were the pockets of officers who resisted the fascist movements in their own countries, the de Gaulles and von Stauffenbergs. The moral repugnance of Nazism and fascism are too well established to require discussion. Fascist regimes and ideologies also acted as impediments to creativity and to clear and realistic thinking on a number of levels. The advent of the Nazis in Germany brought about an extraordinary "brain drain" as Jewish scientists were pushed out of university positions and imprisoned, murdered, or convinced to emigrate. Some scientists remained and worked assiduously for the regime, but other men of conscience who remained may have reined in their efforts to provide the Nazis with the tools of victory. It is still debated, but this may have been the case with Werner Heisenberg, who dismissed the atom bomb project as impractical despite his reputation for brilliance in solving the kinds of problems that development of the bomb seemed to present.

The fascist doctrine of perpetual war may have been an impediment to the kind of full-on commitment of industrial and scientific resources seen in the Allied nations during the pivotal years of the conflict. Although the Nazis developed innovative and important military technology in the form of the V rockets and early jet fighters, they never amassed the intellectual or industrial capital to employ them in a way and on a scale that might have made them decisive. The most crippling deficiency of the Nazi cause

may have been Nazism itself. Unlike Alexander, Napoleon, or other previous conquerors, the Nazis had no guiding idea that could be disseminated
beyond a very narrow range of humanity. They could win collaborators but
few real converts. What the Nazis coveted they stole or destroyed. Although
they made some efforts to make their nationalistic and racist creed more
inclusive, even throwing open the ranks of the SS (Schutzstaffel) to for-
eigners who might cynically be deemed "Aryan," Nazism could never be a
unifying doctrine. In the end what held it together as much as anything was
shame and the fear of exposure and deserved sanction.

The year 1945 had a similar significance for the world as 1648 had for
Europe. In both cases the exhausted combatants might look back on a half
century that had seen much large-scale warfare and ahead to a new international system. The Treaty of Westphalia had created the nation-state system;
the end of World War II saw the most powerful states dividing along ideological lines. In both periods the military profession had been both culprit
and cure. The seventeenth-century profession of arms underwent needed
reform, rejecting the mercenary model that had been dominant for much
of the early half of the century. In the early and mid-twentieth century,
the authoritarian and xenophobic tendencies of the nineteenth century in
some countries blossomed and became enshrined in ideology. Soldiers participated in what came to be called "crimes against humanity," in genocide,
and in the indiscriminate bombing of civilian populations. Finally, the use
of the atom bombs demonstrated that military power was approaching the
theoretical absolute imagined by Clausewitz. As in the seventeenth century,
the military profession of the post–World War II period was at a crossroads;
the profession had been both a tool for tyrants and an abettor of destruction
and disorder as well as a servant of stability and civilization. Which would
be the dominant model for the future?

The redirection of the military profession at this point may be said to
have originated in two sources. The first of these were the Nuremberg trials
and other war crimes trials that followed the war. These went further than
earlier conventions in establishing soldiers' moral obligations beyond the
limited concerns of national loyalty or "military necessity" that had been
allowed to predominate in the era of nationalism. The other development
was the advent of the United Nations. Proposals to establish a standing
UN armed force were never put into practice, but task-organized UN forces

conducted pioneering peacekeeping missions around the world in the years after the UN's formation (and they continue to do so). UN forces set an example that other coalition forces keeping or enforcing fragile peace in troubled areas would follow.[45] A whole family of noncombative, or "other-than-war," military missions developed in the years after World War II. Military forces intervened to ameliorate the effect of natural or man-made humanitarian disasters, to separate warring factions, and to stabilize areas where security and the rule of law had broken down.

The UN "Blue Beret" forces constitute an odd revival of the eighteenth-century "soldier trade." Countries that provide troops for these missions tend to be poor Third World countries themselves, for whom the financial rewards are a strong inducement to send their soldiers to troubled areas. Such soldiers often suffer from deficiencies in training and education. Their equipment may be outdated and poorly maintained. Peace, humanitarian, and stability operations require individual and unit capabilities beyond those required for combat. The soldiers involved must navigate complex political and cultural waters and coordinate with host nation authorities and multiple nongovernmental agencies. The record of success of such operations has been spotty, and on some occasions the failures have been spectacular and much publicized. Still, peace, humanitarian, and stability operations continue to be conducted and are sometimes effective. The conduct of such operations has become part of the professional playbook of many armed forces across the spectrums of region and capabilities.

Counterinsurgency and Wars of National Liberation

In the years after World War II a combination of ideology, awakening national consciousness, impatience with sometimes obtuse or heavy-handed European rule, and the dislocations brought on by the war gave rise to a generation of insurgencies and wars of national liberation against former colonial rulers, their postcolonial proxies, and the United States, which joined the conflict mostly because of an ideological opposition to communism. Over time, Western armies became more proficient at the specialized tasks involved in these kinds of conflicts, which included nation building and rural and urban policing (although they might also involve conventional operations, which dominated the Korean conflict and the latter part of the Vietnam War). Counterinsurgency operations rewarded superiority of information more than preponderance of firepower. The soldier at war has arguably always been in the service of policy and diplomacy, but in counterinsurgency the soldier must actually acquire some of the skills of the politician or diplomat. However, and despite developing proficiency and sometimes deepening commitment, Western soldiers often appeared to be on the wrong side of a historical trend. How much responsibility for the demise of colonial empires was borne by the soldiers who tried to uphold them? Ideology aside, these colonies represented an unnatural state of affairs. Colonial empires could survive only by enfranchising and empowering native people, but to do so meant giving up the colonists' own authority. Ironically, many insurgents had received their initial military training as members of the colonial armies, some even remarking that the colonial armies had made them good soldiers. In the tradition of Friedrich Engels, some insurgent leaders could claim to be members of the profession of arms. Some who had begun in ragged local peasant garb graduated to formal ranks and uniforms. Mao Tse-tung, Vo Nguyen Giap, Fidel Castro, and Ernesto "Che" Guevara were formidable adversaries whose beliefs and methods appeared for a time to be in the ascendant. In their interest in military matters and preference for military solutions and metaphors, Guevara and Mao were as much the descendants of Engels as of Marx. Both wrote insurgent or guerilla treatises that are still read today.[46]

Counterinsurgency called for highly educated officers who were capable of imaginative thought and of communicating with people of different cultures. Language skills were needed not only to gain information but also to articulate a political or ethical position that made sense on the ground. Counterinsurgency required creative solutions to political, economic, and cultural problems that had an impact on the security situation and on the operational and tactical picture. In a sense, counterinsurgency turned the conventional principles of war upside down. Whereas in conventional operations the side that could levy the most force and combat power was usually the winner, in counterinsurgency the goal in both the short and long term was to reduce and eliminate the use of force. Conventional operations also called for the offensive and for mobility, while in counterinsurgency the side that could stay in one place the longest often secured the advantage. Even the principle of unity of command was modified by the need to include numerous parties in decision making. Daunting as they were, the cognitive and doctrinal challenges of counterinsurgency were perhaps outweighed by its ethical pitfalls. The frustrations, sometimes bitter shocks, and setbacks of counterinsurgency could disrupt clear thinking and be an incitement to reprisal, atrocity, and the adoption of vicious methods such as hostage-taking or the shifting of responsibility for one's own war crimes onto the enemy.

Once a military force became embroiled in a counterinsurgency war, the conflict might assume a life, logic, and rationale all its own. This was conspicuous in Algeria and in Vietnam. The French defeat in Indochina at Dien Bien Phu probably only accelerated a withdrawal that the French government had already accepted as inevitable, but it was humiliating nevertheless to members of the French military profession. French soldiers returned to an incipient insurgency in their other traditional colonial stronghold of Algeria determined not to lose again. The French regular army became strongly ideological and collectively convinced that the enemy they faced in Algeria was motivated by communism, as it had been in Indochina. The French army performed impressively in the Algerian War, employing helicopters and airborne forces to overtake and encircle insurgent units in the countryside. The insurgent Front de Liberation Nationale (FLN) fought an especially brutal, deliberately provocative terror campaign, targeting beaches, "milk bars," and other gathering places of young and old, sparing no one and killing far more Algerians than Europeans. The French rose to the bait. Every new attack became a pretext for rounding up hundreds of Algerians, most of them innocent. The French became inured to the use of harsh interrogation and torture, which often were followed by secret executions termed "a walk in the woods." Elite units like the Foreign Legion and paratroopers became heroes to *pieds noir*, as the European colonists of Algeria called themselves, and the soldiers responded with a deepening commitment to the perpetuation of Algérie française.

In 1961 a coterie of four French generals led by Air Marshal General Maurice Challe, the ousted former military commander in Algeria, led a coup in reaction to French president Charles de Gaulle's calls for Algerian self-determination. The coup failed when the majority of French soldiers, most of whom were short-service conscripts, remained loyal to the government.[47] In another example of a paradox of military professionalism, the short-service conscripts served the civil authority more faithfully than did the highly trained, long-service volunteers. With the failure of the coup, some French and Foreign Legion soldiers deserted and went underground, forming the Organisation de l'armée secrète (OAS) and carrying out terrorist raids in support of what was almost certainly a lost cause.[48]

The departure of the Westerners from the scene of an insurgency did not necessarily put an end to conflict. In fact, the end of colonial authority could unleash tribal and other animosities that previously had been held in check, and perhaps even aggravated by the years of outside rule. The new states that had been born of conflict often found it difficult to put aside the sword, and in any case the military establishments usually continued to play a disproportionate share in public life in countries with few other viable institutions and still facing threats to stability, bringing on a revival of praetorianism that was perhaps unmatched in extent and influence since the original.[49] Dirty wars fought with mixes of mercenaries and local levies sometimes followed liberation, especially in Africa, where the situation could recall that of Europe during the Thirty Years' War, or even of late antiquity.

In Vietnam, the departure of the French opened the way for American involvement. Reluctant at first—cautioned by the French example, the casualties of the Korean War, and MacArthur's warning about committing to a ground war in Asia—America began with a slow buildup of intelligence and logistics support in the early 1960s, but after the first commitment of ground combat units in 1965 the escalation was rapid. Like the French army before it, the American military became committed to the war as almost a personal matter, with the elusiveness of victory an affront to manhood and professional credibility. William Westmoreland, the commander of Military Assistance Command Vietnam (MACV) from 1964 to 1968, was an artilleryman whose answer to the communist challenge was the traditional American solution of victory through superiority of fire.[50] Better solutions may have been available in the form of a greater investment in the military effectiveness of the Army of the Republic of Vietnam or in establishing longer-lasting regional security through programs such as the Combined Action Platoons, a promising undertaking by the Marine Corps. The reliance on superior firepower was also reflected in the "Rolling Thunder" bombing campaigns. American bombing in the North and in the rest of the theater was quite discriminating relative to the past practice of aerial bombing and the limitations of available technology. But ultimately the bombing failed the most important test of military effectiveness: it did not shorten or end the war; it merely raised the level of suffering on both sides.

The Vietnam War produced an impressive outpouring of literary works by soldiers, and books by Vietnam veterans continue to appear. As in previous times, the works often contain narratives and reflections that contribute to an understanding of military professionalism. Tim O'Brien's *If I Die in a Combat Zone* (1973) contains observations on the sources and nature of courage, along with frequent references to the Socratic *Laches*. Marine officers Philip Caputo and James Webb wrote books based on their service in Vietnam. Caputo's *Rumor of War* (1977) is an allusive memoir of the deployment to Vietnam of one of the first American ground combat units. Webb's *Fields of Fire* (1978) is a novel. Both books chronicle an American war crime and its aftermath. Webb, a Naval Academy graduate and one of the most highly decorated officers of his generation, went on to become Secretary of the Navy and a U.S. senator, a soldier-writer-statesman in the tradition of Caesar and Grant. Josiah Bunting's *The Lionheads* (1972) is an unusual work in its focus on the often-neglected middle officer ranks. Most of the principal characters are officers of the rank of captain through colonel. Bunting himself had served in Vietnam and was an Army major when his book was published. His novel offers an unsparing critique of the American Vietnam-era officer corps, although the problems of institutional groupthink and blind optimism he depicts are not unique to that time and place. Most telling and universal are his identification of the "divorcement of remorse from power" that can overtake senior officers in command, along with the inability of even enlightened and competent officers to impose order on chaos or to change entrenched beliefs and interests.

It might be fair to say that for the American military establishment and profession, Vietnam was a disaster whose lessons were neither completely ignored nor fully comprehended.[51] Like the French in Algeria, the Americans in Vietnam gave way to some of the demoralization that threatens an organized military force conducting a counterinsurgency campaign against a ruthless enemy. American troops committed war crimes, and in some cases senior officers conspired to conceal the full extent of those crimes. The reliance on "body counts" and other dubious quantitative measurements of success on the part of the Defense Department and the uniformed military not only led to breaches of integrity; it also encouraged a simplistic, number-crunching approach to war that was unworthy of the army of Washington, Grant, Marshall, and Eisenhower. The prestige of the military and the attractiveness of military service were at a low ebb in the years after the war, so the services were induced to lower enlistment standards and compromise on matters of discipline. American officers wanted no more Vietnams, and counterinsurgency yielded in doctrine and training to an emphasis on decisive, mobile warfare quickly brought to a finish.

In some ways this was a misinterpretation of the lessons of the war, since Vietnam had arguably demonstrated that counterinsurgency campaigns might have to be fought, like it or not. Unquestionably, however, with concepts such as "maneuver warfare" in the air, the post-Vietnam U.S. armed forces developed a powerful capability to wage conventional warfare decisively. The use of simulators as well as an increased emphasis on realism also improved training. By the end of the 1970s, enlistment standards had improved and the American military was becoming a force of motivated volunteers who had chosen and who generally enjoyed military life and responded to the demands of discipline and the appeals of esprit de corps. The American military also did some professional introspection, conscious of the ethical and cognitive failures that had accompanied defeat. A new generation of military sociologists, the inheritors of the tradition of Samuel Huntington and Morris Janowitz, formed an organization called the Inter-University Seminar on Armed Forces and Society, which still publishes a scholarly journal.[52] Charles Moskos was the leading figure in this group, and he and other academics—some retired from the military, others still in uniform and teaching at the service academies and schools— consulted with the services on matters of policy and professionalism.

A group of American military professionals who performed creditably in this era were the Vietnam prisoners of war. Most were officers and pilots who had been shot down during the bombing campaigns in the North. Nearly all acquitted themselves honorably, in accordance with the U.S. Code of Conduct that had been developed after the experience of the Korean War. One of the longest-interned and the acknowledged leader of the Hanoi prisoners was Commander (later Vice Admiral) James Stockdale, who was awarded the Medal of Honor for his conduct as a prisoner. A philosophy graduate student before he was deployed to Vietnam, Stockdale came home committed to the idea that military professionals should read works of philosophy and other classic humanities literature as part of their moral development and to strengthen their character. Stockdale and philosophy professor Joseph Brennan designed a course that is still taught at the Naval War College based on these ideas that was later the basis for Brennan's book *Foundations of Moral Obligation*.[53]

Conventional Warfare

For more than forty years after World War II, the opposing forces of NATO and the Warsaw Pact faced each other in strength across the continent of Europe, on its flanks, and in the surrounding seas. The expectation of a major conflict in Europe sometimes ran high, but conventional combined-arms warfare in Western Europe occurred neither on land nor at sea in the second half of the century. It flared up in Korea and in Vietnam, especially in the final offensives that brought on the fall of South Vietnam. Conventional warfare occurred frequently in the Middle East, partly because of the area's terrain, but also because adversaries were often opposing nation-states with symmetrical (although often unmatched) military forces. The fledgling Israeli armed forces achieved a victory in 1948, and then with more highly organized and better-equipped forces defeated their Arab opponents decisively in 1956 and 1967. In 1973 they achieved a less rapid victory against an Egyptian army that had been stung by repeated defeats and equipped with the latest Soviet wire-guided antitank technology.

During this period the Israeli army may be said to have set the standard of military professionalism as measured in battlefield success and in terms of its service and relationship with civil society, perhaps especially in contrast to lowered American military prestige as a consequence of Vietnam. Israel had the grim memory of the Holocaust and a realistic existential threat to focus its attention on the national defense. The fact that the Israeli people tended to be highly educated and had a common religion, traditions, and culture helped them to create a formidable military establishment out of limited population and resources. Israel's limited geographic size made passive, position defense suicidal and encouraged an active, even preemptive approach to defense, most notably in 1967.

The circumstances and response of Israel, a small nation surrounded by larger neighbors and with a disproportionately large and very capable army, might be reminiscent of Prussia in the eighteenth century. The differences are equally significant, however. Prussia faced no existential threat when Frederick launched the first of his series of campaigns in 1740, and Israeli society lacked the militarism—the reification of military trappings and methods for their own sake—that came to characterize Prussian and German society. To this day the Israeli government is civil and democratic. When Israeli soldiers come to wield political power, as in the case of special operations officer, general, and strategist Ariel Sharon, they do so as elected civilians, not as soldiers on horseback.

The largest use of conventional military force in the latter years of the twentieth century was Iraq's invasion of Kuwait and the response of Operations Desert Shield and Desert Storm. A quick, decisive victory by the U.S.-led coalition demonstrated the distance that U.S. forces had come from the post-Vietnam era in terms of equipment and training. The Soviet Union having dissolved in 1989, the United States was unquestionably the greatest military power on land, air, and sea. America's efforts to exert military power in arenas that were less conducive to conventional war were not as successful, however, most notably in Somalia, although they did achieve more success in the Balkans. America went from triumphant to chastened in the 1990s. Then came an event that seemed to change everything, although how much really changed still remains to be seen.

Deterrence, the Cold War, and Its Conclusion

I conclude this chapter on the military profession of the twentieth century by returning to the period of the Cold War in order to note perhaps the greatest accomplishment of the military profession during the century: the stewardship, control, restraint, and nonemployment of the nuclear weapons several countries possessed in the second half of the century. The main Cold War nuclear antagonists were the United States and the Soviet Union, but many other countries possessed nuclear arsenals and delivery systems, and perhaps also the motives or pretext for their use. The nuclear arsenals of the Cold War created a new breed of defense intellectuals, typified by Herman Kahn and chillingly portrayed in the book and feature film *Fail-Safe* (1962).[54] These "endgamesmen," as Stephen Brodsky describes them, thought about the unthinkable and had a different vision of war from that of traditional professionals.[55] Whether their work helped to hold the nuclear holocaust at bay or to normalize nuclear war and therefore make it more acceptable and more likely is subject to debate. As detailed in Eric Schlosser's book *Command and Control*, the nuclear accident was waiting to happen and was averted only by a hundred acts of heroism and initiative on the part of officers and technicians on all sides.[56]

The United States not only had the largest nuclear arsenal; it also had a robust, redundant system of delivery options consisting of ground-based missiles such as the Minuteman, nuclear submarines, and long-range nuclear bombers. The latter were grouped under the Strategic Air Command (SAC). Although there were dire (and not entirely misplaced) predictions of a devastating nuclear mishap or reluctant reciprocal exchange, the hammer always managed to fall on an empty chamber. The SAC motto, Peace Is Our Profession, was the subject of satire, but SAC was perhaps the first military organization in history whose mission was never to wage war. Their long flights and vigils in freezing high-altitude skies went mostly unnoticed. At the end of the Cold War, various rival and Allied military establishments, inheritors of centuries of traditions of discipline and restraint, had successfully held the fearsome weapons in check and the dreaded event never took place.

Conclusion

THE TWENTY-FIRST CENTURY
A Century of the Soldier?

In the midst of the Thirty Years' War and other virulent military activity in the seventeenth century in Europe and beyond, the Italian writer Fulvio Testi wrote that it had been the century of the soldier.[1] A person writing about the twenty-first century may have reason to echo this observation. The lines are being drawn between the democratic and stable nations of the world and the agents and areas of disorder, and these could become battle lines: a coalition of the soldiers of civilization versus the warrior-terrorists in the service of their gods and strange dreams of apocalypse. Another factor of the international scene is the resurgence of a xenophobic nationalism even in "liberal" countries. Arguably, since the Treaty of Westphalia in 1648 the nation-state has been the chief repository of political, economic, and military power on the globe, as well as the main avatar of meaning, art, and narrative.[2] This system has been experiencing some recent changes and challenges. While the global history of the nation-state may not inspire nostalgia in everyone, the national state and the international system of states had certain advantages. It has been said that the nation-state both created and was created by the need to wage warfare on a large scale, but the nation-state could be a source of order and civilization as well as a war-fighting entity. Perhaps most important, the nation-state could eventually be held accountable for its actions; it could be subject to deterrence and reprisal. A rough justice was at work among the nations of the world, one that promised to get slightly less rough and more just with the advent of the United Nations. The secular deity delineated by Thomas Hobbes and enshrined by G. W. F. Hegel has often been a poor neighbor and tenant. Along with disillusionment about nationalism, the nation-state now has competition for loyalties and power in the form of transnational organizations. The most powerful of these is the transnational corporation; the most dangerous is the extremist group dedicated to terrorism as a tactic. These transnationals, the terror-embracing ones in particular, are elusive, hard to identify, and tied to no geography or identifiable population. This very postmodern, information age lack of corporeality is part of their allure and their power. Is the nation-state surrendering its moral authority and its hold on the imaginations of a new generation? If so, what international or transnational angels or demons will come to take its place?

In the twenty-first century the military profession has been challenged to retain both its effectiveness against asymmetrical opponents and its monopoly status (or at least majority share) in the application of armed force, and also to develop unaccustomed capabilities and partnerships. The pace of technological development has accelerated, calling for new methods of assimilation and a closer (if still wary) relationship with science and industry. The privatization of some military functions has accompanied the rise of the non-state-affiliated fighter, terrorist, or insurgent. War is less likely to be between competing armies of soldiers than between soldiers and their various adversaries. The boundaries of the profession of arms have at once been threatened and expanded. This is not new. At all times in history the profession of arms has been encircled by a military profession of administrators, logisticians, manufacturers, scientists, and others who support the military undertaking by providing expertise and services. While also not new, it is the case perhaps to a greater degree than ever before, and the need for the profession of arms to define its special provenance may also be greater than ever.

Soldiers may see themselves as bound to resist the erosion of state authority, but the increasing practice of coalition operations demonstrates that they are part of this trend. The UN doctrine of "Responsibility to Protect" is based on the emerging belief that individual rights can trump national sovereignty. Armies may be becoming transnational themselves in order to unite and effectively fight against transnational opponents. This may call for a new breed of soldier with broader capabilities and even loyalties: a professional peacemaker in the service of civilization. As I have argued in this book, history returns echoes of this role, from Caesar to Marshall, and it may be that peacekeeping will come to be the soldier's most important task of all.

In the 1990s some military professionals in and out of uniform proclaimed a "revolution in military affairs" (RMA) brought on by developments in technology with the potential to provide a commander with unprecedented resources for intelligence, communications, command, and control. The new technology would give the commander instant information on the where-abouts and status of friendly units and nearly as much information on enemy forces. The result would be a revolutionary dispersing of the "fog of war" that Clausewitz describes as one of the immutable factors of armed conflict. Like many heralded revolutions, the RMA was no doubt oversold by some of its enthusiasts, who tended to be associated with the more technologi-cal services of Air Force and Navy rather than Army and Marine Corps.[3] Nevertheless, technology has had an undoubted effect on the warfare of the twenty-first century. Digital technology can give commanders and units a shared picture of the friendly battle space unseen since battles were fought on open fields. Following that historical analogy, it may also be observed that the contemporary commander's encompassing digital view of the battlefield is a revival of an ancient perspective as well as the introduction of a new one, and that neither view was or is perfect or a panacea. As with the earlier adoption of and reliance on wire communications, the new technology can implant a false sense of knowledge and lead to neglect of traditional methods of communication as well as to meddling on the part of senior command-ers.[4] Digital command-and-control systems can also lead to a neglect of the factors in war and in combat that do not fall under their scope, human and cultural factors in particular. It is these very factors that are most significant in counterinsurgency, which has been the most prevalent form of conflict so far in this century and will be at least one aspect of military operations in the years and decades to come. Digital devices can detect groups of people and even individuals, but cannot peer into their hearts. They are better at spotting the heavy equipment of a conventional army than the smaller, less conspicuous or hidden weaponry of an insurgent cell.

Perhaps the most controversial tool of the digital counterinsurgent is the armed drone. Given good intelligence, the drone can be an effective coun-terinsurgency and counterterrorism tool. If intelligence is faulty or incom-plete, however, a drone strike can kill the innocent instead of or along with the targeted. There is something in us that does not love a drone. With each advance in weaponry—the advent of archery, of gunpowder weapons, and of attacks from the air—traditional soldiers and compassionate civilians decried the increase in remoteness between target and shooter. Distance shooters have been branded cowardly and unaccountable, their weapons spelling the end of military virtue. In each case the professional ethos has accommodated itself to the new weaponry, and advances in technique have contrived to put the remote combatant at risk. The use of drones further separates shooter and target, and it can put shooters in positions of safety and insulate them almost completely from the impact of their actions. In such a setting, the possibility of sacrifice is weighted almost all on one side, and war comes to resemble murder. Only a very difficult, even wildly improbable, asymmetrical counterattack might put the controller of a drone at risk.

Cyber operations, another new form of warfare, are less likely than drone attacks to have lethal results, but they keep the soldiers conducting them from harm or even hardship in what may seem a distinctly unsoldierly way. It might be argued that a military professional serving in a drone or cyber operations command could be transferred to a more active front, given the fortunes of war and the vagaries of military personnel assignment. Whether or not this is a realistic possibility in an individual's own situation, it is perhaps a challenge to the distance-battle soldier to cultivate and retain an appreciation for the battlefield that he or she may perceive directly only in the silent images of a remote camera. To paraphrase Winston Churchill, war, which was once cruel and splendid and later cruel and squalid, is becoming for some uniformed military professionals cruel and cyber: very real at one end and virtual on the other.

A further challenge to military professionalism lies in the increasing mechanization of warfare. The pages of this history may suggest that few humans are fully equal to the varied and heavy demands of leadership in war and combat. Like the dreams of the early aviation professionals, robot warfare seems to offer the possibility of war with less error, trauma, and loss of human life. Still, the matter of how much military service can or should be outsourced to machines (or to bioengineered clone-soldiers) is a question to be approached very carefully. It is one that the military profession must address along with the rest of society, since the mechanization of both military and nonmilitary human functions is a prospect with broad, even ontological consequences hard to foresee but somehow more nightmarish than like a dream.

9/11, Afghanistan, and Iraq

The attacks on the World Trade Center and the Pentagon in 2001 seemed to many who lived through them to mark a clear line of departure in history.

That the mainland of America suffered a deadly, large-scale attack from outside without precedent since the War of 1812 was only part of it. Even more disorienting was the nature of the attack, the shadowy organization and almost unfathomable worldview and motives behind it. Part of the U.S. reaction was to retaliate in kind by energizing the nation's intelligence services and resources to conduct covert operations against a covert enemy. But within a few months the United States had also committed conventional forces to a campaign in Afghanistan. This was initially successful, routing the Taliban and appearing to restore much of the country to the control of a secular, antiterrorist government. The early success of the campaign in Afghanistan contributed to a U.S. buildup of forces and the invasion of Iraq in March 2003. In both campaigns, as long as the fighting was mostly conventional America and its allies did well, but once the challenge changed to that of combating a dispersed enemy of insurgents the situations deteriorated. As so often in the past, early optimism had proved to be misleading. Some poor decisions and a conceptual unpreparedness for counterinsurgency worsened what was going to be at best a difficult and complex situation. An overestimation of the advantages conferred by technology contributed to a force being committed that was much smaller than what military planners had originally envisioned.

Failure to plan for the governance and stabilization of Iraq had perhaps the greatest impact, based in part on a lack of understanding of Iraqi society and (more surprising) of the impact of a large-scale invasion on a long-suppressed civil population and an unwisely demobilized Iraqi armed forces. The policy and planning deficiencies exhibited by civilian and military planners (both military professionals and members of the profession of arms) were rescued to a degree by the inspired leadership of officers on the ground at the junior, middle, and senior levels. The Marines dusted off their *Small Wars Manual* and found useful information and even a kind of reflective wisdom in this neglected classic that is too often missing in an age of information frantically acquired and quickly forgotten. Later, a joint U.S. Army–Marine Corps doctrinal publication, *FM 3-24/MCWP 3-33.5 Counterinsurgency*, was published in 2006 (and revised as *Insurgencies and Countering Insurgencies* in 2014).[5]

At the tactical level, leaders began to adopt a more engaged and forthcoming approach to counterinsurgency, at first extemporaneously but later as a matter of doctrine. Such an approach could involve great hazards, but progress was made in securing the cooperation of the Iraqi people and in developing their security and military forces. There were also some conspicuous missteps on the part of the leadership, however, including an excessive tolerance of misbehavior and mediocrity. Maybe even worse than this, the intellectual, doctrinal, and moral limitations of the post-Vietnam rebuilding of the U.S. armed forces were revealed. As Thomas Ricks notes in *The Generals*, the Army in particular had come to focus on tactics at the expense of developing within the officer ranks a capacity for strategic thought, thus bringing about a separation between policy and the military means used to enforce it.[6] The conventional tactical victories of 1991, 2002, and 2003 turned out to be largely hollow. Further exacerbating the problem, in the 1950s and afterward, military officers became increasingly reluctant to relieve subordinates who did not perform, as if a military career were more important than oath, lives, and mission.[7] This amounted to a reversal of the high-minded tradition and war-winning practice of George C. Marshall, who wanted creative strategic thinkers and was not afraid to relieve senior officers found wanting in courage, energy, or performance.

Humanitarian Assistance Operations

Humanitarian assistance operations have become an increasingly important area of military professionalism in the twenty-first century. Such operations may at first appear simple and unproblematic. The immediate enemies in humanitarian operations are hunger, disease, and dislocation. The solutions to these problems would appear to be largely logistical. The challenges are complex and often large in scale, but they lack the innate unpredictability of combat operations. In practice, however, humanitarian operations must usually confront the *causes* of want and suffering, which are often political or cultural issues, nearly intractable and of long standing. The impact of humanitarian relief may be unpredictable and mistakes difficult to undo. Employing the military instrument to solve a humanitarian crisis may resemble Alexander's legendary use of a sword to untie the Gordian knot: the knot is loosed, but the rope is irreparably severed, and any use it may have served is lost. Humanitarian operations have the potential to undermine what little order exists in a fragile society. They can wound already injured pride, provoke resistance, and incite violence. They can come to be seen as examples of self-interested late imperialism rather than as a sincere desire to help. The relief campaign in Somalia is perhaps the classic modern humanitarian operation gone wrong. What had seemed a fairly simple exercise in logistics and security revealed itself to be a complex political problem. Unexpected heavy fighting and American casualties in effect revealed a flawed understanding of the problems and challenges that led to an ignominious retreat and a subsequent reluctance to intervene elsewhere. In addition (and perhaps partly in response) to the many inherent difficulties, some soldiers view humanitarian operations as a distraction, something done better by organizations like the Red Cross, with military forces perhaps limited to providing security and deterrence.

Despite the difficulties and reasonable objections, however, military organizations will probably be called on to conduct humanitarian operations across the spectrum of functions because they possess to an unmatched degree many of the capacities most needed in humanitarian relief. They can move themselves and large amounts of supplies and equipment under adverse conditions; they possess their own organic medical personnel; and they can protect themselves and extend protection to others when a breakdown of order accompanies a humanitarian crisis. Beyond the capacity for logistics and security, what a military organization committed to humanitarian operations will most need is adaptability. Such operations require a military organization to be a learning community that is on a curve often even steeper than required in a flexible tactical situation. Humanitarian operations place a premium on mental agility, and sometimes on subtlety. Societies that appear primitive by American and Western standards may in fact be culturally and politically sophisticated, and what appears to be merely random or atavistic behavior may have complex origins rooted deep in local, regional, and global history. Humanitarian operations might even be perceived as embodying the broad, global goal of the military profession: the preservation of stability, order, human rights, and welfare.

Whatever alternate possible futures for the globe actually manifest, it seems inescapable that the military profession will play a large role in containing and levying force and in keeping the peace. In peace and war soldiers and military professionals will be needed as guardians and agents of civilization. If permanent peace ever comes, the soldier will have a place in that world too. Even today there are officers in military uniform who play strictly noncombatant roles. The officer-scientists of the National Oceanic and Atmospheric Association and the officer-physicians of the National Health Service have no role even in the support of military operations. The cadets of the maritime colleges and midshipmen at the U.S. Merchant Marine Academy might someday become involved in warfare at sea, but very rarely in a combatant role. Nevertheless, these are professionals for whom the military officer's uniform serves as a reminder of the high degree of dedication and liability that are required of them. They are men and women who may have to risk life and limb in the service of their country and professional calling.

Challenges of the Century

To fulfill their role completely, the military professionals of today must know, heed, and apply the examples and narrative of the most successful and exemplary military professionals of the past at their best. Out of the foregoing account of the history of the military profession, a number of lessons emerge. I will discuss these in terms of officer education, civil-military relations and nation building, and global role.

Officer Education

The education of military professionals has been the subject of disagreement since it was first seen as a distinct subject. Perhaps starting with the Roman commander Marius, some have espoused a more minimalist, "hands-on" or technical approach.[8] This has the virtues of efficiency and ability to assess the results, and subjects such as weapons handling and simplified small-unit tactics are often what remain when the education of officers must be compressed into a short period, especially under the demands of a wartime buildup. Still, I side with those who find this approach dangerously reductive. In fact, I am in general agreement with those who find current officer education lacking in depth and rigor. If the potential for military service to be stultifying and dehumanizing is to be averted and the potential for the military professional to be an agent of order and civilization is to be fulfilled, the development of moral character, intellectual curiosity, and creativity should be part of a soldier's education, especially for those who will spend much of their lives in the service, and most especially in the officer ranks. Mentoring, civilian education, and formal professional military education can address this need. The reinstitution of off-duty events combining social and education aspects, "officers calls," as they have been termed, could be quite valuable, following the example set by Eisenhower and others in building teams, staffs, and coalitions. Officer education is a matter of both policy and command climate.

As I have maintained in this work, the military profession, considered most comprehensively, might be viewed as an interdisciplinary branch of the humanities. In any profession, but perhaps most especially in the profession of arms, a soul as well as skills is required. In dark and crowded hours the soldier has need of the inner being who not only acts but also thinks, dreams, and loves. As soldier-intellectuals and soldier-poets have long demonstrated, the contemplative does not rule out the active; indeed it may fuel it as personal resources husbanded and cultivated in times of peace are put into play. Marlborough, Jackson, Patton, and Marshall are examples of men whose rich inner lives served them well in the role of military leader. The education of military professionals should include the history of their own profession. The officer's education should partake of the rhetorical education practiced by the Romans, with its emphasis on the active voice and on public speech, clear and realistic in detail but also inspiring, and not eschewing the arts of the orator or poet. The historical examples of the Greek soldier's involvement with the intellectual currents of his times, of knightly education and chivalry, of Neostoicism and *bildung* offer rich objects of study and of emulation. A consideration of the past can be intellectually liberating, giving wings to thought and imagination.[9]

This does not mean that officer education should merely be rooted in the past. The ability of modern information systems to simulate a complex four-dimensional landscape is probably still underutilized. For instance, some view the use of social media as a threat to security and discipline, but it also has the potential to enhance military knowledge by encouraging the exchange of ideas.[10] Operational research is a capability that is now within the reach of any tactical, operational, or strategic commander or staff officer, like a general staff officer at the elbow of every officer moving and making decisions across space-time. Cutting-edge theories of leadership such as adaptive leadership could be better applied.[11] In officer education, too little attention has been paid to developing the diverse and demanding cognitive requirements of military professionalism. Officers are called upon to think in the structural manner of mathematicians and engineers, and also like poets, philosophers, and politicians.[12] Modern cognitive science could make a contribution to officer education by helping us to better understand the intellectual demands of officership. What is it to "think like an officer"? Attempts have been made in this area—for example, in physician Andrew Wallace's paper "General George Catlett Marshall: A Cognitive Approach to Who He Was and What He Did."[13] Wallace traces the intellectual development (much of it self-cultivated) of America's most thoroughly professional soldier, who transcended his role of war fighter to become a statesman and defender of civilization par excellence. What better blueprint for the education of officers at every level?

The need for a highly educated officer corps is one reason to consider lengthening military careers for both reserve and active-duty officers. Fitness and energy are required for an officer's service, but many of an officer's roles make even greater demands on wisdom and experience. Longer and healthier modern lifespans modify somewhat the traditional advantages and insistence on youth for command in combat. The longer careers could support the greater use of sabbaticals for professional diversification and personal development. Like the Roman officers observing gladiatorial training or serving in the Senate, or the medieval knights spending time on their land, modern officers and senior enlisted members could learn much from their civilian peers. Such an arrangement would also directly address the problem of civil-military relations Admiral Mullen and others have recognized. As Lipsius, Montesquieu, and others have noted, true military reform must be rooted in societal reform. Another, related reform that merits consideration (and that is already receiving respectful attention) is the practice of 360-degree, or "bottom-up," evaluations. Not only would these potentially result in more accurate representations of an officer's fitness and potential, they would enhance the sense of a professional community, a "round table" of younger and older peers in the profession of arms. The greatest deficit in modern officer corps likely exists at the senior level, where the demands are greatest. Senior officers need more than an understanding of mere strategy; they must be prepared to bridge the strategy-policy gap that has so bedeviled us in the past.

Civil-Military Relations and Nation Building

In the life of a nation, the officer corps functions principally as the repository of a historical and evolving understanding of armed conflict. This understanding must be imparted not only to generations of new soldiers but also to the citizenry in general. Unless the civil society has some understanding of war, it will never be capable of the support or oversight the military requires, especially in wartime. Knowledge of war does not flow in one direction only. The profession of arms may bear a disproportionate share of the burdens of war, but there likely have been few wars in which the totality of suffering and death among civilians has not outweighed that among soldiers. The military profession must engage in a discourse with civilians about the impact and perceptions of war and the military on civil society. The profession must be warned of growing rifts and must close them either by adapting its own values, by trying to redirect the perceptions and values of the larger society, or both. The role of veterans and the care of wounded veterans must be a prime concern of every serving and former officer.

A good relationship between civil society and military society is essential if the armed forces are to play their part in peace and in war, but the armed forces also have a contribution to make in civil society itself. The armed forces set an example of service, leadership, and engaged, active citizenship that can benefit the civil community. Civilians act out the role of citizen on occasion and by exception when they engage in the political process, volunteer for community service, and obey the laws. Members of the armed forces act the citizen around the clock. As Donald Downs and Ilia Murtazashvili argue in *Arms and the University: Military Presence and the Civic Education of Non-military Students*, a military presence on a college campus can contribute to the goals of a humanities education.[14] The study of war and the military profession has the potential to raise fundamental questions about the nature of human community, morality, and existence. In order to serve society by addressing these questions, members of the profession of arms in particular must cultivate in themselves the ability to engage in high-order thinking, to communicate in a nuanced and sophisticated way, and to tolerate debate and differing views. That officer education is currently unequal to these demands is a point forcefully made in Timothy Challans' *Awakening Warrior*.[15] Challans' work is a provocative indictment of the shallowness and self-regarding insularity of much military education and discourse. One does not have to accept all of his premises or prescriptions to concede that much of what he says is worth consideration. Some of his points are echoed in *What It Is Like to Go to War* by Marine infantry

WHAT LIES AHEAD? Marines move forward during Operation Iraqi Freedom in 2003. Since then, the perils facing soldiers and those they guard may have diminished, but the uncertainties are even greater. *U.S. Marine Corps photo by Lance Corporal Brian L. Wickliffe*

officer and decorated Vietnam veteran Karl Marlantes, who also wrote the critically acclaimed Vietnam War novel *Matterhorn*.[16] Military officers learn the how of tactics, but less often the whys of strategy, policy, and moral purpose. Just as they are often ill equipped to manage the peace that military victory has secured, they are unable to understand and mitigate the personal costs of war in themselves or among subordinates. Reform is needed if the American military is to go from good to truly great. Its war-making ability gives the West the potential not only to defeat outsiders but also to pull down the temple. If the military instrument cannot be both accountable and self-regulating, if it does not perceive for itself a nonmilitaristic role in society, history teaches that it can destroy itself and the civilization it putatively serves. Will historians someday look back and wonder whether the profession of arms could have done more to save an endangered twenty-first-century civilization? As in the past, real military reform may well demand societal reform. A new *Constantia*, a quality of resolve, "keeping our heads" in challenging times, may be required of soldiers and civilians together. Soldiers and veterans must shake off the fatigue of their campaigning while civilians acquire some of the strength and adaptability of warriors.

Global Role

The future global role of American and other armed forces and the military professionals who lead them is subject to influences and trends that we may not fully understand, and to events still to come in an uncertain future. Broadly, there are perhaps three possible scenarios. The first is a continuation of the trends of the past two decades, with regional conflicts and local encroachments of disorder sometimes addressed by outside intervention (with varying degrees of effectiveness) and other times allowed to simmer or to burn out as they will. This general state of affairs would likely see U.S. and other armed forces, UN and European in particular, continuing to conduct various forms of stability and counterinsurgency operations.[17] It is not hard to predict the trouble spots, sources of terrorism, and centers of disorder over the coming decades, although given the mixed results of recent operations, the will to intervene might be less certain. The continuing disintegration of order in some societies and the acceptance and use of terror as a tactic (rising to the level of a strategy, even an end in itself) raise the specter of a second scenario: a much wider breakdown of order and reign of destruction than we have witnessed, one from which the West would not be spared. Even the limited use of weapons of mass destruction (WMD) by terrorists could have an enormous impact on social order and on economic and physical well-being worldwide. Neither of the first two scenarios, limited or more widespread violence and disorder, would rule out the possibility of a third: large-scale conventional conflict. Likely adversaries in a global conventional conflict would be China, Russia, and the United States. Such a conflict would feature the latest in high-tech precision weaponry, although it could also devolve to a war of attrition or even escalate to involve the use of WMD.

In the worst-case scenario combining widespread terrorism and conventional conflict involving the use of WMD, the military profession might be called upon to preserve values of civilization even after the physical temple has been pulled down. This is a function it has served often in the past. Homer's poem survived the Greek dark ages to inspire later men with its tale of heroic values. Roman military institutions outlived the empire, eventually spawning chivalry and the medieval knights who called themselves *miles*. The neochivalric movement of the seventeenth century and the limitations on warfare that prevailed through most of the next century are other examples of the military profession preserving and reviving the civilizing practices of an earlier time. When the old order of the ancien régime had crumbled, been rebuilt, and again come under attack in the nineteenth century, the military profession helped to create and was largely responsible for enacting a new international code of restraint and relief of suffering. Finally, after 1945 and Nuremberg, the military profession acquired an international character (itself a revival of the past) and undertook peacekeeping and humanitarian relief as major roles.

The moral and intellectual life of humankind as a whole and that of each individual is a race between learning and forgetting, between knowledge and neglect. As a species and as individuals we strive to acquire new knowledge, sometimes forsaking the wisdom of our past and early lives. Ralph Waldo Emerson wrote that he wished he knew as an adult all he knew on the day he was born. This book has been an effort to re-grasp some of the instinctive empathy that, as a young boy, I felt with the soldiers of the past, but most of all it has been an attempt to recall some of the wisdom about war the history of humankind encompasses. This is not to halt the search for new knowledge, but perhaps to place a caveat on the reliance on technological solutions, on the confident assertions of newness without precedent, on bureaucracy over professionalism, and on the preoccupation with the events of the moment that sometimes seem to dominate public discourse on both civil and military matters. Ultimately, it is neither the past nor the present that is our main concern, but rather the future. The Greeks saw the future as being at their backs, unseen and perhaps only to be guessed at by a close regard of what had passed in order to see a reflection of what was to come. The accumulated knowledge of the military profession about war will be our best guide on how to face the conflicts of the future as they arise. The profession of arms is still something that civilization cannot exist without, and perhaps only its unique combination of courage and wisdom in the face of matters of life and death will be sufficient to save us.

Notes

Introduction

1. Gilles Deleuze and Felix Guattari, *Nomadology*, trans. Brian Massumi (New York: Semiotext(e), 1986), 13.
2. See Jared Diamond, *Guns, Germs, and Steel: The Fate of Human Societies* (New York: W. W. Norton, 1997).
3. See Michael Gelven, *War and Existence: A Philosophical Inquiry* (University Park: University of Pennsylvania Press, 1994).
4. Many readers will recognize this phrase as the title of Russell Weigley's *The American Way of War: A History of United States Military Policy* (Bloomington: Indiana University Press, 1973). Weigley's book is associated with the thesis that American military policy and strategy have evolved toward a preference for decisive operations using overwhelming force rather than for limited commitment and protracted campaigns. This view has gained wide acceptance, but it has also been subject to critique and even dissention, most recently and notably in Antulio J. Echevarria II, *Reconsidering the American Way of War: U.S. Military Practice from the Revolution to Afghanistan* (Washington, DC: Georgetown University Press, 2014). Echevarria argues for a more diverse American approach to warfighting.
5. "Military Professionalism: Introspection and Reflection on Basic Tenets and the Way Ahead," conference, 10 January 2011, National Defense University, Fort Lesley J. McNair, Washington, DC.
6. Jeff Geraghty, "The Nature and Nurture of Military Genius: Developing Senior Leaders for the Postmodern Military," Air Force Research Institute, 27 July 2010, 25.
7. See Morris Janowitz, *The Professional Soldier: A Social and Political Portrait* (Glencoe, IL: Free Press, 1960); and Samuel P. Huntington, *The Soldier and the State: The Theory and Politics of Civil-Military Relations* (1957; Cambridge, MA: Harvard University Press, 1960).
8. David J. Ulbrich, *Preparing for Victory: Thomas Holcomb and the Making of the Modern Marine Corps, 1936–1943* (Annapolis, MD: Naval Institute Press, 2011), 5.

9. Russell Weigley, *Towards an American Army: Military Thought from Washington to Marshall* (Westport, CT: Greenwood, 1974); Williamson Murray and Richard Hart Sinnreich, eds., *The Past as Prologue: The Importance of History to the Military Profession* (Cambridge: Cambridge University Press, 2006); William B. Skelton, *An American Profession of Arms: The Army Officer Corps, 1784–1861* (Lawrence: University Press of Kansas, 1992); Christopher McKee, *A Gentlemanly and Honorable Profession: The Creation of the U.S. Naval Officer Corps, 1794–1815* (Annapolis, MD: Naval Institute Press, 1991).

10. Rudyard Kipling, "The Young British Soldier," in *Barrack-Room Ballads and Other Verses* (London: Methuen, 1892).

11. Paul K. Van Riper, "The Relevance of History to the Military Profession: An American Marine's View," in Murray and Sinnreich, *The Past as Prologue*, 53.

12. See Peter Paret, *The Cognitive Challenge of War, Prussia, 1806* (Princeton, NJ: Princeton University Press, 2009); and John Lynn, *Battle: A History of Combat and Culture* (Boulder, CO: Westview, 2003).

13. See Victor Davis Hanson, *Carnage and Culture: Landmark Battles in the Rise of Western Power* (New York: Random House/Anchor, 2002).

14. See Ronald Heifetz and Marty Linsky, *Leadership on the Line: Staying Alive through the Dangers of Leading* (Boston: Harvard Business Review Press, 2002), and other contemporary literature on adaptive leadership authored by Heifetz, Linsky, and others.

15. In sociological writing on military professionalism, the approval of a society for a profession is called "legitimacy." See, for example, James Burk, "Expertise, Jurisdiction, and Legitimacy of the Military Profession," in *The Future of the Army Profession*, ed. Lloyd J. Matthews (Boston: McGraw-Hill, 2002), 19–39.

16. Leo Tolstoy, *War and Peace*, trans. Rosemary Edmonds (London: Penguin, 1978), 1183.

17. John W. Thomason, *Fix Bayonets!* (New York: Scribner's, 1926), xiv.

18. See Michael Ignatieff, *The Warrior's Honor: Ethnic War and the Modern Conscience* (New York: Metropolitan/Henry Holt, 1997).

Chapter 1. Greeks and Macedonians

1. Hans van Wees, *Greek Warfare: Myths and Realities* (London: Duckworth, 2004).
2. Victor Davis Hanson, *Carnage and Culture: Landmark Battles in the Rise of Western Power* (New York: Random House/Anchor, 2002); van Wees, *Greek Warfare*.
3. There is a considerable contemporary literature arguing for the relevance of Homeric literature for an understanding of armed conflict. See, for example, Jonathan Shay, *Achilles in Vietnam: Combat Trauma and the Undoing of Character* (New York: Scribner, 1994); Shay, *Odysseus in America* (New York: Scribner, 2002); and Caroline Alexander, *The War That Killed Achilles: The True Story of Homer's* Iliad *and the Trojan War* (London: Penguin, 2009). John Lendon makes an argument for the influence of the *Iliad* on succeeding generations of Greek and Macedonian soldiers in his *Soldiers and Ghosts: A History of Battle in Classical Antiquity* (New Haven, CT: Yale University Press, 2005).
4. My discussion of *The Iliad* is derived in part from a paper I delivered at a discussion panel that I helped organize at a conference of the Inter-University Seminar on Armed Forces and Society in 2001. References are to the 1997 translation by Stanley Lombardo. This section also owes a debt to my doctoral dissertation, "Served This Soldiering Through: Language, Virtue, and Masculinity in the World War II Soldier's Novel," Boston University, 1999.
5. For a discussion of the place of discourses of warfare, see John Lynn, *Battle: A History of Combat and Culture* (Boulder, CO: Westview, 2003).
6. M. I. Finley, *The World of Odysseus* (New York: Viking, 1954), 46.
7. It is possible that if the historical Trojan War did go on for years, or for a considerable length of time, it was because the missile tactics used at the time were more suited to raids and skirmishing than they were to a decisive engagement. Hanson, in fact, often argues that hoplite tactics were adopted in order to make decisive combat possible.
8. See Finley, *World of Odysseus*, for an example.
9. Simone Weil, "The *Iliad*, or the Poem of Force," in *Simone Weil: An Anthology*, ed. and intro. Siân Miles (New York: Grove, 1986), 162–95; Sheila Murnaghan, introduction to *The Iliad*, trans. Stanley Lombardo (Indianapolis: Hackett, 1997).

10. Gregory Nagy, *The Best of the Achaeans: Concepts of the Hero in Ancient Greek Poetry* (1979; Baltimore: Johns Hopkins University Press, 1999), 26–41.

11. Carl von Clausewitz, *On War*, trans. and ed. Michael Howard and Peter Paret (1832; Princeton, NJ: Princeton University Press, 1984), 119.

12. Homer, *The Iliad*, 17, 660–65.

13. Ibid., 2, 79.

14. Ibid., 18, 111.

15. John Lendon, *Soldiers and Ghosts: A History of Battle in Classical Antiquity* (New Haven, CT: Yale University Press, 2005) 36–38.

16. Victor Davis Hanson, *The Western Way of War: Infantry Battle in Classical Greece* (New York: Knopf, 1989).

17. John Carman, "Beyond the Western Way of War: Ancient Battlefields in Comparative Perspective," in *Ancient Warfare: Archaeological Perspectives*, ed. John Carman and Anthony Harding (Gloucestershire, UK: Sutton, 1999), 39–55.

18. Hanson, *Carnage and Culture*, 93.

19. Oliver Lyman Spaulding, *Pen and Sword in Greece and Rome* (1936; Cranbury, NJ: Scholar's Bookshelf, 2006), 80.

20. Much about Spartan society and military organization is to be found in Xenophon's account of the Spartan constitution. See Naphtali Lewis, "Sparta, an Arrested Society," in *Greek Historical Documents: The Fifth Century B.C.* (Toronto: A. M. Hakkert, 1971), 68–89.

21. Donald Engels, *Alexander the Great and the Logistics of the Macedonian Army* (Berkeley: University of California Press, 1980).

22. Hanson, *Carnage and Culture*, 76–77.

23. Peter Tsouras, *Alexander: Invincible King of Macedonia* (Washington, DC: Brassey's, 2004), xiii, 51, 59.

24. Ibid., xiii.

25. Victor Davis Hanson, *The Wars of the Ancient Greeks and Their Invention of Western Military Culture* (London: Cassell, 1999), 118.

26. Hanson, *Carnage and Culture*, 88–89.

Chapter 2. Romans

1. Victor Davis Hanson, *Carnage and Culture: Landmark Battles in the Rise of Western Power* (New York: Random House/Anchor, 2002), 111.

2. See Eugene McCartney, *Warfare by Land and Sea*. Our Debt to Greece and Rome series, ed. George Hadzsits and David Robinson (New York: Cooper Square, 1963), 27–28.

3. Hanson, *Carnage and Culture*, 123.

4. Edward Gibbon, *The Decline and Fall of the Roman Empire* (Chicago: Encyclopedia Britannica, 1990), 1:4.

5. Adrian Goldsworthy, *In the Name of Rome: The Men Who Won the Roman Empire* (London: Weidenfeld and Nicolson, 2003), 113–37.

6. Antonio Santosuosso, *Barbarians, Marauders, and Infidels: The Ways of Medieval Warfare* (New York: MJF Books, 2004), 14.

7. See Erich Segal, trans., *Plautus: Three Comedies* (New York: Harper and Row, 1963). Segal points out that much of Plautus' Roman audience would have consisted of soldiers or ex-soldiers. These men might have enjoyed the play in a spirit similar to that of American veterans enjoying a comedy that lampoons a stock comic figure of military life, such as the buffoonish Sergeant Carter in the 1960s television series *Gomer Pyle, USMC*.

8. Juvenal, "Satire XVI," in *The Sixteen Satires*, trans. Peter Green (Baltimore: Penguin, 1967), 293.

9. Adrian Goldsworthy, *Roman Warfare* (2000; London: Orion-Phoenix, 2007), 28.

10. Jon C. N. Coulston, "By the Sword United: Roman Fighting Styles on the Battlefield and in the Arena," in *The Cutting Edge: Studies in Ancient and Medieval Combat*, ed. Barry Molloy (Gloucestershire, UK: Tempus, 2007).

11. Polybius, *The Histories of Polybius*, trans. F. Hultsch and Evelyn S. Shuckburgh (Bloomington: Indiana University Press, 1962), 1:481.

12. Oliver Lyman Spaulding, *Pen and Sword in Greece and Rome* (1936; Cranbury, NJ: Scholar's Bookshelf, 2006), 44.

13. Valerie Maxfield, *The Military Decorations of the Roman Army* (Berkeley: University of California Press, 1981), 23.

14. Spaulding, *Pen and Sword*, 84.

15. J. Wright Duff, *A Literary History of Rome in the Silver Age, from Tiberius, to Hadrian*, ed. A. M. Duff (London: Ernest Benn and Barnes and Noble, 1964), 339.

16. Frontinus, *The Strategems*, trans. Charles E. Bennet (1925; Cambridge, MA: Harvard University Press, 1961).
17. Spaulding, *Pen and Sword*, 88.
18. Duff, *Literary History of Rome*, 13–14.
19. Goldsworthy, *Roman Warfare*, 132.
20. Ibid., 56.
21. Coulston, "By the Sword United," 41.
22. Gibbon, *Decline and Fall*, 675n.
23. Goldsworthy, *Roman Warfare*, 28.
24. Maxfield, *Military Decorations*, 22.
25. Spaulding, *Pen and Sword*, 86.
26. Pat Southern, *The Roman Army: A Social and Institutional History* (Oxford: Oxford University Press, 2007), 163.
27. Maxfield, *Military Decorations*, 66.
28. Southern, *Roman Army*, 7.
29. Philippe Contamine, *War in the Middle Ages*, trans. Michael Jones (London: Basil Blackwell, 1984), 6.
30. Graham Webster, *The Roman Imperial Army of the First and Second Centuries A.D.* (1969; New York: Barnes and Noble, 1994), 121–22.
31. Goldsworthy, *Roman Warfare*, 131.
32. Edward N. Luttwak, *The Grand Strategy of the Byzantine Empire* (Cambridge, MA: Harvard University Press/Belknap, 2009).
33. Richard Talbert, *Rome's World: The Peutinger Map Reconsidered* (Cambridge: Cambridge University Press, 2010).
34. Richard A. Gabriel and Karen S. Metz, *From Sumer to Rome: The Military Capabilities of Ancient Armies* (Westport, CT: Greenwood, 1991), 29.
35. Suggested by remarks of Dr. Edward Barrett, Stockdale Center for the Professional Military Ethic, at annual McCain Conference, April 2013, U.S. Naval Academy, Annapolis, MD.
36. See Adrian Goldsworthy, *How Rome Fell: Death of a Superpower* (New Haven, CT: Yale University Press, 2009). Goldsworthy's book is a recent contribution to the long debate over the reasons for the decline and fall of Rome. He avoids simple or dogmatic answers to the question but seems to side with internal decay (as opposed to outside pressures) as the major culprit.

37. Ibid., 409.

38. See Lendon, *Soldiers and Ghosts*, 171, 200–203.

39. H. E. L. Mellersh, *The Roman Soldier* (New York: Taplinger, 1965), 189.

40. Ibid., 187.

41. Geoffrey Best, *Humanity in Warfare* (New York: Columbia University Press, 1980), 8.

42. Theodore K. Rabb, *The Artist and the Warrior: Military History through the Eyes of the Masters* (New Haven, CT: Yale University Press, 2011), 33.

43. Polybius, *Histories*, 2: 55.

44. James J. Murphy, "Rhetorical History as a Guide to the Salvation of American Reading and Writing: A Plea for Curricular Courage," in *The Rhetorical Tradition and Modern Writing*, ed. James J. Murphy (New York: Modern Language Association of America, 1982), 5.

45. Mellersh, *Roman Soldier*, 38.

46. F. E. Adcock, *The Roman Art of War under the Republic* (1940; New York: Barnes and Noble, 1995), 112–13.

47. Tacitus, *Agricola* and *Germania*, trans. Harold Mattingly (1948; London: Penguin Books, 2009), 1–32.

48. Thomas Burns, *Rome and the Barbarians, 100 B.C. to A.D. 400* (Baltimore: Johns Hopkins University Press, 2003), 165.

49. Maxfield, *Military Decorations*, 21.

50. Goldsworthy, *In the Name of Rome*, 327.

51. Ibid., 188–89.

Chapter 3. Late Antiquity

1. John W. Birkenmeier, *The Development of the Khomenian Army, 1081–1180* (Leiden, Netherlands: Brill, 2002), 13–14.

2. Bernard S. Bachrach, *Merovingian Military Organization, 481–751* (Minneapolis: University of Minnesota Press, 1972), vii, italics in original.

3. Birkenmeier, *Development of the Khomenian Army*, 72.

4. Edward N. Luttwak, *The Grand Strategy of the Byzantine Empire* (Cambridge, MA: Harvard University Press/Belknap, 2009), 10, italics in original.

5. Antonio Santosuosso, *Barbarians, Marauders, and Infidels: The Ways of Medieval Warfare* (New York: MJF Books, 2004), 20; and Lars Brownworth, *Lost to the West: The Forgotten Byzantine Empire That Rescued Western Civilization* (New York: Crown, 2009), 87–90.

6. Luttwak, *Grand Strategy*, 415–18.

7. Brownworth, *Lost to the West*, 22.

8. Ibid., 304.

9. Santosuosso, *Barbarians, Marauders, and Infidels*, 139.

10. Burton Raffel, introduction to *Beowulf* (New York: Mentor/New American Library, 1963), xii.

11. Victor Davis Hanson, *Carnage and Culture: Landmark Battles in the Rise of Western Power* (New York: Random House/Anchor, 2002), 137–41.

12. A. V. B. Norman, *The Medieval Soldier* (1971; New York: Barnes and Noble, 1993), 21.

13. Ibid., 12–13.

14. H. W. Koch, *Medieval Warfare* (London: Bison-Dorset, 1978), 28.

15. Santosuosso, *Barbarians, Marauders, and Infidels*, 67.

16. Dorothy Sayers, introduction to *The Song of Roland*, trans. Dorothy Sayers (1957; Hammondsworth, UK: Penguin, 1965), 8.

17. Philippe Contamine, *War in the Middle Ages*, trans. Michael Jones (London: Basil Blackwell, 1984), cited by Santosuosso, *Barbarians, Marauders, and Infidels*, 69.

18. Santosuosso, *Barbarians, Marauders, and Infidels*, 68.

19. Bachrach, *Merovingian Military Organization*, 50–51.

20. Contamine, *War in the Middle Ages*, 267.

Chapter 4. The Middle Ages

1. John France, *Western Warfare in the Age of the Crusades, 1000–1300* (Ithaca, NY: Cornell University Press, 1999), 3.

2. Steven Pinker, *The Better Angels of Our Nature: Why Violence Has Declined* (New York: Penguin, 2011). Pinker supports his thesis on the decline of violence with numerous statistics and charts. A comparison of the charts on pages 53 and 63 of his book supports my claim concerning the fourteenth and twentieth centuries.

3. Sean McGlynn, "The Myths of Medieval Warfare," *History Today* 44, no. 1 (1994), http://www.historytoday.com/sean-mcglyn/myths-medieval -warfare. McGlynn discusses both Oman's contributions and his limitations in addition to debunking or questioning other "myths" about warfare of the period.

4. R. C. Smail, *Crusading Warfare 1097–1193* (Cambridge: Cambridge University Press, 1956); J. F. Verbruggen, *The Art of Warfare in Western Europe during the Middle Ages*, trans. Sumner Willard and R. W. Southern (Suffolk, UK: Boydell, 1997); Philippe Contamine, *War in the Middle Ages*, trans. Michael Jones (London: Basil Blackwell, 1984). Some examples of the work of Prestwich, Keen, and France are as follows: Michael Prestwich, *Armies and Warfare in the Middle Ages: The English Experience* (New Haven, CT: Yale University Press, 1996); Maurice Keen, *Chivalry* (New Haven, CT: Yale University Press, 1984); France, *Western Warfare*.

5. Jonathan D. Spence, *The Memory Palace of Matteo Ricci* (New York: Elisabeth Sifton/Viking Penguin, 1984). In this work Spence discusses the military uses of the Ricci memory garden. Ricci was an early Jesuit who wrote and traveled widely. He recommended that military officers master mathematics and the new technology of the time (31–32).

6. France, *Western Warfare*, 54–55.

7. Nicholas Orme, *From Childhood to Chivalry: The Education of English Kings and Aristocracy, 1066–1530* (London: Methuen, 1984), 57.

8. Ibid., 71–72.

9. Ibid., 87.

10. Frances Gies, *The Knight in History* (New York: Harper and Row, 1987), 72.

11. Juliet Barker, *Agincourt: Henry V and the Battle That Made England* (New York: Little, Brown: 2005), 306.

12. Contamine, *War in the Middle Ages*, 210.

13. See McGlynn, "Myths of Medieval Warfare."

14. Udo Heyn, *Peacemaking in Medieval Europe: A Historical and Bibliographical Guide* (Claremont, CA: Regina Books, 1997), 55.

15. Richard Barber, *The Knight and Chivalry* (1970; Suffolk, UK: Boydell, 1974), 136.

16. France, *Western Warfare*, 3.

17. Matthew Bennett, appendix to Judith M. Upton-Ward, *The Rule of the Templars: The French Text of the Rule of the Order of the Knights Templar* (Suffolk, UK: Boydell, 1992), 175.

18. See Philippe Aries, *Centuries of Childhood: A Social History of Family Life*, trans. Robert Baldick (New York: Random House/Vintage, 1962), 193. Aries argues that the profession of arms retained the apprenticeship model of education after other professions had abandoned it, into the seventeenth century.

19. Orme, *From Childhood to Chivalry*, 80.

20. Clifford J. Rogers, *Soldiers' Lives through History: The Middle Ages* (Westport, CT: Greenwood, 2007), 258–68.

21. John Lynn, *Battle: A History of Combat and Culture* (Boulder, CO: Westview, 2003), 73–109.

22. Keen, *Chivalry*, 31.

23. Orme, *From Childhood to Chivalry*, 120.

24. Heyn, *Peacemaking in Medieval Europe*, 7.

25. Christopher Allmand, "War and the Non-combatant in the Middle Ages," in *Medieval Warfare: A History*, ed. Maurice Keen (Oxford: Oxford University Press, 1999), 253–54.

26. Heyn, *Peacemaking in Medieval Europe*, 36.

27. Ibid., 55.

28. See C. J. Tyerman's review of *To Follow in Their Footsteps: The Crusades and Family Memory in the High Middle Ages*, by Nicholas L. Paul, *Times Literary Supplement*, 14 June 2013.

29. Contamine, *War in the Middle Ages*, 227.

30. Ibid., 226.

31. Jean Froissart, *Chronicles*, sel. and trans. Geoffrey Brereton (London: Penguin, 1968), 131.

32. France, *Western Warfare*, 14.

33. H. J. Hewitt, *The Organization of War under Edward III* (1966; Barnsley, UK: Pen and Sword, 2004), 50–63.

34. Jonathan Sumption, *The Hundred Years' War*, vol. 3, *Divided Houses* (Philadelphia: University of Pennsylvania Press, 2009), 756.

35. Barker, *Agincourt*, 86.

36. Sumption, *Hundred Years' War*, 3: 762.

37. Lecture by Clifford Rogers, "The Soldier's Experience of Battle in the Middle Ages," 25 January 2008, New York Military Affairs Society.

38. Barker, *Agincourt*, 32.

39. See Richard Newell, *Muster and Review: A Problem of Military Administration, 1420–1440* (Cambridge, MA: Harvard University Press, 1940).

40. Ibid., 53.

41. Bennett, appendix to *Rule of the Templars*, 175–88.

42. Contamine, *War in the Middle Ages*, 219.

43. H. W. Koch, *Medieval Warfare* (London: Bison-Dorset, 1978), 161.

44. Rogers, *Soldiers' Lives*, 112–13.

45. Ibid., 121–22.

46. Philip Warner, *Sieges of the Middle Ages* (1968; South Yorkshire, UK: Pen and Sword, 2004), 2–3.

47. Rogers, *Soldiers' Lives*, 126.

48. John Keegan, *The Face of Battle* (London: Jonathan Cape, 1976), 97.

49. John Sutherland and Cedric Watts, *Henry V, War Criminal? & Other Shakespeare Puzzles* (Oxford: Oxford University Press, 2000), 108–16.

50. Barker, *Agincourt*, 24; and Charles D. Blyth, ed., *Thomas Hoccleve, The Regiment of Princes* (1411; Kalamazoo, MI, 1999).

51. Barker, *Agincourt*, 25.

52. Hewitt, *Organization of War*, 32.

53. Clifford Rogers, "The Military Revolutions of the Hundred Years' War," in *The Military Revolution Debate: Readings on the Military Transformation of Early Modern Europe*, ed. Clifford Rogers (Boulder, CO: Westview, 1995), 62.

54. Barker, *Agincourt*, 277.

55. Christopher Hibbert, *Agincourt* (Philadelphia: Dufour, 1964), 150–52.

56. Ibid., 72.

57. Geoffrey Parker, *Success Is Never Final: Empire, War, and Faith in Early Modern Europe* (New York: Basic Books, 2002).

58. France, *Western Warfare*, 1.

59. Sumption, *Hundred Years' War*, 3:745.

60. Froissart, *Chronicles*, 128.

61. Rogers, "Soldier's Experience."

62. Kenneth Burke, *A Rhetoric of Motives* (1950; Berkeley: University of California Press, 1969), 211.

63. This equates closely to the twelve monthly weekend drills and two weeks of annual training expected of members of the American select military reserve today.

64. Warner, *Sieges of the Middle Ages*, 120.

65. Ibid., 131–33.

66. Rogers, "Military Revolutions," 58–76.

67. See the reference to the "vitally important" command of the archers being assigned to the veteran soldier Sir Thomas Erpingham at Agincourt in Barker, *Agincourt*, 277.

68. David Eltis, *The Military Revolution in Sixteenth-Century Europe* (London: I. B. Tauris, 1998), 24.

69. Rogers, "Military Revolutions," 64.

70. See Brett D. Steele and Tamera Dorland, eds., introduction to *The Heirs of Archimedes: Science and the Art of War through the Age of Enlightenment* (Cambridge: MIT Press, 2005), 1–33.

71. Brown quoted in Bennett, appendix to *Rule of the Templars*, 175.

72. Andrew Ayton, "Knights, Esquires, and Military Service: The Evidence of Armorial Cases before the Court of Chivalry," in *The Medieval Military Revolution: State, Society, and Military Change in Medieval and Early Modern Europe*, ed. Andrew Ayton and J. L. Price (New York: Barnes and Noble, 1995), 81.

Chapter 5. The Early Modern Period

1. Michael Roberts, "The Military Revolution, 1560–1660," reprinted in *The Military Revolution Debate: Readings on the Military Transformation of Early Modern Europe*, ed. Clifford Rogers (Boulder, CO: Westview Press, 1995), 13–36.

2. See, especially, Geoffrey Parker, *The Military Revolution: Military Innovation and the Rise of the West, 1500–1800* (Cambridge: Cambridge University Press, 1988); Clifford Rogers, "The Military Revolutions of the Hundred Years' War," in Rogers, *Military Revolution Debate*, 55–94; Jeremy Black, "A Military Revolution? A 1660–1792 Perspective," in Rogers, *Military Revolution Debate*, 95–114; Gunther Rothenberg, "Maurice of Nassau, Gustavus Adolphus, Raimondo Montecuccoli, and

the 'Military Revolution' of the Seventeenth Century," in *Makers of Modern Strategy from Machiavelli to the Nuclear Age*, ed. Peter Paret (Princeton, NJ: Princeton University Press, 1986), 32–63; and David Eltis, *The Military Revolution in Sixteenth-Century Europe* (London: I. B. Tauris, 1998).

3. See Rogers' remarks on "punctuated equilibrium evolution" in Rogers, "Military Revolutions," 76–77.

4. See Robert M. Epstein, *Napoleon's Last Victory and the Emergence of Modern War* (Lawrence: University Press of Kansas, 1994); and Andrew Liaropoulos, "Revolutions in Warfare: Theoretical Paradigms and Historical Evidence: The Napoleonic and First World War Revolutions in Military Affairs," *Journal of Military History* 70 (2006): 363–84.

5. F. L. Taylor, *The Art of War in Italy, 1494–1529* (1921; Cranbury, NJ: Scholar's Bookshelf, 2006), 1–2.

6. Rogers, "Military Revolutions," 75.

7. Historian Geoffrey Parker is unquestionably the master of early modern logistics. In addition to *Military Revolution*, see his *The Army of Flanders and the Spanish Road, 1567–1659: The Logistics of Spanish Victory and Defeat in the Low Countries' Wars* (Cambridge: Cambridge University Press, 2004).

8. It is not difficult to find disparaging references to soldiers as a class during this period. Herbert Langer refers to the "negative perfection" of the image of the soldier in his *Thirty Years' War* (New York: Hippocrene, 1980), citing historical and literary sources. Hans Jacob Christoffel von Grimmelshausen's classic and sardonic *The Adventures of a Simpleton* was published in 1669 but concerns events of thirty years earlier. Soldiers themselves were often repulsed by the increasingly no-holds-barred form of warfare that the larger armies and the Reformation appeared to have ushered in. See Geoffrey Parker, "The Etiquette of Atrocity: The Laws of War in Early Modern Europe," in *Success Is Never Final: Empire, War, and Faith in Early Modern Europe* (New York: Basic Books, 2002), 150–53. Disenchantment with war and soldiers is often vividly reflected in the art of the period, to include Pieter Bruegel's *Massacre of the Innocents*, Diego Velázquez's *Mars*, and Jaques Callot's *Miseries of War* series. Theodore K. Rabb, *The Artist and the Warrior: Military History through the Eyes of the Masters* (New Haven, CT: Yale University Press, 2011), 89, 105–6, 111.

9. For the most complete discussion of the advent and impact of Neostoicism, see Gerhard Oestreich, *Neostoicism and the Early Modern State*, trans. Davis McClintock (Cambridge: Cambridge University Press, 1982). Neostoicism is also discussed in Gunther Rothenberg, "Maurice of Nassau." For the revival of chivalry, see D. J. B. Trim, ed., *The Chivalric Ethos and the Development of Military Professionalism* (Leiden, Netherlands: Brill, 2003). A number of authors discuss the emerging importance of national service among soldiers; see Bruce D. Porter, *War and the Rise of the State: The Military Foundations of Modern Politics* (New York: Free Press, 1994).

10. See Max Weber, *The Protestant Ethic and the Spirit of Capitalism*, trans. Talcott Parsons (New York: Scribner, 1958).

11. Galileo's device was not a magnetic compass but an instrument that could be used to perform the mathematical operations necessary to form infantry units for battle. Brett D. Steele and Tamera Dorland, eds., *The Heirs of Archimedes: Science and the Art of War through the Age of Enlightenment* (Cambridge, MA: MIT Press, 2005), 15; and Thomas F. Arnold, *The Renaissance at War* (London: Cassell, 2001), 72.

12. Eltis, *Military Revolution*, 60.

13. Arnold, *Renaissance at War*, 64. Arnold describes the Swiss as having "a culture of war, not a science."

14. E. M. Lloyd, *A Review of the History of Infantry* (1908; Cranbury, NJ: Scholar's Bookshelf, 2006), 89.

15. Eltis, *Military Revolution*, 63.

16. David Parrot, *Richelieu's Army: War, Government, and Society in France, 1624–1642* (Cambridge: Cambridge University Press, 2001), 40.

17. Rothenberg, "Maurice of Nassau," 42.

18. Geoffrey Parker, cited in David Parrott, "Strategy and Tactics in the Thirty Years' War: The 'Military Revolution,'" in Rogers, *Military Revolution Debate*, 227.

19. Thomas M. Barker, *The Military Intellectual and Battle: Raimondo Montecuccoli and the Thirty Years' War* (Albany: State University of New York Press, 1975), 91.

20. Christer Jorgensen, Michael F. Pavkovic, Rob S. Rice, Frederick C. Scheid, and Chris L. Scott, *Fighting Techniques of the Early Modern*

World, AD 1500–1763: Equipment, Combat Skills, and Tactics (Staplehurst, Kent: Spellmount, 2005), 26.

21. Lee Cardell, *Ill-Starred General: Braddock of the Coldstream Guards* (Pittsburgh: University of Pittsburgh Press, 1986), 137.

22. George Clark, *War and Society in the Seventeenth Century* (Cambridge: Cambridge University Press, 1958), 73.

23. Parrot, *Richelieu's Army*, 58.

24. Ibid., 79.

25. Barker, *Military Intellectual*, 3.

26. Rothenberg, "Maurice of Nassau," 60.

27. Martin van Creveld, *Supplying War: Logistics from Wallenstein to Patton* (Cambridge: Cambridge University Press, 1977), 7.

28. Ibid., 10–14.

29. Geoffrey Parker, "The Treaty of Lyon (1601) and the Spanish Road," in Parker, *Success Is Never Final*, 129.

30. The Spanish Road is an even more remarkable achievement when one considers it in the context of the "first global empire in history," as Geoffrey Parker calls it in *The Grand Strategy of Philip II* (New Haven, CT: Yale University Press, 1998), xv.

31. The term "state commission army" appears to have coined by John Lynn in *Giant of the Grand Siècle: The French Army, 1610–1715* (Cambridge: Cambridge University Press, 1997). In this period the state commission army replaced the aggregate contract armies as the dominant model for army organization in France and the rest of Europe. Instead of contracting nobles or entrepreneurs to raise armies in time of war, monarchs came to support standing armies whose members (the officers in particular) owed them direct allegiance (often in the form of a written commission).

32. For an incisive description of the state of seventeenth-century military ethics, see Parker, "Etiquette of Atrocity."

33. Hew Strachan, *European Armies and the Conduct of War* (1983; London: Routledge, 2002), 8–9.

34. Geoffrey Best, *Honour among Men and Nations: Transformations of an Idea* (Toronto: University of Toronto Press, 1981), 35.

35. Parker, "Etiquette of Atrocity," 163–64.

36. The culmination of this was the requirement of 22 May 1781 that all aspiring officers be able to prove "four generations of full and unimpeachable nobility" in order to qualify for a commission. Christopher Duffy, *The Military Experience in the Age of Reason* (1987; Hertfordshire, UK: Wordsworth, 1998), 38.

37. See Brian M. Downing, *The Military Revolution and Political Change: Origins of Democracy and Autocracy in Early Modern Europe* (Princeton, NJ: Princeton University Press, 1992). For a discussion of the consequences and modification of the national service ethos among mid-twentieth-century soldiers, see Best, *Honour among Men.*

38. Fernando González de León, "*Soldados Platicos* and *Caballeros*: The Social Dimensions of Ethics in the Early Modern Spanish Army," in Trim, *Chivalric Ethos*, 253–59.

39. Edmond Rostand, *Cyrano de Bergerac*, trans. Brian Hooker (1898; New York: Henry Holt, 1923), 240. Rostand's play is based on the life of the historical Cyrano, who was apparently not a genuine Gascoigne, but who in many ways fits the model of the early modern professional soldier who is both literate and committed to fighting.

40. Ibid., 282.

41. González de León, "*Soldados Platicos*," 243.

42. Ibid., 253.

43. Ibid., 256.

44. Ibid., 265.

45. See John Kenyon and Jane Ohlmeyer, "The Background to the Civil Wars in the Stuart Kingdoms," in *The Civil Wars: A Military History of England, Scotland, and Ireland, 1638–1660*, ed. John Kenyon and Jane Ohlmeyer (Oxford: Oxford University Press, 1998), 3.

46. Ibid., 7–17.

47. Ian Gentles, "The Civil Wars in England," in Kenyon and Ohlmeyer, *Civil Wars*, 107–8.

48. Ibid., 110.

49. Ibid., 113, 116.

50. Ian Gentles points out that religious belief was more likely to be an incitement to execution, reprisal, and atrocity after 1648, when the Royalist cause was reignited. Puritans like Cromwell viewed this as an

act of betrayal and impiety, with the result that some of the old restraint disappeared. Gentles, "Civil Wars," 152.

51. Ibid., 149.

52. John Morrill, "Postlude: Between War and Peace, 1651–1662," in Kenyon and Ohlmeyer, *Civil Wars*, 311.

53. Ibid., 328.

54. For a clear account of the culture of amateurism that has inspired the British Army, see G. W. Stephen Brodsky, *Gentlemen of the Blade: A Social and Literary History of the British Army since 1660* (New York: Greenwood, 1988).

55. See John Barratt, *Cavalier Generals: King Charles I and His Commanders in the English Civil War, 1642–46* (Barnsley, UK: Pen and Sword, 2004). Barratt concludes that the Royalist commanders performed as well as their less-elevated Parliamentarian adversaries. It was the failure of their senior leadership, Prince Rupert and especially Charles I, "to control them, and utilize their talents" that brought about defeat (211). The Restoration and later British armies found a means to combine aristocratic values and antecedents with principles of duty and subordination.

56. See Theodore Meron, *Bloody Constraint: War and Chivalry in Shakespeare* (New York: Oxford University Press, 1998). One of Meron's themes is Shakespeare's depiction of the professionalization of chivalry and its appropriation by the monarch or state, so that what had once been a largely individualistic ethos becomes one more dedicated to service and loyalty. Another interesting work is Duff Cooper, *Sergeant Shakespeare* (London: Rupert Hart-Davis, 1949). Cooper, a soldier in World War I, engages in an extended speculation on the possibility that Shakespeare's "missing years" around 1585 may have been spent in the army. His evidence for this largely derives from the frequency, authoritativeness, and respectful understanding of Shakespeare's military references in the plays. If the Spanish had Velázquez as a guide, provocation, and inspiration for their own revival of chivalry (and Cervantes to rein them in), the English could look to Shakespeare during their own renaissance of chivalric and military ideals. The French did not produce an early modern reinterpreter of chivalric ideas of such lasting eminence, although Montaigne writes in his essay "On Experience,"

"There is no calling so pleasant as a soldier's." See Michel Montaigne, *Essays*, trans. J. M. Cohen (Harmondsworth, UK: Penguin, 1958), 382.

57. Clark, *War and Society*, 75.

58. See Parrot, *Richelieu's Army*.

59. Colin Jones, "The Military Revolution and the Professionalization of the French Army under the Ancien Regime," in *The Military Revolution and the State, 1500–1800*, ed. M. Duffy (Exeter, UK: University of Exeter Press, 1980). Jones writes that by the end of Louis XIV's wars, "the anarchic, bloodyminded and entrepreneurial army officer" of the previous century "had given way to an altogether more docile and obedient character" (158).

60. Ibid., 149.

61. A painting by Gemalde von François-Joseph Heim, *The Battle of Rocroi, 19 May 1643*, depicts an episode in the battle in which Conde personally intervened to stop his cavalry from charging the Spanish infantry, who had recommenced firing after their surrender as the result of a misunderstanding of French movements. The respect for chivalric ideals depicted in the painting of Breda in 1625 is not absent even after almost twenty years of brutal fighting in the Thirty Years' War.

62. Jones, "Military Revolution," 162, 164.

63. Oestreich, *Neostoicism*, 76–89.

64. Henry J. Webb, *Elizabethan Military Science: The Books and the Practice* (Madison: University of Wisconsin Press, 1965), 59–61.

65. Oestreich, *Neostoicism*, 80. Oestreich, disagreeing with John U. Nef (*War and Human Progress* [Cambridge, MA: Harvard University Press: 1950]), says that examples of restraint in war such as the surrender of Breda (pictured by Velásquez) in 1625 were less examples of a survival of chivalry than the "quest for a military ethic and discipline essentially oriented toward Neostoic values." My own point is that such examples represent not so much the "remains" of chivalry as a self-conscious effort to revive and reinvent them.

66. C. Duffy, *Military Experience*, 18–32.

67. For examples, see Best, *Honour among Men*; and Michael Glover, *Wellington as a Military Commander* (London: Penguin, 2001). Best's book (actually a collection of lectures) describes the refusal of Prussian general Friedrich Christoph von Saldern to obey Frederick the Great's

instructions to destroy an adversary monarch's hunting lodge (16). In Glover's biography Wellington both expresses regret over past actions perceived at the time as necessary and demurs from cooperating with policy or practice he sees as dishonorable, saying at one point that he would "sacrifice . . . every frontier in India ten times over in order to preserve our credit for scrupulous good faith" (234).

68. C. Duffy, *Military Experience*, 36.
69. For more on the pan-European military culture, see Scott N. Hendrix, "The Spirit of the Corps: The British Army and the Pre-national Pan European Military World and the Origins of American Military Culture," PhD diss., University of Pittsburgh, 2005.
70. Barratt, *Cavalier Generals*, 26.
71. Erik Lund, *War for the Every Day: Generals, Knowledge, and Warfare in Early Modern Europe, 1680–1740* (New York: Greenwood, 1999).
72. Ibid., 158.

Chapter 6. The Eighteenth Century

1. Azar Gat, *A History of Military Thought* (Oxford: Oxford University Press, 2001), 29.
2. Jeremy Black, *European Warfare in a Global Context* (London: Routledge, 2007), 98.
3. Martin van Creveld, *Supplying War: Logistics from Wallenstein to Patton* (Cambridge: Cambridge University Press, 1977), 12.
4. Russell F. Weigley, *The Age of Battles: The Quest for Decisive Warfare from Breitenfeld to Waterloo* (Bloomington: Indiana University Press, 1991).
5. Christopher Duffy, *The Military Experience in the Age of Reason* (1987; Hertfordshire, UK: Wordsworth, 1998), 51.
6. Ibid.
7. Basil Hart and Adrian Liddell Hart, *The Sword and the Pen: Selections from the World's Greatest Military Writings* (New York: Crowell, 1976), 133.
8. T. R. Phillips, "Frederick the Great," in *Roots of Strategy: The 5 Greatest Military Classics of All Time* (1940; Harrisburg, PA: Stackpole Books, 1985), 307.
9. Maurice de Saxe, *Reveries on the Art of War* (1757; Mineola, NY: Dover, 2007), 80.

10. James Wolfe, *General Wolfe's Instructions to Young Officers: Also his Orders for a Battalion and an Army; Together with the Orders and Signals Ufed in Embarking and Debarking an Army by Flat-Bottom'd Boats &c.; and a Placart to the Canadians; to Which is Prefixed the Refolution of the Houfe of Commons for his Monument; and his Character, and the Dates of all his Commiffions. Also the Duty of an Adjutant and Quarter-Master, &c.* (London: J. Millan, 1768).

11. See Patrick Speelman, *Henry Lloyd and the Military Enlightenment of Eighteenth-Century Europe* (Westport, CT: Greenwood Press, 2002).

12. Ibid., 109.

13. Duffy, *Military Experience*, 48.

14. J. A. Houlding, *Fit for Service: The Training of the British Army, 1715–1995* (Oxford: Clarendon Press, 1981), 106.

15. For a discussion of the evolving relationship between military forces and a civilian bureaucracy in this period, see John Brewer, *Sinews of Power: War, Money, and the English State, 1688–1783* (New York: Knopf, 1989).

16. See Bruce D. Porter, *War and the Rise of the State: The Military Foundations of Modern Politics* (New York: Free Press, 1994). For an alternative view, see Brian M. Downing, *The Military Revolution and Political Change: Origins of Democracy and Autocracy in Early Modern Europe* (Princeton, NJ: Princeton University Press, 1992).

17. Downing, *Military Revolution*, 75.

18. Houlding, *Fit for Service*, 59.

19. Ibid., 346, 356.

20. Christopher Duffy, *The Army of Frederick the Great* (New York: Hippocrene, 1974), 149.

21. John Lynn, *Battle: A History of Combat and Culture* (Boulder, CO: Westview, 2003), 128–29.

22. H. W. Koch, *The Rise of Modern Warfare, 1618–1815* (Englewood Cliffs, NJ: Prentice-Hall, 1981), 81.

23. Houlding, *Fit for Service*, 319–21, 281.

24. David Chandler, *The Art of Warfare in the Age of Marlborough* (1976; Staplehurst, UK: Spellmount, 1990), 127. Chandler notes that the French defeat at Dettingen was partly attributed to their fixing bayonets too soon, slowing their rate of fire.

25. The return of the infantry hand grenade in World War I might have set a record for a certain type of institutional memory, since it involved the revival of a weapon that had been discontinued more than two centuries earlier. Although the infantry now has effective grenade launchers and other individual area weapons with high impact and kill radius, the humble hand grenade is still issued and employed, especially for combat in urban areas, in a form of fighting that is perhaps the contemporary equivalent of the siege or attack on a fortified position, where the early grenades were most used.

26. Hew Strachan, *European Armies and the Conduct of War* (1983; London: Routledge, 2002), 23–37.

27. Ibid., 28.

28. Ibid., 26.

29. Ibid., 33–34.

30. See Janis Langins, *Conserving the Enlightenment: French Military Engineering from Vauban to the Revolution* (Cambridge: MIT Press, 2004).

31. Ibid., 35.

32. Ibid., 37.

33. Duffy, *Military Experience*, 318.

34. Ibid., 317.

35. Douglas Southall Freeman, "Leadership," speech delivered at the Naval War College, Newport, Rhode Island, 11 May 1949; printed in *Naval War College Review*, March–April 1979, 3–10.

36. Charles Royster, *A Revolutionary People at War: The Continental Army and American Character, 1775–1783* (Chapel Hill: University of North Carolina Press, 1979), 217. For a discussion of British officer amateurism, see G. W. Stephen Brodsky, *Gentlemen of the Blade: A Social and Literary History of the British Army since 1660* (New York: Greenwood, 1988).

37. Christopher Duffy, *The Army of Maria Theresa: The Armed Forces of Imperial Austria, 1740–1780* (New York: Hippocrene, 1977), 62.

38. Brodsky, *Gentlemen of the Blade*, 1.

39. Corelli Barnett, *Marlborough* (1974; Ware, UK: Wordsworth, 1999), 180.

40. Charles Spencer, *Blenheim: Battle for Europe* (2004; London: Orion-Phoenix, 2005), 148.
41. Weigley, *Age of Battles*, 83.
42. Black, *European Warfare*, 73.
43. Duffy, *Army of Maria Theresa*, 15.
44. Duffy, *Army of Frederick the Great*, 50.
45. Ibid., 58.
46. Ibid., 110.
47. Ibid., 212.
48. Stephen Brumwell, *Paths of Glory: The Life and Death of General James Wolfe* (Montreal: McGill-Queen's University Press, 2006), 113.
49. Duffy, *Army of Maria Theresa*, 15.
50. Ibid., 59.
51. Ibid., 56.
52. Ibid., 46.
53. Royster, *Revolutionary People*, 47.
54. Ibid., 194–95.
55. David Hackett Fischer, *Washington's Crossing* (Oxford: Oxford University Press, 2004), 7–65.
56. Royster, *Revolutionary People*, 226.
57. Fischer, *Washington's Crossing*, 313.
58. Ibid., 369–70.
59. Norbert Elias, *The Genesis of the Naval Profession* (Dublin: University College of Dublin Press, 2007), 88.
60. N. A. M. Rodgers, *The Command of the Ocean: A Naval History of Britain, 1649–1815* (New York: W. W. Norton, 2006), 324–25.
61. Ibid., 288.
62. See Julian S. Corbett, *Fighting Instructions, 1530–1816* (1905; Cranbury, NJ: Scholar's Bookshelf, 2005). Corbett, himself a famous naval theorist, edited, contextualized, and commented on numerous fighting instructions throughout the period and covering several countries.
63. Relman Morin, *Churchill: A Portrait in Greatness* (Englewood Cliffs, NJ: Prentice-Hall, 1965), 35.

Chapter 7. Napoleon and the Nineteenth Century

1. See Trevor N. Dupuy, *A Genius for War: The German Army and General Staff, 1807–1945* (New York: Prentice-Hall, 1977).

2. Geoffrey Best, *Humanity in Warfare* (New York: Columbia University Press, 1980), 77.

3. Hew Strachan, *European Armies and the Conduct of War* (1983; London: Routledge, 2002), 40.

4. Ibid., 43.

5. Peter Paret, *The Cognitive Challenge of War, Prussia, 1806* (Princeton, NJ: Princeton University Press, 2009).

6. Walter Goerlitz, *The History of the German General Staff, 1657–1945*, trans. Brian Battershaw (New York: Praeger, 1953), 34.

7. Charles Edward White, *The Enlightened Soldier: Scharnhorst and the Militarische Gesellschaft in Berlin, 1801–1805* (Westport, CT: Praeger, 1989), 182–85.

8. See, for example, Bernard Brodie, "The Continuing Relevance of *On War*," in Clausewitz, *On War*, ed. and trans. Michael Howard and Peter Paret (1831; Princeton, NJ: Princeton University Press, 1976), 27–58.

9. Ibid.

10. Alfred de Vigny, *The Warrior's Life*, trans. Roger Gard (1835; New York: Penguin, 1996).

11. On the integration of Sepoy units into the British Indian Army, see John Lynn, *Battle: A History of Combat and Culture* (Boulder, CO: Westview, 2003), 145–77.

12. Frank Baum's fantastic, Pygmalion-like characters in *The Wonderful Wizard of Oz* (1900) may indeed be a comment on popular credulousness at professional authority. The Wizard is a humbug who rules through tricks and secrecy.

13. See Max Weber's seminal work in this field, as recorded in a number of titles, including Max Weber, ed., *The Theory of Social and Economic Organization* (New York: Free Press, 1964).

14. Goerlitz, *History of the German General Staff*, 95.

15. Lori Bogle, "Sylvanus Thayer and the Ethical Education of Nineteenth-Century Military Officers in the United States," in *Military Education: Past, Present, and Future*, ed. Gregory C. Kennedy and Keith Neilson (Westport, CT: Praeger, 2002), 67.

16. Ibid., 67–69.

17. Lexington, Virginia, lawyer, militia colonel, and VMI founder J. T. L. Preston envisioned the institute in words since inscribed on the "Parapet" facing the gymnasium at VMI: "The healthful and pleasant abode of a crowd of honorable youths pressing up the hill of science with noble emulation, a gratifying spectacle, an honor to our country and our state, objects of honest pride to their instructors, and fair specimens of citizen-soldiers, attached to their native state, proud of her fame, and ready in every time of deepest peril to vindicate her honor or defend her rights."

18. Russell Weigley, *History of the United States Army* (New York: Macmillan, 1967), 196.

19. A delayed effect of Schlieffen's monograph on Cannae was its influence on Eisenhower and other officers of his generation, who learned from it a preference for ambitious maneuver and decisive battle aimed at the destruction of the enemy army. For these American officers the 1914 German defeat of Russian forces at Tannenberg, not the battle of the French frontier, was the World War I epitome of this approach to operations. See Grant Jones, "Education of the Supreme Commander: The Theoretical Underpinnings of Eisenhower's Strategy in Europe, 1944–45," *War and Society* 30, no. 2 (2011): 108–33.

20. Dupuy, *Genius for War*, 51.

21. Anonymous, *The German Army from within, by a British Officer Who Has Served in It* (New York: George H. Doran, 1914), 138.

22. Cecil Woodham-Smith, *The Reason Why* (1953; New York: McGraw-Hill, 1954), 7. Woodham-Smith says of the young 7th Earl of Cardigan, "The melancholy truth was the glorious golden head had nothing in it."

23. E. B. Greenwood, *Tolstoy: The Comprehensive Vision* (1975; London: Methuen, 1980), 32.

24. Woodham-Smith, *Reason Why*, 54–55, 57–58.

25. John Sweetman, *War and Administration: The Significance of the Crimean War for the British Army* (Edinburgh: Scottish Academic Press, 1984), 128–33.

26. Edward Spiers, "The Late Victorian Army 1868–1914," in *The Oxford History of the British Army*, ed. David Chandler and Ian Beckett (Oxford: Oxford University Press, 1994), 187–210.

27. Ibid.

28. Thomas B. Buell, *The Warrior Generals: Combat Leadership in the Civil War* (New York: Three Rivers Press, 1997), xxvii.

29. Ibid., xxi, 189–91.

30. Brent Nosworthy, *The Bloody Crucible of Courage: Fighting Methods and Combat Experience of the Civil War* (New York: Carroll and Graf, 2003), 592, 549–67.

31. Russell Weigley, *The American Way of War: A History of United States Military Policy* (Bloomington: Indiana University Press, 1973), 97.

32. Ibid., 119–23.

33. Best, *Humanity in Warfare*, 32.

34. Ian Becket, *Victorians at War* (London: Hambledon, 2006), 4.

35. Weigley, *American Way of War*, 127.

36. Michael Howard, *The Franco-Prussian War* (1961; New York: Macmillan-Collier, 1969), 1–2.

37. Michael Howard, "William I and the Reform of the Prussian Army," in *Studies in War and Peace* (1959; New York: Viking, 1971), 65–82.

38. Daniel J. Hughes, ed., *Moltke on the Art of War: Selected Writings* (Novato, CA: Presidio, 1993), 3.

39. Ibid., 116–17.

40. Ibid., 110.

41. Ibid., 9.

42. Howard, *Franco-Prussian War*, 16.

43. Ibid., 32–34.

44. Ardant du Picq, *Battle Studies: Ancient and Modern Battle*, trans. John N. Greely and Robert C. Cotton (New York: Macmillan, 1921).

45. Ibid., 139.

46. Strachan, *European Armies*, 76–89.

47. Lynn, *Battle*, 145–77.

48. Strachan, *European Armies*, 76.

49. U.S. Marine Corps, *Small Wars Manual* (Washington, DC: U.S. Government Printing Office, 1940; reprint, New York: Skyhorse, 2009).

50. Buell, *Warrior Generals*, 25–26.

51. Allan R. Millet and Peter Maslowski, *For the Common Defense: A Military History of the United States of America* (New York: Free Press, 1994), 137–39.

52. Michael J. Brodhead, "James W. Albert: Soldier, Explorer, and Naturalist," *Journal of America's Military Past* 27 (2000): 65–75.

53. Perry D. Jamieson, *Crossing the Deadly Ground: United States Army Tactics, 1865–1899* (Tuscaloosa: University of Alabama Press, 1994), 6.

54. T. R. Brereton, *Educating the U.S. Army: Arthur L. Wagner and Reform, 1875–1905* (Lincoln: University of Nebraska Press, 2000), 13–15.

55. Ibid., 22–25.

56. John M. Gates, "The Pacification of the Philippines," in *The U.S. Army and Irregular Warfare*, http://www3.wooster.edu/History/jgates/pdfs/fullbook.pdf, 2006.

57. Richard Hill, *War at Sea in the Ironclad Age* (2000; New York: Harper-Collins, 2006), 80.

58. Philip A. Crowl, "Alfred Thayer Mahan: The Naval Historian," in Peter Paret, *Makers of Modern Strategy from Machiavelli to the Nuclear Age* (Princeton, NJ: Princeton University Press, 1986), 444.

59. Naval War College web site, usnwc.edu.

60. See Walter Millis, *The Martial Spirit* (1931; Chicago: Ivan Dee/Elephant, 1989).

61. Michael Howard, "Men against Fire," in Paret, *Makers of Modern Strategy*, 521.

62. Sigmund Neumann and Mark von Hagan, "Engels and Marx on Revolution, War, and the Army in Society," in Paret, *Makers of Modern Strategy*, 264–66.

63. Michael Geyer, "German Strategy in the Age of Machine Warfare, 1914–1945," in Paret, *Makers of Modern Strategy*, 530.

64. Best, *Humanity in Warfare*, 193.

65. Meirion Harries and Susan Harries, *Soldiers of the Sun: The Rise and Fall of the Imperial Japanese Army* (New York: Random, 1991), 24.

66. Best, *Humanity in Warfare*, 131.

67. Ibid., 155.

68. David Howarth, *Waterloo: Day of Battle* (New York: Atheneum, 1968), 210. Howarth's book contains an account of the aftermath of the battle and some further discussion of the neglect and even the plundering and murder of the wounded of both sides by the victorious English and Prussians.

69. Ibid.

70. Best, *Humanity in Warfare*, 150–53.

71. H. G. Wells, *Little Wars* (1913; New York: Macmillan, 1970), 100.

Chapter 8. The Twentieth Century

1. Michael Howard, "Men against Fire," in *Makers of Modern Strategy from Machiavelli to the Nuclear Age*, ed. Peter Paret (Princeton, NJ: Princeton University Press, 1986), 516–17.

2. Ibid., 517–18.

3. Allan R. Millet and Peter Maslowski, *For the Common Defense: A Military History of the United States of America* (New York: Free Press, 1994), 338–42.

4. See, for example, Captain Adolf Von Schell, *Battle Leadership* (Fort Benning, Columbus, GA: Benning Herald, 1933, 92; reprint, Marine Corps Association, 1999).

5. Millett and Maslowski, *For the Common Defense*, 316.

6. Howard, "Men against Fire."

7. There is a considerable literature on adaptive leadership. See, for example, Ronald Heifetz and Marty Linsky, *Leadership on the Line: Staying Alive through the Dangers of Leading* (Boston: Harvard Business Review Press, 2002).

8. See Ben Shephard, *A War of Nerves: Soldiers and Psychiatrists in the Twentieth Century* (Cambridge, MA: Harvard University Press, 2003), for details on the rise of psychiatric treatment for combat-induced stress disorders in World War I.

9. Paul Fussell, *The Great War and Modern Memory* (Oxford: Oxford University Press, 1975).

10. For the use of some of this context and terminology, see Anatole Rapoport, introduction to *On War* (Harmondsworth, Middlesex, UK: Penguin, 1968), 11–80.

11. Alan Clark, *The Donkeys* (New York: William Morrow, 1962), 13.

12. See Andrew Gordon, *The Rules of the Game: Jutland and British Naval Command* (1996; Annapolis, MD: U.S. Naval Institute Press, 2000), for a detailed depiction of how habits of obedience and loyalty can have an impact on doctrine.

13. This statement is attributed to Lieutenant General Launcelot Kiggell by Robert Polis and Philip Langer in *Command Failure in War:*

Psychology and Leadership (Bloomington: Indiana University Press, 2004), 143. In their notes the authors cite Leon Wolff, *In Flanders Fields: The 1917 Campaign* (New York: Viking, 1958), 149, as their source. They also note that the story is called into question by Paul Fussell in *Great War and Modern Memory*, 84.

14. Williamson Murray and Allan R. Millett, eds., *Military Innovation in the Interwar Period* (Cambridge: Cambridge University Press, 1996).

15. Trevor N. Dupuy, *A Genius for War: The German Army and General Staff, 1807–1945* (New York: Prentice-Hall, 1977), 216.

16. See Bruce Gudmundsson, *Stormtroop Tactics: Innovation in the German Army, 1914–1918* (Westport, CT: Praeger, 1995).

17. David MacIsaac, "Voices from the Central Blue: The Air Power Theorists," in Peter Paret, *Makers of Modern Strategy from Machiavelli to the Nuclear Age* (Princeton, NJ: Princeton University Press, 1986), 633.

18. See John Masters, *Bugles and a Tiger* (1948; New York: Ballantine, 1968); and Francis Yeats-Brown, *The Lives of a Bengal Lancer* (New York: Viking, 1930).

19. Stilwell made several attempts at beginning a personal account of the war, but he unfortunately never got past "an initial survey of Chinese language and culture." Charles F. Romanus and Riley Sunderland, *United States Army in World War II, China-Burma-India Theater: Stilwell's Command Problems* (Washington, DC: Office of the Chief of Military History, Department of the Army, 1956), 470. The closest among published works we have to a Stilwell memoir is Joseph W. Stilwell, *The Stilwell Papers*, edited and arranged by Theodore H. White (New York: William Sloane, 1948). The standard biography of Stilwell is Barbara Tuchman's *Stilwell and the American Experience in China, 1911–45* (New York: Macmillan, 1970).

20. See Maurer Maurer, *Aviation in the U.S. Army, 1919–1939* (Washington, DC: Office of Air Force History, U.S. Air Force, 1987).

21. For a detailed account of how the bomber and fighter pilot communities have serially dominated the top ranks of the Air Force, see Mike Worden, *The Rise of the Fighter Generals: The Problem of Air Force Leadership, 1945–1982* (Maxwell Air Force Base, AL: Air University Press, 1998). Worden concludes with a warning against "the enduring dangers of parochialism and bias in any organization that is too homogeneous

in its senior leadership and culture" and a call for "broad education and experience and a diversity of views" (238).

22. Examples of superior literary works by military aviators and about aviation in wartime are much too numerous to mention in the context of this work, but should include V. M. Yeates, *Winged Victory* (1934); Ernest K. Gann, *Fate Is the Hunter* (1961); Antoine de Saint-Exupéry, *Flight to Arras* (1942); and James Salter, *The Hunters* (1956). In different ways these works express the paradoxical experience of flight and of aerial combat as liberating but also limiting and often finally fatal. The craft of the flying machine imposes a demanding discipline that makes other forms of human activity difficult, even though it may also inspire literary creativity and its own brand of spirituality.

23. MacIsaac, "Voices from the Central Blue," 624–47.

24. Examples of their work include Giulio Douhet, *Command of the Air* (1921; Washington, DC: Office of Air Force History, U.S. Air Force, 1983); and Alexander Seversky, *Victory through Air Power* (New York: Simon and Schuster, 1942).

25. Alastair Horne, *To Lose a Battle, France 1940* (1969; Harmondsworth, UK: Penguin, 1979), 102.

26. Louis Morton, "Germany First: The Basic Concept of Allied Strategy in World War II," in *Command Decisions*, ed. Kent Roberts Greenfield (Washington, DC: Center of Military History, U.S. Army, 1990), 11–48.

27. Russell Weigley, *The American Way of War: A History of United States Military Policy* (Bloomington: Indiana University Press, 1973), 265.

28. Victor Davis Hanson, *Carnage and Culture: Landmark Battles in the Rise of Western Power* (New York: Random House/Anchor, 2002), 152–55.

29. Stephen Budiansky, *Blackett's War: The Men Who Defeated the Nazi U-Boats and Brought Science to the Art of Warfare* (New York: Knopf, 2013), 89–90.

30. Ibid., 86–87.

31. Robert R. Palmer, Bell I. Wiley, and William R. Keast, *United States Army in World War II. The Army Ground Forces: The Procurement and Training of Ground Combat Troops* (Washington, DC: Historical Division, Department of the Army, 1948), 37–39.

32. Ilaria Dagnini Brey, *The Venus Fixers: The Remarkable Story of the Allied Soldiers Who Saved Italy's Art Treasures during World War II* (New York: Farrar, Straus, and Giroux, 2009), 47.

33. Ibid., 86–87.

34. S. L. A. Marshall is surely an exception to the common neglect of official histories. Marshall expanded the boundaries of official history and went on to write popular military history outside the Army's imprimatur. For an account of his influence within the Army, see F. D. G. Williams, *SLAM: The Influence of S. L. A. Marshall on the United States Army* (Fort Monroe, VA: U.S. Army Training and Doctrine Command, 1999). James Jones' *WWII: A Chronicle of Soldiering* (New York: Ballantine, 1975) provided a best-selling showcase of World War II art.

35. John Ellis, *The Sharp End: The Fighting Man in World War II* (New York: Scribners, 1980), 192.

36. E. B. Sledge, *With the Old Breed at Peleliu and Okinawa* (1981; New York: Oxford University Press, 1991), 38–39.

37. Ibid., 90–91.

38. A more detailed discussion of S. L. A. Marshall's *The Armed Forces Officer* (Washington: Department of Defense, 1950) can be found in my "Reconsidering *The Armed Forces Officer* of 1950: Democracy, Dialogue, the Humanities, and the Military Profession," *Joint Forces Quarterly* 68 (January 2013), 64–69. In this paper I credit Marshall's work with an open-ended, "dialogic" form that is especially appropriate to the education of officers. *The Armed Forces Officer* also sets a very good example of wide, eclectic reading, a practiced facility with language, and openness to ideas.

39. Marshall, *Armed Forces Officer*, 1.

40. See Mark Perry, *Partners in Command: George Marshall and Dwight Eisenhower in War and Peace* (New York: Penguin, 2007). Although Marshall and Eisenhower had seen little of each other before Eisenhower was assigned to the War Department in December 1941, Marshall had apparently seen enough to note young Eisenhower's ability and willingness to speak his mind. Fox Connor was a mutual acquaintance who had enormous hopes for both men. He described Marshall to Eisenhower as "close to being a genius."

41. Geoffrey Perret, *Eisenhower* (New York: Random House, 1999), 379.

42. See Larry I. Bland, "George C. Marshall and the Education of Army Leaders," *Military Review* 68 (October 1988): 27–37; revised article printed from George C. Marshall Library web site, 9 January 2014, http://marshallfoundation.org/marshall/wp-content/uploads/sites/22/2014/04/Education_of_Army_Leaders.pdf.

43. Richard E. Neustadt and Ernest R. May, *Thinking in Time: The Uses of History for Decision Makers* (1986; New York: Free Press, 1988), 247–52. Neustadt and May identify Marshall's ability to think in "time-streams," to see unfolding events in a historical perspective even as they were happening. As early as 1943, with victory still in question, this enabled him to begin to envision the need for a plan for Europe's post-war recovery. This plan would eventually take shape and become known as the Marshall Plan.

44. Gordon Craig, *The Politics of the Prussian Army, 1640–1945* (1955; London: Oxford/Clarendon, 1964). Craig refers to the German officers of this time as "technicians operating in the void to the point of unreason" (470).

45. Geoffrey Best, *Honour among Men and Nations: Transformations of an Idea* (Toronto: University of Toronto Press, 1981), 73, 81–82.

46. The titles of two influential works by Mao and Guevara are usually respectively translated as *On Guerilla Warfare* (1937) and *Guerilla Warfare* (1961).

47. Daniel Moran, *Wars of National Liberation* (New York: Smithsonian Books, 2001), 126.

48. See Alastair Horne, *A Savage War of Peace* (New York: Viking, 1978).

49. For a detailed discussion of mid-twentieth-century praetorianism, see Eric Nordlinger, *Soldiers in Politics: Military Coups and Governments* (Englewood Cliffs, NJ: Prentice-Hall, 1977). Nordlinger discusses the reasons and results of military coups in the Third World, in general giving them low marks for addressing the evils that they set out to cure, even if these were genuine problems. He also makes the interesting and disquieting point that it is often the better-educated officers who participate in coups and military governments, possibly because their

education has given them an increased (if often exaggerated) sense of their own abilities.

50. Lewis Sorley, *Westmoreland: The General Who Lost Vietnam* (Boston: Houghton Mifflin/Harcourt, 2011). Sorley's thesis that Westmoreland's strategy in Vietnam was the principal cause for the American defeat, albeit one nearly averted under Westmoreland's successor at MACV, Creighton Abrams, is not without critics. However, he carefully lays out the shortcomings of Westmoreland's approach, which almost certainly contributed to the defeat, whether it was the main cause or not.

51. Speech by Chairman of the Joint Chiefs of Staff Admiral Michael Mullen at National Defense University Conference on Military Professionalism, Fort McNair, Washington, DC, January 2012. In his remarks Admiral Mullen, who served as a junior officer during the Vietnam era, referred to the military profession's failure to "wring out" some of the challenges and lessons of Vietnam.

52. *Armed Forces and Society*, a quarterly publication, is the official journal of the Inter-University Seminar on Armed Forces and Society. See http://afs.sagepub.com.

53. Joseph Gerard Brennan, *Foundations of Moral Obligation: The Stockdale Course* (Newport, RI: Naval War College, 1992).

54. See Herman Kahn, *On Thermonuclear War* (Princeton, NJ: Princeton University Press, 1960).

55. Stephen Brodsky, *Gentlemen of the Blade: A Social and Literary History of the British Army since 1660* (New York: Greenwood, 1988), xxiv, 165–68, 173.

56. See Eric Schlosser, *Command and Control: Nuclear Weapons, the Damascus Accident, and the Illusion of Safety* (New York: Penguin Press, 2013).

Conclusion

1. Geoffrey Parker, *Success Is Never Final: Empire, War, and Faith in Early Modern Europe* (New York: Basic Books, 2002), 125.

2. Charles Hill, *Grand Strategies: Literature, Statecraft, and World Order* (New Haven, CT: Yale University Press, 2010), 50, 59, 86, 90.

3. See Edward Smith, "The Navy RMA War Game Series: April 1995– 1996," *Naval War College Review* 50 (autumn 1997): 17–31.

4. U.S. Marine Corps, *MCDP 6 Command and Control* (Washington, DC: Department of the Navy, Headquarters, U.S. Marine Corps, 1996).

5. U.S. Army/Marine Corps, *Counterinsurgency* (Washington, DC: Headquarters, Department of the Army, 2006); revised as *Insurgencies and Countering Insurgencies* (Washington, DC: Headquarters Department of the Army, 2014).

6. Thomas Ricks, *The Generals: American Military Command from World War II to Today* (New York: Penguin, 2012), 347–48.

7. Ibid., 213.

8. See Martin van Creveld, *The Training of Officers: From Military Professionalism to Irrelevance* (New York: MacMillan, 1990).

9. Russell F. Weigley, *The Age of Battles: The Quest for Decisive Warfare from Breitenfeld to Waterloo* (Bloomington: Indiana University Press, 1991), 146. Weigley points out that the romantic legacy of the Crusaders, for example, can add breadth to the "strategic outlook" of modern soldiers.

10. See Lieutenant Colonel Seth M. Milstein, "Tactical Tweets, Blogs, Smartphones, and Drones (Oh, My!)," *Marine Corps Gazette* 98, no. 4 (2014): 63–66.

11. Although the U.S. Army's recent *ADP 5-0: The Operations Process* (Washington, DC: Department of the Army, 2012) is purported to incorporate adaptive leadership concepts, it fails to acknowledge the hazards, tradeoffs, and paradoxes of leading for real change. See William J. Cojocar, "Adaptive Leadership in the Military Decision-Making Process," *Military Review* (November–December 2011): 29–34, http://usacac.army.mil/CAC2/MilitaryReview/Archives/English/MilitaryReview_20120630MC_art007.pdf.

12. Glenn Voelz, "Is Military Knowledge 'Scientific'?" *Joint Forces Quarterly* 75 (4th quarter 2014): 84–90. The author makes an argument for eclectic and nondoctrinaire, pseudoscientific thought among military officers, stating that "leaders might benefit from considering methods that are not intuitively similar to military operations such as biology, epidemiology, or meteorology" (90).

13. Andrew G. Wallace, "General George Catlett Marshall: A Cognitive Approach to Who He Was and What He Did," Marshall Foundation, 3 January 2013, http://marshallfoundation.org/marshall/wp-content/uploads/sites/22/2014/04/GeneralGeorgeCatlettMarshallAndrewWallace.pdf.

14. Donald Downs and Ilia Murtazashvili, *Arms and the University: Military Presence and the Civic Education of Non-military Students* (Cambridge: Cambridge University Press, 2012), 57–62.

15. Timothy L. Challans, *Awakening Warrior: Revolution in the Ethics of Warfare* (Albany: State University of New York Press, 2007).

16. Karl Marlantes, *What It Is Like to Go to War* (New York: Grove-Atlantic, 2011), and *Matterhorn* (New York: Grove-Atlantic, 2010).

17. Ralph M. Goodman, *From Warfare to Party Politics: The Critical Transition to Civilian Control* (Syracuse, NY: Syracuse University Press, 1990), 228. Goodman makes some interesting specific recommendations concerning a greater role for the Military Staff Committee that was established as part of the UN charter. These recommendations include calls for an international military academy and the coordination of responses to international terrorist activities.

Bibliography

Adcock, F. E. *The Roman Art of War under the Republic.* 1940. New York: Barnes and Noble, 1995.

Alexander, Caroline. *The War That Killed Achilles: The True Story of Homer's* Iliad *and the Trojan War.* London: Penguin, 2009.

Allmand, Christopher. "War and the Non-combatant in the Middle Ages." In *Medieval Warfare: A History,* edited by Maurice Keen. Oxford: Oxford University Press, 1999.

Anonymous. *The German Army from within, by a British Officer Who Has Served in It.* New York: George H. Doran, 1914.

Aries, Philippe. *Centuries of Childhood: A Social History of Family Life.* Translated by Robert Baldick. New York: Random House/Vintage, 1962.

Arnold, Thomas F. *The Renaissance at War.* London: Cassell, 2001.

Ayton, Andrew. "Knights, Esquires, and Military Service: The Evidence of Armorial Cases before the Court of Chivalry." In *The Medieval Military Revolution: State, Society, and Military Change in Medieval and Early Modern Europe,* edited by Andrew Ayton and J. L. Price, 81–104. New York: Barnes and Noble, 1995.

Bachrach, Bernard S. *Merovingian Military Organization, 481–751.* Minneapolis: University of Minnesota Press, 1972.

Barber, Richard. *The Knight and Chivalry.* 1970. Suffolk, UK: Boydell, 1974.

Barker, Juliet. *Agincourt: Henry V and the Battle That Made England.* New York: Little, Brown, 2005.

Barker, Thomas M. *The Military Intellectual and Battle: Raimondo Montecuccoli and the Thirty Years' War.* Albany: State University of New York Press, 1975.

Barnett, Corelli. *Marlborough.* 1974. Ware, UK: Wordsworth, 1999.

Barratt, John. *Cavalier Generals: King Charles I and His Commanders in the English Civil War, 1642–46.* Barnsley, UK: Pen and Sword, 2004.

Becket, Ian. *Victorians at War: New Perspectives.* London: Hambledon, 2006.

Bennett, Matthew. Appendix to Judith M. Upton-Ward, *The Rule of the Templars: The French Text of the Rule of the Order of the Knights Templar.* Suffolk, UK: Boydell, 1992.

Best, Geoffrey. *Honour among Men and Nations: Transformations of an Idea.* Toronto: University of Toronto Press, 1981.

————. *Humanity in Warfare.* New York: Columbia University Press, 1980.

Birkenmeier, John W. *The Development of the Khomenian Army, 1081–1180.* Leiden, Netherlands: Brill, 2002.

Black, Jeremy. *European Warfare in a Global Context.* London: Routledge, 2007.

————. "A Military Revolution? A 1660–1792 Perspective." In Rogers, *Military Revolution Debate,* 95–114.

Bland, Larry I. "George C. Marshall and the Education of Army Leaders." *Military Review* 68 (October 1988): 27–37.

Blyth, Charles D., ed. *Thomas Hoccleve, The Regiment of Princes* (1411; Kalamazoo, MI, 1999).

Bonadonna, Reed R. "Reconsidering *The Armed Forces Officer* of 1950: Democracy, Dialogue, the Humanities, and the Military Profession." *Joint Forces Quarterly* 68 (January 2013): 64–69.

————. "Served This Soldiering Through: Language, Virtue, and Masculinity in the World War II Soldier's Novel." PhD dissertation, Boston University, 1999.

Brennan, Joseph Gerard. *Foundations of Moral Obligation: The Stockdale Course.* Newport, RI: Naval War College, 1992.

Brereton, T. R. *Educating the U.S. Army: Arthur L. Wagner and Reform, 1875–1905.* Lincoln: University of Nebraska Press, 2000.

Brewer, John. *Sinews of Power: War, Money, and the English State, 1688–1783.* New York: Knopf, 1989.

Brey, Ilaria Dagnini. *The Venus Fixers: The Remarkable Story of the Allied Soldiers Who Saved Italy's Art Treasures during World War II.* New York: Farrar, Straus and Giroux, 2009.

Brodhead, Michael J. "James W. Albert: Soldier, Explorer, and Naturalist." *Journal of America's Military Past* 27 (2000): 65–75.

Brodie, Bernard. "The Continuing Relevance of *On War.*" In Carl von Clausewitz, *On War,* edited and translated by Michael Howard and Peter Paret, 27–58. 1831. Princeton, NJ: Princeton University Press, 1976.

Brodsky, G. W. Stephen. *Gentlemen of the Blade: A Social and Literary History of the British Army since 1660.* New York: Greenwood, 1988.

Brownworth, Lars. *Lost to the West: The Forgotten Byzantine Empire That Rescued Western Civilization.* New York: Crown, 2009.

Brumwell, Stephen. *Paths of Glory: The Life and Death of General James Wolfe.* Montreal: McGill-Queen's University Press, 2006.

Budiansky, Stephen. *Blackett's War: The Men Who Defeated the Nazi U-Boats and Brought Science to the Art of Warfare.* New York: Knopf, 2013.

Buell, Thomas B. *The Warrior Generals: Combat Leadership in the Civil War.* New York: Three Rivers Press, 1997.

Burk, James. "Expertise, Jurisdiction, and Legitimacy of the Military Profession." In *The Future of the Army Profession*, edited by Lloyd J. Matthews, 19–39. Boston: McGraw-Hill, 2002.

Burke, Kenneth. *A Rhetoric of Motives.* 1950. Berkeley: University of California Press, 1969.

Burns, Thomas. *Rome and the Barbarians, 100 B.C. to A.D. 400.* Baltimore: Johns Hopkins University Press, 2003.

Cardell, Lee. *Ill-Starred General: Braddock of the Coldstream Guards.* Pittsburgh: University of Pittsburgh Press, 1986.

Carman, John. "Beyond the Western Way of War: Ancient Battlefields in Comparative Perspective." In *Ancient Warfare: Archaeological Perspectives,* edited by John Carman and Anthony Harding, 39–55. Gloucestershire, UK: Sutton, 1999.

Challans, Timothy L. *Awakening Warrior: Revolution in the Ethics of Warfare.* Albany: State University of New York Press, 2007.

Chandler, David. *The Art of Warfare in the Age of Marlborough.* 1976. Staplehurst, UK: Spellmount, 1990.

Clark, Alan. *The Donkeys.* New York: William Morrow, 1962.

Clark, George. *War and Society in the Seventeenth Century.* Cambridge: Cambridge University Press, 1958.

Clausewitz, Carl von. *On War.* Translated and edited by Michael Howard and Peter Paret. 1832. Princeton, NJ: Princeton University Press, 1984.

Cojocar, William J. "Adaptive Leadership in the Military Decision-Making Process." *Military Review* (November–December 2011): 29–34.

Contamine, Philippe. *War in the Middle Ages.* Translated by Michael Jones. London: Basil Blackwell, 1984.

Cooper, Duff. *Sergeant Shakespeare.* London: Rupert-Hart-Davis, 1949.

Corbett, Julian S. *Fighting Instructions, 1530–1816.* 1905. Cranbury, NJ: Scholar's Bookshelf, 2005.

Coulston, Jon C. N. "By the Sword United: Roman Fighting Styles on the Battlefield and in the Arena." In *The Cutting Edge: Studies in Ancient and Medieval Combat,* edited by Barry Molloy, 34–51. Gloucestershire, UK: Tempus, 2007.

Craig, Gordon. *The Politics of the Prussian Army, 1640–1945.* 1955. London: Oxford/Clarendon, 1964.

Deleuze, Gilles, and Felix Guattari. *Nomadology.* Translated by Brian Massumi. New York: Semiotext(e), 1986.

De Saxe, Maurice. *Reveries on the Art of War.* 1757. Mineola, NY: Dover, 2007.

De Vigny, Alfred. *The Warrior's Life.* Translated by Roger Gard. 1835. New York: Penguin, 1996.

Diamond, Jared. *Guns, Germs, and Steel: The Fate of Human Societies.* New York: W. W. Norton, 1997.

Douhet, Giulio. *Command of the Air.* 1921. Washington, DC: Office of Air Force History, U.S. Air Force, 1983.

Downing, Brian M. *The Military Revolution and Political Change: Origins of Democracy and Autocracy in Early Modern Europe.* Princeton, NJ: Princeton University Press, 1992.

Downs, Donald, and Ilia Murtazashvili. *Arms and the University: Military Presence and the Civic Education of Non-military Students.* Cambridge: Cambridge University Press, 2012.

Duff, J. Wright. *A Literary History of Rome in the Silver Age, from Tiberius to Hadrian.* Edited by A. M. Duff. London: Ernest Benn and Barnes and Noble, 1964.

Duffy, Christopher. *The Army of Frederick the Great.* New York: Hippocrene, 1974.

———. *The Army of Maria Theresa: The Armed Forces of Imperial Austria, 1740–1780.* New York: Hippocrene, 1977.

———. *The Military Experience in the Age of Reason.* 1987. Hertfordshire, UK: Wordsworth, 1998.

Du Picq, Ardant. *Battle Studies: Ancient and Modern Battle.* Translated by John N. Greely and Robert C. Cotton. New York: Macmillan, 1921.

Dupuy, Trevor N. *A Genius for War: The German Army and General Staff, 1807–1945.* New York: Prentice-Hall, 1977.

Elias, Norbert. *The Genesis of the Naval Profession.* Dublin: University College of Dublin Press, 2007.

Ellis, John. *The Sharp End: The Fighting Man in World War II.* New York: Scribners, 1980.

Eltis, David. *The Military Revolution in Sixteenth-Century Europe.* London: I. B. Tauris, 1998.

Engels, Donald. *Alexander the Great and the Logistics of the Macedonian Army.* Berkeley: University of California Press, 1980.

Epstein, Robert M. *Napoleon's Last Victory and the Emergence of Modern War.* Lawrence: University Press of Kansas, 1994.

Finley, M. I. *The World of Odysseus*. New York: Viking, 1954.

Fischer, David Hackett. *Washington's Crossing*. Oxford: Oxford University Press, 2004.

France, John. *Western Warfare in the Age of the Crusades, 1000–1300*. Ithaca, NY: Cornell University Press, 1999.

Freeman, Douglas Southall. "Leadership." Speech delivered at the Naval War College, Newport, Rhode Island, 11 May 1949. Printed in *Naval War College Review*, March–April 1979, 3–10.

Froissart, Jean. *Chronicles*. Selected and translated by Geoffrey Brereton. London: Penguin, 1968.

Frontinus. *The Strategems*. Translated by Charles E. Bennet. 1925. Cambridge, MA: Harvard University Press, 1961.

Fussell, Paul. *The Great War and Modern Memory*. New York: Oxford University Press, 1975.

Gabriel, Richard A., and Karen S. Metz. *From Sumer to Rome: The Military Capabilities of Ancient Armies*. Westport, CT: Greenwood, 1991.

Gat, Azar. *A History of Military Thought*. Oxford: Oxford University Press, 2001.

Gates, John M. "The Pacification of the Philippines." In *The U.S. Army and Irregular Warfare*, chapter 3. http://discover.wooster.edu/jgates/files/2011/11/fullbook.pdf, 2006.

Gelven, Michael. *War and Existence: A Philosophical Inquiry*. University Park: University of Pennsylvania Press, 1994.

Gentles, Ian. "The Civil Wars in England." In Kenyon and Ohlmeyer, *Civil Wars*, 103–55.

Geraghty, Jeff. "The Nature and Nurture of Military Genius: Developing Senior Leaders for the Postmodern Military." Air Force Research Institute, 27 July 2010. http://www.au.af.mil/au/afri/research_full.asp?id=11.

Geyer, Michael. "German Strategy in the Age of Machine Warfare, 1914–1945." In Paret, *Makers of Modern Strategy*, 527–97.

Gibbon, Edward. *The Decline and Fall of the Roman Empire*. Volume 1. Chicago: Encyclopedia Britannica, 1990.

Gies, Frances. *The Knight in History*. New York: Harper and Row, 1987.

Glover, Michael. *Wellington as a Military Commander*. London: Penguin, 2001.

Goerlitz, Walter. *The History of the German General Staff, 1657–1945*. Translated by Brian Battershaw. New York: Praeger, 1953.

Goldsworthy, Adrian. *How Rome Fell: Death of a Superpower*. New Haven, CT: Yale University Press, 2009.

———. *In the Name of Rome: The Men Who Won the Roman Empire.* London: Weidenfeld and Nicolson, 2003.

———. *Roman Warfare.* 2000. London: Orion-Phoenix, 2007.

González de León, Fernando. "*Soldados Platicos* and *Caballeros*: The Social Dimensions of Ethics in the Early Modern Spanish Army." In *The Chivalric Ethos and the Development of Military Professionalism,* edited by D. J. B. Trim, 253–59. Leiden, Netherlands: Brill, 2003.

Goodman, Ralph M. *From Warfare to Party Politics: The Critical Transition to Civilian Control.* Syracuse, NY: Syracuse University Press, 1990.

Gordon, Andrew. *The Rules of the Game: Jutland and British Naval Command.* 1996. Annapolis, MD: U.S. Naval Institute Press, 2000.

Greenwood, E. B. *Tolstoy: The Comprehensive Vision.* 1975. London: Methuen, 1980.

Gudmundsson, Bruce. *Stormtroop Tactics: Innovation in the German Army, 1914–1918.* Westport, CT: Praeger, 1995.

Hanson, Victor Davis. *Carnage and Culture: Landmark Battles in the Rise of Western Power.* New York: Random House/Anchor, 2002.

———. *The Wars of the Ancient Greeks and Their Invention of Western Military Culture.* London: Cassell, 1999.

———. *The Western Way of War: Infantry Battle in Classical Greece.* New York: Knopf, 1989.

Harries, Meirion, and Susan Harries. *Soldiers of the Sun: The Rise and Fall of the Imperial Japanese Army.* New York: Random House, 1991.

Hart, Basil, and Adrian Liddell Hart. *The Sword and the Pen: Selections from the World's Greatest Military Writings.* New York: Crowell, 1976.

Heifetz, Ronald, and Marty Linsky. *Leadership on the Line: Staying Alive through the Dangers of Leading.* Boston: Harvard Business Review Press, 2002.

Hendrix, Scott N. "The Spirit of the Corps: The British Army and the Pre-national Pan European Military World and the Origins of American Military Culture." PhD dissertation, University of Pittsburgh, 2005.

Hewitt, H. J. *The Organization of War under Edward III.* 1966. Barnsley, UK: Pen and Sword, 2004.

Heyn, Udo. *Peacemaking in Medieval Europe: A Historical and Bibliographical Guide.* Claremont, CA: Regina Books, 1997.

Hibbert, Christopher. *Agincourt.* Philadelphia: Dufour, 1964.

Hill, Charles. *Grand Strategies: Literature, Statecraft, and World Order.* New Haven, CT: Yale University Press, 2010.

Hill, Richard. *War at Sea in the Ironclad Age*. 2000. New York: Harper-Collins, 2006.

Homer. *The Iliad*. Translated by Stanley Lombardo. Indianapolis: Hackett, 1997.

Horne, Alastair. *To Lose a Battle, France 1940*. 1969. Harmondsworth: Penguin, 1979.

———. *A Savage War of Peace*. New York: Viking, 1978.

Houlding, J. A. *Fit for Service: The Training of the British Army, 1715–1995*. Oxford: Clarendon Press, 1981.

Howard, Michael. *The Franco-Prussian War*. 1961. New York: Macmillan-Collier, 1969.

———. "Men against Fire." In Paret, *Makers of Modern Strategy*, 510–26.

———. "William I and the Reform of the Prussian Army." In *Studies in War and Peace*, by Michael Howard, 65–82. 1959. New York: Viking, 1971.

Howarth, David. *Waterloo: Day of Battle*. New York: Atheneum, 1968.

Hughes, Daniel J., ed. *Moltke on the Art of War: Selected Writings*. Novato, CA: Presidio, 1993.

Huntington, Samuel P. *The Soldier and the State: The Theory and Politics of Civil-Military Relations*. 1957. Cambridge, MA: Harvard University Press, 1981.

Ignatieff, Michael. *The Warrior's Honor: Ethnic War and the Modern Conscience*. New York: Metropolitan/Henry Holt, 1997.

Jamieson, Perry D. *Crossing the Deadly Ground: United States Army Tactics, 1865–1899*. Tuscaloosa: University of Alabama Press, 1994.

Janowitz, Morris. *The Professional Soldier: A Social and Political Portrait*. Glencoe, IL: Free Press, 1960.

Jones, Colin. "The Military Revolution and the Professionalization of the French Army under the Ancien Regime." In *The Military Revolution and the State, 1500–1800*, edited by M. Duffy, 29–48. Exeter: University of Exeter Press, 1980.

Jones, Grant. "Education of the Supreme Commander: The Theoretical Underpinnings of Eisenhower's Strategy in Europe, 1944–45." *War and Society* 30, no. 2 (2011): 108–33.

Jones, James. *WWII: A Chronicle of Soldiering*. New York: Ballantine, 1975.

Jorgensen, Christer, Michael F. Pavkovic, Rob S. Rice, Frederick C. Scheid, and Chris L. Scott. *Fighting Techniques of the Early Modern World, A.D. 1500–1763: Equipment, Combat Skills, and Tactics*. Staplehurst, Kent: Spellmount, 2005.

Juvenal. "Satire XVI." *The Sixteen Satires*. Translated by Peter Green. Baltimore: Penguin, 1967.

Kahn, Herman. *On Thermonuclear War*. Princeton, NJ: Princeton University Press, 1960.

Keegan, John. *The Face of Battle*. London: Jonathan Cape, 1976.

Keen, Maurice. *Chivalry*. New Haven, CT: Yale University Press, 1984.

Kenyon, John, and Jane Ohlmeyer, eds. "The Background to the Civil Wars in the Stuart Kingdoms." In Kenyon and Ohlmeyer, *Civil Wars*, 3–40.

———. *The Civil Wars: A Military History of England, Scotland, and Ireland, 1638–1660*. Oxford: Oxford University Press, 1998.

Kipling, Rudyard. "The Young British Soldier." In *Barrack-Room Ballads and Other Verses*. London: Methuen, 1892.

Koch, H. W. *Medieval Warfare*. London: Bison-Dorset, 1978.

———. *The Rise of Modern Warfare, 1618–1815*. Englewood Cliffs, NJ: Prentice-Hall, 1981.

Langer, Herbert. *Thirty Years' War*. New York: Hippocrene, 1980.

Langins, Janis. *Conserving the Enlightenment: French Military Engineering from Vauban to the Revolution*. Cambridge: MIT Press, 2004.

Lendon, John. *Soldiers and Ghosts: A History of Battle in Classical Antiquity*. New Haven, CT: Yale University Press, 2005.

Lewis, Naphtali. "Sparta, an Arrested Society." In *Greek Historical Documents: The Fifth Century B.C.,* by Naphtali Lewis, 68–89. Toronto: A. M. Hakkert, 1971.

Liaropoulos, Andrew. "Revolutions in Warfare: Theoretical Paradigms and Historical Evidence: The Napoleonic and First World War Revolutions in Military Affairs." *Journal of Military History* 70 (2006): 363–84.

Lloyd, E. M. *A Review of the History of Infantry*. 1908. Cranbury, NJ: Scholar's Bookshelf, 2006.

Lund, Erik. *War for the Every Day: Generals, Knowledge, and Warfare in Early Modern Europe, 1680–1740*. New York: Greenwood, 1999.

Luttwak, Edward N. *The Grand Strategy of the Byzantine Empire*. Cambridge, MA: Harvard University Press/Belknap, 2009.

Lynn, John. *Battle: A History of Combat and Culture*. Boulder, CO: Westview, 2003.

———. *Giant of the Grand Siècle: The French Army, 1610–1715*. Cambridge: Cambridge University Press, 1997.

MacIsaac, David. "Voices from the Central Blue: The Air Power Theorists." In Paret, *Makers of Modern Strategy*, 624–47.

Marlantes, Karl. *Matterhorn*. New York: Grove-Atlantic, 2010.

———. *What It Is Like to Go to War*. New York: Grove-Atlantic, 2011.

Marshall, S. L. A. *The Armed Forces Officer*. Washington, DC: U.S. Department of Defense, 1950.

Masters, John. *Bugles and a Tiger*. 1948. New York: Ballantine, 1968.

Maurer, Maurer. *Aviation in the U.S. Army, 1919–1939*. Washington, DC: Office of Air Force History, U.S. Air Force, 1987.

Maxfield, Valerie. *The Military Decorations of the Roman Army*. Berkeley: University of California Press, 1981.

McCartney, Eugene. *Warfare by Land and Sea*. Our Debt to Greece and Rome series. Edited by George Hadzsits and David Robinson. New York: Cooper Square, 1963.

McGlynn, Sean. "The Myths of Medieval Warfare." *History Today* 44, no. 1 (1994). http://www.historytoday.com/sean-mcglyn/myths-medieval-warfare.

McKee, Christopher. *A Gentlemanly and Honorable Profession: The Creation of the U.S. Naval Officer Corps, 1794–1815*. Annapolis, MD: U.S. Naval Institute Press, 1991.

Mellersh, H. E. L. *The Roman Soldier*. New York: Taplinger, 1965.

Meron, Theodore. *Bloody Constraint: War and Chivalry in Shakespeare*. New York: Oxford University Press, 1998.

"Military Professionalism: Introspection and Reflection on Basic Tenets and the Way Ahead." Conference, 10 January 2011, National Defense University, Fort Lesley J. McNair, Washington, DC.

Millet, Allan R., and Peter Maslowski. *For the Common Defense: A Military History of the United States of America*. New York: Free Press, 1994.

Millis, Walter. *The Martial Spirit*. 1931. Chicago: Ivan Dee/Elephant, 1989.

Milstein, Seth M. "Tactical Tweets, Blogs, Smartphones, and Drones (Oh, My!)." *Marine Corps Gazette* 98, no. 4 (2014): 63–66.

Montaigne, Michel. *Essays*. Translated by J. M. Cohen. Harmondsworth, England: Penguin, 1958.

Moran, Daniel. *Wars of National Liberation*. New York: Smithsonian Books, 2001.

Morin, Relman. *Churchill: A Portrait in Greatness*. Englewood Cliffs, NJ: Prentice-Hall, 1965.

Morrill, John. "Postlude: Between War and Peace, 1651–1662." In Kenyon and Ohlmeyer, *Civil Wars*, 306–28.

Morton, Louis. "Germany First: The Basic Concept of Allied Strategy in World War II." In *Command Decisions*, edited by Kent Roberts Greenfield,

11–48. Washington, DC: Center of Military History, U.S. Army, 1990.

Murnaghan, Sheila. Introduction to *The Iliad*. Translated by Stanley Lombardo. Indianapolis: Hackett, 1997.

Murphy, James J. "Rhetorical History as a Guide to the Salvation of American Reading and Writing: A Plea for Curricular Courage." In *The Rhetorical Tradition and Modern Writing*, edited by James J. Murphy, 3–12. New York: Modern Language Association of America, 1982.

Murray, Williamson, and Allan R. Millett, eds. *Military Innovation in the Interwar Period*. Cambridge: Cambridge University Press, 1996.

Murray, Williamson, and Richard Hart Sinnreich, eds. *The Past as Prologue: The Importance of History to the Military Profession*. Cambridge: Cambridge University Press, 2006.

Nagy, Gregory. *The Best of the Achaeans: Concepts of the Hero in Ancient Greek Poetry*. 1979. Baltimore: Johns Hopkins University Press, 1999.

Nef, John U. *War and Human Progress*. Cambridge, MA: Harvard University Press, 1950.

Neumann, Sigmund, and Mark von Hagan. "Engels and Marx on Revolution, War, and the Army in Society." In Paret, *Makers of Modern Strategy*, 262–80.

Neustadt, Richard E., and Ernest R. May. *Thinking in Time: The Uses of History for Decision Makers*. 1986. New York: Free Press, 1988.

Newell, Richard. *Muster and Review: A Problem of Military Administration, 1420–1440*. Cambridge, MA: Harvard University Press, 1940.

Nordlinger, Eric. *Soldiers in Politics: Military Coups and Governments*. Englewood Cliffs, NJ: Prentice-Hall, 1977.

Norman, A. V. B. *The Medieval Soldier*. 1971. New York: Barnes and Noble, 1993.

Nosworthy, Brent. *The Bloody Crucible of Courage: Fighting Methods and Combat Experience of the Civil War*. New York: Carroll and Graf, 2003.

Oestreich, Gerhard. *Neostoicism and the Early Modern State*. Translated by Davis McClintock. Cambridge: Cambridge University Press, 1982.

Orme, Nicholas. *From Childhood to Chivalry: The Education of English Kings and Aristocracy, 1066–1530*. London: Methuen, 1984.

Palmer, Robert R., Bell I. Wiley, and William R. Keast. *United States Army in World War II. The Army Ground Forces: The Procurement and Training of Ground Combat Troops*. Washington, DC: Historical Division, Department of the Army, 1948.

Paret, Peter. *The Cognitive Challenge of War, Prussia, 1806*. Princeton, NJ: Princeton University Press, 2009.

———. *Makers of Modern Strategy from Machiavelli to the Nuclear Age*. Princeton, NJ: Princeton University Press, 1986.

Parker, Geoffrey. *The Army of Flanders and the Spanish Road, 1567–1659: The Logistics of Spanish Victory and Defeat in the Low Countries' Wars*. Cambridge: Cambridge University Press, 2004.

———. "The Etiquette of Atrocity: The Laws of War in Early Modern Europe." In Parker, *Success Is Never Final*, 150–53.

———. *The Grand Strategy of Philip II*. New Haven, CT: Yale University Press, 1998.

———. *The Military Revolution: Military Innovation and the Rise of the West, 1500–1800*. Cambridge: Cambridge University Press, 1988.

———. *Success Is Never Final: Empire, War, and Faith in Early Modern Europe*. New York: Basic Books, 2002.

———. "The Treaty of Lyon (1601) and the Spanish Road." In Parker, *Success Is Never Final*, 126–42.

Parrott, David. *Richelieu's Army: War, Government, and Society in France, 1624–1642*. Cambridge: Cambridge University Press, 2001.

———. "Strategy and Tactics in the Thirty Years' War: The 'Military Revolution.'" In Rogers, *Military Revolution Debate*, 227–51.

Perret, Geoffrey. *Eisenhower*. New York: Random House, 1999.

Perry, Mark. *Partners in Command: George Marshall and Dwight Eisenhower in War and Peace*. New York: Penguin, 2007.

Phillips, T. R. "Frederick the Great." In *Roots of Strategy: The 5 Greatest Military Classics of All Time*, edited by T. R. Phillips, 301–400. 1940. Harrisburg, PA: Stackpole Books, 1985.

Pinker, Steven. *The Better Angels of Our Nature: Why Violence Has Declined*. New York: Penguin, 2011.

Polis, Robert, and Philip Langer. *Command Failure in War: Psychology and Leadership*. Bloomington: Indiana University Press, 2004.

Polybius. *The Histories of Polybius*. Vol. 1. Translated by F. Hultsch and Evelyn S. Shuckburgh. Bloomington: Indiana University Press, 1962.

Porter, Bruce D. *War and the Rise of the State: The Military Foundations of Modern Politics*. New York: Free Press, 1994.

Prestwich, Michael. *Armies and Warfare in the Middle Ages: The English Experience*. New Haven, CT: Yale University Press, 1996.

Rabb, Theodore K. *The Artist and the Warrior: Military History through the Eyes of the Masters*. New Haven, CT: Yale University Press, 2011.

Raffel, Burton. Introduction to *Beowulf*. New York: Mentor/New American Library, 1963.

Rapoport, Anatole. Introduction to Carl von Clausewitz, *On War*. Harmondsworth, Middlesex, UK: Penguin, 1968, 11–80.

Ricks, Thomas. *The Generals: American Military Command from World War II to Today*. New York: Penguin, 2012.

Roberts, Michael. "The Military Revolution, 1560–1660." Reprinted in Rogers, *Military Revolution Debate*, 13–36.

Rodgers, N. A. M. *The Command of the Ocean: A Naval History of Britain, 1649–1815*. New York: W. W. Norton, 2006.

Rogers, Clifford, ed. *The Military Revolution Debate: Readings on the Military Transformation of Early Modern Europe*. Boulder, CO: Westview, 1995.

———. "The Military Revolutions of the Hundred Years' War." In Rogers, *Military Revolution Debate*, 55–94.

———. "The Soldier's Experience of Battle in the Middle Ages." Lecture. New York Military Affairs Society, 25 January 2008.

———. *Soldiers' Lives through History: The Middle Ages*. Westport, CT: Greenwood, 2007.

Romanus, Charles F., and Riley Sunderland, *United States Army in World War II, China- Burma-India Theater: Stilwell's Command Problems*. Washington, DC: Office of the Chief of Military History, Department of the Army, 1956.

Rostand, Edmond. *Cyrano de Bergerac*. Translated by Brian Hooker. 1898. New York: Henry Holt, 1923.

Rothenberg, Gunther. "Maurice of Nassau, Gustavus Adolphus, Raimondo Montecuccoli, and the 'Military Revolution' of the Seventeenth Century." In Paret, *Makers of Modern Strategy*, 32–63.

Royster, Charles. *A Revolutionary People at War: The Continental Army and American Character, 1775–1783*. Chapel Hill: University of North Carolina Press, 1979.

Santosuosso, Antonio. *Barbarians, Marauders, and Infidels: The Ways of Medieval Warfare*. New York: MJF Books, 2004.

Sayers, Dorothy, trans. Introduction to *The Song of Roland*. Harmondsworth, UK: Penguin, 1957.

Schlosser, Eric. *Command and Control: Nuclear Weapons, the Damascus Accident, and the Illusion of Safety*. New York: Penguin Press, 2013.

Segal, Erich, trans. *Plautus: Three Comedies*. New York: Harper and Row, 1963.

Seversky, Alexander. *Victory through Air Power*. New York: Simon and Schuster, 1942.

Shay, Jonathan. *Achilles in Vietnam: Combat Trauma and the Undoing of Character*. New York: Scribner, 1994.

———. *Odysseus in America*. New York: Scribner, 2002.

Shephard, Ben. *A War of Nerves: Soldiers and Psychiatrists in the Twentieth Century*. Cambridge, MA: Harvard University Press, 2003.

Skelton, William B. *An American Profession of Arms: The Army Officer Corps, 1784–1861*. Lawrence: University Press of Kansas, 1992.

Sledge, E. B. *With the Old Breed at Peleliu and Okinawa*. 1981. New York: Oxford University Press, 1991.

Smail, R. C. *Crusading Warfare, 1097–1193*. Cambridge: Cambridge University Press, 1956.

Smith, Edward. "The Navy RMA War Game Series: April 1995–1996." *Naval War College Review* 50 (autumn 1997): 17–31.

Sorley, Lewis. *Westmoreland: The General Who Lost Vietnam*. Boston: Houghton Mifflin/Harcourt, 2011.

Southern, Pat. *The Roman Army: A Social and Institutional History*. Oxford: Oxford University Press, 2007, 163.

Spaulding, Oliver Lyman. *Pen and Sword in Greece and Rome*. 1936. Cranbury, NJ: Scholar's Bookshelf, 2006.

Speelman, Patrick. *Henry Lloyd and the Military Enlightenment of Eighteenth-Century Europe*. Westport, CT: Greenwood Press, 2002.

Spence, Jonathan D. *The Memory Palace of Matteo Ricci*. New York: Elisabeth Sifton/Viking Penguin, 1984.

Spencer, Charles. *Blenheim: Battle for Europe*. 2004. London: Orion-Phoenix, 2005.

Spiers, Edward. "The Late Victorian Army 1868–1914." In *The Oxford History of the British Army*, ed. David Chandler and Ian Beckett, 187–210. Oxford: Oxford University Press, 1994.

Steele, Brett D., and Tamera Dorland, eds. *The Heirs of Archimedes: Science and the Art of War through the Age of Enlightenment*. Cambridge: MIT Press, 2005.

———. Introduction to *Heirs of Archimedes*. In Steele and Dorland, *Heirs of Archimedes*, 1–33.

Stilwell, Joseph W. *The Stilwell Papers*. Edited and arranged by Theodore H. White. New York: William Sloane, 1948.

Strachan, Hew. *European Armies and the Conduct of War.* 1983. London: Routledge, 2002.

Sumption, Jonathan. *The Hundred Years' War.* Volume 3, *Divided Houses.* Philadelphia: University of Pennsylvania Press, 2009.

Sutherland, John, and Cedric Watts. *Henry V, War Criminal? & Other Shakespeare Puzzles.* Oxford: Oxford University Press, 2000.

Sweetman, John. *War and Administration: The Significance of the Crimean War for the British Army.* Edinburgh: Scottish Academic Press, 1984.

Tacitus. *Agricola* and *Germania.* Translated by Harold Mattingly. 1948. London: Penguin Books, 2009.

Talbert, Richard. *Rome's World: The Peutinger Map Reconsidered.* Cambridge: Cambridge University Press, 2010.

Taylor, F. L. *The Art of War in Italy, 1494–1529.* 1921. Cranbury, NJ: Scholar's Bookshelf, 2006.

Tolstoy, Leo. *War and Peace.* Translated by Rosemary Edmonds. London: Penguin, 1978.

Trim, D. J. B., ed. *The Chivalric Ethos and the Development of Military Professionalism.* Leiden, Netherlands: Brill, 2003.

Tsouras, Peter. *Alexander: Invincible King of Macedonia.* Washington, DC: Brassey's, 2004.

Tuchman, Barbara. *Stilwell and the American Experience in China, 1911–45.* New York: Macmillan, 1970.

Tyerman, C. J. Review of *To Follow in Their Footsteps: The Crusades and Family Memory in the High Middle Ages* by Nicholas L. Paul. *Times Literary Supplement,* 14 June 2013.

Ulbrich, David J. *Preparing for Victory: Thomas Holcomb and the Making of the Modern Marine Corps, 1936–1943.* Annapolis, MD: Naval Institute Press, 2011.

U.S. Army. *ADP 5-0: The Operations Process.* Washington, DC: Department of the Army, 2012.

U.S. Army/Marine Corps. *Counterinsurgency.* Washington, DC: Headquarters, Department of the Army, 2006. Revised as *Insurgencies and Countering Insurgencies.* Washington, DC: Headquarters, Department of the Army, 2014.

U.S. Marine Corps. *MCDP 6 Command and Control.* Washington, DC: U.S. Department of the Navy, Headquarters, U.S. Marine Corps, 1996.

———. *Small Wars Manual.* 1940. New York: Skyhorse, 2009.

Van Creveld, Martin. *Supplying War: Logistics from Wallenstein to Patton.* Cambridge: Cambridge University Press, 1977.

———. *The Training of Officers: From Military Professionalism to Irrelevance.* New York: Macmillan, 1990.

Van Wees, Hans. *Greek Warfare: Myths and Realities.* London: Duckworth, 2004.

Verbruggen, J. F. *The Art of Warfare in Western Europe during the Middle Ages.* Translated by Sumner Willard and R. W. Southern. Suffolk, UK: Boydell, 1997.

Voelz, Glenn. "Is Military Knowledge 'Scientific'?" *Joint Forces Quarterly 75* (4th quarter 2014): 84–90.

Von Schell, Adolf. *Battle Leadership.* Fort Benning, Columbus, GA: Benning Herald, 1933. Reprinted by Marine Corps Association, 1999.

Wallace, Andrew G. "General George Catlett Marshall: A Cognitive Approach to Who He Was and What He Did." Marshall Foundation, 3 January 2013. http://marshallfoundation.org/marshall/wp-content/uploads/sites/22/2014/04/GeneralGeorgeCatlettMarshallAndrewWallace.pdf.

Warner, Philip. *Sieges of the Middle Ages.* 1968. South Yorkshire, UK: Pen and Sword, 2004.

Webb, Henry J. *Elizabethan Military Science: The Books and the Practice.* Madison: University of Wisconsin Press, 1965.

Weber, Max. *The Protestant Ethic and the Spirit of Capitalism.* Translated by Talcott Parsons. New York: Scribner, 1958.

———, ed. *The Theory of Social and Economic Organization.* New York: Free Press, 1964.

Webster, Graham. *The Roman Imperial Army of the First and Second Centuries A.D.* 1969. New York: Barnes and Noble, 1994.

Weigley, Russell F. *The Age of Battles: The Quest for Decisive Warfare from Breitenfeld to Waterloo.* Bloomington: Indiana University Press, 1991.

———. *The American Way of War: A History of United States Military Policy.* Bloomington: Indiana University Press, 1973.

———. *History of the United States Army.* New York: Macmillan, 1967.

———. *Towards an American Army: Military Thought from Washington to Marshall.* Westport, CT: Greenwood, 1974.

Weil, Simone. "*The Iliad,* or the Poem of Force." In *Simone Weil: An Anthology,* edited and introduction by Siân Miles, 162–95. New York: Grove, 1986.

Wells, H. G. *Little Wars.* 1913. New York: Macmillan, 1970.

White, Charles Edward. *The Enlightened Soldier: Scharnhorst and the Militarische Gesellschaft in Berlin, 1801–1805.* Westport, CT: Praeger, 1989.

Williams, F. D. G. *SLAM: The Influence of S. L. A. Marshall on the United States Army.* Fort Monroe, VA: U.S. Army Training and Doctrine Command, 1999.

Wolfe, James. *General Wolfe's Instructions to Young Officers: Also his Orders for a Battalion and an Army; Together with the Orders and Signals Ufed in Embarking and Debarking an Army by Flat-Bottom'd Boats &c.; and a Placart to the Canadians; to Which is Prefixed the Refolution of the Houfe of Commons for his Monument; and his Character, and the Dates of all his Commiffions. Also the Duty of an Adjutant and Quarter-Master, &c.* London: J. Millan, 1768.

Wolff, Leon. *In Flanders Fields: The 1917 Campaign.* New York: Viking, 1958.

Woodham-Smith, Cecil. *The Reason Why.* 1953. New York: McGraw-Hill, 1954.

Worden, Mike. *The Rise of the Fighter Generals: The Problem of Air Force Leadership, 1945–1982.* Maxwell Air Force Base, AL: Air University Press, 1998.

Yeats-Brown, Francis. *The Lives of a Bengal Lancer.* New York: Viking, 1930.

Index

About the Author

REED BONADONNA served in the Marine Corps as an infantry officer and field historian, retiring with the rank of colonel. He earned a doctorate at Boston University with a dissertation on the World War II soldier's novel that was published by VDM. He has published journal articles on military ethics and leadership. He recently retired as director of ethics and character development at the U.S. Merchant Marine Academy.

The Naval Institute Press is the book-publishing arm of the U.S. Naval Institute, a private, nonprofit, membership society for sea service professionals and others who share an interest in naval and maritime affairs. Established in 1873 at the U.S. Naval Academy in Annapolis, Maryland, where its offices remain today, the Naval Institute has members worldwide.

Members of the Naval Institute support the education programs of the society and receive the influential monthly magazine *Proceedings* or the colorful bimonthly magazine *Naval History* and discounts on fine nautical prints and on ship and aircraft photos. They also have access to the transcripts of the Institute's Oral History Program and get discounted admission to any of the Institute-sponsored seminars offered around the country.

The Naval Institute's book-publishing program, begun in 1898 with basic guides to naval practices, has broadened its scope to include books of more general interest. Now the Naval Institute Press publishes about seventy titles each year, ranging from how-to books on boating and navigation to battle histories, biographies, ship and aircraft guides, and novels. Institute members receive significant discounts on the Press' more than eight hundred books in print.

Full-time students are eligible for special half-price membership rates. Life memberships are also available.

For a free catalog describing Naval Institute Press books currently available, and for further information about joining the U.S. Naval Institute, please write to:

Member Services
U.S. Naval Institute
291 Wood Road
Annapolis, MD 21402-5034
Telephone: (800) 233-8764
Fax: (410) 571-1703
Web address: www.usni.org